LINGUISTICS & BIBLICAL INTERPRETATION

PETER COTTERELL & MAX TURNER

INTERVARSITY PRESS
DOWNERS GROVE, ILLINOIS 60515

Published in the United States of America by InterVarsity Press, Downers Grove, Illinois, with permission from SPCK, London, England.

InterVarsity Press is the book-publishing division of InterVarsity Christian Fellowship, a student movement active on campus at hundreds of universities, colleges and schools of nursing. For information about local and regional activities, write Public Relations Dept., InterVarsity Christian Fellowship, 6400 Schroeder Rd., P.O. Box 7895, Madison, WI 53707-7895.

Distributed in Canada through InterVarsity Press, 860 Denison St., Unit 3, Markham, Ontario L3R 4H1, Canada.

The cartoon (Figure 1. The Electronic Serenade) on p. 86 is taken from J. D. Bransford and M. K. Johnson, "Considerations of Some Problems of Comprehension" in W. G. Chase (ed.), Visual Information Processing, New York: Academic Press, 1973, and used by permission.

ISBN 0-8308-1751-4

Printed in the United States of America

Library of Congress Cataloging-in-Publication Data

Cotterell, Peter, 1930-
    Linguistics and biblical interpretation.

    Bibliography: p.
    Includes index.
    1. Linguistics.   2. Bible—Hermeneutics.   3. Languages
—Religious aspects—Christianity.   I. Turner,
Max, 1947-   .   II. Title.
P123.T87   1988   220.6'014   88-32868
ISBN 0-8308-1751-4

17	16	15	14	13	12	11	10	9	8	7	6	5	4	3	2	1
99	98	97	96	95	94	93	92	91	90	89						

Abbreviations

AV	Authorized (King James) Version
Bib	*Biblica*
BJRL	*Bulletin of the John Rylands Library*
BT	*Bible Translator*
ET	*Expository Times*
EvQ	*Evangelical Quarterly*
IDB	*Interpreters Dictionary of the Bible*
JBL	*Journal of Biblical Literature*
JSOT	*Journal for the Study of the Old Testament*
JTS	*Journal of Theological Studies*
KuD	*Kerygma und Dogma*
NEB	*New English Bible*
NIDNTT	*New International Dictionary of New Testament Theology*
NIV	New International Version
NovT	*Novum Testamentum*
NTS	*New Testament Studies*
RSV	Revised Standard Version
SIL	Summer Institute of Linguistics
TDNT	*Theological Dictionary of the New Testament*
TLZ	*Theologische Literaturzeitung*

Preface

Linguistics is concerned with the formal study of human language. The Bible is written in human languages and so linguistics as a discipline should be relevant to everyone who is trying to understand and to interpret it.

Unfortunately our system of higher education seems designed to keep the disciplines of biblical studies and linguistics isolated from each other, and few theologians have been exposed even to those aspects of linguistics which are of most obvious relevance to them.

This book will help to bridge that gap. It introduces the interested student in a non-technical way to some aspects of linguistics which are relevant to biblical exegesis. We explain why some approaches to biblical texts may give misleading results, and how linguistics sometimes points the way to better methods.

The book is decidedly not an introduction to linguistics: John Lyons, *Language and Linguistics* (Cambridge University Press, 1981) or perhaps R. H. Robins, *General Linguistics* (first published by Longmans back in 1964 but updated in 1978) can be recommended to the reader looking for such a work.

Nor did we intend writing about every aspect of linguistics that bears on biblical exegesis. We have not included any discussion of tense or mood, for example, and there is nothing on the phonology of the biblical languages. We have concentrated on three main areas: first, the concept of *meaning* (semantics), and especially on the vexed question of lexical semantics, the meaning of words; second, the particular significance to be assigned to author, text, and reader in the search for the meaning of any particular part of the Bible; and, third, the significance of the recognition of the role of the discourse *as a whole* (a conversation, a parable, an anecdote, an epistle) in determining meaning.

Over the pulpit of a church in Blackpool, England, is a text, 'I have a message from God for you' (Judges 3.20). If this book enables the reader to understand the relationship between the words used in that text, the meaning intended by Ehud, the speaker, the meaning perceived by Eglon, the hearer, the meaning extracted by the unknown individual who erected the pulpit text (by isolating the words from the accompanying text and its sociological context), and the diverse ways in which various people have perceived the text in its new context, and if the reader is able to identify the *correct* meaning of the text, then we shall be not dissatisfied.

A difficulty inseparable from a young and rapidly growing discipline is the absence of an agreed terminology. We have done our best to be consistent in our own terminology, but in general we have refrained from commenting on alternative terms used by some linguists for the same phenomena, or on their use of the same terms for slightly different phenomena.

It is helpful to have some way of drawing attention, when necessary, to *meanings*. In this work we have used single quotation marks around words and around expressions which have both form and meaning. When the *meanings* of such words or expressions are introduced we use double quotation marks. For example we suggest in chapter 5 that in a particular Bible text the word 'head' means "origin" or "source". The importance of distinguishing the *meaning* of an expression from its *form* is one of the concerns of linguistics. Where quotations include within them other quotations this convention has inevitably been breached.

1. Language, Linguistics & Biblical Interpretation

1.1 THE PHENOMENON OF HUMAN LANGUAGE[1]

1.1.1 Introductory

Few of us even think of the extraordinary complexity of the speech process. Most of us simply talk. True enough we talk with varying degrees of fluency, but every normal child learns to talk, and this is quite a remarkable achievement.

Consider the simple fact that there is an infinite number of sentences potentially available in each language known to us. The sentence which stands at the beginning of this paragraph has probably never before been written down or spoken or even thought. Very similar sentences have been produced before, and other similar sentences will be produced again, but it is probable that until this chapter was written no one had ever before written or said: 'Consider the simple fact that there is an infinite number of sentences potentially available in each language known to us.'

And yet we were able to produce the sentence and you were able to understand it.[2] What is more, if we had written '. . . consider the fact simple . . .' you would have known that the sentence was 'incorrect'. You would not have needed any formal grammatical training to have enabled you to spot the mistake in the sentence. From your own acquaintance with the English language you would have known that 'fact simple' is incorrect, and 'simple fact' is correct. If you have had formal grammatical training you might have commented that adjectives in English precede the nouns they qualify, or even that qualifier precedes qualified or, more carefully still, that qualifier usually precedes qualified. But that would merely have been a technical explanation of a practical observation of how the English language functions.

It is when we try to explain how languages work that we become aware to some extent of just how complex language is. Consider, then, secondly, the fact that any sentence is produced linearly, starting at the beginning and going on until the terminus is reached. And yet we are often not quite sure what the terminus will be when we commence the journey, when we start the sentence. And as a result it is not uncommon to encounter ill-formed sentences lacking elements we would have expected to find.

For example, Archbishop Bernard draws attention to the omission of the second main verb in John 1.8, what is termed *ellipsis: ouk ēn ekeinos to phōs, all' hina martyrēsē(i) peri tou phōtos,* 'He was not the Light, but (he came) to bear witness to the light'.[3] Or possibly we end the sentence with a conclusion that is grammatically inappropriate (what is called *anacoluthon*) perhaps because if we ended it 'correctly' it wouldn't say what we wanted it to say. For example, 'My Uncle George, the one who owned a garage, his father never really understood him.' In this example of *anacoluthon* we introduce the subject 'Uncle George' but half way through the sentence discover that the real subject is Uncle George's father, and that discovery forces us into making a fresh start . . . without having completed the part already begun. Grammatically the result is chaos: two elliptical sentences, and the long noun phrase 'My Uncle George, the one who owned a garage', left hanging (which is why it is called a pendent nominative). In terms of communication, however, there is no real problem: badly formed sentences can usually still be understood quite readily.

We do not, in practice, produce our sentences one word at a time. We seem to produce them a chunk at a time, dropping in ready-made chunks as they seem to fit. Even so, sentences are produced linearly, and we need to have reasonably good memories if we are to speak intelligibly. We need to recall what we *have* said already so that what we are saying and what we *will say* fit together. The memory clearly plays an important part in the speech process.

And that is one of the reasons why some people handle language more efficiently than others. Some of us have very good memories and can remember where our sentences began, even if they are very long ones, while others would get lost with a long sentence and so tend to be content with correctly formed and intelligible short sentences:

I, who am I, and no man shall deny it,
I, who am I, and none shall bid me nay;
I, who am I, lo! from the hills I cry it. . . .
I have forgotten what I meant to say!

1.1.2 The Study of Signalling Systems, or "Semiotics"[4]
A third factor that makes our command of language so remarkable is the complexity of the total signalling system that we are using. The word semiotics comes from the Greek *sēmeion*, 'a sign'. Semiotics is the study of signs, or signalling systems, of which, obviously, human communication is just one. The human communication system relies very heavily on speech, but communication in real life depends not only on speech but also on the many features which accompany the speech act: what people are wearing, how those who are trying to communicate are related, what gestures they use to accompany the speech, and so on. It is convenient to divide the semiotics of human communication into two related areas, one dealing with the actual language used and the other dealing with the accompanying circumstances. The first area is termed *semantics* and the second area is termed *pragmatics*. In traditional biblical exegesis it has been customary to focus attention almost exclusively on semantics, and within semantics there has been concentration on the meaning of words, lexical semantics. But the human communication semiotic is more complex than this approach supposes. What we wear signals to the people around us certain information about our character or our business. Thus in Esther 5.1, when Queen Esther determines to seek an audience with the king we are told that she 'put on her royal

robes', signalling both her own status and the formal nature of the occasion.[5]

Proxemics. A further area of complexity is supplied by the fact that each society has conventions regarding the use of personal space,[6] and these conventions further modify the spoken signals. The close proximity of two individuals may signal great intimacy and affection between them, or may represent a threat by one to the other. So we have to take account of proxemics, the significance of proximity, as we observe or participate in dialogue. Luke tells us that when Jesus was in the house of a Pharisee a woman of the city 'who was a sinner' stood behind Jesus, her tears falling on his feet. She then wiped the tears away with her own hair, and when she was still not repulsed kissed his feet and anointed them with the ointment she had brought with her. The Pharisees were outraged: 'If this man were a prophet, he would have known who and what sort of woman this is who is *touching* him' (Luke 7.39). In the proxemic of the Pharisee there could be no physical contact between a prophet and a 'sinner' (presumably the woman was a prostitute). Similarly in the account of the two men who went up to the Temple to pray, the tax collector is seen 'standing far off', a position appropriate to his status as perceived by his contemporaries.

Gesture. Again, the words that I employ, the sounds that I produce, may be heavily modified by what may generally be labelled 'gesture'.[7] Winking is a good example. In the English culture the wink may be a warning not to take what has been said at its face value or may, indeed, signal that the opposite of what has been said is intended. In other cultures winking has other meanings. In Proverbs 6.13 winking is associated with the worthless person, who goes about 'with crooked speech, winks with his eyes, scrapes with his feet, points with his finger, and with perverted heart devises evil'. We have here three distinct gestures, and we cannot be certain of the significance of any one of them. Proverbs 10.10 says that 'He who winks with the eye causes trouble, but he who boldly reproves makes peace', which suggests that winking at that time meant closing the eyes to sin, refusing to rebuke sin where it occurred.[8] The Psalmist prays, 'Let not those rejoice over me who are wrongfully my foes, and let not those wink the eye who hate me without cause.' The idea of winking being mere facetiousness is nowhere apparent in the Scriptures. Winking is 'always associated with sin'.[9] In modern Ethiopia, which has an essentially Semitic culture, to wink at a woman is to invite her to have sex.

1.1.3 The Imprecision of Human Language

We might decide to focus our investigation of human communication on a consideration of the sounds we produce. We might have written 'by considering the words we use', but some of the sounds we use in communication could scarcely be called 'words' at all. A grunt is a sound signal, and may well be a complete and meaningful response to a carefully constructed question or statement. And our actual vocabulary of 'grunts' is enormous, each of them communicating. Paradoxically part of the meaning content of a grunt may be its non-specificity. That is to say, if my wife asks me if I like her new dress and I don't, I may respond with a grunt which commits me neither to an untruth nor to an act of socially unacceptable rudeness. Once again we recognize the complexity of the human semiotic.

The fact is that because of the enormous complexity of human communication we are practically never in total control of the communication process. We use words that mean slightly different things to different people, we wear clothes that signal different things to different generations, we stand too close to people or too far from them without always being aware of the signals we are using, we employ gestures that are very open to being misunderstood, and we are all the time unaware of the imprecision of what is being signalled. We think that what we mean is clear. It is rarely so.

Once we become aware of the imprecision of human language we may feel ready to study the phenomenon so as to use it better. It is relatively easy to study theoretical, artificially constructed, language: the kind of language that might be produced so as to provide examples for a book on English grammar, for example.[10] It is relatively easy since that kind of language is susceptible of more or less rigorous analysis. It is also easy to analyze because it has no immediately relevant context. There is a real author constructing artificial sentences, but there is no other context for the sentences themselves. And so analysis yields reasonably precise results. In fact much of the imprecision of language is related to what we would call 'real' language, language as it is actually, practically, used in spoken or written communication. We shall be primarily concerned with 'real' language (so that the example above, on page 12, is a genuine utterance referring to a real Uncle George, and is not an artificially devised example). We shall try to maintain a distinction between real language and artificially contrived language, and concern ourselves primarily with real language and therefore with both semantics and pragmatics. Some linguists use the term *utterance* to refer to sequences of real language, whether written or spoken and we shall use that convention here. Leech suggests that the difference between semantics and pragmatics is that semantics answers questions of the form 'What does X mean?', while pragmatics answers questions of the form 'What did you mean by X?'[11] The latter question directs attention to utterances.

In attempting the exegesis of Scripture we are dealing with utterances, not with artificial context-less text. It is intuitively obvious that a proper understanding of Paul's correspondence with the church at Corinth will come from a study of the letters themselves, of the vocabulary and sentences as we now have them, and from as detailed a reconstruction of the actual context within which the letters came to be written and of the relationships between all of the individuals and groups named in the correspondence as can be determined. The first is the task of semantics, the second of pragmatics. In fact we shall have cause to emphasize this observation: the understanding of *utterances* requires some measure of understanding of the *text*, the actual words used; the *cotext*, the sentences, paragraphs, chapters, surrounding the text and related to it; and the *context*, the sociological and historical setting of the text. These three contributions to our understanding of any utterance demand the dual study involving semantics and pragmatics.

The Pauline correspondence is not the only biblical literature to demand this dual study of the exegete. For example, if we take John chapter 3, the account of the conversation between Jesus and Nicodemus,[12] the sentence 'We know that you are a teacher . . .' is an utterance. It was spoken by Nicodemus,[13] a Jewish rabbi, to Jesus, apparently an itinerant preacher, but presented by the writer of the Fourth Gospel as the 'Son of God' (1.34 etc.), at evening time in Jerusalem, almost certainly spoken in the presence of followers of both men (see below, 8.6). All of that information is important in understanding the utterance. In fact we understand any utterance only by noting all the circumstances associated with it. By contrast, an artificially contrived sentence, 'The cat sat on the mat', may be employed by the teacher to explain the concept of grammatical subject and verb without any reference at all as to the time of day when the cat sat on the mat. But we may go further: if the context of the utterance is changed, then the content of the utterance also is changed. Thus if the 'identical' grammatically well-formed sentence, 'We know that you are a teacher . . .' is taken to represent not the words of a genuine Nicodemus, but part of a heavily coded representation of the first-century dialogue between Church and synagogue (as C. K. Barrett in his commentary on St John supposes),[14] then that sentence is still an utterance, but a totally different utterance. A new set of questions must be constructed with regard to its context, and a new meaning for the new utterance will necessarily emerge. Each utterance is unique. The same sentence may be written down in a book again and again. But the same utterance never occurs a second time. Quite literally so: the time at which the utterance is spoken or written must be different, and so the utterance itself is different.

In interpreting any utterance we would like to know not only the words that were used, the ordering of those words, the intonation pattern imposed on the words, and the pattern of stress used, but also we would like to have details of any accompanying gesture, the speech habits of the speaker and of his hearers, the relationship between speaker and hearer, the nature of the occasion, the expectation of each participant, their proxemic relationship and how they were dressed. The more of this information we have so the more accurate are we likely to be in understanding the utterance. Conversely, the less of this information that is available to us so the less confident can we be that we have correctly and fully perceived the communication.

Take, for example, the utterance 'Punch'. It was the name of our dog. It is also the name of Judy's husband in the English 'Punch and Judy' show, also the name of a drink, and of a tool used in a workshop. It is also a verbal form, possibly an imperative, 'Punch!' Written down in isolation it is simply impossible to know what the word means. Assuming it to be an utterance we simply cannot tell how to differentiate between the numerous possible ways of understanding it:

'Punch!',   an instruction to a boxer,
'Punch!',   a request for a tool,
'Punch!',   "Come here, Punch, you rascal",

'Punch?',   "But how could it have been Punch?"
            "What a strange name to give a dog!"
            "Could it be Punch who stole the bone from the kitchen
            table?"
'Punch!',   (accompanied by a pointing finger), "Get outside, Punch!"
'Punch!',   "Great, I enjoy a glass of punch",

and so on, through a very large number of possibilities. However, once
we are given enough cotext and enough information about the context
the imprecision disappears.

1.2 PRAGMATICS AND EXEGESIS

There has been a tendency to interpret the text of the Bible in terms
of sentences rather than in terms of utterances, although all responsible
commentators have taken some account of the socio-historical setting
of the texts they expound. However, English exegesis in the past has
excelled in the study of the meaning of words, lexical semantics, rather
than in the study of chunks of text, because of the assumed precision
of such studies. It was James Barr more than any other scholar who first
seriously challenged this preoccupation with words.[15]

There is, in fact, a fine balance to be maintained between two ex-
tremes as we consider the role of words in human communication.
Words are signals, and they form part of a signalling system. So, the
significance of the words cannot arbitrarily be changed by the individual
if his signals are to be correctly perceived by others. On the other hand
it is not possible arbitrarily to insist that the significance of the signs
shall not change. The signs change in their meaning as society insists
collectively that they should change. For example the word 'gay' has
been changed by society and given a meaning, "homosexual", that it did
not have before. It would be simply absurd to insist that the word does
not mean "homosexual" because of its derivation from an Old French
word which did not mean "homosexual". But still we cannot change the
meaning of words arbitrarily, individually, and still expect to use those
words in a useful signalling system. Humpty Dumpty thought that he
could:

'The question is', said Alice, 'whether you CAN make words mean
different things.' 'The question IS', said Humpty Dumpty, 'which is
to be master, that's all.' Alice was too much puzzled to say anything,

so after a minute Humpty Dumpty began again. 'They've a temper, some of them—particularly verbs, they're the proudest—adjectives you can do anything with, but not verbs—however, I can manage the whole lot.'[16]

We must return to the question of the meaning of words in the chapter on lexical semantics.

Linguistics is aimed at helping us to understand human language. Pragmatics concentrates on the interpretation and explanation of utterances. But whether we speak of linguistics in general or pragmatics in particular we are dealing with subjects which are of enormous importance to the correct understanding of the Bible.

1.3 UNIVERSALS OF LANGUAGE[17]

Linguistics is the study of language, not the study of any particular language. This at once indicates an assumption: that the languages of the world have a great deal in common. If that were not so we could not have the comprehensive and generalized discipline designated 'linguistics', and we could not produce a book which attempted to apply general linguistic theory to specific languages. In this section we shall look briefly at the hierarchy of language and at those features of spoken human language which are generally recognized to be universals, without attempting to justify each statement.

For convenience we may organize the phenomenon of human language into a hierarchy of decreasing generality. At the top of the hierarchy is language: the general phenomenon of human speech. Next down is the language family: the Semitic family, including Hebrew and Arabic and Amharic (the principal language of modern Ethiopia) and Maltese; Indo-European (including Italian and German and English and Swedish and Hindi and Bengali); and perhaps twenty other families.[18] Then come the individual languages: French and Norwegian and Swahili. Next are the dialects: Cockney, and Scouse, and Geordie.[19] And finally, at the lowest level of the hierarchy, and with the least generality, comes the idiolect, the unique speech habits of the individual.[20]

Obviously the speech of the individual is a complex blend of the idiosyncratic and the commonplace, a mixture of words pronounced and employed as no one else does, and words pronounced and employed more or less as most other people do. If this were not the case then the individual would not be understood. But just as idiolects have something in common with other idiolects of the same dialect, and just as dialects have something in common with other dialects of the same language, and languages have something in common with other languages of the same language family, so at the top of the language hierarchy it is true that one language family has much in common with other language families. It is not easy to see why this should be so. The range of semiotic systems is enormous, and yet the semiotic systems related to human language show remarkable similarity. The explanation may be found in actual historical relationships between the languages, just as Guthrie was able to demonstrate that the Bantu language family could be explicated in terms of a historical development from two parent languages.[21] Less rigorously, perhaps, we might explain the relationship in terms of intermittent contact between the families: Indo-European with Semitic, Semitic with Cushitic, Cushitic with Nilotic, Nilotic with Bantu and so on. Alternatively one might wish to explain the general homogeneity of the phenomenon of language in terms of human mental processes: that the ability to speak is a function of the brain (more particularly of the left hemisphere of the brain), and that the nature of language is in a sense genetically predetermined.[22] Of course we don't *know* that, but it represents one possible explanation of the homogeneity of language.

That phrase must sound rather hollow to anyone who finds language learning difficult. To such people the 'homogeneity' may well appear to be very elusive. So we turn to a consideration of universals of language.

1. *A limited range of sounds is used.* If we move into a country where the languages are all novel to us, we will always find that a large part of the inventory of sounds being employed is already familiar to us. The way the sounds are put together to produce strings may be unfamiliar, but it is usually not difficult to make at least a reasonable attempt to mimic what is heard. Of course there will almost certainly be some unfamiliar sounds: the 'clicks' of Xhosa, the ejective [t'] of Amharic, the laryngals of Arabic. But still the actual range of sounds used in human language is limited.

This is readily explained: the range of sounds available is simply determined by the means we have of producing them. The so-called speech organs all have other functions, but the lungs, the diaphragm, the tongue, the mouth cavity and the nasal cavity, the vocal chords, all have important functions in producing sounds. However their function is not primarily or exclusively the production of sounds, and in fact the range of sounds they are capable of producing is physiologically limited.

All languages demonstrate a distinction between vowels and consonants and all languages have at least two different vowels.

2. *All languages have sounds grouped together into units* which appear again and again, corresponding to our idea of words. Perhaps the simplest definition of a word is the smallest cluster of sounds repeatedly employed in a language which may be surrounded by a pause, or juncture or silence. Palmer calls it 'the smallest speech unit capable of functioning as a complete utterance'. Unfortunately the pause, the juncture, is not an objective feature of human speech: many rapid speakers are perceived as simply running their words together. However, even they may be invited to slow down, and when they do so the junctures become more apparent.

Some words, but only some, may stand alone. This draws attention to two different classes of words, those which may stand alone and those which (normally) do not. For example, 'this' or 'of' are clearly different in some essential way from 'book' or 'walked'. The former are sometimes termed 'functors', words which function grammatically rather than the latter, which carry the main semantic content. Functors do not normally stand alone in a speech sequence, where the others sometimes do. These functional words are also sometimes termed 'empty', as having no lexical meaning.[23] So we may identify two distinct word classes. But we may approach the question of the nature of the word from the standpoint of the linguist. What does the linguist mean by the term 'word'?

If I begin learning New Testament Greek and learn *ergou* and *ergōn* (the singular and plural genitive forms of the noun meaning 'a work'), have I learned one word or two? It depends on what we mean by 'word'. 'Word' is a simple but elusive term, and linguists make all kinds of attempts to bring some measure of precision into its use. In answer to my question, I might refer to the fact that in my Greek lexicon I would find both *ergou* and *ergōn* under a single entry for the basic form of the two words. The basic or root form of any set of related words (*who, whom, whose,* in English, or the various declined forms of Greek *polis, poli, polin, poleōs* and so on) is termed a *lexeme,* while the derived forms of the lexeme are termed *word-forms*.

In our everyday use of language, words such as 'man', 'boy', *'gynai'* (Greek for 'woman') are labels waiting to be attached to something in the real world. Listed in a dictionary they are of very general application: the word 'boy' *could* be applied to any person of the right age and sex. But once the word is removed from the lexicon and brought into actual use its application may become specific. Thus the same *label*, 'boy', could be attached to several distinct but quite specific objects, boys. The label now has a particular meaning, it applies to *this* boy. In this book, where we wish to draw attention to meaning rather than to a word-form, we use double quotation marks. This represents a minimal distinction required by linguistics, but in an introductory work such as this might be seen to be sufficient.

3. *In all languages comparatively brief sequences of speech* are used corresponding to our notion of sentences. Speech does not simply go on and on until a second speaker interrupts the flow by starting a new flow of words. A point is reached at which it seems appropriate to stop. And this point is not arbitrary. Something has been completed, and the 'something' is what we would mean by 'sentence'. Of course some sentences are enormously long. Some speakers are particularly adept at producing long sentences. But most sentences are reasonably brief: whatever 'reasonably' may mean for speaker and audience.

It has proved to be impossible to define 'sentence' in a way that satisfies all linguists. The main requirement of a sentence, however, is that it should be 'complete'. Not necessarily semantically complete: if a sentence begins 'Therefore' (cf. Romans 12.1) it is impossible to explain the sentence completely without going back to whatever the 'therefore' points to. But it should be possible to produce a complete grammatical analysis of a sentence without going beyond the boundaries of the sentence.

As we have already seen, we distinguish in this book between *sentences* and *utterances*. The term 'sentence' is appropriate to meta-language, language about language, but when a sentence is used in the real world, whether it is spoken or written, it is referred to as an *utterance*. If a grammatically complete sequence of words is encountered twice then meta-linguistically we may refer to the *same sentence* being used because the same *word-forms* appear in each. In real life, however, we would have two different *utterances* because the *word-forms* would be attached to different objects or events in the two usages.

4. *In all languages there are ways of asking questions,* giving commands, making statements. The actual way in which this is effected will differ from language to language. Some languages use interrogatives, words that signal questions. Some do the same thing by using intonation. English does both. The intonation feature is of no use to us when we are attempting to understand written sentences rather than spoken utterances, since we are rarely told anything about the intonation of the written word. But the very fact that intonation may be used to turn a statement into a question should warn us against the naive assumption that the form of a sentence necessarily determines its meaning: 'Is that window open?' has the form of a question, but it may, in fact, be a command, an instruction to close the window.[24]

Questions are used so as to obtain information. But something like seventy per cent of the 'questions' which appear in the New Testament are rhetorical: they are not in fact intended to obtain information, but to convey information. Thus when the writer to the Hebrews asks: '. . . how shall we escape if we neglect such a great salvation?' (Hebrews 2.3), he does not expect his readers to suggest a few possibilities. He is, in fact, strongly affirming by means of the rhetorical question that under the circumstances considered there can be no escape from judgement. Note also John 7.51, where Nicodemus asks, 'Does our law judge a man without first giving him a hearing and learning what he does?', not because he does not know the answer to his question, but to remind his hearers of a principle of the law which they seem set on ignoring.

5. *There are at least two word categories,* the one used to denote objects, corresponding to our notion of nouns, and the other used to denote actions, corresponding to our notion of verbs. These two categories are often labelled nominals and verbals, useful terms since they are very similar to the terms we are already familiar with in traditional grammar, but slightly different so that we do not assume too readily that we are quite certain of what nominals or verbals are.

6. *All languages have word classes* which allow for the modification of the nominals and verbals: let us call them adjectivals and adverbials. These words introduce a kind of 'fine tuning' into language, so that the precision of a communication is potentially increased, depending, of course,

on the speaker's ability to use the adjectivals and adverbials correctly.
A person may be represented simply as walking, or as walking quickly,
or nervously or very slowly, so adding precision to the communication.

7. *All languages have a class of 'pro-forms',* words that stand in the place
of other words or groups of words. In English we have a whole range
of proforms which deliver us from the monotony of repeating 'Uncle
George' each time we talk about (Uncle George) him. This introduces
into language the notion of reduction, producing a more economic use
of language by eliminating clumsy and possibly lengthy repetition:

'I like Uncle George, and I went to see Uncle George yesterday.'

'I like Uncle George, and I went to see him yesterday.'

The noun of a preceding phrase or sentence is usually assumed to be
the antecedent of the pro-form, the noun to which the pro-form refers.
Although the introduction of pro-forms produces by reduction a more
economic and more elegant form of writing, it may also have the effect
of reducing the precision of the language. It is by no means always clear
what the antecedent of a pro-form actually is. In John 3, Nicodemus
begins by saying to Jesus, 'Rabbi, we know. . . '. But who is the 'we'?
Does Nicodemus speak for the Sanhedrin, for his own disciples, for
everyone who had seen Jesus' signs, or for whom? The introduction of
the pro-form leaves the answer to this question unclear (but see below,
8.6).

8. *All languages have the means of expressing negatives:* of expressing a positive
by means of an appropriate negative ('You will not go tomorrow'), or
of saying what did not happen: 'Uncle George did not inherit the garage
from his father', of giving negative commands: 'Don't touch it!'

9. *All languages have some means for the deletion* of tiresome repetitions,
especially repetition of verbal forms. In the passage about women being
subject to their husbands, in Ephesians chapter 5, Paul writes, 'Be subject to one another out of reverence for Christ, wives . . . to your
husbands as to the Lord.' The absence of a verb in the second part of
the sentence is not an invitation to us to supply any 'appropriate' verb,
conjured up from our own prejudices, but a requirement that we find
the parallel antecedent verb and, with appropriate grammatical emendation, use it to fill the blank.

10. *All languages demonstrate morphemic*[25] *structure.* Languages make use of
limited numbers of transferable semantically significant units called

morphemes. In English we have free morphemes, morphemes which can stand alone, such as 'walk', 'think', 'sail', and we have bound morphemes, morphemes which make no sense by themselves but give a precise sense when added to some other morpheme: '-ing', for example. In isolation it means nothing, but when added to the three free morphemes given above changes them to 'walking', 'thinking', and 'sailing', in each case making a similar contribution to the meaning of the resultant word.

1.4 SYNCHRONIC AND DIACHRONIC LINGUISTICS[26]
When we begin to study any given language we quickly discover that it is not homogeneous. There are varieties of accents and a range of dialects and a mass of idiolects. But we will also quickly discover that this kaleidoscope is continually changing with time. The pattern won't stay still. A language has been compared with a river: take a cross-section here and the river can be described, or there and again it can be described, although the description will be different. If we see the length of the river as signifying time then taking a cross-section at different points along the river, and comparing what is found, corresponds to *diachronic* linguistic study, while the examination of a single cross-section corresponds to *synchronic* study. So we might wish to study a particular word, say 'presently', in a language. Synchronically we would examine all the ways in which the word is used at a particular point in time: say *now*. Diachronically we would want to discover how its meaning had changed over the centuries, from the time when it clearly meant "present-ly", "in the present", "now", to the time when it meant "soon", but *not* "now".

cf. Proverbs 12.16: 'A fool's wrath is presently known.' (AV)
'The vexation of a fool is known at once.' (RSV)
(Hebrew *ba-yyōm*, 'in (the) day')

In this example, the AV translation was correct when it was made but is no longer correct because of the shift of meaning of 'presently'.[27] As perceived in the twentieth century the AV rendering of Proverbs 12.16 suggests that a fool is able to bottle up his anger for a while, but eventually it will be shown. That is *not* the nature of a fool's wrath.

The two studies of language, synchronic and diachronic, are important to us in that they warn us against two errors in studying words: the error of thoughtlessly explaining one writer's use of a word by

reference to another person's use of the 'same' word, and the error of
explaining one person's use of a word by reference to how it was used
by someone else and at a different time.

Of course reference to how someone else uses a particular word may
be helpful. But the existence of dialects and idiolects should remind us
that words are mere tokens, tokens which mean something to those
who use them, but which have no meaning in themselves. We cannot
therefore unthinkingly explain the Pauline use of *dikaios* by referring to
John's use of the 'same' word,[28] or Matthew's, or its usage in the Septuagint. These comparisons may be interesting, suggestive, illuminating,
puzzling, but they must always be made with care. Synchronically or
diachronically language is non-homogeneous.

1.5 LINGUISTICS AND THE BIBLE
Having read this far you might still be asking, What, if anything, has
linguistics to do with the Bible? Is the application of the findings of this
rapidly growing discipline to the Bible just another attempt to keep up
with the academic fashion? Can it serve a useful role in biblical interpretation? Or might linguistics merely provide a new bed for contemporary sons and daughters of Procrustes; a device by which we may
stretch areas of the biblical message that don't tell us enough, or lop off
those limbs we deem unnecessarily to protrude?

As we have seen, linguistics is the study not of individual languages,
but of the phenomenon of language itself, and certain of its disciplines
are particularly concerned with the relationship between language and
'meaning'. Since the Bible undeniably comes to us in language, it might
be said the real question is not 'Has linguistics anything to do with the
interpretation of the Bible?', but 'How is it that biblical interpretation
has so far survived without involving itself in the relevant aspects of
linguistics—and even now seems almost wilfully to ignore them?'[29]

A twofold answer might be given to the question. In the first place,
it might be retorted that we are able to understand people and make
ourselves understood without actually being able to give a scientific
account of how we accomplish this; and, by analogy, we can understand
what the biblical writers are saying without knowing how the communication comes about. And secondly, it may be said that many of the
aspects of understanding that would be covered by a course in linguistics

have already been the object of considerable scholarly activity in disciplines with other titles. Would the great philologists of the past, such as Bauer, Blass, Deissmann, and Norden, really have produced significantly better works with the benefit of a course in, say, Lexical Semantics, such as is given today in the Linguistics Department of one of our universities? And have the giants of grammatical research such as Schwyzer, Robertson, Moulton, and Blass at last been buried; felled by pebbles from the sling of the (comparatively) youthful new discipline?

Even to ask such questions seems in a sense irreverent; we owe an incalculable debt to the patient and meticulous work of such scholars. And it is true that the concerns of the science of linguistics are not entirely new; many of them have been faced by earlier generations, and with no mean success. But neither of these responses can be taken as an excuse for ignoring the new discipline.

Linguistics May Afford Further Precision, System and Breadth of Analysis to Some of the Older Disciplines.

Linguistics has a contribution to make even in those areas of past research of which we might justifiably feel most proud. No one can fail to be impressed by, and learn enormously from, Walter Bauer's immense work, *A Greek-English Lexicon of the New Testament and Early Christian Literature*. But even an elementary knowledge of lexical semantics throws up some sharp questions about the book. Not only is the structure of the layout of the entries in the dictionary perceived to be somewhat haphazard, but the entries themselves often fail to give some of the most useful information, for example how any one sense of the word in question differs from other words with a closely related meaning.[30]

The developments in our understanding of this field of study are now such as to justify the publication[31] of a quite different *kind* of dictionary—a dictionary in which entries are classified by field of meaning—not as a replacement for Bauer, but certainly as a necessary adjunct to it. And if there are shortcomings in the major works of the masters themselves, much more may this be said of the average scholar who has neither the time nor the expertise to match Bauer.

To turn to another major work, it has been said that the earlier volumes of the most prestigious *Theological Dictionary of the New Testament* are deeply flawed with what can only (with the benefit of hindsight!) be

called linguistic 'howlers'; theological statements of far-reaching significance were made by a wide range of illustrious scholars on the basis of
a sheer misunderstanding of the way in which language actually functions (for examples see Chapters 4 and 5). The attention of academic
theologians was drawn to the flaws in the work by James Barr in 1961
in his important work, *The Semantics of Biblical Language*, which has been
called 'a trumpet blast against the monstrous regiment of shoddy linguistics',[32] and, at least in principle, the scholarly world has accepted the
rebuke Barr offered. Unfortunately the myths about language that
flawed much academic work before Barr's book was published still per-
sist, and not merely at student and more popular levels of interpretation.
Part of the reason for this is that the positive findings of linguistics have
not been made readily available to those who are engaged in biblical
study. Indeed, Barr himself went little further than pointing out abuses,
and pointing to the potential importance of a study of the field of linguistics. He told us how not to do word-study, and not to confuse word-
study with a study of concepts; but he offered little positive help to those
who approached him asking, 'Make me a disciple, on the condition you
teach me Semantics while I stand on one foot.' And since Barr no one—
at least until very recently—has offered to make up the lack. There is
of course an extensive literature within the discipline of linguistics; but
there are all too few attempts to mediate the results to theological students.[33]

Linguistics Has Also Pioneered New Methods of Text Analysis.
Linguistics may also be able to offer help in familiar areas where biblical
interpretation has not yet charted the theoretical ground. What we have
said so far about the possible relevance of linguistics to biblical interpretation relates primarily to the question of use and abuse of word studies.
But one of Barr's most important emphases was that it is not words
which provide the basic unit of meaning, but the larger elements of
discourse, sentences and paragraphs. We could extend that affirmation
to embrace whole discourses.

Of this we need not pretend biblical scholars have been entirely unaware. Even the scholars whom Barr criticized most strongly appealed
more than occasionally to the context to elucidate verbal meaning. And
the whole science of Old Testament and New Testament introduction,

with its lengthy discussion of the purposes of the writings under consideration, is built on the assumption that to understand, say, Galatians is to understand how the parts relate to the whole, and that in turn requires understanding how 'the whole' relates to the situation Paul addresses. Strenuous attempts are therefore made to analyze the argument and development of themes in the letter in order to penetrate its coherence. This task is undertaken by every commentator of any stature, and numerous monographs have been spawned to deal more precisely with individual elements within the argumentation. H. D. Betz, meanwhile, has also sought to break new ground by attempting to explain the structure of the *whole* epistle in terms of the rhetoric of Hellenistic apologetic letters.[34]

But for all this, it is surely strange that there is little *theoretical* analysis of structuring. In what way does the word order effect the sense? How does a speaker or writer communicate his meaning through the fine texturing of the verbal structure of his material? And in what different ways do smaller units, such as individual propositions, cluster together to make larger ones, and how do these larger units relate in turn to each other to make up whole discourses? These considerations (as well as those of 'style') are surely relevant to an understanding of a text, and yet they receive little discussion in theological works.

The unwary might assume from its name that the recent attention paid by biblical scholars to *structuralism* is an attempt to answer such issues. The term 'structuralism' is currently used in several different ways. It is used, for example, to describe the approach to language which was essentially the fundamental contribution of the father of modern linguistics, Ferdinand de Saussure,[35] though its elements can perhaps be found earlier in Herder, von Humboldt and Leibniz. Saussure's central thesis was that every language is a unique structure or system, and that the units (whether sounds, words or meanings) derive their essence and existence purely from *their relationship to other units in the same language system*. The effects of 'structuralism' in this sense will be traceable throughout this book, though we are neither strictly Saussurean structuralists, nor do we wish to identify with any one post-structuralist school.

But the term is also now used to describe a particular approach to literature based in the social anthropology of Claude Levi-Strauss. It was he who formalized a framework of contrasts, oppositions, similarities and identities by which the significance of any activity might allegedly be measured. Applied to literature by A. J. Greimas, and to *biblical* exegesis by Roland Barthes and others, this basically meant analyzing any plot into the interaction between about twenty stereotyped roles (such as 'Sender' and 'Receiver', 'Helper' and 'Opponent', etc., each a unit; the interaction making the 'structure'). This approach has made surprising inroads into biblical exegesis,[36] surprising because it seems to the authors of this work to have rather little to offer. Its theoretical basis appears to be less-than-adequately substantiated, and its application to texts in practice may well be thought to be little more than the imposition of an arguably alien interpretative framework. Worse, its tendency to reduce all 'plots' to a minimal number of universal 'roles', and all 'meaning' to the pattern of interaction between the role-players, may be suspected of reductionism. Enough has probably been said to make it clear why we doubt this *structuralism* offers the key to analyzing the structure of an author's argument. Indeed structuralism of the literary-critical type is not primarily concerned with the *author's* intention, with literary cotext and historical *context*, at all, but with alleged universal features in texts which make them meaningful *for us*. Its aims are thus very much removed from the concerns of this book, and of traditional exegesis, even if it may offer occasional insights.

Where biblical scholars have attempted to write *methodologically* about the analysis of the structure of larger units they have done so mainly within the confines of their own discipline; dealing with such criteria as the presence of *chiasmus*, of repetition and of other types of parallelism, or with general thematic, form- and redaction-critical considerations. But while theologians have largely neglected a theoretical discussion of semantic and discourse structuring, and how this relates to meaning, *these have become a prime concern for the study of linguistics, especially in the area of the discipline which deals with discourse analysis.*

Unfortunately such studies appear largely to have been overlooked by those engaging in exegesis. At present the application of, say, discourse analysis techniques to biblical materials appears virtually to be confined to the circle of professional Bible translators,[37] and when one member of a colloquy of professors and senior scholars recently offered a careful exegesis of 1 Cor. 14 from the perspective of textlinguistics (an analysis of the factors which structure a discourse) it was greeted as a novelty, and an almost total lack of awareness of the approach was widely evinced by the hearers.[38]

This apparent lack of awareness should perhaps surprise us; especially when we bear in mind that for several decades now scholars have been aware of the potential importance, for interpretation, of correctly elucidating the structure of such sections as Col. 1.15-20, Eph. 1.3-14 and John 1.1-18, for which a myriad of mutually incompatible and often highly subjective analyses have been offered. Discourse analysis may not be able to *solve* the problem of the structuring of these passages (which are uncomfortably short for such analysis), but it at least offers some further and more objective criteria on the basis of which to make decisions. Despite this, it seems that only one scholar has tried to anchor his exegesis of the latter passage in a textlinguistics analysis (and *that* of an attenuated variety).[39] And the more successful application of the techniques to *whole* discourses (such as Colossians or Hebrews)[40] by Bible translators has gone largely unnoticed. Careful work has achieved a measure of success in distinguishing the backbone of these longer discourses from the sections of discourse embedded in it; in distinguishing the paragraph boundaries of the discourse on the basis of such relatively firm criteria as lexico-semantic cohesion, use of particles, discourse function, back reference (e.g. tail-head transitions), change in verb form (tense, mood, person), etc; and in making an important contribution to the elucidation of the semantic structuring of the whole and of its parts. In short, discourse analysis can contribute not only to our understanding of the fine structure of meaning in small units, but can also help us to distinguish the wood from the trees in large units; and it does so by pointing to signals in the text that have all too often been overlooked.

The situation, then, appears to be as follows: biblical scholars are aware they need new tools the better to accomplish some of the interpretative tasks they attempt daily to perform. Several of the disciplines within linguistics have begun to fashion some of the tools required. And yet, for the most part, they are left to stand untried on the workbench! It is surely time for biblical scholars to engage linguistics.

We have suggested that a study of linguistics may afford new precision, system and depth to older disciplines, such as word study, and also provide new criteria for analyzing whole discourses. We must beware, however, of making claims for linguistics that go beyond its competence. Neither linguistics, nor any other discipline, can provide certainty in interpretation. We are as disturbed by Bible translators who seem to think they can penetrate the translatable meaning of a New Testament writing by discourse analysis, *without* reference to the findings of historical-grammatical exegesis, as we are by biblical exegesis that proceeds to talk about the meaning of the same writing without any apparent awareness of theoretical discussions of the variety of ways in which the elusive 'meaning' relates to the surface structure of the text before them.

Establishing the 'meaning' of a text is a complex task for which there are no short cuts, and, in the end, all too few absolute certainties. Linguistics may make us more aware of what we are looking for in general—how texts or spoken utterances 'mean' something. It may also open our eyes to features of the way people use language that we had not considered, and to signals of meaning in our text which we had not previously observed, or of which we had not appreciated the significance. Like historical study, the use of linguistics in biblical interpretation, is not so much to provide assured answers as to *clarify the important questions*. What *kind* of language is the speaker or writer using (literal, metaphorical, affective?), and how can we tell? If it is metaphorical how may we decide what correspondence with reality is intended; if affective language, how do we gauge its significance? What *could* this or that word mean at the time of the speaker, and why has he chosen this particular word here rather than another with closely related meaning? In what ways *might* such and such a proposition relate to those around it, and what signals are there in the text to suggest one possibility is more probable than another? These (and many besides) are the sort of questions linguistics helps us with. It broadens the horizons of our search, and makes suggestions as to what sort of evidence we might look for. But ultimately it is the interpreter who has to put *all* the relevant evidence together—linguistic-semantic, cultural, and historical—in coming to a conclusion about the meaning of a text. And that 'conclusion' is only a hypothesis about the relation of such pieces of evidence as he has considered.

In a book of this size and scope the authors will not be able to break significant new ground on either linguistic or exegetical matters; nor even to give a comprehensive account of the possible relations of the two disciplines. But we may hope to make plain *some* of the potential benefits to be gained from bringing together linguistics and biblical interpretation. And we hope to be able to offer a measure of guidance to students as to how they can use linguistics to develop more nuanced approaches to exegesis.

Notes

[1] R. W. Langacker, *Language and its Structure*, New York, Harcourt, Brace, Jovanovich, 1973[2], chap.2.

[2] Noam Chomsky comments at greater length on this phenomenon in *Current Issues in Linguistic Theory*, New York, Humanity Press, 1964, pp.7-8.

[3] *St John* (ICC), vol.1, p.9. Archbishop Bernard refers to similar ellipsis at 9.3; 13.18; and 15.25. For the reader who is unfamiliar with the technical terms of grammar in general and linguistics in particular we would recommend the work by David Crystal, *A Dictionary of Linguistics and Phonetics*, Oxford, Blackwell, 1985.

[4] J. Lyons, *Language and Linguistics*, Cambridge, CUP, 1981, 1.5, and the more technical discussion of his *Semantics*, vol.1, ch.3, 'Language as a Semiotic System'.

[5] See below, p.237, for a more detailed exegesis of the passage.

[6] See David Hesselgrave's invaluable *Communicating Christ Cross-culturally*, Grand Rapids, Zondervan, 1978, pp.282-4.

[7] J. Corner and J. Hawthorn, *Communication Studies*, London, Arnold, 1980, chap.6: 'Historical Changes in Gestural Behaviour'. See also C. H. Spurgeon, *Lectures to my Students*, London, Marshall, Morgan & Scott, 1954, chaps. 19 and 20, 'Posture, Action, Gesture', for an amusing, informative, and typically Spurgeonic account of the role of gesture in preaching. See further 2.1.7 below.

[8] But note that this translation falls back on LXX for the balancing and explanatory clause; NIV concludes the saying, 'and a chattering fool comes to ruin', which sheds no light on the significance of winking.

[9] On winking see, for example, Prov. 6.12; 10.10; Job 15.12; Ps. 35.19; and the *International Standard Bible Encyclopedia*, art. 'Winking'. In AV Acts 17.30 refers to 'winking' but this is simply an aberration of the translators: the verb *huperoraō* means to overlook in the sense of "to forgive" (although, obviously, not in the sense of "fail to notice").

[10] See G. Brown and G. Yule, *Discourse Analysis*, Cambridge, CUP, 1983, p.19 and J. Lyons, *Semantics*, 1.6. Lyons uses the terms 'System-sentence' for contrived language, and 'Text-sentence' for naturally occurring language.

[11] G. Leech, *Principles of Pragmatics*, 1.2. Formal semantics is sometimes differentiated from the study of meaning in *utterances*. See J. Lyons, *Language and Linguistics*,

5.5 and 5.6; and see below, 1.3, section 3. But on the whole subject of the semantics of utterances see S. C. Levinson, *Pragmatics*, chap. 1, 'The scope of Pragmatics'.

[12]See section 8.6 below.

[13]It is certainly presented in John's Gospel as being spoken by Nicodemus, but firstly it must be recognized that the original words spoken by Nicodemus, presumably in Aramaic, are lost to us, and secondly it must be recognized that the majority of modern scholars would question the historicity of the Nicodemus pericope and would not take very seriously the suggestion that Nicodemus *did*, say 'We know that you are a teacher come from God'.

[14]*The Gospel According to St John*, London, SPCK, 1978[2], p.202.

[15]Stephen Neill gives a lucid and very readable summary of Barr's criticisms in *The Interpretation of the New Testament, 1861-1961*, Oxford, OUP, 1964. On Barr, see below, 1.5.

[16]*Alice Through the Looking Glass*, quoted in E. D. Hirsch, *The Aims of Interpretation*, Chicago, University of Chicago Press, 1976, p.52. On words see also J. Faur, *Golden Doves with Silver Dots*, p.71.

[17]Langacker, *Language and its Structure*, pp.246ff.

[18]See the definitive *The World's Major Languages*, edited by Bernard Comrie. The proposed language families, or *phyla*, are not seen as independent of each other but as related in more or less tenuous ways. The classification is principally the work of J. H. Greenberg and M. Ruhlen, but it may fairly be said that it has not received universal acceptance.

[19]Properly speaking, dialects differ from each other in vocabulary, in grammar, and in pronunciation, not merely in this last feature. Thus Geordie 'Wheer ye gangin hinny' ('Where are you going, honey?') is in vocabulary and grammar indistinguishable from southern English. But note by contrast the Yorkshire use of 'while' to mean 'until', a true indicator of dialect. Words used in games are a good guide to dialect: 'skinch' in Newcastle, 'fainites' in Essex are words used by children to take what the American dialect calls 'time out' from a game.

[20]See particularly the fascinating 'Introduction' to Ronald Wardhaugh's *An Introduction to Sociolinguistics*, Oxford, Blackwell, 1986. See also Lyons, *Language and Linguistics*, pp.17-27 and 9.2, 'Accent, Dialect and Idiolect'.

[21]Malcolm Guthrie was Professor of Bantu Languages in London University's School of Oriental and African Studies. See his four volumes, *Comparative Bantu*, London, Gregg International, 1964.

[22]Noam Chomsky, for example, believes that the complexity of language rules out the possibility of any child merely *learning* it; language ability must, in some sense, be part of a child's genetic inheritance. See Lyons, *Language and Linguistics* 1.2, and Langacker, *Language and its Structure* pp.12-15. See also Noam Chomsky,

Language and Responsibility, Hassocks, Sussex, Harvester Press, 1979, chap. 3, 'A Philosophy of Language'.

[23]See David Crystal, *A Dictionary of Linguistics and Phonetics*, articles on 'Word' and 'Functor'. On 'empty' words see F. R. Palmer, *Grammar*, Harmondsworth, Penguin Books, 1984, chap.2.

[24]For the wider implications of this distinction between 'form' and meaning see especially E. A. Nida and C. R. Taber, *The Theory and Practice of Translation*, Leiden, Brill, 1969, chap.2 , and Leech, *Principles of Pragmatics*, 2.4 and 2.5.

[25]On morphemes, see Langacker, pp.74-8, and R. H. Robins, *General Linguistics, an Introductory Survey*, London, Longmans, 1980[3], 5.4.

[26]Robins, ibid., 1.1.2 and Lyons, *Language and Linguistics*, 2.5. The distinction goes back to de Saussure.

[27]Although in some North American and other dialects of English (including Scottish) the word does still mean "now".

[28]Moises Silva, *Biblical Words and their Meaning*, Grand Rapids, Zondervan, 1983, chap.1. The clearest expression of the distinction between synchrony and diachrony we owe to the linguist Ferdinand de Saussure.

[29]See Güttgemanns' lament that theology has ignored linguistics to its cost: *Studia Linguistica Neotestamentica*, München, Kaiser Vig, 1971, 'Introduction'. For a most readable account of the scope of linguistics, and a plea that its relevance be taken seriously, see R. Hudson, *Invitation to Linguistics,*Oxford, Robertson, 1984, especially chap.9.

[30]For an appreciation and criticism of Bauer see, for example, M. Silva, *Biblical Words and their Meanings*, pp.171-7.

[31]The forthcoming United Bible Societies' *Greek New Testament Lexicon*, edited by J. P. Louw; for details see 5.2.6 below.

[32]Silva, op.cit., p.18.

[33]Notable exceptions are offered in the excellent introductory articles by A. C. Thiselton, 'Semantics and New Testament Interpretation', in I. H. Marshall (ed.), *New Testament Interpretation*, Exeter, Paternoster, 1977, pp.75-104, and by C. Taber on 'Semantics' in *IDB*, and more fully in J. P. Louw, *Semantics of New Testament Greek*, Chico, Scholars Press, 1982.

[34]H. D. Betz, 'The Literary Composition and Function of Paul's Letter to the Galatians', *NTS* 21(1975), pp.353-79. See also his commentary on the letter in the Hermeneia series. But note especially the critique by D. Aune in *The New Testament and its Literary Environment*, Philadelphia, Westminster, 1987, and more fully in his review article in *Religious Studies Review*, 7,4(1981), pp.323-8.

[35]See Tuckett, *Reading the New Testament*, p.152; de Saussure's work *Cours de Linguistique Générale* was published posthumously only in 1916, a fair indication of the comparative youth of serious linguistic study.

36There is a very useful chapter, 'The New Testament and Structuralism' in C. Tuckett, *Reading the New Testament*, London, SPCK, 1987. See also A. M. Johnson (ed.), *Structural Analysis and Biblical Exegesis*, Pittsburg, 1974, and A. C. Thiselton, 'Structuralism and Biblical Studies', *ET*,89(1978). See also Daniel Patte, *What is Structural Exegesis?*, Philadelphia, Fortress Press, 1976.

37See J. P. Louw's essay, 'Discourse Analysis and the Greek New Testament' in *The Bible Translator*,34(1973), pp.101-18, and his *Semantics of New Testament Greek*, chaps.9 and 10. Work on Discourse Analysis of biblical texts for translators has been pioneered by J. Beekman and J. Callow, *Translating the Word of God*, Grand Rapids, Zondervan, 1974; J. Beekman, J. Callow, and M. Kopesec, *The Semantic Structure of a Written Communication*, Dallas, SIL, 1981, W. Pickering, *A Framework for Discourse Analysis*, Dallas, SIL, 1978, and Kathleen Callow, *Discourse Considerations in Translating the Word of God*, Grand Rapids, Zondervan, 1974. See also the relevant work of E. Nida et al. *Style and Discourse*, Capetown, BSSA, 1983.

38L. Hartman, 'I Co. 14.1-25: Argument and Some Problems', in L. De Lorenzi, *Charisma und Agape (1 Ko 12-14)*, Rome, Benedictina, 1983, pp.149-169.

39R. Schnackenburg, 'Die Grosse Eulogie Eph.1.3-14, Analyse unter textlinguistischen Aspekt', *BZ*, 21(1977), pp.67-87. His EKK commentary reflects throughout some of the fruits of his approach, although he does not use it overtly. The only commentaries of which we are aware that constantly appeal to approaches informed by linguistics are W. Schenk's *Die Philipperbriefs des Paulus*, Stuttgart, Kohlhammer, 1984, and J. P. Louw, *A Semantic Discourse Analysis of Romans*, 2 vols, Pretoria, University of Pretoria Press, 1979.

40See, for example, W. Pickering, *A Framework for Discourse Analysis*, Dallas, SIL, 1978, on Colossians, and L. L. Neeley, 'A Discourse Analysis of Hebrews', *Occasional Papers in Translation and Textlinguistics* 3-4(1987), pp.1-146.

2. Semantics
& Hermeneutics

2.1 SEMANTICS[1]

In this chapter we approach an issue that is fundamental both to linguistics and to biblical exegesis: the question of meaning. We shall set out a brief introduction to the issues involved in 2.1, and then develop the more important of them in some detail in 2.2 and in later chapters.

Semantics is that aspect of linguistics which deals with meaning in language. Perhaps surprisingly not all linguists have assigned any particular priority to meaning. Noam Chomsky produced the most innovative development in linguistic theory, generative grammar, in 1957,[2] a theory which was notable for the rigour of its method. But of set purpose he omitted semantics from his system.[3]

But we feel, intuitively, that any linguistic theory that fails to integrate meaning into its analysis is to that extent already flawed. It is not at all surprising that those involved in developing the theory of generative grammar rapidly recognized the need to incorporate semantics into the system, so that as early as 1963 J. J. Katz and J. A. Fodor had published 'The structure of a semantic theory'[4] which initiated the search for an integrated generative grammar.

Although the question of meaning is highly elusive, and the study of semantics far more complex than we might initially suppose, meaning remains a central issue for linguistics.

2.1.1 The Meaning of Meaning[5]

We use the word 'meaning' in various ways, and for that reason we need to decide how we intend using that word here. Consider some possible usages of the words 'mean' and 'meaning':

S1 'You never say what you mean.'
S2 'What do you mean by "rationalization"?'
S3 'I did not mean to insult you.'
S4 'She means well.'
S5 'This means war!'
S6 'The root meaning of the word 'holy' is "separate".'

The first five of these sentences could, without too much difficulty, be provided with appropriate contexts and even cotexts so as to produce convincing real-life scenarios. Sentence six is clearly metalinguistic, but even so a real-life scenario within which it might occur could be created. The creative act would take into account the non-technical nature of the definition offered.

Sentences 3 and 4 both seem to point to 'intention', the intention of whoever produced the sentences, and sentence 5 points to 'implication and not to the (absurd) suggestion that the word 'this' means "war". Sentence 6 involves some process of clarification. The first two sentences suggest that a communication is taking place between two people, that each is aware of an intention to communicate which, for different reasons, is not satisfactorily being realized.

How is it possible to speak without satisfactorily and unambiguously communicating meaning? A rather trivial explanation might be found in the speaker's or the hearer's lack of facility in the language. It is a simple fact that some speakers have a better control of language than others, constructing well-formed sentences and sequencing the sentences in a logical order. Much more interesting, however, is the situation where both speaker and listener have good control of the language but still the communication is perceived to fail: meaning is not perceived, or if it is, it is recognized that the perception is inadequate.

This commonplace experience, the experience of inadequate perception of 'meaning', is not, at this point in our study, altogether surprising.

A little introspection might lead us to the conclusion that the effectiveness of our attempts at communication is somehow related to our actual experience of the communication process and our ability to learn from that experience. To quote John Lyons again: 'The fact remains that the meaning of words and sentences is learned and maintained by the use to which language is put in communicative situations.'[6] 'Meaning' is to be related to the human communication process. This directs attention to three aspects of that process: the (two) participants and the communication. There are correspondingly three aspects to 'meaning' as it is applied to the process: meaning$_1$, *author's* meaning; meaning$_2$, receptor's meaning, or *perceived* meaning; meaning$_3$, sentence meaning, or *textual meaning*.

2.1.2 Authorial Meaning

Author's meaning is necessarily subjective: only the author can ultimately[7] and authoritatively respond to remove my confusion if I fail to perceive his communication. In reality very few human communications are entirely misperceived. But most human communications are in some sense partially opaque, even where the words used present no particular problem. John records that Jesus told the crowd: 'You will seek me and you will not find me; where I am you cannot come' (John 7.34), to which the crowd responded, 'Where does this man intend to go that we shall not find him? . . . What does he mean by saying "You will seek me and you will not find me," and, "Where I am you cannot come"?' The text here is concerned with dialogue, with real language, with repartee.[8] In repartee it is necessary to go beyond the *text* to the total *context*, and to the full *cotext* if meaning is to be satisfactorily discerned. In the above example the *text* would be the words spoken by Jesus, 'You will seek me and you will not find me', the *cotext* would be the surrounding account of the discussion, at least John 7.32-6, and the context is first-century Jerusalem grappling with the problem of understanding the person of Jesus. And even when we have studied text, cotext, and context we may still be left with no more than the probability that we have correctly perceived meaning, in the above example the meaning intended by Jesus.

There is a further potential problem to be considered: the problem posed by a speaker's occasional unwillingness to make his meaning clear, possibly even his unwillingness to make it clear to himself. We live in society, and it is important that we live peaceably in society. We may find ourselves caught out in a statement which we would rather not have made. If it has not been understood . . . so much the better: let it remain not understood. If it has been understood let us by all means dis-clarify it. To some extent apocalyptic literature is of this genre. To those who hold the interpretative key to the symbols employed, the literature may be entirely clear. To those who do not hold the key, the literature is simply perplexing. The casual reader of Revelation who first encounters chapter twelve would almost certainly find the unexpected introduction of a pregnant woman and a red dragon incomprehensible (see below, 9.6), and the reference in Revelation 13.18 to 'the number of the beast', six hundred and sixty-six, has tested the ingenuity of innumerable commentators, although presumably both the Seer and his potential readers would have understood the symbolism.

Some societies have developed a distinct literary genre which serves to conceal meaning. The Ethiopian 'Wax and Gold'[9] is a striking example. A sentence, perceived at the surface level, is mere wax, innocuous. But perceived at a deeper level, through an awareness of a subtle system of coding, the sentence becomes gold. In the closing years of the Ethiopian Empire anecdotes could safely be told of lion hunts, but the elaboration of some of these anecdotes made it at least possible that the 'lion' was Emperor Haile Selassie, the 'Lion of Judah'. However, the identification could always be denied if it was politic to do so, and the 'wax' meaning could be asserted by the speaker.

In considering authorial intention it is important to be able to identify the author's intended literary genre. Was it 'Wax and Gold', or was it poetry, or metaphor, or parable, or hyperbole, or cold history? Where, as in the New Testament, a passage is explicitly labelled by the author as 'Parable', it could be misleading and even absurd to treat it as history, although this is not to dismiss the possibility of an historical event being turned into parable. Even if a passage is not specifically labelled it is still important to attempt to determine in cases of ambiguity what the intention of the author was. Luke 15.3-7 is parabolic. But what is to be said about Luke 16.19-31, which begins 'There was a rich man' without the preceding formula indicating that we are being offered a parable? Clearly the structure of the story should indicate its literary genre, but this at once presents a problem: the structure appears to be composite, as though there were two stories with two applications. This complexity requires explanation. Howard Marshall indicates[10] that the story itself appears to be a parabolic development of a folk tale which had its origin in Egypt but which had been modified and incorporated into Jewish oral literature. The original teaching of the story, that a man's status in life might be reflected in his funeral, but might well contrast with his after-life, is retained, but the story is extended to develop a second point absent from the original. The new point is that the refusal of the Pharisees to accept the teaching of Jesus is an absolute refusal: no imaginable level of miracle would suffice to convince them of his true status, not even a witness from the dead.

Thus although the story is not designated a parable it *is* a parable, uncharacteristically[11] demonstrating two distinct teachings, the one to be attributed to the source story, and the other to the requirements of the context within which the story was told by Jesus.

The importance of *context* in the elucidation of meaning was central to the semantic theories of J. R. Firth,[12] who used the term 'contextualization' to describe that part of the process of discerning meaning which consisted in the identification of the total context of any utterance. Once set in a specific and defined context the author's intended meaning, the speaker's intended meaning, could be determined. Without that context a 'sentence' was, for Firth, little more than a trivial string of symbols to which no semantic significance could be given.

It is arguable that no string of words can be context-less: that any string is produced by someone, somewhere, somehow. Thus if I sit down and write 'The sentence "The cat sat on the mat" is an example of a grammatically well-formed sentence' then the sentence quoted ('The cat sat on the mat') has a perfectly well-defined context (the writer, producing an example of a well-formed sentence). The reader will not be foolish enough to ask the cat's name or the address of the house, or whether it was raining at the time, precisely because he will have correctly identified the context of the sentence, which is not that of any real cat sitting anywhere. The point that is being made here is an important one: that language is produced in context by particular people, and both a knowledge of the general context and of the specific individual generating the language is usually involved in the process of discerning meaning.

As we shall see below (2.2.2) an energetic debate continues on the importance of author's meaning. Is author's intended meaning the only correct meaning, or is it legitimate to insist on some other meaning, possibly even contradicting an author's claimed intended meaning? E. D. Hirsch is perhaps the leading proponent of the theory of the determinacy of author's intention; he insists,

> A text cannot be interpreted from a perspective different from the original author's. Meaning is understood from the perspective that lends existence to meaning. Any other procedure is not interpretation but authorship.[13]

In attempting to relate these matters to biblical interpretation we must be aware of the existence of further levels of complication. Thus Luke writes down what was said, let us say, by John the Baptist, and at once we are confronted with two authors, John and Luke, and two quite different contexts, the context of John's original speech and the context of Luke's compiling the Gospel. In fact the position is more complex than this: Luke did not hear what John said; he (probably) used Mark and (possibly) Q as his source(s). And again, those who believe in inspiration will need to add a fourth level of authorial intention, that of the Holy Spirit, while others might wish to eliminate *Luke* from the list of authors altogether.

2.1.3 Text Meaning

When we use language we produce more-or-less objective strings of morphemes, together with a superimposed collection of modifiers: stress, intonation pattern and accompanying gesture both instinctive and paralinguistic. The subjective element may be disowned, but still there remains in verbal communication an objective element to which appeal must always be made in any attempt to elicit meaning. No matter what the intonation or accompanying gesture, the utterance 'Send for John Smith' cannot readily be interpreted to mean "I had bacon for breakfast on Christmas Day".

In the exegesis of written texts, such as Bible texts, we are confronted with an objective reality: these (so far as textual criticism has been able to determine them) are the words that were written down. They are the ultimate authority, the principal objective evidence available to us, and attempts to make sentences mean something other than what they clearly do mean must be resisted.[14] In elucidating meaning, here, we would clearly be involved in lexical semantics, and in the study of grammar and of syntax. The meaning we eventually identify as attaching to any sentence is perceived through those linguistic disciplines.

The problem of biblical interpretation lies precisely in the recognition that most ancient texts do not have clear meanings readily discernible by us today. The sheer chronological distance separating the modern commentator from the text, the cultural gulf yawning between text and modern commentator, as well as the problems of Greek and Hebrew grammar, ensure that even certainty of text cannot guarantee clarity of meaning. In the matter of context outstanding work has been done towards providing us with a comprehensive and synthesized view of the state of our present knowledge about the background to the biblical texts. The text-narrative approach of, for example, Gerd Theissen,[15] the detailed work of E. P. Sanders, especially in his *Jesus and Judaism*[16] and the varied writings of Martin Hengel[17] have served to bring together in readily accessible and notably memorable ways just that information which is needed for the responsible exegesis of the text. And it is certainly a step in the right direction to find contemporary commentators concentrating attention on the objective text confronting them, and attempting to discern meaning in the text, rather than concentrating primarily on the subjective task of recreating some supposed ur-text.[18]

For the fact is that someone, somewhere, put this text together in this way and in so doing intended to convey a meaning, a meaning, moreover, which has a value and an authority which could not be accorded to the ur-text except in those rare cases where the new text is accorded near-unanimous approval.

John 20.17 provides a useful illustration of the point. Jesus is represented as saying to Mary '*mē mou haptou*', the negative of a present imperative. The verb *haptesthai* appears again only at 1 John 5.18, and means "to touch". But this presents an apparent inconsistency: in 20.27 Thomas is positively invited to touch the risen Jesus. In his 1928 commentary Bernard suggested a textual emendation which removed the inconsistency, building on the admitted textual variations at this point. Some texts omit *mou* altogether, and Codex Vaticanus has *mē haptou mou* and Bernard suggested that the original text was *mē ptoou*, "Do not be afraid", which through a scribal error became *mē aptou*, which then became *mē mou aptou* and *mē aptou mou*, by way of clarification. The emendation is ingenious and resolves the apparent problem, but it has not won acceptance. The reason is that further consideration of the objective text, and especially of the significance of the negative form of the present imperative,[19] resolved the problem without any need for textual emendation. R. Schnackenburg reminds us that 'When the act of touching has already begun, the negative present imperative can also mean, Do not hold on to me any longer, let me go!'[20]

For biblical interpretation the nature of the objective text is important. In the Bible we are always confronted with a text which was created within a context. It has long been recognized that the identification of that context is vital to the correct interpretation of the text. There are at least two contexts to be taken into account: the milieu within which the actual events underlying the text took place, and the context of the creation of the text itself. To Paul Ricoeur, who is both philosopher-linguist and theologian,[21] we owe what might be termed a spiral model of textual exegesis. Ricoeur notes the three principal stages in the development of a text: the occurrence of an event, the recording of the event to create a Word, and the study of the Word in order to discern meaning and significance. Between event and Word, and between Word and interpretation there inevitably stand longer or shorter periods of time. Between event and Word there stands a period of time during which a potential writer must decide on the principles which will stand behind his work. He will decide on the literary genre to be used, on the level of language to be adopted, and on the general character of the editing process, the redaction process,[22] that must inevitably take place. Some details must be omitted, others included, and appropriate emphasis given to each. But then there is the time lapse between the creation of a Word and the approach to that Word by an interpreter. In the case of biblical material this time lapse may be of the order of hundreds of years, during which the text remains constant but language and culture change, leading to increasing possibilities of polysemy: multiple meaning. Ricoeur saw that the task of the interpreter must be to get back even behind the word to the event so that the contemporary significance of the event might be correctly perceived.

2.1.4 Perceived Meaning

We may sometimes be assisted in our elucidation of meaning in texts by the observation of perceived meaning at the time. Thus in Luke 22.70, Jesus' response to his accusers with regard to whether he was or was not 'Son of God' is an enigmatic *humeis legete hoti egō eimi*, which is translated

> by NIV as 'You are right in saying I am'
> by RSV as 'You say that I am'
> by NEB as 'It is you who say I am'.

It is significant at this point to note that his interrogators perceived his response as affirmative:[23] 'Why do we need any more testimony? We have heard it from his own lips.' The situation being depicted is very dramatic but linguistically unclear. Any credible attempt to understand what Luke signals when he thus records the words of Jesus must take into account the way in which he describes the perception of those words by those who then heard it. For his hearers were well qualified to understand it, better qualified, indeed, than the modern exegete could possibly be.

The highly complex matter of the relationship between author's intended meaning and audience perceived meaning is discussed below, 2.2.2 and 3.3.

2.1.5 Denotation[24] and Connotation[25]

But we have still by no means exhausted the question of the inherent complexity of 'meaning'. In the real world within which human language must be used words and phrases do not only have a context: they also have a history. Meaning, whether authorial, textual or audience-perceived is usually affected by this historical aspect of language, the social context of language. So we recognize two further distinctions in semantics, the distinction between denotative meaning and connotative meaning.

Many lexemes have rather clear denotative meaning. Nominal forms such as 'man', 'cat', 'tree', 'house' and so on can be applied to real objects, quite distinct from other real objects. The lexeme does have a distinctive denotation: a cat is not a house. A dog is a canine quadruped.[26] Of course the denotation is not always as clear as we might wish it to be. Thus 'shoe', 'sandal', 'slipper', 'plimsoll', 'boot', 'clog', 'pump' and 'welly' all refer to footwear, and in translation, at least, we may need to find some reliable means for differentiating one from the other, and finding an appropriate equivalent to some particular footwear referred to in the Bible.[27] We might then consider some kind of comparative inventory of properties: made of leather? with laces? worn indoors? over the ankles? and so on, producing distinctive distributions of each feature which may then be matched with similar or even identical distribution patterns in the receptor language. Thus it is possible when handling a text to develop a reasonably objective method for determining denotative meaning.

However, when we come to the study of language as it is actually used, we find a second category of meaning intruding itself: connotative meaning. Here we move away from objectivity to subjectivity, away from cold grammar to flesh-and-blood utterances. Words are not, in fact, the neutral entities we might intuitively assume them to be. Each of us develops a relationship towards words, based on repeated experiences of their usage and of the referents which lie behind the words. We know the word 'father' and we know also our own experience of 'father': a kindly figure, a bullying figure, an absent figure, a suffering figure or whatever. We also have some experience of other people's fathers, and we have our attempt to formalize this diverse experience. Inevitably then the word 'father' carries for each individual a connotation.

Connotation is also in some cases determined by society. Animals are usually treated in some sense anthropomorphically, in fairy stories, for example. The fox is cunning, the jackal despicable, the monkey sharp, the mule stubborn, the elephant never forgets. Human beings are treated in the same way: mothers-in-law are figures of fun, step-mothers are inevitably cruel. The interpreter of the Bible must be aware of the real danger of importing into an ancient culture the connotative perceptions with which he is familiar in his own culture. There is, after all, no particular reason why a fox (Luke 13.32) should be always and everywhere 'cunning'. It is true that in classical and Hellenistic Greek the fox was presented as crafty, and this characteristic eventually moved into rabbinic literature[28] but in Ezekiel 13.3-4 (RSV) the *foolish* prophets are likened to foxes, and there is the further possibility that Jesus had in mind the pretentions of Herod to the lordly status of a lion when he was in reality no more than a puppet king, better compared to a cringing fox.[29] Louw, on the other hand, suggests that the English 'rogue' or 'rascal' is closer to the intended meaning of 'fox' in Luke 13.32.[30]

Connotative meaning is elusive. I may be able to find out the general societal view of the fox, but I may not know your particular view of mothers-in-law. Nor do you know my particular view. If I tell a story involving mothers-in-law and my attitude is sympathetic, I may well be confused to discover that you have perceived my story very differently because of your connotative relationship to 'mother-in-law'. In exegesis it is clearly important to ensure that the connotative meaning assumed for a word in the text is preserved in the exegesis by the choice of an appropriate equivalent. Take for example John 2.4, Jesus' response to Mary's information about the inadequacy of the wine supply at the Cana wedding. The English translations vary considerably:

AV 'Woman, what have I to do with thee?'
RSV 'O woman, what have you to do with me?'
NIV 'Why do you involve me?'
NEB 'Your concern, mother, is not mine.'
GNB 'You must not tell me what to do, woman.'[31]

To the modern reader of this story in English, the word 'woman' here has an odd connotation. It is either abrupt, rude, and certainly un-filial, or else it is coarse, familiar and again un-filial. The introduction by NEB of 'mother' is clearly more appropriate to the context and is connotatively equivalent to *gynai* even though it might be argued that *gynai* does mean "woman". Denotatively it does. Connotatively and in this particular context the rendering will not do.

For exegesis this question of connotation is of great importance. In explaining a text the connotation of any particular rendering must be considered and must be considered *for the audience being addressed*.

2.1.6 Implicature

Language is interesting in that what is implied may be as informative as what is said. Thus if I ask my wife, 'Did you get the beans and the ice cream for supper?', and she replies 'I got the beans', then there is an implication that she did not get the ice cream.[32] Notice that this implication is not the same as a logical entailment: an implicature may be shown to be not, in fact, realized.

The notion of implicature is of importance in the interpretation of utterances in general and of conversations in particular. As we shall see below (8.2) conversations are governed by certain principles, amongst which is the expectation of co-operation. Another is the principle of context-appropriateness. The actual words used in conversation might appear to run contrary to those principles. My wife asked me: 'Are the girls in yet?', and I replied, 'The porch light is still on.' Taken out of context the two utterances appear to be unrelated, and my response would appear to disregard both principles. However my response had an implicature which did not require to be expressed: 'The porch light is still on, *the girls would have switched it off had they come in, and so I can say that they are not yet in.*' The conversation principle that I should not include unnecessary information is observed and so are the two earlier principles.

In John 1.35-9 we have a sequence of utterances which illustrate the notion of implicature:

'Behold the Lamb of God!'
which was more than a command to *look* at Jesus. This is clear from what followed: two of John's followers left him to follow Jesus. The utterance may be glossed somewhat as follows:

'I told you that a prophet was coming who is greater than I, and you seemed interested in him. Well, behold the Lamb of God, *so if you wish to find out more about him go and talk to him.'*
The next part of the conversation is between the two disciples and Jesus:

'What do you seek?'
and they replied:

'Rabbi, where are you staying?'
to which Jesus responded:

'Come and see.'
Again there is an implicature in the words of the disciples. They did not want the address of the house in which Jesus was staying and so Jesus did not give it to them. Their utterance might be glossed:

'Rabbi, we would like to know more about you. May we spend time with you? Where do you live? If you tell us then perhaps we might come to talk with you?'
Again, when James writes 'Don't show favouritism' (James 2.1), the sentence itself carries the implicature that the Christians to whom he wrote

SEMANTICS & HERMENEUTICS   **49**

did, in fact, show just that kind of discrimination against which he
wrote. The recognition of implicature enables us to recognize the legitimacy and even the necessity of understanding the meaning of utterances as extending beyond the evident meaning of the actual words used.

The assertion of an implicature is not merely a matter of the imagination. It must be shown to be required as an explanation of the sequence of utterances under consideration. We might ask 'Why did John's
disciples go after Jesus when they heard what John had to say about
him?' We might ask 'Why did James tell Christians not to discriminate
against the poor?' Or we might ask 'Why does the author of The Acts
of the Apostles say "we made a direct voyage" in Acts 16.11, but "they
went down to Troas" in verse 8?' It is in the answers to such appropriate
questions that implicatures are identified.

2.1.7 Gesture[33]

Although gesture is usually separated from the science of linguistics it
is in fact an accompaniment to every utterance. It is quite impossible not
to add to verbal communication some gestural component. As Freud put
it: 'No mortal man can keep a secret. If his lips are silent he chatters with
his fingertips; betrayal oozes from him at every pore.'

More than 130 distinct body movements[34] have been identified associated with the English culture, and these relate to the eyes, the fingers,
the legs, the lips and so on. The eyes open wide, close to a slit, offer a
sideways glance, stare fixedly, close firmly, or perhaps wink. The mouth
is particularly mobile. As Bolinger expresses it, 'Language is embedded
in gesture', and our comprehension of any *written* text is in some sense
simplistic since we lack many of the vital clues to the meaning because
gesture is not consistently indicated to us.

The general phenomenon of gesture is commonly divided into two
categories, *paralinguistic gesture* and *instinctive gesture*. Paralinguistic gesture
is again divided into two categories, *learned* and *instinctive*. Each principal
category may further be subdivided, learned into *lexical* and *iconic*, and
instinctive into *involuntary* and *voluntary*, although the boundary between
these two latter categories is imprecise.

Learned lexical gesture is close to being a complete paralanguage. In
situations where noise is undesirable we may nod to indicate agreement,
put a finger to the lips to urge quietness, put a hand to the ear to signal

inability to hear, point to signal a relevant feature or use the thumbs-up gesture to indicate that all is well. In Acts 21.40 Paul 'motioned with his hand to the people', an iconic gesture which apparently resulted in 'a great hush'. In Acts 22.23 we find two actions described: the crowd 'waved their garments' and they 'threw dust into the air', actions indicative of violent disapproval of Paul's speech. All three of these gestures would be learned, and the latter pair would be culture-specific. Iconic gesture is frequently transferable across cultures.

In general, however, gesture does *not* transfer across cultural boundaries without change of meaning. The same facial expression or the same hand gesture may have quite different meanings in different societies. Even the 'smile' is to be seen as essentially no more than a signal produced by a particular state of the facial muscles. It may indicate pleasure or it may indicate embarrassment and actual displeasure. Even within a single culture laughter may signal amusement, incredulity, cynicism, embarrassment, hysteria and mockery.

Instinctive gesture begins with a range of involuntary actions, including laughter and tears. These and other features of instinctive gesture tend to be cross-culturally transferable. However most adults learn to transform these involuntary and instinctive actions into controlled voluntary gesture. Both smiles and tears, although in origin instinctive, may become learned and to that extent potentially deceptive.

In biblical texts some indication is occasionally given of gesture which accompanies speech. Thus in Acts 26.1 we are told that Paul 'stretched out his hand' and then began his speech in defence. Here we simply do not know the significance of the gesture: unlike the earlier passage, Acts 21.40, no indication is given of any response to the gesture. In the same context we are told that Paul's accusers 'stood up' (25.18). In Acts 13.3 we note that the leaders of the church 'laid their hands' on Paul and Barnabas before sending them off to Cyprus. Galatians 2.9 refers to James, Peter and John giving 'the right hand of fellowship' to Paul and Barnabas, apparently a particular symbol of association. On the other hand we read in Acts 13.51 of Paul and Barnabas 'shaking off the dust' from their feet as a signal of rejection of the Jews of Pisidian Antioch.

2.1.8 Body Language[35]
Body language is to be distinguished from gesture, and belongs properly

to the heading *kinesics*. Here we are concerned with a whole language of communication of which most people are overtly unaware. The juxtaposition of two speakers, their movements nearer to and further from one another chart the progress of the conversation. The posture of the participants is certainly important. In Nazareth Jesus received the scroll of Isaiah from the synagogue attendant and read it standing. He then gave it back to the attendant and sat down. It was this action, apparently, which signalled to the congregation that he was about to expound the passage he had read. And so 'the eyes of all in the synagogue were fixed on him' (Luke 4:20).

The narrative passage Luke 4.16-21 describing Jesus' participation in synagogue liturgy at Nazareth usefully illustrates many of the issues relevant to the careful exegesis of any written record of a historical event. The most obvious problem is the inescapable redactional activity of the author. We know that in synagogue worship there were regular liturgical constituents. Luke in his account of Jesus' Nazareth address makes no mention of the Psalm, of the recitation of the *Shema'* or the Blessings, nor of the Torah reading. The immediate impression given is that events commenced with the reading from the Prophets (the *haptārāh*).[36] Again, we are not told the circumstances under which Jesus came to read that day: presumably it had been arranged with the Ruler of the synagogue.[37] Nor are we told why he read from that particular passage: almost certainly there was at that time no fixed lectionary.[38] We are not told how it was that Jesus came to give the commentary on the Prophets.[39] However, Luke's redaction, those parts of the incident which he chooses to record, is entirely in accord with what we know from other sources of synagogue worship of the day.

2.1.9 Meaning and Significance[40]

The modern reader of the Bible is, presumably, hoping to understand what is read and, possibly, to apply it to the decision-making process that is an inescapable part of life. This second part of the reader's concern is not necessarily present when the same reader studies other forms of ancient, or even modern, literature. Practical exegesis requires us to take seriously these two aspects of the reader's concern: to enable the reader to understand the text in its original setting and to discern its significance *now*.

The careful study of a text allows us to determine its meaning with a greater or lesser precision depending on the information available to us. We may, for example, study the Lucan account of the Lord's Supper and determine its meaning by reference to contemporary practice, indications of time given in the cotext and the grammar and syntax of the actual text of the account. But this leaves the event firmly in the first century. In determining meaning we have completed a first stage in interpretation, indeed a decisive stage. Anything that is done beyond this stage must be controlled by the meaning that has been identified in the first stage. Careful exegesis will take account of the contemporary reader's tendency to import into the text knowledge which is available to him but which was not available to the original reader of the same text, and so to misrepresent the text.

Thiselton makes reference to the parable of the Pharisee and the Tax Collector in Luke 18.9-14.[41] The fact is that the perceptions of the story by a first-century Jew and by a twentieth-century Englishman will be vastly different. For one thing the Jew knows that the Pharisee is a good and godly man, while the Englishman knows that the Pharisee is a hypocrite. The Jew, therefore, is astonished when Jesus concludes that the Tax Collector is justified but the Pharisee is not. The Englishman finds nothing surprising in this conclusion. He has been expecting it. But by this process of understanding the point being made by Jesus is lost. Jesus is saying that the Pharisee who, it seemed, deserved God's grace, didn't get it, while the Tax Collector who did not deserve God's grace did get it. We know from the start that the Pharisee does not deserve God's grace. As a result we miss Jesus' point entirely and substitute a new significance for it. Jesus was saying that grace comes to the undeserving. We perceive him as warning us not to be hypocrites like the Pharisees.

The parable allows us to see what Hirsch and Thiselton are driving at. We must as a vital preliminary establish the meaning of a text, and only then may we determine the significance of the text for the present reader *in conformity with that determined meaning*. If we fail to take this second horizon seriously then we may well allow the reader or listener to import into an anecdote or parable a significance not intended by the author at all.

The imagery of two horizons has been employed by Hans-Georg Gadamer, a philosophical linguist who described himself as not so much a theoretician as a describer[42] of the way things are. It is difficult to argue with Gadamer's pragmatic assertion that any text must necessarily relate to two horizons: the horizon of the original event of bringing the text into existence, and the horizon of the reader of the text. It is out of this recognition of two horizons that the distinction between meaning and significance arises. Hirsch defines significance as 'textual meaning as related to some context, indeed any context beyond itself'.[43]

We turn now to a more detailed investigation of some of the aspects of meaning which have been thus far only superficially introduced.

2.2 THE TASK OF EXEGESIS AND THE NATURE OF 'MEANING'

We have outlined some of the aspects of semantics which bear on the interpretation of texts, including biblical ones. Our purpose in this section is to consider in more detail some of the dimensions of the question of textual 'meaning'. The hermeneutical issues raised may then be developed more systematically in the chapters which follow.

Hermeneutics can be defined simply as the study of how we determine what a discourse means. By 'discourse' we mean any form of oral or written communication; from a legal summons to Tennyson's 'The Lady of Shalott', and from the snatch of an utterance in Acts 5.30, 'The God of our fathers raised up this Jesus—whom you killed by hanging him on a tree', to the whole of Acts. And we shall use the word 'text' to denote a written record of the words of such a communication, or copies or editions thereof.

How do we come to an understanding of these discourses? That is the question which is the particular concern of hermeneutics. The answer to the question is neither easy to formulate nor uncontroversial when it has been formulated. The problem appears in perhaps its most acute form when readers perceive quite different meanings in one and the same text. Perceived meaning is often not singular.

John Donne wrote a poem called 'A Valediction Forbidding Mourning'. Its opening lines run:

> As virtuous men pass mildly away
> And whisper to their souls to go
> While some of their sad friends do say
> 'Now his breath goes', and some say 'No' . . .

Later in the poem we read:
    Our two souls therefore, which are one,
    Though I must go, endure not yet
    A breach.
Finally we read:
    Thy firmness makes my circle just,
    And makes me end where I began.
E. D. Hirsch describes how his class, on reading this, became convinced
that the poem portrayed a dying speaker giving comfort to his loved
ones before his death. Hirsch himself, however, argued strongly that it
was about no such thing, but about the sorrow of a temporary physical
absence from a friend, a view which seems to be confirmed in the lines
in the final three verses of the poem, the details of which need not
concern us. What is of more significance is that Hirsch records that he
failed to convince his class that his view was the right one. Having
arrived at their provisional conclusion about the meaning of the poem
they could not see it in any other way.[44]

For those of us who regularly attend churches, listen to sermons, or
read theological works, the example could readily be multiplied. We do
not need to be reminded of the fact that different readers understand
texts not merely in different ways, but actually in ways which are mutually incompatible. The question is, why do they do so, and of what
significance is the phenomenon for hermeneutics?

2.2.1 Different Interpretations of the Fact of Contradictory Readings of a Text

Let us begin by outlining two possible responses to the problem posed
by mutually contradictory readings of a single text. On the one hand it
could be argued that both Hirsch and his students might be correct. This
could, perhaps, be justified by arguing that texts do not have meaning
in themselves: they have meaning only for readers. 'Meaning' lies entirely in the reader's own perception. At the opposite extreme it might
be affirmed that only the writer's intended meaning is correct; the interpreter's task would then be to adjudicate between Hirsch and his
students as to which of the two (if either) faithfully reflected John
Donne's meaning.

The first of these two options might not sound particularly inviting (although it is found in the typical church usage of Bible texts!). However, it turns out to have serious supporters in more academic circles at the extreme end of the Reader-Response interpretative school as represented by, for example, Roland Barthes, Jacques Derrida and Stanley Fish. According to their understanding, meaning is merely potential in any text; it only becomes actual in relation to a reader. Stanley Fish comments on the way he thought before his conversion from the more common critical views:

> I did what critics always do; I 'saw' what my interpretive principles permitted or directed me to see, and then I turned around and attributed what I had 'seen' to a text and an intention.

This position Fish has now abandoned. He came instead to 'see' that it is the way we read a text which 'discovers' traits which we take to be the key to meaning. However, they were not there, themselves, in the text:

> There are still formal patterns, but they do not lie innocently in the world [in texts!]; rather, they are themselves constituted by an interpretive act. The facts one points to are still there . . . but only as a consequence of the interpretive . . . model that has called them into being.[45]

These writers are not saying that a text may mean absolutely anything we care to read into it. 'Send for John Smith' cannot mean "I had bacon for breakfast on Christmas Day", and Donne's 'Valediction' cannot be read as a eulogy on the joy of eating baked beans. Fish, for example, explains the agreement between readers on the 'meaning' of a text by appealing to a dialectic relationship between the text and the linguistic, conceptual and literary conventions of the community of readers. Our conventions predispose us to read predictable meanings into any given text. For Fish, then, any one community is capable of recognizing a 'normative' reading, and even of pointing out that by its linguistic conventions certain alternative perceptions are simply aberrant. In fact Fish might himself attempt to persuade Hirsch's students that their perception was 'wrong'; but on a quite different basis from that of Hirsch. They would have to abandon what would be their own normal, conventional use of language and idiom in order to make the actual wording of several parts of the poem conform to their general perception of it as applying to death. At heart, Fish is saying to them: 'Given your

conventions of language and literature you should surely read this particular text in this particular way.' But this recognizes that a reader from
another community with a different set of literary conventions might
quite 'rightly' perceive the text differently and discern another 'meaning', possibly even something incompatible with the other. Let us take
a second example, a couplet which is capable of being perceived in several ways:

The shooting of the hunters she heard
But to pity it moved her not.

This could be taken to mean either that the woman had no pity for the
animals which the hunters shot, or, alternatively, a more sinister reading might be that the woman had no pity for the men the hunters were
pursuing. Again, it could be taken to mean that she failed to pity the
hunters who were being shot (or, conceivably, both, the hunters were
shooting each other!). It is not difficult to contrive alternative readings
which would still make sense: that the hunters were noisily 'shooting'
drugs, or that they were 'filming' someone in compromising circumstances. On a reader-response theory none of these perceptions could
be said to be 'wrong'. The same kind of perception analysis could be
applied not merely to couplets, as in the above example, but to whole
works, and a similar assertion still made: that no *possible* meanings could
be dismissed as 'incorrect' (although the word 'possible' itself indicates
the subjective nature of this kind of thinking). Meaning then becomes
something with which the *reader* clothes a text, not something which is
already inherent in it; and so the *meaning* of the text must necessarily
be indeterminate. The consequence of such a view of the interpretative
task for our understanding of the biblical text should be apparent. At
the other extreme stands the view of Hirsch. In one sense Hirsch can
agree with the presupposition that texts do not have meanings of their
own: they can only receive meaning from people. But emphatically he
does not accept that it is the *reader* who provides the meaning. Instead
he argues the more traditional position that a text, as a record of a
discourse, has just one correct meaning, and that is *the meaning intended
by the author*. In fact he defines discourse meaning in terms of what he
calls 'verbal meaning', and elucidates this as follows:

*Verbal meaning is whatever someone has willed to convey by a particular sequence
of linguistic signs and which can be conveyed by means of those linguistic signs.*[46]

According to Hirsch, then, meaning is determinate. A real-life author will have intended just one of the possible senses of the couplet, 'The shooting of the hunters she heard, but to pity it moved her not', and only that meaning is 'correct'. Another author, on another occasion, using 'the same' words but of a different situation may intend some other sense and *that* will be the meaning of the new discourse.

For Hirsch it is fundamental that we distinguish between 'meaning' and 'significance'. The text of a discourse has only one viable 'meaning'—the meaning intended by the author—but it may have a multiplicity of significances for different readers as they attempt to relate that one meaning to their own situation. Indeed the work may even come to have a different significance for the author himself as he reads it on some later occasion. A Shakespeare play or a single stanza from it, or a Bible text, may be allowed different significances to succeeding generations because each new generation perceives new relationships between the discourse meaning and the changing world. According to Hirsch, part of the reason for multiple accounts of the alleged *meaning* of a work, is confusion between the *significance* of a work, its meaning *to the readers*, and the author's original, intended, meaning. But Hirsch would also insist that we may only legitimately assert that we have brought to light the significance of, say, King Lear, for our lives if we have first discovered Shakespeare's intended meaning, and then related *that* meaning to our world. Without this important control, we are not discovering the significance of Lear, but of our parody of Lear.

Significance is the relationship of meaning between authorial meaning and the world of a reader, or some aspect of that world. And, of course, the same would be true of our approach to John's Gospel, or Romans. Ultimately we may only be interested in the significance of these works for our own times, but we cannot ascertain that significance without first knowing the one determinate meaning of John or Romans as originally given by their authors. So we have two conflicting theories of meaning: that the meaning of a text is only what it means to its readers, or that meaning is only what the author meant, reader perception against author intention. How are these two theories to be evaluated?

2.2.2 Refining the Question
Proponents of each view are able to point out supposed weaknesses in

the alternative position. In this section we shall direct our attention to three types of argument commonly advanced against the position advocated by Hirsch, and then respond to them in the next.

1. It is a fallacy to identify author's intended meaning with the meaning of the resultant text because it is entirely possible that an author might not succeed in saying what he *means*. In Lessing's *Emilia Gallotti*, for example, Emilia's mother is made to say: 'My God! If your father knew that! How angry he was already to learn that the prince had seen you *not without displeasure!*' It is quite clear from the context that Lessing meant that the Prince was pleased to see Emilia. Lessing obviously intended to write either 'not without pleasure' or 'not with displeasure', but in fact he has Emilia say the opposite—and we are told that no one noticed for a century!

This is, of course, a rather trivial case,[47] but it is clear that here the words of the text do not mean what the author intended. In such instances it would certainly be paradoxical to define the meaning of the *text* as 'the author's intended meaning'; one would have to recognize that the *text* of the discourse has one meaning and the author's intended meaning is the opposite.

2. A further objection to Hirsch's view might be the fact that we are able to understand texts even when we don't know the identity of the author. We are able to do this because once a writer has committed himself and published his discourse it is firmly in the public domain and the words and sentences of the text 'mean' whatever linguistic convention allows them to mean. In other words, we would not be forced to silence about the meaning of a poem merely because it was anonymous. To chain the meaning to the author's inscrutable (because unavailable) 'intention' was vigorously denounced as 'the Intentional Fallacy' in the now famous essay by Wimsatt and Beardsley.[48]

3. Again, it might be argued, Hirsch appears to assume that we have an objective way of getting back to authorial meaning, a meaning which he distinguishes sharply from the 'significance' of the discourse, its 'meaning for us'. But this is not only practically impossible: it is also theoretically impossible, as modern hermeneutical philosophers from Schleiermacher and Gadamer onwards have insisted.[49] We can only understand another person's discourse by relating what he says to the world we already know, and by asking questions from within that

world. When we first attempt to read a discourse about a subject of which we know nothing (a computer magazine, for example), we fail to understand it because we are incapable of relating its world to the world we know.

C. S. Lewis captured the problem in his account of Ransom's first view of the planet Malacandra:

> He gazed about him, and the very intensity of his desire to take in the new world at a glance defeated itself. He saw nothing but co-lours—colours that refused to form themselves into things. *Moreover, he knew nothing yet well enough to see it: you cannot see things until you know roughly what they are.* His first impression was of a bright, pale world—a watercolour world out of a child's paint-box[50] [our italics].

Or consider the attempt of Ezekiel to describe 'the glory of the Lord':

> Above the expanse . . . was *what looked like* a throne of sapphire, and high above on the throne was a figure *like that* of a man. I saw that from *what appeared to be* his waist up he *looked like* glowing metal, *as if* full of fire, and that from there down he *looked like* fire; and brilliant light surrounded him. *Like the* appearance of a rainbow in the clouds on a rainy day, so was the radiance around him. This was *the appearance of the likeness of* the glory of the Lord. (Ezekiel 1.26-8)

In fact, the criticism goes, the Cartesian or Baconian ideal of 'objective' exegesis, an exegesis that is unaffected by the world of the analyst, is unattainable. Every attempt to define author's intended meaning actually only discovers a meaning which is somehow related to 'meaning-for-me'. In brief, the sharp distinction between 'author's-intended-meaning' and 'significance' cannot be maintained: the former is an abstraction incapable of being recovered.[51]

These counters to Hirsch's position may assist us in establishing a more nuanced position, without forcing us into the extreme reader-response position. Let us consider the three criticisms in turn.

2.2.3 A Response to the Three Objections

2.2.3.1 The Problem Posed by Author's Incompetence It does seem necessary to accept that author's intended meaning may not be precisely the same as the meaning of the text itself, and it is the textual meaning from which we must begin. We are not so much interested in what the writer to the Ephesians may have meant to say, but failed to bring to clear expression, as in what he actually wrote. Hirsch is himself fully aware of the problem posed by an author's failure intelligibly to express what he means.[52] In reply to this particular criticism of his position Hirsch insists that meaning is a property of utterances—conscious acts of bringing meaning to expression in words—and so can be attributed only to *people*, not to texts. We may infer from a text what its author meant even where he fails, through a momentary linguistic incompetence, to express himself clearly or 'correctly'. In such a situation the author has merely failed to bring the evident intended meaning to successful completion. Of course it is arguable that every human communication is only more-or-less competent and might have been made more effectively, more precisely, less ambiguously.

But while this observation saves Hirsch's theory in cases where an author merely says what is not intelligible (for example, Poe's writing 'my most immemorial years', when he meant 'my most memorable years') it is less easy to see how it can be applied to, say, Lessing's slip. The problem there is not that the sentence in question is unclear, but that it is all too clear, and says the opposite of what the author intended. It would be artificial to suggest anything other than that the text of the utterance 'means' one thing and that Lessing 'meant' something else, and that the two are clearly distinguishable.

And yet again we are, in fact, dealing with the question of linguistic competence. Assuming (as we must, from a consideration of the rest of the text) that Lessing had a clear intention, but that his text did not fulfil that intention, we must further assume that had he carefully considered his text he could have (would have?) perceived the textual error and corrected it. For some reason at the time of producing the text his linguistic competence failed him: and we all of us share in that experience from time to time. But there can be no evading the fact that there are two 'meanings' here, authorial meaning, which the reader perceives from text and cotext by reference to linguistic conventions, and the more limited sentence meaning, also perceived by the reader and also from a consideration of literary convention.

We must emphasize that to allow that authorial meaning and text meaning are potentially distinguishable is *not* to say that the text is completely autonomous—that the text, being public, can mean whatever the speech community takes it to mean, irrespective of the author's intention. Indeed it is very difficult to believe that a text could have meaning in itself, independent of the author's meaning. For example if we were told that Wordsworth's lines,

> No motion has she now, no force;
> She neither hears nor sees;
> Rolled round in earth's diurnal course,
> With rocks, and stones, and trees

had been produced by chance by monkeys playing with a typewriter, what sort of meaning could we attribute to them? As Juhl observes,[53] we would normally assume, here, that 'rolled round' referred to the slow motion brought about by the rotating earth (rather than 'spun round', like a top). We assume such a meaning for the expression 'rolled round' because we believe that the piece has been written as a coherent whole, that the author has *intentionally* modified the verbal expression with the prepositional phrase 'in earth's diurnal course', and that he did so knowing the nature of the earth's motion. Monkeys simply could not be suspected of any such intention. If the text were, indeed, randomly produced rather than intentionally created we could scarcely assume that it had any coherence or, indeed, that it *meant* anything at all.[54] Coherence is a consequence of *purpose*, and Hirsch is surely right—it is the author who gives the stamp of coherence through his organization of the material: it is not merely potentially there, waiting to be added to the poem by lesser lights.

2.2.3.2 The Problem Posed by the Anonymity of an Author
The second argument against Hirsch probably tilts at a straw man. The fact is that Hirsch does not claim that we need to know the author and have an account of his intention before we can understand what he writes. Indeed he specifically denies it.[55] Rather, we usually *infer* the intention from the writing. And we clear up the meaning of any ambiguous passage in a novel, or history, or poem, by referring to what we *infer* to be the meaning of the work as a whole, as deduced from the relatively clear passages. We need to observe that we can do this only because we assume the work to be a coherent whole, and it can only be a coherent whole because a *person* has *intended* coherence. Such coherence could not be reckoned as a property of a truly autonomous text. It must at once be admitted that this argument does not protect Hirsch's view from

Fish's understanding of the process of interpretation. Fish would say that coherence is simply a reader's assumption: he 'discovers' coherence because his own analysis assumes it, not because it is objectively there before the interpretative act. Those who regard the text as autonomous effectively thereby treat texts as they would treat isolated context-less sentences and we need not be surprised when they discover multiple meanings originating wholly with readers.

In contrast to such an approach, Hirsch and Juhl develop an analogy between texts of sometimes lengthy discourses and texts of short utterances. They rightly observe that in any one *utterance*, any one instance of speaking, *only one of the admittedly multiple possible meanings is liable to be correct.*[56] That meaning may be entirely clear from the context. Taking again the couplet,

> The shooting of the hunters she heard,
> But to pity it moved her not,

we may imagine the speaker and hearer observing the non-reaction of the lady in question as she watches the hunters being executed by firing squad, or we might find the speaker subsequently clarifying what he means by some such assertion as 'She didn't bat an eyelid when the hunters were shot!' But in either case it would be nonsense to continue to affirm that the couplet is still ambiguous, or that some other meaning is still possible. It is clear that here the speaker's meaning, whether elucidated by context or by his own further comment, is absolutely determinative. It makes no sense in such cases to maintain that the couplet itself remains ambiguous. When once the context or the speaker himself has clarified meaning no one may reasonably seriously ask the question: 'But is that what the couplet really meant?'

Strangely enough, Fish devotes an entire essay to analyzing a similar problem, without apparently seeing the implications for the determinacy of textual meaning.[57] He discusses an occasion when a colleague was asked by a student, on the opening day of term, 'Is there a text in this class?' The teacher answered, 'Yes, it's the *Norton Anthology of Literature*', whereupon the student clarified the question: 'I mean, in this class do we believe in poems and things, or is it just us?' On the basis of this, Fish distinguishes two different sentences, 'Is there a text in this class'$_1$, corresponding to the first meaning divined by the teacher, and 'Is there a text in this class'$_2$, corresponding to his second reading (according to which the girl was asking the more philosophical question 'Does a poem have a meaning, or do we invest it with one?'). Fish goes on to discuss how the situational context of shared academic convention has enabled both the first and the subsequent readings to be made.

Curiously he argues against Hirsch that it is only the situation which has fixed the reading, and that the meaning of the words themselves is not determinate. He does not appear to realize that having said this he has conceded the case Hirsch seeks to establish, namely that *in the situation* the meaning of the sentence has been rendered determinate. Once the girl has clarified the matter there is clearly only one true meaning of her initial question, and it is the *girl's* intended meaning. Whatever conventions might force some eavesdropper to conclude that her words meant something else, that conclusion would be a false conclusion, a misunderstanding, neither more nor less and *not* an equally viable reading of a sentence of indeterminate meaning. Contrary to Fish's understanding, Hirsch would not claim that the words used by the girl have determinate meaning *despite* context; for he allows what is in fact the norm, that the speaker's context (indicated by such referring expressions as 'this class') is a component of the communication that supplies the determinacy of the utterance. Indeed, from the standpoint of linguistics it is precisely the total context of an utterance (cotext and social context) which generally gives determinacy to a speaker's meaning. Isolated, contextless *sentences* may have many possible meanings, but *utterances* do not. And it may be argued that texts are more like utterances in this respect.

Now comes the vital point: by analogy, Hirsch, Juhl[58] *and Thiselton*[59] *would maintain that texts of written discourses are not to be interpreted as if they were contextless sentences to be read in the abstract and so capable of multiple meanings.* Rather, they are to be interpreted as we interpret utterances (or records of them). For, like the latter, they are representations of definite acts of communication given in particular contexts by specific people, for definite purposes, and this matrix of properties is determinative for at least some levels of their meaning. If 1 Corinthians is taken as being like a contextless sentence then no doubt it would be capable of many different meanings. But it was written by Paul because he couldn't go to Corinth to deal personally with the issues being raised there. What he writes has, thus, the character of an utterance and not that of a contextless sentence.

Its meaning is fundamentally determined by the context and by Paul's intended meaning. We may not, with Hirsch, be able to claim that the meaning of the text of 1 Corinthians is *by definition* Paul's intended meaning *simpliciter*, but neither may we simply strip the letter of its Pauline context and rip it out of Paul's hand, so that the intention which originally gave shape to the letter becomes irrelevant to its meaning. Paul's letter forms part of an on-going conversation between Paul and Corinth, and to decontextualize it would be to alter its meaning. Or put another way, if it were *recontextualized* and given the context of some twentieth-century reader's world, its meaning would necessarily change even though the words of the text were not changed at all.

Like an utterance, the letter can only be understood aright by reference to the one context from which and in which it has its meaning. We may therefore state that our goal is to discover what we may call the *discourse meaning* of, say, 1 Corinthians. We are searching for the meaning of what Paul expressed when it is understood as the record of an (admittedly lengthy) contextualized utterance. We wish to know not what the wording of 1 Corinthians could be taken to mean by a reader without knowledge of the context, but what it would necessarily mean to a competent judge from the contemporary Corinthian church; to one who grew up knowing Hellenistic Greek, who was aware of the church situation to which Paul was addressing his remarks, and who would know the history of the relationship between Paul and that church and what Paul had taught there. All these factors will have a bearing on the total meaning of the letter as it is read at Corinth: they make up the context shared by Paul and his readers, a context which governs what Paul writes and consequently what his readers discern. We shall discuss the question of just how context shapes the meaning of discourses or utterances more fully later.

As far as the Pauline letters are concerned we may safely ignore Ricoeur's insistence on the *fundamental distinction* between utterances and written works.[60] For Ricoeur the former are determinate, their meaning defined by the event and context of the utterance, but the latter are not determinate because they lack the essential element of situational self-reference and contextual reference. However, these features are notably *not* missing from the epistles. As R. W. Funk has shown, Paul's letters are an immediate substitute for his personal presence, and, what is more, the apostle can expect his intention to be more fully elucidated, if necessary, by the bearer of the letter.[61] In such circumstances there can be no measure of semantic autonomy granted by the mere act of writing.

Ricoeur's distinction may, however, need to be taken more seriously with respect to other biblical writings. Can we also treat Exodus, or Psalms, or Jonah, in the same way as 1 Corinthians? Ricoeur has himself gone part way towards providing an answer to this question. He insists that we must not fall prey to the fallacy of the absolute text—of hypostasizing the text as an authorless entity:

> If the intentional fallacy overlooks the semantic autonomy of the text, the opposite fallacy forgets that a text remains a discourse told by somebody to someone else about something. It is impossible to cancel out this main characteristic of discourse without reducing texts to natural objects, i.e., to things which are not man-made, but which, like pebbles, are found in the sand.[62]

His point concerning the fallacy of the absolute text is well taken; we need only doubt what he says about the *intentional fallacy*. Given what he affirms concerning the former, semantic autonomy should be seen for the mirage that it is. A text may *appear* to have semantic autonomy for any reader who does not share the author's context, but the text does not achieve semantic autonomy over its author merely by virtue of its having been written down and published. The reader who knows *that* will recognize that any apparent semantic autonomy is purely illusory.[63] He will know that the author was saying something to someone about something, even if (because he does not share the author's context) the referents are less clear to him than they would have been to the originally intended audience.

Even fictional literary compositions are not semantically autonomous. As Juhl points out, critics of all schools *in practice* attempt to explain obscure passages in a work by appealing to other works by the same author handling similar motifs in a more transparent fashion. In doing so they are clearly grounding 'meaning' in *author's intended meaning*,[64] however much they may protest the text's autonomy.

Nor need we be beguiled into a belief in total semantic autonomy of literary discourses by authors who tell us that they do not know the meaning of their own works.[65] The claim has a certain superficial appeal when related to sections of abstract poetry, but we must be careful in our understanding of such claims. In the case of abstract poetry it may mean no more than a recognition that the poem is vague in sense and ambiguous in reference. It is not so much a matter of the author being unaware of some sharply definable 'meaning' transparent to others, but of there being no sharply definable meaning at all—only sharply definable 'applications' of the vague meaning to different readers' worlds.

Similarly, when C. S. Lewis tells us of his own book *Till We Have Faces* that 'an author doesn't necessarily understand the meaning of his own story better than anyone else',[66] we need not doubt that in the book Lewis has carefully portrayed a world, that he has indicated his evaluation of aspects of that world in the development of his story, and that he intends an (admittedly oblique) comparison with our world and a corresponding evaluation.[67] Indeed he virtually says as much in his own comments on the Narnia chronicles. All this indicates that much of the meaning of Lewis's work is determinate, some of it being consciously planned, some being fully intended even if not consciously planned,[68] and that Lewis himself would (and does!) label contradictory interpretations 'wrong'.[69]

So then, the claim that an author is not a privileged interpreter certainly cannot be taken to mean that the text stands in an entirely autonomous relation to the author's own intention, although we must allow that the author might not be specifically conscious of all the possible entailments and potential implications of his imagery, and that he cannot determine the ultimate scope of the significance of his work for our world. With this, of course, Hirsch would not disagree.

And most importantly, it has to be noted that the issue we are discussing is primarily, although not exclusively, a problem of literary and fictional works where the element of correspondence between the world of the writing and our world is oblique. We may not find the 'meaning' of Job, or Jonah, to be as readily accessible to us as that of Paul or Mark, but we have no reason to assume because of that that the text is autonomous and indeterminate. It is still the author's intended meaning which must be the first object of our enquiry.

We have already made passing reference to the question of author's meaning as it applies to a text considered to be an inspired Scripture.

Which author do we mean when we refer to a work which the Church confesses to be of divine origin: is it Paul's or is it God's meaning which is determinative for the believer's exegesis of 1 Corinthians?

To put the question in this way is, however, misleading. Arguably there are places in Scripture where a writer claims to be offering God's wording *rather than* his own. Such is probably the case with the messenger formula 'Thus says the LORD . . .' in the prophets. But this is not advanced as the paradigm of the relationship between the human author and the divine in the rest of Scripture: indeed, not even as the exclusive paradigm for all that the prophets themselves have to say. Moreover in the New Testament Paul does not request Corinthian obedience on the grounds that he is merely God's scribe, writing God's words to them, but on the ground that he is a spiritual man (1 Cor. 7.25,40), their father in the gospel (1 Cor. 4.15). Similarly, Luke does not commend his Gospel to Theophilus on the basis that it has been divinely revealed word for word to him, but on the more mundane grounds that he has carefully researched the material (Luke 1.1-4).

It is not surprising, therefore, that when scholars confess the divine origin of Scripture they do so primarily within some form of doctrine of complementary authorship, stating that God was in some way sovereign over the otherwise ordinary, human and intentional act of authorship. In conservative circles such a view entails that what Paul says—and as *Paul meant* it—is simultaneously God's word to Corinth. In a less conservative understanding the relationship between Paul's meaning and God's revelation is much more oblique, but the latter is still regarded only as some function of *Paul's* meaning, and only accessible, if at all, through it.

If someone wishes to assert that God's meaning is not only an extension of Paul's, but actually different from it, then two consequences follow. Firstly he robs Paul's meaning of any divine authority at precisely the point where the divine meaning is alleged to differ from the apostle's meaning (and so, at least potentially, from all Paul's meaning). Secondly he loses the hermeneutical key provided by context; Paul's contextualized meaning is potentially accessible. We can probably elucidate it with some degree of success. Important aspects of his teaching on spiritual gifts and ministry for example can be discerned from 1 Corinthians 12—14, always provided that we allow for contingent factors; for example the fact that he is writing to correct misuse of gifts at Corinth, and that he is speaking to their understanding. We can judge the significance of what he says by comparing it with what he says elsewhere on a similar subject but in other circumstances. If we believe Paul to be a divinely inspired writer, we could affirm that the main lines of his teaching in 1 Corinthians are also what God intended to be said to the Corinthian situation, and that God speaks to other parallel situations through what is said to Corinth (and, of course, through what is said elsewhere in Scripture, addressed to other contexts). But what God might mean by the wording of 1 Corinthians taken *out* of the historical Pauline context is not at all clear. These considerations would not rule out the possibility of a *sensus plenior*, some fuller sense intended by God in, say, Isaiah's contextualized words, but going beyond them. However, even in such circumstances the human author's intended meaning remains primary for our understanding of the Scripture, and the fuller sense is recovered from canonical or redemption-historical perspectives.[70] *Sensus plenior* may perhaps be defended as an extension by God through the Spirit of the author's intended meaning, but not as a merely verbally related alternative to it.

To summarize this part of the argument we may now affirm that the second objection raised against Hirsch, that a complete account of author's intention is not available to us, is not a theoretical barrier to the belief that author's meaning is determinative for discourse meaning. The context of writing and author's intention are closely related, and together they provide the decisive factors for establishing the meaning of a text just as they do for fixing the meaning of an utterance.

2.2.3.3 The Problem Posed by the Intrusion into the Interpretative Act of the World of the Interpreter
The third criticism of Hirsch carries some weight. The original meaning is hidden from us, and we have no way of resurrecting it—again, Hirsch would agree to that. All that we can do is to infer the meaning, and that will in some measure be affected by our present understanding of our world. This may lead to a distortion in our understanding of Paul's world: and Hirsch may underestimate the significance of this. But at least we would agree with Hirsch that it is the meaning of the discourse as Paul delivered it to, for example, Corinth, that is the meaning we are after—not just any meaning, nor are we looking merely

for an immediate significance for us. We are concerned to discover the meaning of Paul's letter as it would be understood by a competent reader, fully aware of the linguistic conventions of Hellenistic Greek, after a careful hearing and reading of the entire letter and fully aware of the total situational context shared by Paul and the Corinthians.

We shall call this meaning the 'discourse meaning', on the one hand to protect ourselves against the misunderstanding that a text means precisely and only what the author meant (so qualifying Hirsch), and on the other hand to stave off the view that we really can speak of 'text meaning' as though the text were autonomous.

The term *discourse meaning* points us back to the event of the utterance or act of writing which is contextually informed and determinative for meaning. With respect to Lessing's slip, an analysis in terms of discourse meaning would be free to affirm that while conventionally the wording of Emilia's mother's utterance must mean "without pleasure" (and that is the meaning of the text as it stands in isolation from its context), nevertheless the broader context of the utterance within the work clearly indicates the opposite meaning, which should be regarded as the 'discourse meaning' (and, indeed, the author's intended meaning).

We may never know whether we have fully grasped the 'discourse meaning' of any particular writing. It is often hard enough to be certain of the meaning of something written by a colleague whom we know. And time and again an author today justifiably complains he has been misunderstood by his highly competent reviewers! They have read what he has written incorrectly because they have read it through the spectacles of their own knowledge and experience: the interpreter's world has intruded into the interpretative act. How much more serious is the potential problem, then, when we are separated by a gulf of time, language, culture and presuppositions such as exists between the biblical writers and ourselves.

If we often find we have misunderstood our contemporaries, what chance do we stand of recovering the discourse meaning of the correspondence between Paul and his Galatian readers, let alone the discourse meaning of the final form of Genesis or Job when we know all too little of the author or intended readership? Here, surely, the danger of the interpreter reading his own world into the text is all the greater because he knows correspondingly less about the world of the writing itself, and the danger of distortion is all the greater because the two worlds are very different. Any confidence in the 'objectivity' of our findings must be further called into question by the frank recognition that many if not all scholars would be prepared to admit they are *ultimately* studying Paul (or Calvin or whomever) *in order to understand themselves and their God*. Does this not necessarily imply a very active engagement between the world of the interpreter and that of the text, with all the attendant dangers of misunderstanding and distortion?

It does indeed. But the observations need not lead to paralysis, far less to an abandoning of the quest for the discourse meaning such as occurs in most Structuralist and New Hermeneutic approaches to biblical interpretation. Rather, awareness of the problem should generate the appropriate caution, both in respect of method and in the degree of certainty we attach to our 'conclusions'. We need fully to recognize that *our* reading of the letter to Philemon (or whatever), however certain we may feel it is what Paul meant, *is actually only a hypothesis*—our *hypothesis*—*about the discourse meaning*. It is the result of seeing certain aspects of the text and of providing what *we understand* to be the meaning that provides coherence to the evidence. Unfortunately, like Hirsch's students we may easily have jumped to premature conclusions which then grip us like a spell and bind the rest of our interpretation. We all need, perhaps daily, to take to heart the message expressed so admirably by Oliver Cromwell in a letter to the General Assembly of the Church of Scotland (3rd August 1650), 'I beseech you, in the bowels of Christ, think it possible you may be mistaken'!

The obvious dangers of allowing our world to distort our attempt to elucidate discourse meaning requires that we find ways of testing our reading or hypothesis with respect to any passage. This is not just a problem for Hirsch's view, it applies to some extent to Fish's approach as well, because, as we pointed out, he allows that some readings are simply bizarre *misreadings* and others are more correct (i.e. more in accord with a conventional understanding of the language and themes of the text). Where they will differ is in the nature of the tests to be applied, and the choice of these reflects the different types of 'meaning' they are seeking to establish. Because Hirsch is in quest of the 'original meaning' he would require us to check whether the various aspects of our reading of Philemon were in conformity with what we otherwise have reason to believe about the linguistic, cultural, conceptual and historical situation in which the letter was written. Fish, who does not regard the discourse meaning as determinative, would appear to be content if our interpretation could be proved to match what a conventional American reader would make of the language and themes of the letter today, without historical enquiry.

Unquestionably Hirsch's demands are the more difficult to meet; and indeed, as Hirsch recognizes, they are impossible for any one reader—or even a generation of readers—to meet *completely*. No one has the competence (and energy!) fully to research every aspect of his interpretation of even so short a letter as Philemon, and to check it exhaustively against what we can know of Paul and his context. Were some superman to try it, the very attempt would only turn up up further questions to be answered. At best we can hope to approximate to the discovery of the author's meaning as different commentators and the writers of various monographs attempt to elucidate the situation, and as we compare the models they offer with the text itself. Each creative contribution will highlight some traits of the text unnoticed, or poorly explained before. And even if the interpreter's explanation of them may be judged unconvincing, his highlighting of these phenomena brings to our attention further significant factors in the discourse that need to be taken into account in giving an overall explanation of it. Unfortunately it is true we do not have the 'original meaning' to hand, but we do have critical methods for adjudicating between alternative readings or interpretations; ways of testing whether—to the limits of our present knowledge—specific aspects of a reading are more or less probable.

The problems we have mentioned do not invalidate the insight that it is the *discourse meaning* (in the sense defined above) that we should be seeking. It may be difficult to establish even the strong probability (let alone certainty) of any single hypothesis about the 'original meaning' of an ancient text. And such advances as we are able to make will usually pertain only to *some* specific *aspects* of our reading rather than to the whole. But the gains may be considered worthwhile if they are understood as contributing to the discovery of some determinate meaning, rather than as just another move in an eternal game of reinvesting neutral texts with new but indeterminate meanings.

2.2.4 Defining the Task of Hermeneutics

After this refinement of these questions we may offer a new definition of the task of hermeneutics in lieu of a summary of our argument so far. Hermeneutics is a study of the theoretical basis and methodology of two separable processes:

1. The determination of what we call the Discourse Meaning of the text, that meaning which can be arrived at by competent judges with sufficiently extensive knowledge of the *linguistic context*, the *discourse cotext* (the contribution of all the other parts of the text to that part under immediate consideration) and the *situational context* shared by the writer and his intended readers. This is what we mean by *exegesis*.[71] Exegesis is the bringing to expression of an interpreter's understanding of an author's intended meaning (or, more precisely, though they are very closely related, of the discourse meaning) of the text.

2. The interpreting of the text. That is the bringing to expression of the interpreter's understanding of the significance for his own world of the discourse meaning of the text.

We are now in a position to analyse more carefully what we mean by 'meaning', and of what elements it is composed.

Notes

[1]See J. Lyons, *Semantics,* Cambridge, CUP, 1977, and J. Hurford and B. Heasley, *Semantics: A Coursebook,* Cambridge, CUP, 1983. At a more introductory level see chap. 5 of J. Lyons, *Language and Linguistics,* and chap. 2 of G. B. Caird, *The Language and Imagery of the Bible,* London, Duckworth, 1980.

[2]Noam Chomsky, *Syntactic Structures,* The Hague, Mouton, 1957. What Chomsky was aiming at was the creation of a new type of grammar, synthetic instead of merely analytic, with the capability of *generating* all the grammatical sentences of a language, but no ungrammatical sentences.

[3]John Lyons surveys the almost endless ramifications of semantic theory in his two-volume *Semantics.* On Chomsky's foundational work he comments: 'When Chomsky first put forward his theory of generative grammar (in a version that has since been substantially modified), he had little to say about the possibility of integrating phonology, morphology, syntax and semantics within a unified model of a language system' (p.409).

[4]*Language,* 39(1963), pp.170-210.

[5]See Caird, *The Language and Imagery of the Bible,* chap.2 and J. Lyons, *Semantics,* 1.1, 'The Meaning of "Meaning" '. See also E. D. Hirsch, *The Aims of Interpretation.*

chap.1, 'Meaning and Significance' for an important distinction made by him (and generally adopted here) between meaning and significance.

[6]*Semantics*, p.4.

[7]Although this is not to suggest that without the presence of the author we cannot determine, within reasonable limits, the meaning of his text. See below, 2.2.3.2 and note also Paul's use of Titus in transmitting the 'Painful' letter (2 Cor. 7.6ff) and of Timothy (1 Cor. 4.17) and of Tychicus (Eph. 6.13): although Paul could not have been accessible to those who received his letters, still his messengers would have been able to elucidate Paul's meaning to them.

[8]R. E. Longacre, *The Grammar of Discourse*, chap.2.

[9]D. N. Levine, *Wax and Gold*, Chicago, University of Chicago Press, 1965.

[10]*The Gospel of Luke*, Exeter, Paternoster, 1978, p.633f., referring to the original suggestion by H. Gressmann and to J. Jeremias, *The Parables of Jesus*, pp.182-7.

[11]But note also the parable of the Prodigal Son which also displays two principal teaching points. Here again the explanation of the complex structure is to be found in context. The second teaching point of the churlishness of the elder brother arises out of the attitude of the Pharisees towards the 'sinners' who thronged to listen to Jesus (Luke 15.1-2).

[12]See the valuable summary of Firthian semantics in J. Lyons, *Semantics*, 14.4.

[13]*The Aims of Interpretation*, p.49.

[14]An observation which is not intended to deny the existence of texts where the meaning is unclear.

[15]*The Social Setting of Pauline Christianity*, Edinburgh, T. & T. Clark, 1982, and *The Shadow of the Galilean*, London, SCM, 1987.

[16]London, SCM, 1985.

[17]Note especially his *The Charismatic Leader*, Edinburgh, T. & T. Clark, 1981, hailed by Sanders, op.cit., p.133, as the best single treatment of a synoptic pericope ever done, and *Between Jesus and Paul*, London, SCM, 1983.

[18]See however the fine commentary by W. Brueggemann, *Genesis*, Atlanta, John Knox Press, 1982; the reader might care to compare this commentary with E. A. Speiser's *Genesis* (Anchor Bible), New York, Doubleday, 1964.

[19]J. H. Moulton and Nigel Turner, *A Grammar of New Testament Greek*, vol.III, Edinburgh, T. & T. Clark, 1963, pp.75-6.

[20]R. Schnackenburg, *The Gospel According to St John*, vol.3, London, Burns & Oates, 1982, p.318.

[21]On Ricoeur see, for example, Lewis Mudge(ed.), *Essays on Biblical Interpretation*, London, SPCK, 1981; P. Ricoeur, *The Conflict of Interpretations*, Evanston, Northwestern University Press, 1974, especially 'Structure, Word, Event', and *Semeia* 4 (1975), 'Paul Ricoeur on Biblical Hermeneutics'.

[22]Christopher Tuckett's *Reading the New Testament: Methods of Interpretation*, London,

SPCK, 1987, deals very neatly and competently with such matters as textual criticism, source criticism, form criticism, and redaction criticism. See also John H. Hayes and Carl R. Holladay, *Biblical Exegesis: A Beginner's Handbook*, Atlanta, John Knox Press, 1982, and London, SCM, 1983.

[23]'The form of expression is not a direct affirmation: but it is certainly not a denial', I. H. Marshall, *The Gospel of Luke*, Exeter, Paternoster, 1978, p.851. See also G. Vermes, *Jesus the Jew*, London, Collins, 1973, pp.147-9 for a more detailed discussion of the interpretation of Jesus' words.

[24]J. Lyons, *Language and Linguistics*, 5.3. E. Nida and C. R. Taber, *The Theory and Practice of Translation*, Leiden, Brill, 1969, prefer the term 'Referential Meaning' to 'Denotation'.

[25]Nida and Taber, ibid., chap.5.

[26]David Crystal, *A Dictionary of Linguistics and Phonetics*, article 'Denotation'.

[27]See the section on Componential Analysis in 5.2.7 below.

[28]See J. A. Fitzmyer, *The Gospel According to Luke* (Anchor Bible), vol.2, New York, Doubleday, 1985, p.1031.

[29]*Pirke Aboth*, 4.15.

[30]*Semantics of New Testament Greek*, p.55. See also Kenneth Bailey's discussion in *Through Peasant Eyes*, Grand Rapids, Eerdmans, 1980 , p.24.

[31]The sentence is what is termed a *minority-pattern* sentence: see 6.1.3 below.

[32]Hurford and Heasley, *Semantics*, Unit 26. See especially S. C. Levinson, *Pragmatics*, chap.3, for a detailed study of Grice's theory of implicature.

[33]See particularly D. Bolinger and D. A. Sears, *Aspects of Language*, p.5. See also David Efron, 'Historical changes in gestural behaviour' in J. Corner and J. Hawthorn, *Communication Studies*, London, Edward Arnold, 1980.

[34]D. Hesselgrave, *Communicating Christ Cross-culturally*, Grand Rapids, Zondervan, 1978, p.295.

[35]Ibid., especially chap.31, 'Seven Aspects of the "Behavioural Dimension" '.

[36]Cf. J. A. Fitzmyer, *The Gospel According to Luke I-IX*, p.531.

[37]According to E. Schürer 'The scripture readings . . . could equally be undertaken by any member of the congregation', *The History of the Jewish People in the Age of Jesus Christ*, vol.2, rev. edn, ed. G. Vermes, F. Millar and M. Black, Edinburgh, T. & T. Clark, 1979, p.450.

[38]'In the course of time a regular pattern of reading was established, so that the whole of the Pentateuch was read in a three-year cycle and the other parts of the canon ordered in relation to it. Despite various attempts to show that various lectionary patterns antedate the fall of Jerusalem . . . there is no evidence to suggest that the three-year cycle was in existence during the Second Temple period' (C. Rowland, *Christian Origins*, London, SPCK, 1985, p.45).

[39]'Preaching, too, was not restricted to particular persons, but . . . was open to

any competent member of the congregation', Schürer, ibid., p.453.

40See A. C. Thiselton, *The Two Horizons*, Exeter, Paternoster, 1980, chap.1; and E. D. Hirsch, *The Aims of Interpretation*, chap.1.

41*The Two Horizons*, pp.12-15.

42Ibid., p.28.

43*The Aims of Interpretation*, p.3.

44E. D. Hirsch, *Validity in Interpretation*, London, Yale University Press, 1967, pp. 73f.

45S. Fish, *Is there a Text in This Class: The Authority of Interpretive Communities*, Cambridge, Mass., HUP, 1980, pp.12f.

46Hirsch, *Validity in Interpretation*, p.31.

47We are grateful to Silva, *Biblical Words and Their Meaning*, p.140, for the example.

48Reproduced in W. K. Wimsatt, *The Verbal Icon*, Lexington, University of Kentucky Press, 1954.

49For an account of the significance of modern philosophical discussion for hermeneutics see, *inter alios*, R. E. Palmer, *Hermeneutics: Interpretation Theory in Schleiermacher, Dilthey, Heidegger and Gadamer*, Evanston, Northwestern University Press, 1969; A. C. Thiselton, *The Two Horizons: New Testament Hermeneutics and Philosophical Description with Special Reference to Heidegger, Bultmann, Gadamer and Wittgenstein*, Exeter, Paternoster, 1980; and J. Bleicher, *Contemporary Hermeneutics*, London, RKP, 1980.

50C. S. Lewis, *Out of the Silent Planet*, London, Pan, 1952, p.46.

51Cf. D. C. Hoy, *The Critical Circle: Literature, History and Philosophical Hermeneutics*, London, University of California Press, 1978, pp.11-40.

52Hirsch, *Validity in Interpretation*, pp.233-5.

53P. D. Juhl, *Interpretation: An Essay in the Philosophy of Literary Criticism*, Princeton, Princeton University Press, 1980, chap.4, esp. pp.69ff.

54We would have no way of knowing whether the 'she' of line 2 was the 'she' of line 1 and the subject of lines 3-4; indeed we would have no way of knowing that 'she' is semantically different from 'he' or 'xy4'; for semantic difference is a property of lexical *choice*.

55Hirsch, *Validity in Interpretation*, pp.14ff.

56Juhl, *Interpretation*, pp.54-8.

57S. Fish, *Is There a Text in This Class?*, pp.303-21.

58*Interpretation*, pp.52f., 54ff., and chap.5.

59R. Lundin, A. C. Thiselton, and C. Walhout, *The Responsibility of Hermeneutics*, Exeter, Paternoster, 1985, pp.101-13.

60P. Ricoeur, *Interpretation Theory: Discourse and the Surplus of Meaning*, Fort Worth, Texas Christian University Press, 1976, chaps. 1 and 2.

61Funk, 'The Apostolic Parousia' in W. R. Farmer, C. F. D. Moule, R. R. Niebuhr (eds.), *Christian History and Interpretation*, Cambridge, CUP, 1967, pp.249-68.

62Ricoeur, *Interpretation Theory*, p.30.

63Cf. the criticism of Ricoeur by T. W. Gillespie in D. K. McKim (ed.), *A Guide to Contemporary Hermeneutics*, Grand Rapids, Eerdmans, 1986, pp.201f.

64See Juhl, *Interpretation*, pp.214-19.

65For a discussion of this phenomenon see, for example, Hirsch, *Validity in Interpretation*, pp.19ff. and pp.44-56.

66In W. H. Lewis (ed.), *Letters of C. S. Lewis*, New York, Harcourt, Brace & World, 1966, p.273. I am grateful to D. C. Steinmetz's essay in D. K. McKim (ed.), *A Guide to Contemporary Hermeneutics*, p.74, for this reference, whilst not agreeing with the very general conclusions he draws from it.

67For a good analysis of levels of meaning in fiction, and their relation to author's intent, see Walhout's essay in R. Lundin, A. C. Thiselton, C. Walhout (eds.), *The Responsibility of Hermeneutics*.

68For a discussion of the significance of this distinction between planned meaning and meaning which is fully intended even if not planned, see Juhl, *Interpretation*, pp.128-37.

69See, for example, C. S. Lewis, *Christian Reflections*, London, Bles, 1967, pp. 152ff.

70For a good recent discussion and bibliography on the issue see D. J. Moo, 'The Problem of *Sensus Plenior*,' in D. A. Carson and J. D. Woodbridge (eds.), *Hermeneutics, Authority and Canon*, Grand Rapids, Zondervan, 1986, pp.175-212.

71The discerning reader will appreciate how much the form of the definition owes to the two essays by V. S. Poythress, 'Analysing a Biblical Text: Some Important Linguistic Distinctions', *Scot. JT* 32(1979), pp.113-37, and 'Analysing a Biblical Text: What are we After?', *Scot. JT*, 32(1979), pp.319-31. It will also be clear that we allow less autonomy to the text than Poythress appears to.

3. Dimensions of the Meaning of a Discourse

We have now defined exegesis in terms of the bringing to expression of the interpreter's understanding of the author's intended meaning (or, more accurately, the 'discourse meaning') of a text. We must now elucidate more carefully various aspects of what we mean by 'meaning'. The verb 'to mean' and its allied substantive 'meaning' are catch-all terms which demand careful attention. In 2.1 we looked briefly at some of the many and diverse ways in which these terms are commonly used. We must now examine these in more detail.

3.1 MEANING AS 'SENSE'

3.1.1 Word Sense

When we ask such questions as 'What does "sesquipedalian" mean?' we are asking about the sense of the word in question. We are inviting the hearer to match the word 'sesquipedalian' with some other word or expression which has the same sense (but one we will recognize). A reasonable reply would be something like ' "Sesquipedalian" means "prone to use long words" '. Indeed we may provisionally and very roughly define the 'sense' of a word as 'how that word (or expression) relates in meaning to other words or expressions in the language'. For example, we could affirm that one sense of the word 'bachelor' is defined by its synonymous relation to a combination of three other words, namely the words 'unmarried', 'adult' (we would not call a baby a bachelor), 'male'. Of course this is only one sense of the word, for the same word, 'bachelor', can mean "person holding the academic status of 'Bachelor of Arts' " (whether or not that person is married or male). Most words have several senses; and dictionaries compile the various possible senses of each word, by indicating each sense in terms of synonymous words or expressions. We shall discuss the use and abuse of word studies and the grammar of words in more detail in chapters four and five.

3.1.2 Sentence Sense

We speak not only of the sense of words (or expressions) but also, in an untechnical (and slightly different) way, of the sense of sentences and of paragraphs. If we are asked the sense of a word we will probably attempt to provide a synonym; if someone asks, 'What does the sentence, "Ontogeny recapitulates phylogeny," mean?', we might attempt to offer a *paraphrase*, that is another sentence expressing the same proposition(s). So we might offer: 'It means, "The development from a fertilized egg to a foetus mirrors the alleged stages of evolution from lower types of animal to higher types." ' The two sentences might then be said to mean the same in that they carry roughly the same sense, or convey approximately the same propositions.

Of course we could approach the question another way and first give a synonymous expression for the word 'ontogeny'. Then we could explain that it is the subject of the sentence before going on to provide a synonym or explanation of 'recapitulates', indicating that it is the verb in a generalizing present tense, before finally explaining the grammatical object 'phylogeny'. This would provide a more fully analytic approach (which could be considerably refined), but the most immediately helpful answer might be the paraphrase of the meaning. Indeed a good way of finding out whether people understand sentences is to ask them to provide paraphrases.

3.1.3 Paragraph Sense

In the case of complex sentences, and those clusters of such sentences which collectively constitute *paragraphs*, we might still legitimately inquire about their sense: 'What does this paragraph mean?' And again, a paraphrase might still provide the most readily useful answer. However, the task of providing a paraphrase is now much more difficult.

The problem is partly created by the fact that complex sentences not only make several propositions (rather than one single proposition), but also that each proposition stands in its own special type of relationship to another, or to several others. For example, Col. 1.21-23a (which is, in fact, part of a longer sentence) contains the following basic propositions:

(i)   You were formerly alienated from God.

(ii)   You were hostile towards him in mind.

(iii)   You did evil deeds.

(iv)   God has now reconciled you.

(v)   Christ suffered physical death.

(vi)   God will present you holy before him (at his tribunal).

(vii)   You continue to have faith.

(viii) You continue stable.

(ix)   You do not lose the hope the gospel announces.

Each of these could be paraphrased separately to clarify it; indeed some are already paraphrases of what is in the text. But the *sense of the paragraph* lies not merely in the individual propositions but in the relationships of those propositions to each other. We may attempt to state the relationships within the added square brackets.

(i)   [Although] You were formerly alienated from God

(ii)   [and as a consequence of (i)] You were hostile towards him in mind

(iii)   [and as a consequence of (i) and as an expression of (ii)] You did evil deeds.

(iv)   [Nevertheless (i.e. contraexpectation to (i)] **God has now reconciled you.**

(v)   [The means used to accomplish the result (iv) was] Christ suffered physical death.

(vi)   [The purpose of (iv) was] God will present you holy before him (at his tribunal).

(vii)   [The condition attached to (vi) is] You continue to have faith.

(viii)   [To clarify matters; (vii) means] You continue stable.

(ix)   [To clarify again; (vii) and (viii) mean] You do not lose the
           hope the gospel announces.

What we have placed in the square brackets is every bit as important
to the understanding of the passage as the individual propositions. The
outline provides a *structure of meaning (or sense) relationships* into which the
individual propositions are slotted, and indicates which element is central (here [iv]). The propositions and the structure of relationships are
together called the *semantic structure* of the passage; but we might as easily,
though less precisely, refer to it as the sense of the passage.

Interestingly, commentaries are often quite good at explaining the
individual propositions, and even (in the technical works) of giving detailed analysis of the possible relationships between one proposition and
its immediately adjacent proposition, whilst much more rarely commenting on the 'shape' of the whole cluster, the structure of meaning
relationships. If so the result is usually that we do not see the wood for
the trees. We do not see where the passage is *going*. We shall discuss
semantic structure analysis in some detail in Chapter 6.

3.1.4 Discourse Sense

The paragraphs in Paul's letter to the Colossians, or, say, in a monograph on the New Testament, stand in the same sorts of meaning relation as those that exist between the individual propositions within the
paragraph; that is, one paragraph may give a reason for the main assertion in another, or a clarification of it, or a purpose for it. By spelling
out the sense relationships *not merely within the paragraph*, but also *those that
connect the paragraphs themselves*, we establish the *development* of the work or
its *argument*.

We usually do this intuitively as we read, without attempting formally
to identify the individual relationships as such. However, when we come
to a complex technical argument we may find ourselves struggling to
perceive just how the argument is progressing; we begin to get the
feeling that we cannot understand the paragraph just now being read
because we do not see how it relates to what has been said previously
and to what follows. Taking notes often helps us to clarify the issues,
because the very process of summarizing makes us tease out the main

point of each paragraph, and it is *then* easier to see how the paragraphs relate together and how they then fit into some larger, overarching, structure. Until we have some such overarching understanding of the whole discourse we may not feel confident that we have understood the individual sections.[1]

Strangely enough, although this should all be obvious, people do attempt to explain, for example, individual passages in Romans without relating what they have to say sufficiently carefully to the overall structure of Paul's argument there. Certainly at the popular level one is accustomed to hearing it said that Rom. 7.7-25 must be about the Christian's relation to the Law, because it follows what Paul says about reconciliation in chapter five, and sanctification in chapter six, and precedes what Paul says about the Christian and the Spirit in chapter eight. The commentators are naturally more cautious, and if they adopt this position support it with other arguments.[2] But this 'structure' does not appear to represent the logic of Paul's development of themes at all. Rom. 7.1-6 is about the Christian and the Law, culminating in the statement that we are now discharged from the Law which held us captive, so that we may now serve God in obedience. But Rom. 7.7-12, far from expanding on the Christian's freedom, takes up rather the questions raised by 5.20; 6.14; and 7.6; namely, If we need to be freed from the Law to be free from sin's mastery does this mean the Law is sin?

Paul's answer to this question, in Rom. 7.7-12, would raise a further question for any good Jew who regarded the Law as the badge of the covenant and of God's grace. He would ask (probably heatedly), 'Paul, do you really mean to say God's holy Law brought death rather than life?!' And it is this question Paul faces in 7.13-25. It would seem to follow that neither the questions nor the answer are about Christian experience of the Law, but about how Paul can assert that the Law brought death to Israel, and so why Israel had to be freed from it.[3] For our present purposes we do not need to claim that this interpretation of Romans 7 is the *right* one;[4] we merely point out that how we understand the sense relations of paragraphs in a section *considerably* affects the sense of the paragraphs themselves.

We need to emphasize that the types of relation between propositions and paragraphs which we have just introduced (and which will be discussed more fully in Chapter 6) are characteristic only of certain types of discourse; primarily of the kind that seek to present a connected argument, or to elucidate a theme. And even in these writings there are additional important structural factors.

We have already made mention of H. D. Betz's attempt to demonstrate that Galatians is structured as an apology letter. The structural factors which govern *narrative discourses* are an entirely different matter again. Of the Gospel writers, Luke exploits structure more dramatically than the others, so as to bring across the significance of the material he has chosen to relate.[5] So, for example, in Luke 1—2, he sets stories of the annunciation and birth of John and Jesus in a deliberate and staggered parallelism (to clarify their respective roles). Again, he makes the sermon at Nazareth (4.16-30) paradigmatic, by making it Jesus' first public speech (similarly Peter's Pentecost speech is paradigmatic for Acts). He organizes the whole of 9.51—19.28 as a journey towards Jerusalem, and death-and-ascension (cf. 13.32, etc), which thus provides an interpretative framework for the material contained within the section. The Gospel ends, and Acts begins, with the ascension of Jesus which is of pivotal importance for Luke (and set at the midpoint of his twofold work). He also orchestrates a careful and extensive set of parallels between Jesus, Stephen, Peter and Paul, which both makes the point that the true disciple is the one who suffers with Jesus, and that Paul was a true apostle of Christ; at one with and of similar stature to Peter.[6] These are only a few of the devices Luke employs to guide his readers to what he regards as the important elements of his story; the parts that govern the rest. Narrative strategies will be discussed further in Chapter 7.

In sum, when talking about 'sense' we are talking about such things as the relationship of meaning between a word and other words in the language; the relation between a simple sentence and possible paraphrases of the sentence, and that between clusters of sentences and other ways of expressing the same propositions in the same logical relation to each other. In each case 'sense' is a different sort of relationship of meaning between words and *other words in the language*.

3.2 MEANING AND REFERENCE
A clever Martian who had memorized the *Oxford English Dictionary* might be able to give a synonymous word or expression for any word that was

put to him, without having any idea at all about the entities to which the words usually apply. He might, in other words, be able to define 'boy' in terms of other words ('human', 'male', 'non-adult'), and those words in turn in terms of yet other words, without being able to distinguish a real flesh-and-blood boy from a statue or even a cow. He would have the ability to offer different 'senses' of various words, but not know the real entities to which the words are actually applied. And we might expect him to evince the same confusion between people who are 'out of sight, out of mind', and 'invisible idiots' that translating machines are supposed to make.

By contrast *we* grow up associating words with objects, events and processes in the world around us, and so become aware which kind of object in the world the word 'statue' denotes, and what type of activity going on in the world would be denoted by the word 'sculpting'. *Denotation* is the term used for the relationship which exists between words and the corresponding entities in the world; between words like 'statue' and the objects we denote as statues, and between words like 'sculpting' and the activity in the world which we recognize to be sculpting (cf. our discussion in section 2.1.5). Our knowledge of the real entities denoted by the words we use seems to be important for our perception of discourses using those words. This is notably so in discourses about specialized or technical areas of knowledge. For example, a talk on the benefits of different makes of transmission systems, intended for an audience of car mechanics, might be crystal clear to them, and yet entirely opaque to me if I happen to become a casual overhearer. This is at least in part due to the fact that many of the words being used denote real entities in the world, but entities (mechanical devices) which I have never seen and of which I know nothing.

On the whole we do not meet this sort of problem in biblical interpretation. Predictably some of the OT cultic terminology is opaque to us (we still do not really know what the *teraphim* [cf. Gen. 31.34 and 1 Sam. 19.13!][7] were), and in the New Testament we are uncertain as to what entities should be included in the denotation of the language of principalities and powers (just existential forces? political powers? planetary powers? angels?). However, broadly speaking our attempt to understand the text of the Bible does not founder because of denotational problems.

Much more significant is the related, but more specific, question of *reference*. I may know the sense and possible denotation of all the words in a discourse and *still* not be able to understand the meaning of the discourse at all. Take the following example:

If the balloons popped the sound wouldn't be able to carry, since everything would be too far away from the floor. A closed window would also prevent the sound from carrying, since most buildings tend to be well insulated. Since the whole operation depends on a steady flow of electricity, a break in the middle of the wire would also cause problems. Of course the fellow can shout, but the human voice is not loud enough to travel that far. An additional problem is that a string could break on the instrument. Then there would be no accompaniment to the message. It is clear that the best situation would involve less distance.[8]

We have no problem here with the denotation of such words as 'wire', 'floor', 'sound', 'operation', 'string', 'instrument', 'message', and so on. Our problem is created by the fact that the speaker/writer is referring to a specific instance of all these things (as indicated by his use of the definite article). He has in mind a particular set of balloons, *the* balloons; a specific floor in a building, *the* correct floor; as well as a previously-identified piece of wire and a particular instrument which has already been introduced earlier in the discourse and to which he is referring back. He has clearly given his auditors a complete description at some earlier stage in the discourse (or he can assume they know the situation in some other way) and he is referring back to it. Our problem is that we don't know what he is referring to. But since we do not know the situation we are at a loss to gauge its meaning. A possible solution is offered in figure 1 (p. 86).

We may now define *reference* more closely: the *referent* of a word or expression in an utterance is the *thing in the world which is intentionally signified by that word or expression*.[9] The *thing* in question may be an object, an event or a process.

We must emphasize that reference is entirely a property of *utterances*, or of discourses which may be regarded as utterances because we envisage them as being spoken by the writer to his potential reader. A contextless sentence, for example, a sentence produced to illustrate a point in a grammar, does not have intentional reference. Even a sentence such as 'London is one gigantic chaos', if it is contextless, can have no reference. It might appear to have, provided that we are prepared gratuitously to assume that 'London' is an intentional reference to London, England. But firstly 'London' could in fact be the name of a house, a boat, a pet, or some other city: London, Ontario, for example. And we have no context which would enable us to say what in the world, real or imaginary, the sentence signifies. Second, and more important still, we have no specific author *intending* any reference.

Equally we might note that utterances often contain expressions which denote real entities but without having true *referents*. If the gamekeeper tells me, 'I'm off to shoot a pheasant', we may assume readily enough that he believes there are real birds corresponding to that species in the vicinity, but unless we have reason to know he has a *particular* pheasant in mind there is no *intended referent* for the word. He might, of course, add, 'It keeps scaring the bairn': and that would immediately change the analysis. We would now infer from the whole context that a particular bird was intentionally signified, and so was the referent intended when the gamekeeper first mentioned 'a pheasant'.

There are cases where the issue is rather more difficult to decide. For example, in a letter Johnson wrote to Boswell[10] he penned the famous quip, 'When a man knows he is to be hanged in a fortnight, it concentrates his mind wonderfully.' If this were genuinely meant as a *universal affirmation*, then it has reference—it intentionally refers to the whole class of condemned men on the fourteenth day before their execution. But if we feel it difficult to believe that Johnson intends to offer anything more than a teasing generalization, then his quip amounts to little more than a comment about what might be true of perhaps most condemned men, or of a typical condemned man. In that case the sentence has no *referents*, for there is no *particular* group of men (nor of minds, hangings or fortnights) intentionally signified. In fact, Johnson's original fortuitously commenced 'Depend upon it, *Sir . . .*', and 'Sir' is a referring expression, the referent being the addressee. But had he not added that word there would have been no referent in the utterance at all.

A further theoretical problem arises with such a description as follows:

Something was coming up behind them. What it was could not be seen: it was like a great shadow, in the middle of which was was a

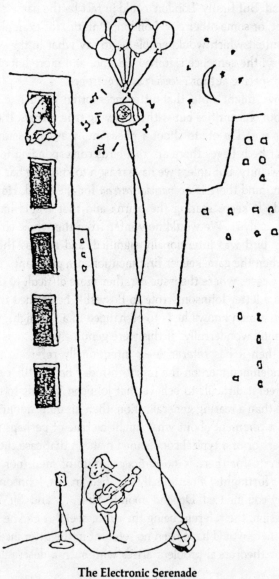

The Electronic Serenade

Figure 1.

dark form, of man-shape maybe, yet greater; and a power and terror seemed to be in it and to go before it. [J. R. Tolkien, *The Fellowship of the Ring*, 313]

At first there would appear to be clear and intentional reference in the pronouns 'something' and 'it'. But, not least because we doubt the existence in the real world of such creatures as Balrogs, we might, in the final analysis, be more inclined to say that there is *no* referent to the description. And similarly, an atheist or agnostic might wish to deny referential status to all expression in the New Testament which purport to refer to God, or angels, or other supernatural beings or events.

To avoid the endless philosophical haggles that could ensue it is probably worthwhile to speak of such 'reference' as appears to be indicated (in the passage quoted) as reference *within Tolkien's universe of discourse*. That is to say we may admit that the pronouns in question do indeed have reference, at least within the 'world' the author has created; and there may then be no pressing need to raise the further question of whether the creature specified exists (or existed) in the world we acknowledge as 'real'. Similarly with the more serious problem of Biblical reference to supernatural beings and events: we may talk of the referents of Paul's discourse *within the universe of that discourse*, if we so wish, without getting bogged down each time in metaphysical questions.

Referential questions are frequently encountered in biblical interpretation, both within the Bible itself and in discussions of it. When, for example, in Acts 8.34, the Ethiopian asks Philip concerning the Suffering Servant of Isa. 53, 'About whom, pray, does the prophet say this? About himself or about another?' it is not the *sense* of the passage he is querying; he wants to know *the referent*. And when Philip replies that the passage is referring to Jesus, he is enabling the Ethiopian to put together the sense of the prophecy and his newly acquired knowledge of the referent in a mutually interpretative fashion so as to lead to a new synthesis of meaning.

Similarly New Testament scholars might be willing to sacrifice a right arm to know the identity of the 'false apostles' referred to in 2 Cor. 11.13. For on their identity, and on the nature of their claims, hangs the interpretation of the whole of 2 Corinthians 10—13 if not, indeed, of the whole of 2 Corinthians (and much of the New Testament beside). Does this term refer to the same people Paul calls 'super-apostles' in 11.5

and 12.11? And were they Judaizers (so Barrett), gnostic pneumatics (Bultmann, Schmithals), the Jerusalem apostles themselves (so F. C. Baur!), delegates from Jerusalem, championing Jewish Christianity, but not directly authorized by the Jerusalem apostles (as most commentators hold), or triumphalist miracle-working Hellenistic Jews regarding themselves as 'divine men' (Friedrich, Georgi and R. P. Martin), or something else yet?

The same sort of *referential* questions apply to the agitators in Galatia (and to the gospel they preached), and to those whom Paul envisages might attempt to 'disqualify' the Colossians 'insisting on self-abasement and the worship of angels' (2.18). So the correct interpretation of whole books seems to depend on an understanding of the referents of certain allusions to people and their teachings, or to events that have occurred, and which are not further explicated by the writer simply because he can take it for granted that his readers already *know* those referents, and will be able to put together their referential knowledge and the new information or argument he is now offering. How many chapters of Paul's letters would at once be rendered crystal clear (or at least far clearer) if only we knew the referents of Paul's assertions and allusions as well as the apostle could assume his readers did.

To mention but a few more examples: the whole of 1 Cor. 1—4 (and perhaps beyond) would be clarified if we once knew who the 'parties' of 1.12ff. were, and what each stood for; our understanding of Philippians would be considerably enhanced if we knew the identity of the enemies of the cross of Christ against whom Paul guards, and of whom he has already warned the addressees (3.18ff.). Similarly, our understanding of 2 Thessalonians would be considerably enriched if we knew the teaching Paul had already given to the Thessalonians on the 'Man of Lawlessness', and 'the Restrainer', teaching to which he merely refers allusively from 2.4 onwards. Similarly, as we have already indicated, Romans 7 would be much clearer if we could be sure of the real referent of Paul's 'I' in 7.14ff.: Is it Paul before conversion? Is it Paul as a Christian struggling in his own power apart from the Spirit's help? Or, indeed, is it Paul the Christian even *with* the Spirit's help? Or is the 'I' merely a literary projection whose real referent is *Israel*—and *her* experience of the Law?

Our knowledge of the *referent* of an utterance is usually important, even vital, for understanding the intended *sense* of what is said. But we must not allow this to lead us into a confusion of sense and reference. As a very rough and ready rule, the *referent* is the extra-linguistic entity[11] about which something is being asserted, while the *sense* is the linguistic meaning of the assertion itself. Scholars are not above confusing the two. Thus Caird points out that one of the arguments against the Pauline authorship of Ephesians is that the writer allegedly uses Pauline words with non-Pauline senses. As an example, the use of *mystērion* ('mystery', 'secret') in Eph. 1.9; 3.3,4,9 is contrasted with that in Col.1.26f. With respect to this Caird aptly comments:

> In Colossians . . . the mystery is God's secret plan to incorporate all men into Christ, whereas in Ephesians . . . it is God's secret plan to break down the barrier between Jew and Gentile . . . There is a discrepancy here only if we commit the elementary linguistic error of confusing a word's meaning [i.e. its sense] with its reference . . . In each case the word means 'secret' and it is the *content* of the secret [i.e. the referent] that is different. [Our italics][12]

A more subtle case is evidenced in E. Käsemann's essay on ministry in the New Testament. Käsemann appears to assume that Paul gives a technical sense to the word *charisma*, using it to denote a gift that is inseparable from the gracious power which bestows it, and is indeed the manifestation of that power. And he gets to this point at least in part from the statement in Romans 6.23 that 'the charisma of God is eternal life in Christ Jesus our Lord', concerning which he can even maintain:

> Other charismata only exist because of the existence of this one charisma to which they are all related, and they only exist where the gift of eternal life is manifested in the eschatologically inaugurated dominion of Christ.[13]

Käsemann goes on to say many things about Paul's understanding of *charismata* with which we would not disagree, but the argument that a technical sense has attached to the word is improbable, and certainly no evidence has been advanced for it. One cannot easily avoid the suspicion that Käsemann has merely read properties of the *referent* of the word *charisma* (in the utterance in Rom. 6.23) into the *sense* of the lexeme. In fact the word *charisma* need mean no more here than 'gift' (i.e., the thing given); and it is merely a property of the particular gift in question— of the referent—that it is a quality of life that is eschatological and Christocentric in character. Neither here, nor elsewhere in Paul, is there good evidence that the word *charisma* had a technical meaning.[14]

3.3 MEANING AS SIGNIFICANCE AND PRESUPPOSITION POOLS

The significance of an utterance is related to its sense, but may go well beyond it. Let us say an electronic eavesdropper hears me say, 'That wretched animal over there chased me right across the field.' If he can only hear my words, but cannot see the referents, he will necessarily have far less of my meaning available to him than would the person to whom I am directly speaking. The latter can see for himself that the 'wretched animal' is a hot-hoofed snorting bull, that the field is extensive and completely open, with nothing convenient to hide behind, and that the surrounding hedge is prickly and uninviting. So he will readily recognize that my experience was both unpleasant and dangerous.

He is aware of the significance of my comment in a way the eavesdropper cannot be, because he is aware of the implications of what he both hears and sees; and thus of the total event concerned. Without being told he can deduce what being in that field with that particular animal would be like. My utterance successfully conveys much more than I actually say because I share with my hearer a 'Presupposition Pool'[15] which contains information constituted from the situative context (how big the bull is, the layout of the field, and also the normal nature of bulls), as well as the new information from the completed part of the discourse itself.

Now let us suppose that the person I am addressing is actually the farmer who owns both the field and the bull, and that my tone of voice indicates mild annoyance. The significance of the message is now quite different from what it would have been if the same words were no more than a passing comment to a walking companion. Addressed to the farmer they may well mean, "You should tether your bull, or at least put up a warning sign!" This 'meaning', the real significance of my statement, on the surface has very little to do with what was actually said. Indeed there is not a single word in common between the suggested 'meaning' and the original speech. What relates the spoken words to the intended meaning, the implicature, is rather a set of *assumptions*, some logical *entailments*, and other, more conventionally based, implications.

The assumptions would include: (a) that charging bulls are dangerous, (b) that the farmer is responsible for charging bulls if he owns them, (c) that he knows that he is responsible. And the conventional implications would at least include: (a) that the farmer is in the wrong and should apologize; (b) that he should take steps to rectify the situation. If the farmer were to understand my communication—as surely he would—it would be because we share a common presupposition pool from which he furnishes the necessary background information to add to my words. From my look, and from the tone of my voice, he infers that I am intending a rebuke, not the mere transmission of a piece of information. From the situational context, and from his general knowledge (including a knowledge of the English conventions regarding a farmer's responsibilities for his animals) he deduces both the content of the rebuke and its probable implications.

We often use our speech to perform actions (such as the action of *rebuking* someone, *warning* a companion of some danger, *informing* of a situation, etc.). In linguistics, such uses of speech are called *illocutionary acts*. These may be *direct* illocutions (as when I use the words 'I do apologize for . . .' to make an apology) or *indirect* ones—as when I use the question 'Is it a little chilly tonight?' as an act of requesting my host to turn on the heater: here the *force* of my utterance is only *indirectly* related to its grammatical sense. If I roll down my window and call 'I'm running out of petrol' to a passerby, she will probably correctly perceive the implicature in my indirect illocution; namely that I request clear directions to the nearest garage. The factors involved in elucidating such conversational implicature are extremely interesting, but beyond the scope of this section. They are a prime concern of that discipline of linguistics to which the name Pragmatics is given; and the issues involved are introduced at section 2.1.6 above, and dealt with in more detail in Chapter 8. Our only concern here is to indicate the importance of our presupposition pools in our perception of the significance of an utterance.

If, in a quite different situation, I fail to understand a discussion on the comparative benefits of different types of word-processor, it may be due not to a failure on my part to understand the *words* used but rather to my not having an adequate presupposition pool to be able to see all the relevant implications of a sentence such as, 'It has a built in font-editor'.

Turning to a biblical example, let us consider Acts 5.30: 'The God of our fathers raised up Jesus—whom you killed by hanging him on a tree.'

The complex verb 'to hang on a tree' was at the time beginning to be used as an idiom for 'to crucify', and here certainly the referent is Calvary. But why does Peter use *this* idiom, replete as it is with connotations of Deut. 21.22-3 and notions of the display of an executed corpse by hanging it on a tree, to refer to Calvary? And we note that the Deuteronomy passage concludes with the sombre injunction to remove the body by nightfall because 'anyone who is hung on a tree is under God's curse'. Why did Peter not simply use the verb 'to crucify' and thereby avoid the offensive thought of Jesus coming under God's curse? One very real possibility is that his wording is deliberate, and reflects such unstated presuppositions as:

(1) Jesus' resurrection-exaltation demonstrates him to be Israel's Messiah.

(2) If God allows his righteous Messiah (Israel's representative king) to suffer death it must be to accomplish some redemptive purpose through it.

(3) Jesus had himself taught that his forthcoming suffering would be representative and fulfil an atoning function with respect to *Israel's* sin (so Mark 10.45 and the Last Supper tradition).[16]

(4) The crucifixion (a 'hanging of a person on a tree') relates Jesus to the curse of God on sin in Deuteronomy 21 and elsewhere. Hence

(5) the Messiah died under God's 'curse' on sin as Israel's representative and in her place.

In other words, the description 'hanged upon a tree' is quite possibly deliberately chosen to point to the theological significance of the crucifixion as Peter (or Luke) understood it (cf. 1 Peter 2.24).

In the earlier example, the implied assumptions and consequences would be so transparent that the farmer would be bound to perceive the message intentionally conveyed in the complaint concerning his bull. In that instance, the significance of my message is the same as the significance to the farmer. In the situation envisaged in Acts this is not necessarily the case; the implicature was open to two sorts of failure.

On the one hand some hearers might easily fail to perceive any theological significance in Peter's choice of the verb 'to hang on a tree', and so not deduce any implicature in this statement. Others, on the other hand, might successfully connect Peter's words with the Deuteronomic background of the language only to find in the connection a confirmation that Jesus must be cursed of God, and so could *not* be Israel's Messiah (and such a view has sometimes been inferred of *Paul's* pre-Christian understanding of the matter from his wording in Gal 3.13).

The majority might be expected successfully to perceive the implicature (whether or not they accept it as *true*). After all they will know from the cotext that Peter holds presupposition (1), and from his language that he assumes (4). As premise (2) would also be *generally* held [and (3) only clarifies it in a contextually predictable direction], hearers could be *expected* to perceive that Peter held the unstated conclusion (5).

These nine little words, then, 'whom you killed by hanging him on a tree', could have *different significance* for different people. This leads to two important observations.

First, *significance is a relation of meaning between the sense of an utterance and some* person's *world*, or at least some aspect of that world. We may thus appropriately talk both of the significance of the discourse *for the speaker/writer* (involving the premises and consequences he considered immediately relevant, and focused by it) and of the (possibly quite different) significance *for his hearers or readers*. As Hirsch put it, significance is always meaning-*for*-someone.

In the case of the speaker we may need to make a further distinction. To return to the example of Acts 5, to judge from his choice of wording Peter (or at least Luke) probably *intended* to point to the theological significance of the cross as an atoning death when he chose the particular idiom 'by hanging him on a tree'. If so, this theological inference is genuinely part of the discourse meaning itself. If, however, on reflection, Peter later went on to relate Jesus' accursed death to, say, the Suffering Servant motif, or to see it as fulfilment of the cultus, these new considerations could *not* be regarded as part of the significance of the discourse meaning itself. They may indeed be legitimate theological conclusions drawn from it, but they can only be drawn from it by engaging a new and further set of presuppositions—ones neither explicitly offered in the discourse, nor evidently present by implicature, nor so generally held by Jews that they could be assumed. The new significance Peter might see, reflecting on his earlier words, was not part and parcel of the original communication, but results from an extension of the discourse meaning to a new set of questions and assumptions; i.e. to a new context or 'world'. We should have to speak rather of the *subsequent significance for Peter* of the meaning of the discourse he had uttered.

When we talk about the 'meaning' of Acts 5.30 *today*, this usually means the *significance for us* today. That significance will depend partly on what we think the discourse meant (its sense, its reference, and its intended significance then), and partly on our theological and critical assumptions, and the entailments and implications we believe follow from them. It would be relevant, for example, to consider in what sense, if any, we believe that God 'curses' executed criminals. And it would be relevant too to consider the extent to which we believe Luke's account of Peter's discourse 'authoritative' for *our* theological thinking. A radical so-called 'liberal' reader and a strongly conservative one might agree entirely as to what *Luke* thought *Peter* meant, without agreeing for a moment on the significance for *us*, today.

Second, *the significance an utterance has for any hearer depends* not only on the *sense* of what is spoken, and on the shared presupposition pool, *but also on presuppositions held by the hearer that he does not share with the speaker*. For example, as we have suggested above a Jew might consider that anyone whom God sovereignly allowed to be crucified could *not possibly* be Israel's Messiah. If he held such an assumption, the significance of Peter's speech for him would inevitably amount to a confirmation that Jesus is *not* Israel's Messiah. Here clearly speaker's meaning and hearer's meaning are antithetical to each other, and the reason for the difference lies in the role played by elements in the presupposition pools of both. The presupposition pool we engage as we listen to any particular discourse has immediate consequences for our perception of that discourse. Brown and Yule complain:

> One of the most pervasive illusions which persists in the analysis of language is that we understand the meaning of a linguistic message solely on the basis of the words and structure of the sentence(s) used to convey that message.[17]

Such a view clearly does not account for the entirely different conclusions concerning Peter's discourse that could be reached by his hearers on the basis of his use of the expression 'to hang on a tree'. Nor does such a view explain the ease with which we recognize the difference between literal and non-literal utterances. If my wife tells me, 'I ate Duncan for breakfast this morning', it is not *lexical* and *grammatical* analysis that suggest to me she is not speaking literally. I recognize she is informing me she has taken up the issue of the state of tidiness (or, rather, untidiness) of Duncan's bedroom with him in a very determined manner through our shared presupposition pool.

In this section we have been trying to show that it is in fact largely due to factors other than merely the *sense* of sentences that we understand discourse. One further example may suffice to illustrate the significance of presupposition pools. Revelation 3.14-21 (RSV) reads as follows:

(3.14) And to the angel of the church in Laodicea write: 'The words of the Amen, the faithful and true witness, the beginning of God's creation. (3.15) I know your works: you are neither cold nor hot. Would that you were cold or hot! (3.16) So, because you are lukewarm, and neither cold nor hot, I will spew you out of my mouth. (3.17) For you say, I am rich, I have prospered, and I need nothing; not knowing that you are wretched, pitiable, poor, blind, and naked. (3.18) Therefore I counsel you to buy from me gold refined by fire, that you may be rich, and white garments to clothe you and to keep the shame of your nakedness from being seen, and salve to anoint your eyes, that you may see. (3.19) Those whom I love, I reprove and chasten; so be zealous and repent. (3.20) Behold, I stand at the door and knock; if anyone hears my voice and opens the door, I will come in to him and eat with him, and he with me. (3.21) He who conquers, I will grant him to sit with me on my throne . . . .'

Most of the commentators in the standard series are aware that Laodicea was renowned for three things:[18] for its rich banking facilities, for its wool and textile industry, and for its medical school with its widely exported 'Phrygian powder' used as an eye-salve. These were all objects of pride to the population; and the note of arrogant self-sufficiency struck in 3.17 is matched by the city's own response when it was devastated by earthquake circa A.D. 60—Laodicea refused imperial assistance, and rebuilt the city 'from her own resources'.[19] If the reader comes unaware of these facts about the city he will not understand the dramatic irony of the prophetic utterance. The church has identified itself spiritually with the strengths and self-sufficiency of its city; but the heavenly Lord addresses it as the opposite—as the poor, the blind and the naked, who need the spiritual counterparts of the very things the city regards as its pride. The power of the message, as well as its significance, rests in its denial of elements in the Laodicean presupposition pool.

There are other aspects of the message which also clearly depend for their significance on the presupposition pool. In the Near East, to eat with others was a token of full acceptance of them, and so of reconciliation with them, and a token of the forgiveness of estranged parties. This is the significance of Jehoiachin's being released and then being given permission to eat regularly at the table of the king of Babylon (2 Kings 25.27-30). This too is why the Pharisees were incensed by Jesus' eating with 'tax-collectors and sinners'. The cultural significance of table-fellowship is then part of the presupposition pool of the church at Laodicea which gives significance to 3.20; the point is that if the church repents and reopens the door to the Lord, to let him back into her citadel (the allusion is to the massive city gate, closed at dusk, and reopened only in the morning), then she will be forgiven her backsliding and be reconciled.

If we do not share the presupposition pool of the intended hearer/ reader we are prone to misunderstand; perhaps even totally. In this respect it is interesting to see how the commentators cope with 3.15-16. The older standard works take 'hot' to mean zealous for the Lord. Because 'cold' is an antonym to 'hot', we might expect them to take 'cold' to mean "indifferent to", or "cool towards", but of course they don't because that is precisely the significance that is attributed to 'lukewarm'. 'Cold' is therefore taken to denote actual antagonism (almost 'hot' or zealous *against* the Lord!). The resulting exegesis of 3.16 can be summed up in Morris' words, 'There is more hope for the openly antagonistic than for the coolly indifferent'[20]—which is not impossible, but should at least surprise us. And it does not fit very well with 3.15 which was about *works* not disposition.

However, a consideration of the Laodicean presupposition pool may lead to a quite different understanding. The city of Hierapolis stood within clear view of Laodicea. There the hot mineral waters cascaded over cliffs, encrusting them with glistening calcium salts that gave a great white gash to the landscape. These waters were renowned for their healing properties. Very near to Laodicea, but in another direction, lay Colossae, a city that boasted a cold stream, something of a rarity in this volcanic region, the water of which was prized for its deeply refreshing quality.

The trouble with Laodicea was that as the city had grown it had quickly outstripped its immediate water-supply and had been forced to pipe it in from afar.[21] The water was carried across the plain through great stone pipes and arrived warm and with a sludgy deposit that made it barely drinkable. In fact, fit to be spat out! The Laodiceans of course would be fully aware of all this; the knowledge would be part of their presupposition pool. Putting these elements together, Rudwick and Green[22] made the attractive suggestion that the point of the prophetic address is that (once again) the Laodicean church are being compared with their city; they do not have its strengths (gold, wool and eyesalve), but they do have its weakness! While the cold water of Colossae brings refreshment, and the hot water of Hierapolis is famed for its healing, the works of the Laodicean church bring neither healing nor spiritual refreshment; they are like their water supply—fit to be spat out!

This interpretation has the advantage of making sense of why the Lord might be said to prefer 'cold' to 'lukewarm'. In other respects, too, we consider it to be along the right lines, but of course our real point does not depend on whether the interpretation is actually correct. The point we are making is that it must be elements in the presupposition pool (not merely those in the text) that are potentially determinative of significance.

We shall draw out some of the implications of all this for exegesis below. Here it is sufficient to reiterate that utterances have determinate meaning (albeit sometimes also determined ambiguity!), and that part of that meaning is fixed by the context. Further, that, in turn, one of the major contextual influences is what the speaker assumes to be the relevant presupposition pool he shares with the hearer.

3.4 MEANING AS SIGNIFICANCE AND GENRE CONSIDERATIONS

We have already noted that significance is a dimension of meaning that cannot always simply be read off from the literal sense of an utterance. In this respect genre considerations can be very important. Hirsch recounts the reception accorded Daniel Defoe's tract, *The Shortest Way with Dissenters*, which was published anonymously in 1702. Taken at face value it looked like a serious argument for the extermination of dissen-

ters by any and all judicious means including execution. But in fact it
was sustained satire and irony: Defoe was himself a clever dissenter. *The
Shortest Way* was, however, so subtly written that it took all too many
readers in. Hirsch describes the incident:

> There is an anecdote in Oldmixion's History of England of 1735
> which tells of a bookseller who 'having an order from a Fellow of a
> College in Cambridge for a parcel of books, just at the time of pub-
> lishing this Shortest Way put up one of them in the bundle, not
> doubting it would be welcome to his customer, who accordingly
> thanked him for packing so excellent a treatise up with the rest, it
> being next to the Sacred Bible, and Holy Comments, the best book
> he ever saw.' Only later, after it had been discovered that the author
> of this excellent plan to oppress, banish, and hang the dissenters, was
> himself a clever dissenter with a clever pen, did the Cambridge don
> change his view and, in Oldmixion's words 'forbade his bookseller to
> send him any more pamphlets without particular orders.'
>
> . . . We know that Defoe did indeed mislead for a while some very
> clever men who were excellent stylists, even if not stylisticians. This,
> of course, only inflamed the subsequent rage against the pamphlet
> and against its author, the anonymous ironical dissenter. Parliament
> ordered the pamphlet to be burned by the common hangman, and
> issued a proclamation offering the sum of fifty pounds for the dis-
> covery of the author, who subsequently spent time in the pillory and
> in jail.[23]

The story is vivid testimony that at the time 'author's intended meaning'
was accepted as the meaning of the text. No incipient Reader-Response
theorists were called to defend Defoe (or the pamphlet) on the grounds
that his ironic intention had nothing to do with the meaning of the
writing as it stood. Rather, people were angered to find what Defoe
must have meant, and thereby what the pamphlet must have meant.
But our point here is not so much a matter of the history of criticism,
but the reason why the mistaken interpretation was made at all. It arose
because readers assumed that the writing was intended literally, when
in fact its significance lay in the opposite direction. It was a deliberate
piece of irony; and the failure in perception lay in misunderstanding the
genre of the writing—in this instance a failure which was positively
invited.

A 'literary genre' has been defined as 'a group of written texts marked by distinctive recurring characteristics which constitute a recognizable and coherent type of writing'.[24] Our identification of what we take to be the genre to which a particular text belongs raises certain expectations about how the contents of the writing are to be understood. Of a song we expect a certain hyperbole we would not tolerate in a historical text. When the psalmist says he cried out in his affliction, and the earth trembled, smoke and fire belched from God's mouth, the Lord parted the heavens, shot bolts of lightning at the enemy, laid bare the very foundations of the sea, and finally picked the psalmist up out of his trouble (so Psalm 18), we do not flinch; we may be awed by the language, but not entirely surprised by it—at least not as surprised as we would be if we found the account in prose amongst the histories of Israel!

And again, when St John tells us:

> I saw . . . one like a son of man, clothed with a long robe and with a golden girdle round his breast; his head and his hair were as white as wool, white as snow; his eyes were like a flame of fire, his feet were burnished bronze, . . . and his voice was like the sound of many waters . . . (Rev. 1.12-15),

or

> From the throne issue flashes of lightning, and voices and peals of thunder, and before the throne burn seven torches of fire . . . (Rev. 4.5a-b),

we need not, perhaps, doubt that he 'saw' these things; but equally we must recognize that John is not describing what he considers the heavenly Jesus really looks like, or what phenomena surround the divine throne. This should be clear from the way he continues each of the descriptions. The first he concludes:

> In his right hand he held seven stars, from his mouth issued a sharp two-edged sword . . .

and we are surely not intended to believe that the risen Lord really walks amongst candlesticks (so 1.12), holding stars, and with a sword protruding from his mouth! Indeed both the stars and the candlesticks are eventually identified (differently) with the seven churches (cf. 1.20). Similarly, the seven fires burning before the throne are identified as 'the seven spirits of God' (4.5c). In other words, what is 'seen' is apocalyptic symbolism, rather than the true referents of the symbolism. This is a recurrent feature of the book; one of the traits of its genre. And if we fail to understand that, we are liable to misconstrue the whole book.

Psalm, history, and apocalyptic are such obviously different genres that they are not usually confused. The more subtle differences of genre reflected in the Scriptures—both as whole writings and as parts thereof—more frequently succeed in trapping the unwary.

However, the subject of the genre of individual writings is well treated in standard introductions,[25] and need not be dealt with in this book. We merely point out that genre is a dimension of a literary unit which is, once again, of decisive import for assessing (not the sense, but) the intended significance of the writing.

3.5 MEANING AS 'SIGNIFICANCE' AND THE EXEGETICAL TASK

If the biblical books were regarded as autonomous texts, and if the task of exegesis were seen merely to analyze the sense-meaning of passages of Scripture, we could readily hand over the academic guild of biblical scholars to our erstwhile friends, the hunters, for shooting. But because discourse meaning is shaped by situational factors, and because this is especially true of 'significance', we cannot dispense with specialist expertise. The scholar is needed not merely to tell us what the individual words mean, to advise us what sort of entities they denote, and to help us identify the referents of the myriad referring expressions—a difficult enough task—but to guide us towards an understanding of the intended significance of the writings, and of their individual parts.

Theoretically this is a Herculean task; the precise extent of which is not entirely clear. For all our agreement with Hirsch about the determinacy of authorial meaning, and although some areas of significance are clearly definable, it must nevertheless be very hard indeed to define the invisible boundary between what is an intended significance and what is not. In practice we do not need to spell out every possible intended significance of a work (and of each of its parts); we are interested only in those areas potentially of most importance.

In terms of the vocabulary we have been introducing, the greatest task is to define the relevant presupposition pools. Johannes Weiss was able to break new ground in clarifying Jesus' teaching on the Kingdom of God, because he was able to show that central concepts involved were best explained in terms of beliefs already circulating in apocalyptic Judaism; that is to say that apocalyptic ideas were part of the presupposition pool shared by Jesus and his hearers, and that this pool of presuppositions would have been actively engaged by the language Jesus chose to employ. In terms of the language of New Testament scholarship, one of the aims of exegesis is to provide 'parallels' against which the significance of particular New Testament statements becomes more clear. This hunt for parallels is fundamentally right, just so long as it stops short of what Sandmel dubbed 'Parallelomania'.[26] It is right, in other words, as long as the speaker or writer was so geographically, historically, culturally and ideologically placed that it becomes probable he was aware of, and influenced by, the alleged parallels.

It is right, in short, if there is a good probability that the alleged parallel was actually part of the presupposition pool shared by the writer and his intended readers; not merely ideas current either later, or elsewhere, or in a different social or conceptual milieu. By such criteria, the attempt to 'explain' (e.g.) Paul's baptismal teaching in terms of ideas in the Mystery Religions,[27] or to elucidate John (or Ephesians) in terms of gnostic ideas, must remain at best highly controversial. However, the use of Qumran material to elucidate aspects of the description of the Christian community as the new Temple in Ephesians 2.18-22 may be pertinent, as long as the shared concepts are traced back to the common milieu of Judaism rather than specifically and genetically to the Dead Sea Community as such (which, on other grounds, is much less probable).[28]

'Parallels' assist us, provided that they point us to the presupposition pool the writer shares with his reader; they help us to 'read between the lines' of a discourse, and so to understand the significance of the assertions made in it. They must not be permitted to rule the interpretation with a rod of iron (as when Weiss and his followers excluded the possibility that Jesus spoke not merely of the future coming of the Kingdom of God, but also of its arrival in his own ministry): we have no reason to assume that the ideas evidenced in allegedly parallel discourses were taken over lock, stock and barrel, into any speaker's presupposition pool.[29] He may already have accidentally modified them in the very act of seeking to understand them—and beyond that he may have deliberately transformed what he read or heard.[30]

And beyond the search for conceptual parallels, presupposition pools

will also need to be elucidated by careful historical, archeological, sociological[31] and cultural-anthropological[32] research. We need, for example,
to know what responsibilities convention laid at the feet of a Near-
Eastern son or daughter before we can possibly say what 'Honour your
father and your mother!' entailed; what it signified to be slapped on the
cheek, before we can grasp what it means to be asked to offer the other
(the point is *not* passivism); how Jews related to Samaritans in the first
century to understand the radical teaching of Jesus' parable of a Good
Samaritan; how people bought fields and farm animals (let alone took
to themselves wives) in order to see the excuses offered the host in the
parable of the Great Banquet (Luke 14.15-24) for the calculated insults
they were, and so forth.[33] Almost every page of the New Testament
(and not a few in the Old) offers examples where a careful elucidation
of the presupposition pool shared by the writer and reader has thrown
new light—sometimes startling new light—on the significance of an
incident or saying.

CONCLUSION

This chapter has introduced different dimensions of the meaning of a
discourse, and has given some indication of how a knowledge of linguistics (or at least of some of its consistent disciplines) may help an interpreter in the task of commenting on texts. We have not, however, spelt
out in any detail how, for example, lexical semantics might clarify word
sense, how discourse analysis might illuminate the development or argument of a passage, or how pragmatics could elucidate the mechanisms
involved in our perception of implicature. These are the subject of later
chapters in this book. This chapter has only attempted, in provisional
fashion, to indicate *some* of the *kinds* of clarification we may require in
order to be sure we have discovered the discourse meaning of a text.

Notes

[1]Perhaps one of the best examples of the importance of this overarching structure is provided by G. K. Chesterton's *The Man Who Was Thursday*. It is the story
   of a group of anarchists, each named after a day of the week. Their leader is
   code-named Sunday. The identity of Sunday is not revealed until the final
   chapter, at which point the reader is compelled to reinterpret the entire work.
[2]For a brief review of the types of interpretation see J. C. Beker, *Paul the Apostle,*

Edinburgh, T. & T. Clark, 1980, pp.65ff. and 83ff.

[3]And it is not unprecedented for such argument to be presented in autobiographical style (using 'I').

[4]Cf. Beker, *Paul the Apostle*, pp.83ff. For the argument in more detail see e.g. D. J. Moo, 'Israel and Paul in Rom. 7.7-12', *NTS* 32 (1986), pp. 122-3.

[5]See e.g. C. H. Talbert, *Literary Patterns, Theological Themes and the Genre of Luke-Acts*, Missoula, Scholars Press, 1974, though this is an exaggerated statement of the position.

[6]See, for example, A. J. Mattill, 'The Jesus-Paul Parallels and the Purpose of Luke-Acts', *NovT* 17 (1975), pp.15-46; 'The Purpose of Acts: Schneckenburger Reconsidered' in W. W. Gasque and R. P. Martin (ed.), *Apostolic History and the Gospel*, Exeter, Paternoster, 1970, pp.108-22.

[7]See Caird, *The Language and Imagery of the Bible*, pp.10f.

[8]From 'Cognitive Processes' in Bourne and Ekstrand, *Psychology*, New Jersey: Holt, Rinehart & Winston, 1979[3], p.208.

[9]I am aware that many works on semantics use 'reference' more loosely, and so as a synonym for denotation. J. Lyons, *Introduction to Theoretical Linguistics*, Cambridge, CUP, 1968, pp.424ff., used 'reference' in this general sense, but he has since argued for the more sharply defined use of the term: see his *Semantics*, Cambridge: CUP, 1977, chap. 7. Compare J. R. Hurford and B. Heasley, *Semantics*, Cambridge, CUP, 1983, chaps. 1 and 2.

[10]*Letters to Boswell*, 19th September 1777.

[11]Note, however, that if we discuss the use of a particular instance of a word, or expression, we may be treating it as an object in the world, and so it may become the referent of an expression even though it is itself a linguistic entity, not an extra-linguistic one. Thus if I say, 'Romans 8.13 surprises us by its "deeds of the *body*" where we might have expected "flesh" instead', I have made Paul's words *('tas praxeis tou sōmatos')* the main referent of my utterance.

[12]*Paul's Letters From Prison*, Oxford, OUP, 1976, p. 14.

[13]*Essays on New Testament Themes*, London, SCM, 1964, p. 64.

[14]For the argument in more detail see M. M. B. Turner, 'Spiritual Gifts Then and Now', *Vox Evangelica* 15 (1985), pp.30-1, and the literature cited there.

[15]The term is that used by T. Venneman; for a brief review of his development of the concept see G. Brown and G. Yule, *Discourse Analysis*, Cambridge, CUP, 1983, pp.79-83.

[16]We are aware the authenticity of Mark 10.45 and the Last Supper tradition has been widely challenged: but on the former see the discussion in G. R. Beasley-Murray, *Jesus and the Kingdom of God*, Exeter, Paternoster, 1986, 278-82; on the latter see I. H. Marshall, *Last Supper and Lord's Supper*, Exeter, Paternoster, 1980, chaps. 2 and 3, and on the more general question of whether Jesus interpreted

his death see M. Hengel, *The Atonement*, London, SCM, 1981, chap. 2.

[17]G. Brown and G. Yule, *Discourse Analysis*, p.223.

[18]This is not to suggest that all commentaries are equally aware of the significant issues. The watershed is theoretically 1970; for in 1969 C. J. Hemer submitted his Ph.D. thesis to Manchester University under the title 'A Study of the Letters to the Seven Churches of Asia with Special Reference to their Local Background'. R. H. Mounce's commentary *The Book of Revelation*, Grand Rapids, Eerdmans, 1977, is in fact the first to make extensive use of its findings. Hemer's thesis has been revised and is published as *The Letters to the Seven Churches of Asia in their Local Setting*, Sheffield, JSOT Press, 1986.

[19]Tacitus, *Ann.* 14.27

[20]Leon Morris, *The Revelation of Saint John*, London, IVP, 1969, p.82; similarly e.g. M. Kiddle, *The Revelation of St John* (Moffatt NT Commentaries), p.58 and G .B. Caird, *A Commentary on the Revelation of St John the Divine* (Black's NT Commentaries), p.57.

[21]But not from Hierapolis, as is commonly asserted (most recently by G. R. Beasley-Murray, *The Book of Revelation*, London, MMS, 1974, p.105); it came from Denizli. See Mounce, *The Book of Revelation*, p.125, or (in more detail) C. Hemer, *The Letters to the Seven Churches of Asia in their Local Setting*, ad. loc.

[22]M. J. S. Rudwick and E. M. B. Green, 'The Laodicean Lukewarmness' *Expository Times* 69 (1957-8), pp.176-8. The view is taken up and developed by Hemer in his Ph.D. thesis and in *The Letters to the Seven Churches of Asia in their Local Setting*.

[23]E. D. Hirsch, *The Aims of Interpretation*, London, University of Chicago Press, 1976), pp.24f.

[24]So J. J. Collins, *Semeia* 14 (1979), p.1.

[25]The best general account of genre is that by D. Aune, *The New Testament in its Literary Environment*, Philadelphia, Westminster, 1987; or in massive detail in K. Berger's article in W. Haase (ed.), *Aufstieg und Niedergang der Römischen Welt*, 25.2, pp.1031-432.

[26]S. Sandmel, 'Parallelomania', *JBL* (1962) 81, pp.1-13.

[27]See not only G. Wagner's thesis, *Pauline Baptism and the Pagan Mysteries*, London, Oliver & Boyd, 1967, but also B. Metzger, 'Methodology in the Study of the Mystery Religions and Early Christianity', in *Historical and Literary Studies*, Leiden, Brill, 1968, pp. 1-23.

[28]Cf. S. Sandmel, 'Parallelomania', p.6. On the theme of the new Temple in Ephesians and Qumran see e.g. B. Gärtner, *The Temple and the Community in Qumran and in the New Testament*, Cambridge, CUP, 1965, pp.60-6; R. J. McKelvey, *The New Temple*, Oxford, OUP, 1969, chap.8.

[29]See the caution of T. L. Donaldson, 'Parallels: Use, Misuse and Limitations', *EvQ* 55, pp.193-210.

[30]For this thesis in relation to Jesus' teaching see J. Riches, *Jesus and the Transformation of Judaism,* London, SPCK, 1980.

[31]For an introductory account of the possible significance here see D. Tidball, *An Introduction to the Sociology of the New Testament,* Exeter, Paternoster, 1983; J. E. Stambaugh and D. L. Balch, *The New Testament and Its Social Environment,* Philadelphia, Westminster, 1987, and especially W. Meeks, *The First Urban Christians,* New Haven, YUP, 1983.

[32]For suggestive insights here see B. Malina, *The New Testament World: Insights from Cultural Anthropology,* London, SCM, 1983.

[33]For the examples cited see the respective chapters of e.g. K. E. Bailey, *Poet and Peasant,* and *Through Peasant Eyes: A Literary-Cultural Approach to the Parables in Luke,* Exeter, Paternoster, 1983.

4. The Use and Abuse of Word Studies in Theology

4.1 WORD STUDY FROM CREMER TO KITTEL

Future generations may well call the last hundred years or so the Era of Theological Word Studies. Its birth could perhaps be traced back to the publication in Germany of Cremer's *Biblico-Theological Lexicon of New Testament Greek* in 1867. Its *floruit* should certainly be identified with the period of massive industry, from the late twenties to the early seventies of this century, which produced Kittel's justly renowned *Theological Dictionary of the New Testament (TDNT)*. The precise date of its decease would be uncertain; perhaps all that could usefully be said of it is that in 1961 Dr. James Barr pronounced the patient severely ill, and gave it but a short time to live.

To call this period the Era of Theological Word Studies is not to imply that there was no interest in lexicography before and that there has been none since. Cremer was certainly not the first to write a Greek lexicon: twenty-seven were written between 1510 and 1568 alone![1] But Cremer did add a new dimension to the endeavour. Several decades of discussion had taken place as to whether the Greek of the NT was classical or Hebraizing, and the suggestion had recently been made (by Schleiermacher) that New Testament Greek was not actually either, but what amounts to a special 'language of the Holy Spirit'.[2] It was suggested that in some way Christianity had so remoulded men's understanding of God and the world that ordinary Greek terminology had necessarily come to bear new meaning, and even new terms had necessarily to be created, in order to express the new concepts. And this represented a process of linguistic transformation which had already got under way when the Hebrew Old Testament had been translated into Greek.

What Cremer undertook was not to write a theology of the New Testament ordered round its lexical stock (though many have misrepresented him as doing this),[3] but to provide a dictionary of those words which the Septuagint and the advent of Christianity had renewed, transformed or created. His dictionary thus examined only 600 of the New Testament's 5000 or so words (and the last edition from his pen no more than doubled that). In it he attempted to show where Septuagintal and New Testament Greek vocabulary *differed* (in form or sense) from that attested in classical literature, and occasionally to highlight some of the exegetical and theological significance of such distinctive words or meanings. The entries in his dictionary thus amounted to mini-articles and did not confine themselves merely to word-usage, but also elucidated aspects of the broader biblical *concepts* of (e.g.) love, justification, Kingdom, Son of man, Son of God and so on.

Cremer's dictionary was criticized on a number of counts,[4] not least by the great philologist A. Deissmann, who considered it wrong-headed to talk of a special language of the Holy Spirit. Deissmann was able to show that the great majority of so-called examples of distinctively 'biblical Greek' were in fact attested in the then little-researched papyri.[5] These scraps and oddments from account books, wills, bills, private letters, magical texts, and horoscopes that had been preserved in the Egyptian sands, represented the language of the common people—the *koinē*—and it was this that was closest to and best explained the nature of the New Testament writings. The apostles preached and wrote in the everyday parlance of the non-literary world, not in the esoteric and inscrutable private language of a religious coterie.[6] Despite the criticisms, and making allowance for some of them, Cremer's dictionary went through some nine revisions, and a tenth was added by Julius Kögel (1915).

The mantle was then transferred to Kittel, and the massive *Theological Dictionary* was under way. But the conception of a theological dictionary had shifted. With Kögel and Kittel less attempt was made to claim that the Christ event had called into being new *words*. Instead, greater emphasis was placed on elucidating what was believed to be the distinctive theological significances of New Testament words—even, that is, of words that were commonplace in the classical literature. Thus Kittel's dictionary offers major articles of some pages in length on the majority of the words of the New Testament; even on such ordinary and apparently innocent words as the prepositions 'in', 'into', 'before', 'towards'. Not untypically a nine-page entry on 'one' is broken up under the headings 'The Understanding of Uniqueness in the New Testament'; 'Adam and the Common Destiny of the Race'; and 'Christ and the Unity of the Church'; and provides virtually a terse potted summary of biblical monotheism and of the integrity of salvation-history.

Clearly we have moved far from Cremer's originally mainly *lexical* enquiry towards the generation of an *encyclopaedia* of New Testament theology organized alphabetically on the basis of its lexical stock. Let us clarify the distinction. The essential task of a language dictionary or lexicon is usually considered to be the listing of the words of a language (giving relevant morphological information), and the clarification of the respective senses of each word (usually by providing a synonymous expression or range of synonymous expressions for each sense). When Bauer's lexicon under *thyreos*, . . . *ho* gives 'a long oblong *shield;* fig. . . . *shield of faith* Eph. 6.16', he is giving us purely lexical information: he is telling us that the appropriate English word-substitution for *thyreos* is *shield;* he is warning us that a particular *type* of shield is denoted—a long oblong one, as distinct from circular types—and he is informing us that in the New Testament literature the word is used *figuratively* for (the protective function of) 'faith' in Ephesians. By contrast the so-called *New International Dictionary of New Testament Theology (NIDNTT)* under the same Greek word informs us:

> . . . the Roman *scutum*. It had an iron frame and sometimes a metal boss. *thyreos* is linked etymologically with *thyra*, door. It was a large door-shaped or vaulted shield in contrast with the small, round *aspis* or *pelta*. With its several layers of leather soaked in water before battle it was a formidable protection against flaming darts.

Here the information given—which is undoubtedly more *useful* for exegesis than the bare entry in Bauer—nevertheless goes well beyond the
purely *lexical*. NIDNTT does not merely indicate the *sense* of the Greek
word, but tells us extra-linguistic, circumstantial information about the
objects-in-the-world that the word is used to denote. This traditionally
is what we mean by encyclopaedic information, as distinct from lexical,
or dictionary information.[7] The distinction has become blurred by the
production of many works giving encyclopaedic information (i.e. information about objects in the world or concepts, rather than about word-
sense) which, nevertheless, call themselves *dictionaries*: both Kittel and
the NIDNTT are obvious examples.

But Kögel and Kittel did not explain their works in these terms. Kögel
spoke rather of the difference between 'external lexicography' (that concerned with morphology and sense, such as found in Bauer, or Liddell
and Scott) and what he termed 'internal lexicography' (a distinction
taken over by Kittel too). By the latter Kögel meant something approx-
imating to the structure of thought or conceptual context with which
the word was *associated*; the historical and conceptual stage on which
word played its role. It was with this so-called 'internal lexicography'
that Kittel explicitly stated the *Theological Dictionary* to be primarily concerned.[8] This aim was undoubtedly simultaneously both the strength
and the weakness of the 'dictionary'. It was a strength in so far as what
students and interpreters of the New Testament were looking for was
more than merely English word-substitutions for the Greek words *agapē*,
dikaiosynē, *pneuma*, etc. They also wanted a compendium of information
about how people at the time of the writing of the New Testament
conceived of love, or righteousness or whatever, and how the New Testament writers evaluated such conceptions theologically in the after-
math of the Christ event. Unfortunately, this also led to what has been
perceived by many as one of the dictionary's greatest weaknesses; namely that neither the editor, nor his contributors, always managed clearly
to distinguish between the discussion of word-meaning and the elucidation of concepts.

4.2 JAMES BARR AND THE CRITICISM OF WORD-STUDY AP-
PROACHES TO THEOLOGY

1961 saw the publication of James Barr's *The Semantics of Biblical Language*, a work that shook the foundations of the then many attempts to provide theology in the shape of word-studies. The purpose of this work was not to provide a text-book of linguistics, far less to suggest that 'biblical language' was a special sort of language (indeed he vigorously opposed such a view), but 'to criticise certain methods in the handling of linguistic evidence in theological discussion'. Yet the aim was not primarily destructive, but 'to clear the way for a reassessment of biblical language, of the use that may be made of it in theology, and of the possibility of understanding the language of the Bible to-day [sic]'.[9]

Barr's work is not confined to criticizing word studies as such, but is much more broad ranging. Nevertheless, most of what he has to say is relevant to the theme of this chapter, for it concerns misunderstandings about the nature of the biblical languages which are very relevant to word studies.

4.2.1 Barr's Criticism of the Theory that Hebrew Language Structure is a Ready Index of Hebrew Thought

Barr's initial chapters take sharp issue with those who try to correlate an alleged gulf between Greek and Hebrew ways of thinking with characteristics of the lexical stock, morphology and syntax of the respective *languages*. Greek is all too often said to be static, abstract, analytic and anthropologically dualistic (man consists of body and 'soul'), where by contrast Hebrew is alleged to be essentially dynamic, concrete, synthetic and anthropologically monist (man is a body, and is a 'soul'; they are two aspects of the whole, not two separable parts). For example, G. A. F. Knight[10] had partially grounded this allegation of the concrete nature of Hebrew thinking in the observation that Hebrew has few abstract nouns and only a rudimentary adjectival system. This claim of Knight's is open to at least three objections. In the first place, the claim about the paucity of abstract nouns is exaggerated.[11] Second, as Knight himself noted, Hebrew has an alternative to the adjective, namely the construct state, a construction in which two nouns are linked together in such a way as to make the second function adjectivally: e.g. 'a man-(of)-strength' (= 'a strong man'). With respect to these extremely common constructions Barr dryly comments:

We must ask how this demonstrates the non-abstract character of either Hebrew language or Israelite thinking. For it is hard to see how such characteristic Hebrew phrases as 'the mountain of my holiness' or 'a man of strength' or 'words of truth' are signally less abstract than 'my holy mountain' or 'a powerful man' or 'true words'.[12]

Third, and most important, as the example above illustrates, it is difficult to show that there is a *necessary* correlation between language structures and the thought structures of the people who use them. Somewhat mischievously Barr objects:

> The idea that the grammatical structure of a language reflects the thought structure of those speaking it, and that it correspondingly reflects the differences from the thought of those speaking a language with different grammatical structure, has very great difficulties. Of these difficulties we may first of all point out the existence of numerous grammatical structures (or absences of such) which clearly do not correspond to thought structure. The clearest example is grammatical gender. . . . No one would suppose that the Turks, because they nowhere distinguish gender in their language, not even in the personal pronouns as we do in English, are deficient in the concept of sexual difference; nor would we seriously argue that the French have extended their legendary erotic interests into the linguistic realm by forcing every noun to be either masculine or feminine. The absence of correlation between the linguistic types of masculine, feminine and neuter and the real or conceptual distinctions of male, female and inanimate is very obvious in German and other languages.[13]

Barr goes on to criticize in more general and serious terms, albeit still tangentially, the Humboldtian thesis that the 'unique character' of a people finds expression in its language, and that development of it by E. Sapir and B. L. Whorf that came close to affirming that we are 'in all our thinking and forever, "at the mercy of the particular language which has become the medium of expression for [our] society" '.[14] We need not question that it is possible to find occasional traits of a language that are specific to a culture and to the environment in which it is spoken. It need not surprise us that Eskimos have no single word for snow, but a number of different lexemes denoting different kinds of snow, while some African languages have no word for snow at all. But, as Barr again puts it,

> . . . in general the idea that differences of thought structure will

correspond to differences of language structure seems to be contra-
dicted by facts. No doubt the Finns think somewhat differently from
the Swedes, but is it probable that the difference is as great in extent
as the very great difference between their linguistic structures? . . .
Or, working the other way, did Jewish thought in (say) the fourth
century B.C. differ as little from that of the Phoenicians as would be
suggested from the slight and merely dialectal difference of their
languages?[15]

We need not doubt that there are genuine and radical differences of
world view and self-understanding between much Israelite and Greek
thinking, differences such as Knight, Boman and Pedersen, and many
others have observed (albeit that those who describe the contrasts often
greatly oversimplify), but there are no firm grounds offered in the literature for concluding that such differences arise from (or produce!) the
differing linguistic structures with which the respective peoples express
their thought. There are perhaps as deep (or even deeper) divisions of
thought between, say, Aristotelians and Platonists *within* the Greek-
speaking world, as there are between so-called 'Hebrew' thinking and
'Greek'.[16] And it is very difficult indeed to find any thought structure
expressed in the Greek literature that could not (for linguistic reasons)
be expressed in Hebrew (albeit in a different way): there is more than
one linguistic way to skin a conceptual cat.[17] In these comments Barr is
neither simply ignoring Humboldtian and Idealistic Semantics, nor positively taking sides with Empirical and Structuralist Linguistics against
them (though it is perfectly clear where his sympathies lie),[18] but assessing the quality of the actual linguistic evidence advanced.

   Already in these early chapters, Barr touches on the related subject
of misuse of word study. J. A. T. Robinson, in a monograph on the
concept of the Body in New Testament theology, had concluded from
the observation that Greek has two words (*sōma* [body]and *sarx* [flesh])
for the one Hebrew *(basar)* that

   the Hebrews never posed, like the Greeks, certain questions, the
   answer to which would have forced them to differentiate the 'body'
   from the 'flesh'.[19]

This sort of argument, and its associated generalizations—'they have
not got a separate word for it, so they do not have the idea' and 'they
have several words for it, so they must have a rich understanding of it'—

are (as Barr points out)[20] linguistic nonsense. Are we, by the same token, to assume that the French are intrinsically incapable of distinguishing weather and time because they have only the one word *temps* for both? Or that Mexicans cannot tell the difference between a key, a wrench and a faucet, because they happen to use the same Spanish word, *llave*, for all three? The factors which determine whether or not a language produces a separate word for some particular concept are many and varied,[21] but no surprise should be engendered when new concepts are described from within the existing lexical stock (by extension of the meaning of a word in current use) rather than by the creation of a new word. Most of the words of our language are used with several or many quite distinct senses (the phenomena of *polysemy* and *homonymy*, discussed at section 5.1.3 below), and it would be outrageous to argue that because we used one word for a variety of senses we were probably incapable of distinguishing between them.

4.2.2 Barr's Criticism of Etymology as Determinative for Word-Meaning

Barr's discussion of word-studies begins in earnest, however, with his sixth chapter, entitled 'Etymologies and Related Arguments'. He commences with a discussion of the widespread popular view that the 'original' meaning of a word is its 'proper' meaning. In Linguistics this is fully recognized for the nonsense it is (see section 5.1 below). Words take on new meanings in the life of the language, and original meanings are often lost sight of, and come to contribute nothing to the understanding of the word. And yet, as Barr observes, we are still commonly told that 'history' 'properly' means "investigation" (Gk. *historia*), 'person' 'basically' means "mask" (Lat. *persona*), that 'holy' originally (and so properly) means "whole, healthy, sound" (which is not even *historically* true),[22] and so forth. The recent history of a term may be significant for understanding its present range of uses, and occasionally the distant history is important. For example, a knowledge of how the Greek Fathers understood *prosōpon*, and the Latin fathers *persona*, is significant for understanding modern theological discussion of "person" in relation to Christology and Trinity—but historical usage cannot play the role of policeman or judge in relation to modern usage.

One would have thought the etymological fallacy—that word sense is determined by original meaning—was a sufficiently dead horse in educated theological circles to spare it the humiliation of further flogging. However, Barr was able to provide a long chapter of examples to demonstrate that the horse in question, far from being dead, was actually enjoying rude health in even some of the most learned pastures.

Thus, for instance, according to Barr,[23] no less a writer than T. F. Torrance simply ignores the semantics of the words actually used, and builds entirely on etymological fallacy, when he tells us, for example, that (a) the special use of *ekklēsia* in the Septuagint gives the New Testament its technical term for the Church; (b) in the LXX *ekklēsia* refers to the congregation regarded collectively as a people and as a whole, rather than to the actual assembly or meeting of the people; (c) the Hebrew word *qahal* (for which *ekklēsia* is a translation) comes from the same root as *qol*, the word for "voice", and this suggests that the Old Testament *qahal* was the community summoned by the divine voice, the word of God, and (d) *ekklēsia* is an apt translation of *qahal*, indicating as it does the community as 'the called' *(klētoi)* of God.

The aside (d) simply ignores the fact that the Greek word *ekklēsia* was already long established in Greek use for an "assembly" or "meeting" before it ever came to be used to render *qahal*. It is thus no more likely that any Greek speaker would reflect on the possibility that the word was derived from other words meaning "to call" or "called" than we would today consciously bring to mind that (e.g.) Parliament comes from a word meaning "speaking"; or 'pencil' from a word meaning "brush", when we use these words. And if a Greek writer *had* thought of such a connection between his word for "meeting" and words for "to call", he would certainly not surmise that his assemblies or meetings were called together *by gods,* far less by Israel's God! The translation *ekklēsia* is indeed apt for *qahal,* but only because it was the general word for an 'assembly' or 'meeting', not for any etymological connection with 'calling'.

Second, we need to note that Torrance's assertion (c) is also suspect, for similar reasons. Even if *qahal* derives from *qol,* "voice", (which is no more than merely *possible*) it remains highly questionable whether anyone would have been aware of this etymological connection at the time of writing the Old Testament, and even less probable that it would be assumed that the voice which called the gathering together was the

Divine Elective Voice, rather than a human caller. Torrance's etymologizing and subsequent theologizing makes nonsense of such expressions as 'the assembly *(qahal)* of evil doers' (Ps. 26.5); are the wicked too called together of God?

As for Torrance's affirmation (b), Barr rightly points out there is no good evidence that *qahal* ever means more than "assembly," "congregation" or "meeting"; it has not become *'the* Assembly', a technical term for "the people of Israel", except by virtue of Torrance's gratuitous use of an absolutizing definite article—a use which possibly arises out of his conviction that *qahal* denotes the people called together by *God*, rather than the assembly of Israel as called together by e.g. Moses, the king (etc.), on various occasions.

Linked with the fall of (b), the assertion (a) also tumbles; for it becomes questionable whether there is a *special* use of *ekklēsia* in the Septuagint; it, no more than *qahal*, can be shown to mean the congregation regarded collectively and as a whole, rather than the actual assembly or meeting of the people. It need not be doubted at all that the New Testament has a rich theological conception of the Church, nor that it regarded itself as enjoying the fulfilment of promises made to Israel, but these conclusions do not follow from the linguistic properties of the words *qahal* and *ekklēsia*.

Barr mercilessly elucidates the etymologizing and related errors of a panoply of scholars. He includes a substantial chapter cataloguing widespread linguistic misunderstandings of Hebrew and Greek words for faith, which in biblical interpretation are too often wrongly accommodated to "faithfulness" on a spurious etymological basis. The same is true of 'truth', which is usually said in the Bible to be concerned not with the truth-falsity distinction (which is labelled 'Greek' in character) but to be anchored primarily in the Hebrew concept of God's faithfulness. And this is supposedly the result of the etymological link between words for truth and those for steadfastness and reliability.

4.2.3 Barr's Criticism of the Kittel Dictionary
Finally, in two chapters, Barr turns his major guns onto Kittel's *Theological Dictionary of the New Testament*. The fundamental criticism (from which the others may largely be derived) is the surprising confusion amongst the contributors as to whether they are describing *words*, or

concepts, or the *realities in the world* which the words denote, and which the concepts isolate and focus. Since Ogden and Richard's work in 1923 there has been considerable discussion about the so-called triangle of signification (figure 2).

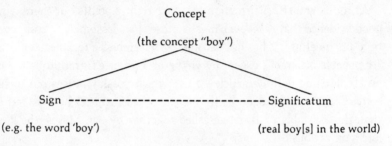

Concept

(the concept "boy")

Sign ------------------------------- Significatum

(e.g. the word 'boy')   (real boy[s] in the world)

Figure 2.

The triangle is an attempt to diagram an essentially triadic relationship that is usually recognized as existing between the verbal signs (the words) of a language, the concepts associated with them, and the things in the world to which both (separately) relate. Much discussion has ensued as to how these entities relate, but that they are potentially distinguishable is fundamental, and that words do not simply relate *directly* to things-in-the-world is also to be accepted (else there would have to be some reality in the world to correspond to each of the words in this sentence, including 'to', 'be', 'the', 'not', 'relate', 'directly', etc.).[24]

Usually it is maintained that 'concepts' mediate between the two somehow. The word 'boy' might thus be said to lexicalize for English speakers the concept "boy" that could have been indicated in other ways, e.g. by the expression 'male child' or 'lad' in English, by 'loon' or 'loonie' in Aberdonian, or by the German word *'Junge'*, or the French *'garçon'*. The concept "boy" is a mental construct, part of the tapestry of mental constructs that we arrive at by segmenting our apprehension of our world (real or imaginary) into identifiable and communicable portions. Words that themselves have no denotation (like 'there', 'the', 'over', etc.) relate to things-in-the-world only by participating in the verbalizing of the concept; e.g. in such expressions as 'the three boys standing over there . . .' (which is sufficiently defined to be called one concept, albeit that it consists of several component concepts).

Two important refinements may be added for clarification. These distinctions are not made by Barr, but sharpen the problem he seeks to elucidate. *First*, we must clarify what we mean by 'the concept "boy" '. It could be taken in a broader sense to mean my understanding of the nature of boys, and of their character and significance in society. Or it could be taken in a minimal sense to denote the bundle of elements of meaning which are necessarily or conventionally entailed by use of the word 'boy'—such as 'non-adult, male, human'. In the context of contemporary discussions of the triangle of signification, it is the latter of these uses of 'concept' alone that is meant. It should be clear that this type of 'concept' is closely related to what otherwise is called the 'sense' of a word, and indeed in some versions of the diagram of the triangle of signification the word 'sense' appears at its apex where we have 'concept'.[25] We shall refer to this type of concept, roughly equivalent to the sense of a word, as a *lexical concept*. It must be sharply distinguished from the broader usage of concept: my concept of 'boy' in the more general usage may include very many features concerning the range of their features and physique, their hygiene, their habits of play, their social abilities and limitations, and so forth, none of which is *linguistically* attached to the word 'boy' as such at all. The sentences

(1) Boys are usually male,

(2) Boys are usually unkind,

illustrate the difference. The first will be recognized as semantically anomolous, for the qualifier 'usually' implies there are exceptions; but a boy that was not a male would appear to be a *contradiction of the sense "boy"*. The second sentence is *linguistically* acceptable (even though we consider it wholly untrue) because nothing about the sense of the word 'boy' overlaps in meaning with either 'kind' or 'unkind'. The sense "male" is *linguistically* attached to 'boy'; "kind" or "unkind" is not.

Second, the fact that we have a concept of 'boy' that we can lexicalize either with the word 'boy' or with 'garçon', suggests to many that the *concept* must somehow transcend language, and provide a structure of meaning independent of language which we can use to compare whether 'boy' means the same as 'garçon'. On the basis of this, and other considerations, Heger and Baldinger (amongst others) have preferred to speak of a *trapezium* of signification, rather than a triangle. They would distinguish between a 'sense', which is the expression of a concept in a particular language, and the supra-linguistic entity, the concept, itself[26] (figure 3).

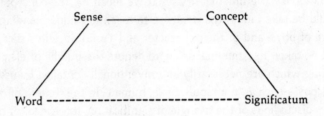

Figure 3.

It cannot be said there is much consensus as to the precise nature of the relations between words, senses, concepts and things-in-the world. But this does not excuse Kittel's repeated failure to distinguish them;[27] not only do the authors frequently talk about concepts when they appear to mean words, but the editor himself has been thought to come close to confusing words with *things-in-the-world*, even in theoretical statements about the relationship between them. Consider the assertion:

> The words and sentences of New Testament language cease to exist for themselves and become, as it were, vessels of transparent crystal which have one sole purpose, that of making their contents visible.[28]

Barr rightly complains that had Kittel contented himself with speaking only of 'the sentences' of the NT the description would have been less misleading. Unfortunately, Kittel wants the message declared in sentences to be ascertainable from the *word studies* that make up his dictionary. Thus *words* become the vessels, and their *content*—that which is to be made visible—is (according to Barr) none other than the Christ event itself. Kittel's wording is perhaps capable of being interpreted to make a less startling claim, but such imprecision in a work on the purpose of TDNT itself is still worrying.

Nor is it a minor matter of occasional infelicities of expression concerning the task of the so-called 'inner lexicography'. The effects of the imprecision of thought are felt throughout the volumes that were written before Barr's book. The contributors fall between two stools; they are not sure whether they are writing articles about the usage of particular *words* or about the history of *ideas* or of broad concepts; whether they are writing a dictionary or an encyclopaedia; and this confusion is built into the very structure of the articles, as some early reviewers were quick to point out.[29]

Thus the article under *agapaō* in its Old Testament section has such headings as 'The Profane and Immanent Conception of Love' (3½ pages) and 'The Religious Conception of Love' (8 pages). These are followed by sections on 'The Words for Love in Pre-biblical Greek' (3 pages), 'Love in Judaism' (7 pages), 'Jesus' (4 pages: subdivided 'The New Demand' and 'The New Situation'), 'The Apostolic Period' (5 pages), and 'The Post-Apostolic Period' (1 page).

It is at once clear that this article is concerned with much more than merely lexical issues, as such are normally understood, and is attempting (despite the title *Theologisches* Wörterbuch *zum Neuen Testament*) to provide a history of ideas. But if this is the case, *why* is the article written under the lexical head *agapaō*, and why does it not treat other words (like *philein*, *erōs*, *storgē*, *philanthrōpia*, etc.) pertinent to New Testament understanding of "love", not to mention whole passages in the New Testament which are highly germane to the concept of love even if they do not mention the word itself? The parable of the Prodigal Son in Luke 15.11ff, for example, has more to teach about Jesus' understanding of love than most passages which use the word! One suspects that the reason for this lack is the failure adequately to distinguish between words and concepts, and a resultant tendency to use the terms interchangeably. And there is also an apparent confusion between whether the discussion is supposed to be about the lexical concept of 'love' or the broader notion of 'the concept of love'.

So long as a writer cherishes the presupposition that a word corresponds directly to a concept (in the broader sense), he is free to talk of the *concept agapān*, and to elucidate it only from passages which use the lexeme *agapān* (or its cognate noun). This leads to a dual error: in the first place it means that the writer will restrict his scope too narrowly by excluding the study of other words and expressions which are immediately relevant to the broader concept in question. A parallel would be the attempt to ascertain Kant's concept of knowledge merely by doing a study of the occurrences in his writing of the German verb *wissen* 'to know', and of its cognate noun, [30] or the attempt to ascertain Le Carré's general concept of spying merely from those passages in his books where he uses the verb 'to spy'.

The other error to which the presupposition leads is a failure to observe that a single lexeme may be used by a writer in different sentences with several quite distinct senses, and in relation to a range of the broader type of concepts. Stauffer can thus happily tell us that 'Johannine *agapē* is quite explicitly condescending love, or rather a heavenly reality which in some sense descends from stage to stage into this world'[31] or that it is 'the principle of the world of Christ which is being built up in the cosmic crisis of the present',[32] as though John had never written such sentences as 'but men loved (*agapān*) darkness more than the light' (3.19); 'they loved (*agapān*, again) praise from men more than praise from God' (12.43) or 'he who loves (*agapān*, once more) the world, love of the Father is not in him' (1 John 2.15). The apparent presupposition that John's word *agapān* will correspond with a single concept appears to have blinded the author to part of John's linguistic usage and its related conceptual realm. Barr is able to show the same phenomenon time and again (without suggesting that all the contributors make the same sort of mistake).

The confusion between words, concepts and realities-in-the-world— and especially the confusion between lexical concepts and the broader notion of concepts—has fathered other undesirable children in Kittel's dictionary, chief of which perhaps is an enormously exaggerated view of the semantic contribution of individual words to the discourses of which they are composed. The fault almost certainly goes back to the potentially misleading terminology 'internal lexicography'. This invites the unwary to assume that all the theology of, say, the discourse in John 1 about Jesus as the Word is 'properly' part of the new meaning of the Greek word *logos*, brought to it by the 'language-moulding power of Christianity'. Reference to '*internal* lexicography' is thus apt to suggest that words are like transporters, crammed with theological-conceptual freight, which they dump into the otherwise featureless field of the sentence and wider semantically barren landscape of the discourse context.

This, of course, would be a complete misunderstanding (and it must be said that Kittel's scholarly commonsense triumphs over his semantic theory in this instance, and prevents him from perpetrating such an error). *Per contra*, it is in fact rather only what is said in the *whole paragraph* (John 1.1-14), and what we know about how certain Jews were thinking about God's wisdom/word at the time, that clarifies John's broad *concept* of "the Divine Word who is the Son". And this *concept* is not under any circumstances to be identified as a sense of the lexeme *logos*, as though its meaning here might 'properly' be lurking everywhere or anywhere else the word *logos* is used. It is not even to be identified as the sense of the semantically distinct collocation (noted by Kittel) *'ho logos'* ('*the word'*)—for this collocation is elsewhere used frequently by John without any reference to Christ (see, e.g., 2.22; 4.37, 39, 50, etc.). And even when the linguistic expression *'ho logos (tēs zōēs)'* is used with christological reference (in 1 John 1.1) the sense is rather "The Message about Life (embodied in Christ)".

The danger of identifying the content of *concepts* understood in the broader sense with *lexical concepts* or *senses* should be clearly seen here. Of the numerous New Testament occurrences of the collocation *'ho logos'*, few are directly christological, and none (including Rev. 19.13)[33] clearly means precisely the same as John 1. However, the place where arguably we find the closest approximation to John's general *concept* of Jesus as the pre-existent Divine Wisdom/Word is in Col. 1.15ff,[34] where the expression *ho logos* is not used at all! John's conception of "the Divine Word, the Son" is not the inner content—and so available to the scrutiny of 'inner lexicography'—of the word *'logos'* (nor in fact did Kittel suggest it was), nor even of the expression *'ho logos'* at all; it is rather the product of whole *sentences* making up a passage.

The actual semantic contribution of the expression *ho logos* itself, to the total meaning, is difficult to judge—mainly because we do not know whether or not it was already in use in Judaism as a term to denote Divine Wisdom. But whether or not it already carried a certain amount of conceptual freight, its contribution to the Johannine concept "the Divine Word, the Son" was still much less than the whole. And it is the propositions John affirms about Jesus, as the Divine Word,—i.e. whole sentences—that make the major semantic contribution to 'John's concept of Jesus as the Logos', not the linguistic expression *'ho logos'* as such.

Of course, with time, and with the acceptance of John as canonical, the expression *'ho logos'*, when used christologically, would become a technical term denoting the concept described by the discourse. But this was not so in the first instance, and is not so for the majority of the words and expressions in the New Testament.

Tångberg well summarizes the issue here (starting with a quote from Barr):

> 'One essential character of language is the capacity to combine a finite number of lexical items occurring in a finite number of grammatical constructions in an all but infinite number of combinations. By the shaping and reshaping of lexical items to particular contexts, a certain suppleness and adequacy are achieved, whatever the apparent limitations of the lexical inventory. In this respect, language may be considered to be a descriptive calculus of a very adequate sort and capable, for all we know, of indefinite refinement.' Words, then, function in constructions and sentences. Here they combine in a countless number of ways. On this level the possibilities of meaningful expression are unlimited. Innumerable nuances can be brought out by the larger units of speech. *Instead of overinterpreting interesting but isolated linguistic facts, biblical theology must concentrate on carefully interpreting the sentence and still larger discourse units that are able to convey theological information.*[35] [Our italics]

Two other errors are traceable to possible confusion over the relation of words and concepts. There is, first, what Barr termed the 'illegitimate identity transfer'; an inelegant term for the mistake of assuming that because two words or expressions apply to the same referent, they therefore mean the same thing. For example, we have Torrance's apparent assumption that because Israel is 'God's people', and because Israel is described as *'laos'*, as opposed to *ethnos* ('nation'), the word *laos* carries the sense "God's people". It does not—this sense is only possible of the fuller expression *'ho laos tou theou'* ('the people of God'), not of *laos* or *ho laos* alone (unless there are other contextual markers connecting these expressions with the fuller one).[36]

The second error, that of assuming, for example, that the full New Testament concept of "the Church" can be read into any one occurrence of the *word ekklēsia*—such as Matt. 16.18—Barr dubbed the 'illegitimate totality transfer'.[37] This has been regarded as Barr's *main* complaint against Kittel by A. C. Thiselton,[38] although in fact Barr uses the expression on only two pages. As Barr states the issue he is undoubtedly right, though if he should be understood as suggesting that 'the correct meaning of any term is that which contributes *least* [our italics] to the total context', as Thiselton almost appears to take him, [39] then we surely have an overreaction. When the author of Ephesians states that it is Christ's intention 'to present the church to himself in splendour' (5.27), it is certainly dangerous to elucidate this in terms of what is said in the Book of Revelation (as though Paul[40] knew the substance of what was said there). But it would be equally misleading to affirm that 'the *ekklēsia*' here means only "the assembly of the people of God", or the like (the minimal contribution); for the writer has built up a concept of "the church" in the progression of his discourse, which the reader is not expected to ignore. We shall later introduce a distinction between lexical concepts and discourse concepts to cope with this sort of case (see 5.2.2.1 below): but here we may simply distinguish between the *lexical concept* or *sense* of the expression 'the *ekklēsia*'—i.e. "the assembly of the people of God"—and the broader concept of 'the church' in Ephesians. They are related, but they are not to be confused. By the former the writer may refer to the latter; but the lexical concept is not interchangeable with the broader concept, or *vice versa*.

In sum, Barr was saying that the then current volumes of Kittel frequently (but not always) confused words with concepts, with dire results, and that the whole enterprise of trying to establish theology on the basis of *word studies* was fundamentally mistaken. The theology of the Testaments lies in the propositions asserted in sentences, paragraphs, and whole discourses of its writings, not in individual words. If a dictionary was to be written at all, it would need to be of a different kind, leading from the linguistic data to the theological significance by a more cautious route.

> [The] procedure would be to group the words in groups each representing a related semantic field, e.g. the 'holy' group with its chief representatives in *hagios, hagnos,* and *hieros*. Within a general field thus loosely defined an attempt would be made to mark off the semantic oppositions between one word and another as precisely as possible; and from this to proceed to special contexts and word-combinations in which each word occurred—bringing in, of course, the words from outside the loosely defined field freely.[41]

4.3 RESPONSES TO BARR

Reactions to Barr have on the whole been positive;[42] and his sharpest critic, T. Boman, appears simply not to have understood him.[43] Something of the same criticism (but not to anything like the same degree) may be levelled at David Hill, who responded with a complete monograph, *Greek Words and Hebrew Meanings*. In this, while accepting many of Barr's points, he nevertheless accused him of implying that *words* are not the bearers of meaning, and not the proper object of semantic analysis.[44] In 'reply', Hill argued that while the context of the sentence gives semantic precision, it is nevertheless true that words themselves have semantic autonomy (they carry their own meaning) to a far greater extent than Barr was willing to recognize. He went on to show, in detailed word studies, that terms like *hilaskesthai* ('propitiate'), *lytron* ('ransom'), *dikaiosynē* ('righteousness'), *pneuma* ('spirit'), etc. were often used in the New Testament with senses that were dependent on specifically Hebraic, apocalyptic or, indeed, distinctively Christian development of thought. In short, these words carried with them into the sentences that used them some considerable conceptual baggage, and so Barr's radical questioning of the relationship between words and concepts looked less than convincing; Kittel was on the right lines after all (even if not always sufficiently careful in detail).

Hill's studies were a model of scholarly caution, but as a reply to Barr they were misconceived.[45] Barr had not denied that words conveyed definite areas of meaning, nor that there was a relationship between words and concepts. He had only argued that there was a *wide variety* of relationships between words (or larger linguistic expressions) and concepts, and that these entities should not be *confused*, and that discourse context was usually decisive for elucidating meaning. Indeed, Hill's word studies so ably demonstrated the variety of meanings attached to any one word, and the importance of other linguistic and contextual markers for a decision about meaning, that Barr was able to claim that Hill's finding entirely supported his own position, and that Hill had simply drawn the wrong conclusions from his otherwise valuable if unspectacular findings.[46] In this judgement of the significance of Hill's work, Barr was not without support.[47]

The new editor of Kittel's dictionary, G. Friedrich, who took over from volume 6, also mounted an attack. Friedrich published a number of articles essentially arguing (to put his case extremely crudely) that Barr's view of Semantics in particular, and of Linguistics more generally, was by no means the only one in the field; that von Humboldt's ideas still found champions in Continental scholarship, if fewer in England; and that Kittel's understanding of the relationship between words and concepts was not far from that of the great pioneer, L. Weisgerber, and could not so lightly be dismissed.[48] But, on the one hand, Friedrich actually accepted many of Barr's points, and, on the other, he has not persuaded all his readers that Linguistics and Semantics are in quite the disarray he suggests. Nor is it apparent that an appeal to Weisgerber's view of 'concepts' (and their relation to words) is relevant to the defence of Kittel. For by 'concept' Weisgerber appears to have meant a *minimal* set of salient features which allow individual examples to be identified as belonging to the semantic class, i.e. *lexical concepts*, while Kittel meant a full descriptive analysis, including not only the lexical concept, but also its relation to associated ideas, and its theological significance. That is, Kittel was nearly always working with the broader notion of 'concept'. Words may be closely related to what Weisgerber meant by 'concepts' (because 'concept' is then very close to 'sense'),[49] while not being nearly so obviously related to what Kittel had in mind.

Broadly speaking, Barr's points have been accepted, and the volumes of Kittel from 6 onwards allow for somewhat less complaint than Barr was able to register with respect to the earlier volumes. The next major dictionary to emerge was quite explicitly a *Begriffeslexicon* not a *Wörterbuch* (A dictionary of concepts, not of word studies)—even if it still poses methodological problems,[50] and is often little more than a summary of earlier Kittel articles. And the OT counterpart to Kittel, the *Theological Dictionary of The Old Testament* (edited by G. J. Botterweck and H. Ringgren), is altogether a more carefully linguistically nuanced enterprise. As Brevard Childs predicted in his 1961 review,[51] Barr's *Semantics* signalled the end of a phase of research. It did not put an end to word study any more than Schweitzer's work put an end to the 'Quest of the Historical Jesus'; but it did transform it, and redirect it. In future there was to be less reliance on word studies as a foundation for biblical theology, and where word study was pursued there was a greater call for an understanding of linguistics and semantics.[52] We shall indicate some further developments as we now move to a presentation of the main elements of a linguistics understanding of the nature of words, and so of the task of word study.

Notes

[1]For a history of lexicographical endeavour before Cremer see G. Kittel and G. Friedrich (eds.), *Theological Dictionary of the New Testament*, X, pp.613-40.

[2]The expression is that of R. Rothe, *Zur Dogmatik* (1863), p.238.

[3]See *TDNT*, X, p. 624.

[4]See the evaluation by Friedrich in *TDNT*, X, p.644.

[5]See A. Deissmann, *Light From the Ancient East*, London, Hodder, 1910, 1911[2], pp. 54-142.

[6]Deissmann's case was no doubt overstated; though he showed that many of Cremer's 'distinctive' words were in fact common to the lexical stock of *koinē*, it could still be argued that the New Testament was using them in some new senses—see *TDNT*, X, p.650f., for criticism of Deissmann.

[7]See further in J. R. Hurford and B. Heasley, *Semantics: A Coursebook*, Cambridge, CUP, 1983, pp.184ff. This is only a work-book, not a work of reference, but as it is perhaps the best available introduction to semantics for theological students we shall refer to it more frequently than would otherwise be expected.

[8]See *TDNT*, I, vii: compare also G. Kittel, *Lexicographia Sacra, Theology Occasional Papers*, 7, passim.

[9]J. Barr, *The Semantics of Biblical Language*, Oxford, OUP, 1961, pp.6 and 4, respectively.

[10]G. A. F. Knight, *A Biblical Approach to the Doctrine of the Trinity*, London, Oliver & Boyd, 1953, pp.8, 89.

[11]See Barr (1961) 28, pointing to the findings of L. Gulkowitsch, *Die Bildung von Abstraktbegriffen in der hebräischen Sprachgeschichte*, Leipzig, 1931.

[12]Ibid., p.29.

[13]Ibid., p.39.

[14]For W. von Humboldt's position see his *Über die Verschiedenheit des Menschlichen Sprachbaues*, Berlin, 1836. For an introductory account of the Sapir-Whorf position see J. Lyons, *Language & Linguistics*, Cambridge, CUP, 1981, pp. 303-12, from whom the quotation is taken (p.304). See also E. Sapir, *Selected Writings in Language, Culture & Personality*, Berkeley, University of California Press, 1947, and B. L. Whorf, *Language, Thought & Reality*, Cambridge, MIT, 1956. Both are reprints of earlier material.

[15]Ibid., p. 42f.

[16]So Barr, *Old and New in Interpretation*, London, SCM, 1966, p.39f.

[17]Compare the defence of Barr's (implicit) rejection of the Humboldtian linguistic philosophy and the Sapir-Whorf thesis by K. A. Tångberg, 'Linguistics and Theology', *BT* 24 (1973), pp.308-10.

[18]He is accused of this by T. Boman, *Sprache und Denken: Ein Auseinandersetzung*, Göttingen, VR, 1968, pp.200ff, and more seriously by G. Friedrich, 'Semasiol-

THE USE AND ABUSE OF WORD STUDIES IN THEOLOGY   **127**

ogie und Lexikologie', *TLZ* 94 (1969), pp. 805-7. 'Idealistic Semantics' in this context may roughly be equated with the more traditional view that the sense of a word is the associated *idea* or mental concept. Structuralist linguistics, by treating sense as a relation of meaning between different words in a language, avoids the necessity of relating word meanings to concepts. See e.g. Lyons, *Language & Linguistics*, pp. 216-23, and the further discussion below, sections 4.2.3 and 5.2.

[19]J. A. T. Robinson, *The Body: A Study in Pauline Theology*, London, SCM, 1952, p.13.

[20]*The Semantics of Biblical Language*, pp.34-8.

[21]See J. Lyons, *Semantics*, 8.4 for discussion and literature.

[22]See the long treatment by Barr, *The Semantics of Biblical Language*, pp.111-4.

[23]Ibid., pp. 119-29.

[24]See the discussion in J. Lyons, *Semantics*, chaps. 4, 5, 7, and 8. Compare L. Zgusta, *Manual of Lexicography*, The Hague, Mouton, 1971, pp. 27ff.

[25]So, for example, S. Ullmann, *The Principles of Semantics*, Oxford, Blackwell, 1957[2], p.69ff.

[26]K. Baldinger, *Semantic Theory*, Oxford, Blackwell, 1980, part II, passim.

[27]See e.g. Barr, *The Semantics of Biblical Language*, p.210f., for examples.

[28]Cited by Barr, *The Semantics of Biblical Language*, p. 212 from Kittel's *Lexicographia Sacra*, London, 1938, which unfortunately was not available to us at the time of writing.

[29]See C. H. Dodd's complaint about the article on *hamartanō* and *hamartia* in *JTS* 34 (1933), pp.280ff. See also Barr, *The Semantics of Biblical Language*, pp.229ff.

[30]We are grateful to M. Silva, *Biblical Words and Their Meaning: An Introduction to Lexical Semantics*, Grand Rapids, Zondervan, 1983, p.27, for this example.

[31]*TDNT*, I, p.53.

[32]Ibid. p.52.

[33]See e.g. J. D. G. Dunn, *Christology in the Making*, London, SCM, 1980, p.246f.

[34]*Against* Dunn (1980) 187-94, who does not think Col.1.15ff. implies pre-existence, see e.g. the essays by I. H. Marshall and J. F. Balchin in H. H. Rowdon (ed.), *Christ the Lord*. Leicester, IVP, 1982.

[35]K. A. Tångberg, 'Linguistics and Theology', *BT* 24(1973), p.304.

[36]Barr, *The Semantics of Biblical Language*, pp. 218, 235.

[37]Barr, *The Semantics of Biblical Language*, pp. 218, 222.

[38]See A. C. Thiselton , 'Semantics and New Testament Interpretation' in I. Howard Marshall (ed.), *New Testament Interpretation*, Exeter, Paternoster, 1977, p.84.

[39]Ibid. The quotation itself is from Nida.

[40]Or the writer of Ephesians, if that is different, which we doubt.

[41]Barr, *The Semantics of Biblical Language*, p.235; his own later book, *Biblical Words for Time*, London, SCM, 1962, attempted something like this. The expression

'semantic field' here is a technical expression, but roughly meaning "a group of words closely related in meaning, often subsumed under a general term" e.g. 'Colour Terms' (this working definition is that of A. Lehrer, *Semantic Fields & Lexical Structure*, London, North-Holland, 1974, p. 1). The type of analysis concerned builds on the pioneering work of J. Trier, *Der Deutsche Wortschatz im Sinnbezirk des Verstandes*, Heidelberg, Winter, 1931, (for an account of whose work see e.g. J. Lyons, *Semantics*, pp. 250-261). Semantic Field analysis will be introduced at section 5.2.2.2 below.

[42]For an account of these see R. J. Erickson, *Biblical Semantics, Semantic Structure, and Biblical Lexicology: A Study of Methods, with Special Reference to the Pauline Lexical Field of "Cognition"*, unpublished Ph.D. dissertation, Fuller Theological Seminary 1980, [available from University Microfilms International, 30/32 Mortimer Street, London W1N 7RA], pp. 28-60.

[43]R. J. Erickson, op.cit., pp.39 (n.93), 41, 43, 44, 45 (!), etc.

[44]D. Hill, *Greek Words and Hebrew Meanings: Studies in the Semantics of Soteriological Terms*, Cambridge, CUP, 1966, p.7.

[45]For a more nuanced discussion of Hill than space here allows see Erickson, op.cit., pp. 29-60.

[46]Barr, 'Common Sense and Biblical Language', *Bib* 49 (1968), pp.377-87.

[47]Cf. J. Sawyer's review *SJT* 21 (1968), p.353f.

[48]See especially his 'Die Problematik eines Theologischen Wörterbuchs zum Neuen Testament', in K. Aland (ed.), *Studia Evangelica*, Berlin, Akademie Vlg., 1959, pp.481-6; 'Semasiologie und Lexikologie', *TLZ* 94 (1969), pp.801-16, and 'Zum Problem der Semantik', *KuD* 16 (1970), pp.41-57.

[49]See the detailed work of K. Baldinger, *Semantic Theory*, passim, and compare also the recent vivacious and controversial work *Lexicography and Conceptual Analysis* by Anna Wierzbicka, Ann Arbor, Karoma, 1985, who, too, tends to maximize the semantic content of concepts associated with words.

[50]See the review of the English edition by M. M. B. Turner in *Themelios* 2 (1977) pp.61-3.

[51]*JBL* 80 (1961), pp. 374-7.

[52]See e.g. J. Sawyer, *Semantics in Biblical Research: New Methods of Defining Hebrew Words for Salvation*, London, SCM, 1972.

5. The Grammar of Words: Lexical Semantics

We may now turn our attention more to the relation between words and meaning. It is beyond the scope of this book to discuss so complex and controversial a question in anything approaching a satisfactory manner; but an introduction of some sort is required if the student is to be able to understand the hidden agendas that lie behind Biblical Word Studies, and if he is to be able to avoid the traps that await the unwary.[1]

5.1 INTRODUCTION

5.1.1 The Conventional Nature of Language, Word Formation, and Transparency

We may begin by reminding ourselves that the relation of the word stock of a language to meanings is for the most part not iconic, nor physiologically nor psychologically necessary, but 'arbitrary' and conventional. Nothing about the form or sound of the word 'tree' makes it especially appropriate as a lexeme to denote a large woody-stemmed perenniel plant, and the French no less appropriately call the same botanical entity *'un arbre'*, the Greeks *'dendron'*, and the Germans *'ein Baum'*. In short, meaning is society's usage.[2]

In most languages there is, however, a large measure of 'transparency' in the lexical stock. That is to say that the meanings of many words can be understood from a knowledge of some basic form, and appropriate rules of word formation and inflection. We can thus guess what 'unadventurousness' might mean from a glance at how the word is made up,[3] even if we have never actually encountered the word before. We should not, however, be beguiled by this facility into thinking that compound lexemes always, or even usually, bear a meaning that is little more than a summation of the separate meanings of the elements of which the word is composed.

In the case of such compound lexemes as (for example) 'afterlife', 'counter-attack', 'downstroke', 'foredeck', 'overcrowded', 'upthrust', and 'watchdog', we appear to have relatively transparent instances. Much more 'opaque' (i.e. less clearly related in meaning to the words from which the compound is formed) are a very large number of others including such common examples as 'backwater', 'butterfly', 'outfit', 'overjoyed', 'pineapple', 'undertaker', and 'upstart'. The meaning of compound words cannot simply be predicted from a glance at the constituents—as the very considerable semantic difference between different compounds made of the same words should indicate: the distinction, for example, between an 'overhang' and a 'hangover' is not the subtle one a comparison of their forms might suggest to the unwary. The meaning of the whole compound usually has a semantic content different from a mere summation of the meaning of the constituent words. Sometimes the difference is small, as in 'blackbird', at other times it is considerable, as in 'ladybird'. In the former case both *black-* and *-bird* serve as relatively full semantic indicators, affording considerable transparency to the compound. In 'ladybird', however, there is only one indicator (in *-bird*) and that only a partial and potentially misleading one. Between them in the spectrum between transparency and opacity we encounter cases such as 'greenhouse' where both *green-* and *-house* serve as partial semantic indicators (i.e. a greenhouse is not a house, but like one it is a building).[4]

Special instances of opacity are *idioms* like 'to pull someone's leg', 'to kick the bucket', 'to run somebody down' (in the sense "to belittle" them), or 'to take coals to Newcastle'. It is not entirely surprising that an 'idiom' has traditionally been defined as an expression whose meaning *cannot* be inferred from the meaning of its parts. A rather more precise definition (offered by D. A. Cruse) is that idioms are complex lexemes acting as a single semantic constituent,[5] but the traditional formulation at least sounds a warning against too ready an assumption of transparency in language.

As with English, word-formation is *often* a fair guide to the original meaning of a Greek word, but certainly *not always*.[6] Thus, for example, while many Greek compound lexemes are relatively transparent (*haimatekchousia* ["shedding of blood"]; *theosebēs* ["God-worshipping"] and *anthrōpareskos* ["man-pleaser"], to take but three examples at random), it would surely be less predictable that *egkaleō* (from "in" + "to call") should mean "to accuse", that *glōssokomon* (from "tongue" + "to keep, hold") should mean a container for the mouthpiece of a flute, and that *probaton* (from a prefix suggesting "forwards", a verbal root meaning "go" and a suffix indicating a concrete noun; hence cumulatively suggesting "thing that goes forward") should mean "sheep".

5.1.2 Changes in Language and Lexical Stock: Diachronic and Synchronic Analysis

In practice, all languages change gradually with time, and words come to have new meanings, older meanings often becoming obsolete. Hence the appeal to 'original' meaning as authoritative or normative involves fundamental misunderstanding. The English word 'nice', originally meaning "simple", "ignorant", added in the thirteenth century the sense "foolish, stupid", in the fourteenth "wanton", and in the fifteenth "coy" or "shy", but each of these is obsolete, and even some of the sixteenth-century senses, "subtle, precise, minutely accurate" are only preserved in such constructions as 'a nice distinction'. It would thus be entirely inappropriate to insist that when I say I have a 'nice doctor' I 'properly' mean he is an ignorant one.

Various *types* of change may be listed, amongst which the most important are: (1) *Shift*—changes in sense by relatively small steps such as *restriction* (e.g. from 'meat' originally meaning "food [generally]" to 'meat' meaning "flesh of an animal") and *generalisation* (e.g. from 'manuscript', which originally meant a "hand-written document" to its present more general sense which could include a typed document, or a computer print-out too; or from *'glōssokomon'*, as above, originally meaning "reed-box" to the more general sense "container" in the NT period [cf Jn 12.6]); (2) *Metaphorical Transfer* (as when, for example, 'spine', earlier denoting the anatomical backbone, came to be used for the back of a book—to highlight correspondence between the two; cf. 'leg' [for part of a table]; 'leaf' [for a flat piece of paper] etc.), and (3) *Metonymic Transfer*, 'a figure in which the name of an attribute or adjunct is substituted for that of the thing meant' (e.g. the introduction of 'the crown' to refer to the monarch, or monarchial power; 'the bench' for the magistracy; 'gate' for the movable barrier that closes a gap [originally it was the gap itself that was the 'gate'], and, in the reverse direction, 'door' [originally the barrier that closed the doorway] for "doorway").[7]

The history of a word (a *diachronic* study of its use) may explain *how* a word came to be used with some particular sense at a specified time, but in order to find out *what* a lexeme means at that particular time we have only to look at the contemporary *usage*. The state of a language, and of its lexical stock, can be understood entirely by direct observation of usage at the time in question (synchronous study). We no more need to know the *history* of the language, or of its lexical stock, to understand the sense of utterances today, than we need to know precisely what moves have been made in a game of chess in order to understand the state of the game and its potentialities now.[8]

5.1.2.1 *The Consequent Dangers of Etymologizing*

Appeal to etymology, and to word formation, is therefore always dangerous. Even if a word did originally mean what etymology and word formation suggest, there is *no guarantee whatever* that the word has not changed meaning by the time a particular biblical writer comes to use it.

The Greek word *baptizein* ("to baptize") derives *originally* from a verb *baptein* which can mean "to dip", "to sink into", and "to dye". But this purely historical observation no more necessitates that the word *baptizein* was used in the New Testament period to denote initiation *by immersion* than that it should suggest that Christians emerged from the process a new colour. The all-important question is what *baptizein* meant *in the New Testament period itself*; and as the evidence suggests it came to mean "deluge with", "overwhelm by", as readily as "immerse into" or "sink", the rite may equally have been performed by affusion (e.g. in John's case, the pouring of a large quantity of water over the candidate, as a symbol of the coming deluge with Spirit-and-fire).[9] There may be good linguistic (and other?) arguments to support the conclusion that Christian baptism was by immersion, but the argument from word formation, and from the original meaning of *baptein*, is not one of them.

Sermons, semi-popular writings, and even some more serious works, evince frequent examples of improbable conclusions drawn from etymologizing or from word-formation considerations. A celebrated example is that a generation of preachers have explained the lowly attitude appropriate to Christian service from the Greek word for servant—*hypēretēs*—on the understanding that the word derived from *hypo* + *eretēs* ('under' + 'rower'), and so meant "under-rower", i.e. a rower from the *lowest* level of a trireme.[10] But there is no hard evidence that the word *ever* meant any such thing, and by the time of the New Testament the word is in wide usage for all types of servants (including those in relatively high-ranking military and 'civil' service), and without any connection with boats.[11] One may wonder too whether the New Testament concept of sin really has anything to do with Homeric arrows falling short of their targets, as many suppose (on the basis that the word *hamartia* is common to both), and however much *parakaleō* looks as though it should mean "to call someone alongside to assist" (from *para* "alongside" and *kaleō* "to call")—and it did once have this sense—in the New Testament period it means simply "to request", "to encourage", or "to cheer up". The fault of relying on etymology lies less with the preachers, of course, than with some of the scholarly commentaries and monographs on which they depend. As Barr was able to show, the error was rampant.[12]

5.1.2.2 The Corresponding Danger of Anachronism

One's understanding that the lexical stock is continuously subject to change should also prevent the corresponding error to etymologizing, namely anachronism; that is, the explanation of biblical meanings in terms of senses which only developed *later*.

Once again this is not uncommon in the devotional literature and in the less technical commentaries, where, for example, the fact that *modern* Greek uses the word *arrabōn* for 'engagement ring' is allowed to explain the use at 2 Cor. 1.13, where in fact the word means either "pledge" or more probably "first instalment", and modern Greek *charismata* (in the sense "birthday presents") is invoked to illustrate the term at 1 Cor. 12.3 (etc), where it simply means "gift" (with perhaps even a deliberate contextual play on the transparency of the word, so "result or event of grace"[13]).

We have even come across an appeal to the modern Greek for 'airline pilot' to illustrate the use of *kybernēseis* ('administrations' or 'acts of direction or guidance') at 1 Cor. 12.28. Now this might be both etymologizing error and anachronism simultaneously. The writer assumes that *kybernēsis* inevitably carries a nautical sense, even in the New Testament period, derived from the word *kybernētēs* ('helmsman','pilot'), where in fact this is unsure; both *kybernēsis* and its cognate verb had been used for a long while as metaphors for a wide range of leadership, administration and direction without necessarily retaining any direct nautical sense. They were probably faded, if not dead, metaphors; a 'nautical' sense would certainly be difficult in the Greek OT where it is used at Prov. 1.5; 11.14 and 24.6. The assumption of a semantic connection with seafaring pilots at 1 Cor. 12.28 is therefore possibly an etymologizing error; and there is no doubt about the anachronism of the reference to airline pilots. The same work goes on delightfully to add:

> The dictionary definition of the modern business science of *cybernetics* (the word comes from the same Greek root) affords fascinating insight into this matter.[14] [our italics]!

One may reasonably hope that most writers and speakers who use such illustrations do not *seriously* mean that twentieth-century usages should be allowed to determine New Testament exegesis, and that their comments are playful or rhetorical asides. Even more is this the case when Greek words like *dynamis* ('power'—as at Rom. 1.16) and *hilaros* ('glad', 'cheerful'—as at 2 Cor.8.9) are 'explained' in terms of the modern English 'dynamite' and 'hilarious'.[15] The problem with such illustrations is that they are too often taken, by the unwary, as revealing meanings that are somehow 'true' to the Greek words illustrated.

The phenomenon of changing meaning commits us to the synchronic analysis of the language of any piece of writing we are examining. Older meanings may not be relevant, later ones almost certainly are not. The only exception to this rule is the possibility that some senses only certainly attested in the period shortly after the New Testament, might actually have been current in the New Testament period itself, although not witnessed to it in any extant writing. A case in point is the Greek expression *stoicheia (tou kosmou)* used at Gal. 4.3, 9 and Col. 2.8, 20. The term could be translated literally 'elements (of the world)', but this is meaningless. The real question is whether the sense is "basic principles" (so NIV) or "elemental spirits" (i.e. planetary powers—so RSV). The latter sense is not certainly attested until after the NT in the late third century (or later) Pseudo-Callisthenes (1,12,1), and in the (probably earlier, but undatable) *Testament of Solomon* (8.2; 18.2). But despite the lack of definite attestation, many scholars feel, both from the way Hellenistic Judaism associated the elements and the planets with angelic powers, and from what Paul actually says in these contexts, that something like 'elemental spirits' must be what Paul meant.[16]

5.1.3 Words and the Multiplicity of their Senses: Polysemy and Homonymy[17]

Students who are learning a new language consult the vocabulary lists at the back of their course book and can easily come away with the impression that each foreign word has one, or at the most two, senses. Such an impression is, of course, a considerable oversimplification of reality. *Most* words in a language have not a single sense but a whole range of senses. Words occupy a domain of meanings and only *rarely* have a single point meaning.

In fact, single point meanings usually arise only temporarily with neologisms, words freshly minted. Thus when Michael Faraday was experimenting in the field of electro-chemistry he invited a classics friend to create new words for his science. It is to this unusual partnership that we owe words such as anode and cathode and diode, which appear to have retained point meanings. The word 'field', however, is applied to agricultural land; to the area of influence of a magnet or an electric current; to an area of human activity or knowledge; to a grouping of words related in meaning; to the place away from laboratory, office, library, etc., where practical work is done, and to the placing of the men in the bowling side in a game of cricket, as well as to the whole collection of horses competing in a race. This phenomenon—that one (phonological) word has a multiplicity of senses—allows considerable economy. If a language required to lexicalize every possible different sense with a distinguishable new word its lexical stock would become enormous, and unmanageable.

Having admitted the general idea of a word having a variety of senses we must now introduce some important distinctions. The command 'Get to the bank as fast as you can' is potentially ambiguous because the word 'bank' could mean *(inter alia)* either a financial institution or the side of a river. In this instance, however, linguists would not say we have one word with two (or more) meanings, but that we have two quite distinct words each spelt 'bank'; 'bank₁' from the Italian *banca* and 'bank₂' from Middle-English respectively. That is, the one (phonological) word is considered to stand for *two* words; or more technically, for two *lexemes*. The phenomenon of two or more lexemes having the same spelling (lexical *form*) and pronunciation is called *homonymy*.

The sentence 'Put the money in the bank!' is also ambiguous. While it suggests 'bank₁' is meant, it remains uncertain whether the 'bank' in question is (a) an institution (e.g. "the Bank of England"); (b) a particular building as the local office of some bank, or (c) the funds held by the banker or dealer in a gambling game. The single lexeme 'bank₁' has itself these several distinct senses (and others beside). The phenomenon of a single lexeme having a multiplicity of senses is called *polysemy*.

Few linguisticists today give exclusive weight to the *etymological* criterion for establishing *homonyms* such as 'bank₁' and 'bank₂' above. After all, if we trace further back, both the Italian and the Middle English 'bank' derive ultimately from a common source—so does etymology point to two words or one? Anyway most language *users* are entirely unaware of the etymology of the words they use, and for languages which have no written history the criterion of etymologically different origins is inapplicable. So distinction of *meaning* has also come to be regarded as a sufficient basis for claiming homonymy. This should be seen to follow not unnaturally from a linguist's conception of a word as a combination of both form *and* meaning. One *form*, *bank*, with two quite distinct *meanings*, on this understanding, implies two different *words*. Potentially this could lead to a swallowing up of polysemy—for what we have called three different senses of the one lexeme 'bank₁' could then as easily be analyzed as three distinct *lexemes* 'bank₁', 'bank₃' and 'bank₄'. Most, however, feel such an approach would lead to an unjustifiable proliferation of lexemes in the dictionary.

Alternatively, at the other extreme, we might insist that the etymological criterion for distinguishing two separate words 'bank₁' and 'bank₂' is inadequate, and that we really have but *one* lexeme ('bank') with at least four different senses ([1] = financial institution; [2] = river bank; [3] = building as local office of a bank, etc.). This would be to make polysemy swallow up homonymy.

In practice, it would be usual to take a mediating position; and to use *homonymy* where we have to do with distinct and apparently *unrelated* senses, while using *polysemy* to refer to occasions of multiple *related* senses of a word. Thus, the (phonological) word 'bank' is capable of the senses (a) "a raised mass, especially of earth"; (b) "the slope (e.g.) of a hill", and (c) "the ground beside a river". Because these senses are all *related in meaning*, we would tend to explain them as different senses of a *single* lexeme, 'bank₂': i.e. we have to do with *polysemy*. Similarly the senses "financial institution", "building (as the local office of a bank)", and "fund (held by a banker in a game)" are all once again related together in meaning; but none is related to any of the senses of 'bank₂'. So here we may conclude on the grounds of unrelated sense that we have here three polysemous senses of a *different lexeme*, 'bank₁'; and as it happens different etymological histories also support the distinction. 'Bank₁' and 'bank₂' are then relatively confidently labelled *homonymous* lexemes. If we now define a *lexical unit* as the combination of a lexical form (e.g. *bank* [plus its merely inflectional variants such as *banks*]) with a *single* distinct sense (e.g. "financial institution"), we may then think of *lexemes* as families of lexical units related to each other in sense.[18]

On purely *syntactic* grounds it would be usual for linguisticists also to distinguish as a third lexeme, 'bank₃', the word 'bank' used as a *verb*. This would be regarded as a different word (even though related in sense to 'bank₁'), distinguished by its different set of word-forms: they include not only *bank* and *banks*, but also *banked* and *banking*.

In sum, what at first might appear (on the basis of form and pronunciation) to be a single word may prove on closer analysis to represent several quite distinct lexemes each with a plurality of senses. This should alert us to the danger of the widespread popular assumption that even if a word has several senses these are liable to share some common core or overarching meaning. That may occasionally be true of *polysemy*, but it is by no means always so, and it takes no account of *homonymy*: what shared meaning could possibly be postulated for 'bank₁' and 'bank₂', or for the various meanings of 'run' in

1. 'We run the engine.'
2. 'We run for Scotland.'
3. 'We run the company.'
4. 'We run stock in that field' [i.e. we leave the animals to graze there].
5. 'We run guns for the rebels.'
6. 'Our noses run when we are cold.'
7. 'The colours run in hot water.'
8. 'Both leases run for two years.'
9. 'The papers run his story tomorrow.'

Any attempt to find some single overarching 'meaning' for *run* here would not only be subjective, but bound to fail.[19] It is the *lexical form* which is held in common, not any major component of sense. Rather we have a number of different lexemes here (and one complex lexeme, or idiom, [4]), with meanings belonging to different semantic domains;[20] movement through use of limbs, internal movement of related parts, movement of liquid and dry masses, operation of organization or enterprise, and so forth.

5.1.3.1 Is There a Single 'Basic' or 'Core' Sense in Polysemous Words?
We have spoken of *polysemy* in terms of a single lexeme having multiple but semantically *related* senses. But that does not mean there is always some 'basic' or 'core' meaning that holds all the senses together. Sometimes there is; for example, the different senses of 'bank₂' appear to include "slope (e.g. of earth)" as an important component meaning. But the relating factor between polysemous senses of a lexeme is sometimes quite tangential to some of the senses. Consider the following (polysemous) uses of 'chair':

1. a seat with a back on which one person sits
2. an official position of authority
3. a person holding an office of authority (cf. 'Please address your questions to the chair!')
4. a professorship
5. an iron or steel socket designed to take a rail and secure it to the sleeper

It may be surmised that the 'core' meaning is (1), that all the others involve sitting in such a chair, and that (5) perhaps *looks* like a chair. But a moment's reflection will show this is both unconvincing and unhelpful. In respect of (5) the surmise is simply untrue; the relation is rather one of *metaphorical transfer* (the rail 'sits' in the 'chair' of a sleeper). And with respect to (2), (3), and (4) the surmise misses the point. 'Chair', in the sense (1), is now *entirely incidental* to sense (4), if part of it at all; for professors are no longer presented with any special item of furniture when they are given their 'chair', and they usually teach standing. Something similar may be said for senses (3) and (2). All three are examples of *metonymic transfer*. The item of furniture that was originally an adjunct of professorship, or of more general types of authoritative office, has been transferred to the office itself, or to the office-holder.

In short, the proposed 'core' meaning actually turns out to focus on an element which may have been historically important, but which is semantically *marginal* to four of the senses. The five uses of 'chair', here, are related polysemously, not because they share some basic 'core' meaning *central* to all five, but because they share *some* element in common (by metaphorical and metonymic transfer) even though the shared element is only marginal to the meaning of four of the senses.

5.2 ANALYZING THE DIFFERENT SENSES OF A WORD

We have just spoken of words having multiple senses, and in Chapter 3 we defined 'sense' in a general and provisional way as a relationship of meaning which exists between a word and *other words* in the language, appealing particularly to the idea of synonymy. There we distinguished 'sense' from 'denotation', 'reference', and 'significance'. We shall now need to take a more careful look at both what we mean by 'sense', and how we analyze the sense of particular lexical units. Before doing so, however, we should introduce an important distinction.

5.2.1 Distinguishing 'Lexical Senses' from 'Word Usages'

In his introductory *Exegetical Fallacies*, D. A. Carson, points to the potential scope of meaning of almost any lexeme by taking the example of 'roller coaster' and noting the possibility of its employment in such an utterance as 'My love life is a roller coaster!' The speaker might successfully be understood to be lamenting that his romance was blowing hot and cold. But, as Dr Carson was fully aware, we could not say this was a 'lexical sense', or the 'lexical meaning', of 'roller coaster'. It would not be found in a lexicon, listed as a meaning, and if we asked the proverbial man on the street whether or not 'roller coaster' means "blowing hot and cold" or "subject to vacillation", or whatever, the answer would be in the negative; it is merely an instance of (metaphorical!) *usage*. Only if this particular usage became widespread, such that it became a standard public idiom, and so *conventional*, would we say it was becoming, or even had become, part of the lexical meaning of the word. The lexical meaning is the range of senses of a word that may be counted on as being established in the public domain.

There is obviously a grey area here. When, for example, Acts 27.17 tells us 'they used *boētheiai*, undergirding the ship', are we to follow Louw (who tells us the word simply means "helps", i.e. "supports", and that *in the context* the plural word may *refer* to cables but that the word itself does not carry such a sense) or are we to follow the hint in Bauer (whom Louw is criticizing) that this word had probably already been used sufficiently frequently with 'supporting cable' as its referent for this to have become a proper sense of the word (by habitual denotation), a nautical technical term?[21] The available evidence for making the decision is not exactly overwhelming. We simply have to take the caution: not all contextual senses and usages are actually lexical meanings. We need to distinguish between usages which are *conventional* (at least to a group), and so an established 'sense' of a word (for that group, or more widely), and those which are not.

It is not always easy to separate lexical meanings from mere usages, and these in turn from what is simply contextually associated information. And even the great dictionaries occasionally read the context of a usage into the lexical meaning of a word. Thus P. W. G. Glare can complain of Liddell and Scott:

> *Baptō* in general means 'dip', but it has a special sense [i.e. usage] 'dip in poison' for two passages in the *Trachiniae*. Certainly we know, and the audience knew, but Deianeira, who actually used the word, had no idea there was any poison.[22]

So there was no justification for the dictionary to list "dip in poison" as a sense of the verb. This is only what is entailed by the context, not by the use of the word itself.[23]

The exegete is naturally interested in both lexical meaning and discourse usage, but the difference is a significant one. Take, for example, Paul's complaint in Col. 2.19 that those holding to a certain brand of teaching 'do not have a grasp of *the Head, from whom the entire body . . . grows with a growth which is from God*'. A plausible interpretation of the underlined elements of the assertion (adopted by some of the Fathers from Athanasius onwards) is that Paul regards Christ as *the source* of the Church—'head' of it in something like the sense that waters flow from the head of a river. This view is set over against the interpretation that 'head' means rather "ruler", "authority (over)", and it has obvious implications both for Paul's talk elsewhere of husbands being 'heads' of wives (cf.1 Cor. 11.3ff.; Eph. 5.23), and for the relation envisaged between Christ and the Church at Col. 1.18; Eph. 1.22, 5.23, etc.). Now contextually it is by no means certain that Col. 2.19 presents Christ as the origin, rather than as the Lord of the Church,[24] but clearly it would considerably strengthen the thesis if the sense "source" was part of the lexical meaning of the Greek word *kephalē* ('head'); that is, if it were one of its *established* senses. Several authors claim precisely that this is so,[25] indeed even that "source" or "origin" is the *normal* sense[26] of the word.

Now this last can only be a mistake; the normal meaning of *kephalē* is certainly "head" in the anatomical sense. The real question is whether the sense "lord" is not so rare as to make it an unlikely reading here, and whether the sense "source" is not so common that this is the one readers would naturally think of. In fact, as Wayne Grudem has recently shown, the sense "ruler", "chief", "authority over", etc. *is not* that unknown amongst the non-literal uses of the word in Greek[27] (and it is *well established* in the Septuagintal Greek),[28] while an extensive and representative sampling of the pre-Christian literature *showed no occasion at all* when *kephalē unambiguously* meant "source" or "origin", and those (very few) contexts which *had* been appealed to failed to substantiate such a sense.

Excursus on the Argument that Kephalē Carries the Sense 'Source' The issue of the sense of *kephalē* is not an uncomplicated one, but it is worthwhile setting out in a little detail as it well illustrates the complexity of the problem of establishing senses in 'dead' languages. The evidence on which the claim that *kephalē* means "source" is based is essentially fourfold.

(a) S. Bedale[29] had argued that as the Septuagint used *archē* and *kephalē* to translate the Hebrew *rosh* ('head'—with *[inter alia]* the senses "anatomical head", "first or beginning", and "chief, captain or ruler"), and as *archē* usually had the sense "beginning" or "source", it followed that *kephalē* was likely to take over this sense. But his argument involves a number of implausibilities. It is true that *kephalē* and *archē* are used interchangeably to translate the Hebrew *rosh* when the latter has the sense "chief" or "head over". It is also true that *archē* was used to translate the Hebrew *rosh* when the latter had the sense "beginning". But there is surely no reason to assume that anyone could confuse or conflate the two entirely distinct *homonyms archē₁* (= "chief" or "ruler") and *archē₂* (= "beginning" or [perhaps] "source")—for both were well established in Greek, and no OT context seriously offers any ambiguity as to which is intended. So the fact that *kephalē* was used interchangeably with *archē₁* (= "chief" or "ruler"), to translate *rosh*, does not itself increase the probability that *kephalē also* came to have the sense of *archē₂* (= "beginning" or "source"). In English, for example, we have the homonyms 'spirit₁ (= "a distilled alcoholic beverage") and 'spirit₂' (= "a supernatural incorporeal being" or "demon"), but that does not predispose English speakers to believe that "demon" is a sense of the word 'whisky'. Because *kephalē* was a synonym for the one homonym would not imply it was also a synonym for the other. In fact the evidence leads in the opposite direction; for in the LXX *kephalē* was never used to translate *rosh* when the latter meant "beginning" (of a time sequence), nor was it used on the one occasion where *rosh* perhaps meant "source" (Gen. 2.10),[30] and this suggests that the translators were aware *kephalē* did not carry these senses of either *rosh* or *archē*.

(b) *kephalai* (the plural of *kephalē*) is cited *once* to refer to the sources of the Tearus in Herodotus (4.91; cf. the same quotation preserved in *Anthologia Graeca* 9.703.2). However, the singular word is also used of the *mouth* of the river (cf. Callimachus, *Aetia* 2.46 [A.D. 270?]), and the easiest explanation of both of these usages of *kephalē* is that they derive from the lexeme's established sense of "extreme end" (both ends of the poles used to carry the ark of the covenant are called the 'heads' in this sense: 3 Kings 8.8 LXX). We do not need to posit that they represent *new senses*, "source" and "mouth" respectively, for which we have no corroborating evidence. Just because one 'extreme end' *(kephalē)* of a river happens also to be the "source" or "origin" from which flow its waters, does not mean the two expressions—'extreme end' and 'source'—are closely related in *sense:* they merely have the same potential referent. It is clear that the expressions do not have the same *sense* in *English* (not all 'extreme ends' or even 'starting points' are also 'sources'), and there is no reason why they should in *Greek.* To assume otherwise is a co-referential error (the assumption that two words used to refer to the same entity will carry the same sense). And the fact that we do not come across frequent examples of *kephalē* in relation to either end of rivers throws particular doubt on the view that "origin" and "mouth" had become lexical senses of the word.

Even if by continual denotation (of which there is no evidence) *kephalē* perchance came to carry the lexical sense "(river) source", we would need to posit another stage—that of further figurative extension (or metaphoric transfer)—before we could speak of *kephalē* having a more general lexical sense "source or origin of something". And where have we evidence of this? Where do we find instances of such statements as 'cows are the *kephalē* of milk'; 'Egypt is the *kephalē* of papyrus', etc. Only such a range of evidence could confirm that *kephalē* had the lexical sense "source" or "origin", generally understood, rather than being specifically collocated with nouns referring to linear entities that have two ends. And we do not appear to have this kind of evidence.

(c) Arguably all the evidence offered so far in favour of the view that *kephalē* means "source" is irrelevant to the specific issue at hand; namely whether the word could be used with this sense when referring to relationships between personal entities. Often cited in favour of the view that *kephalē* had such a sense is the fifth-century B.C. adoration of Zeus contained in *Orphic Fragments* 21a:

Zeus was first, Zeus is last with white vivid lightning: Zeus the head, Zeus the middle, Zeus from whom all things are perfected.

But this is too ambiguous to be useful. What sense attaches to 'head' here? If we already *knew* that 'head' *could* carry the sense "source", that would undoubtedly be an attractive meaning. And both Barrett[31] and Fee[32] point to the fact that some manuscripts have *archē,* instead of *kephalē* here, as strong evidence that the sense "source" is meant. But once again the conclusion is too easily reached. *Archē* like *kephalē* can certainly mean "beginning" (without meaning "source"), and this meaning is arguably the best suited to the context of the other statements in the line.[33] As we are able to explain *kephalē* here along the lines of a perfectly well-established sense of the word, it is barely legitimate to use the fragment as evidence of an otherwise unattested sense "source".

Yet no *other* evidence seems to be forthcoming for the view that *kephalē* means "source" or "origin" in relation to personal entities. To be sure, Payne[34] and Fee[35] have cited Philo's description of Esau as the progenitor of his clan and '"head" as it were to the whole creature'.[36] And taken out of context this looks like a possible case of 'head' meaning "source", for Esau was the seminal source of his clan. But closer examination reveals that the 'clan' or 'whole creature' Philo has in mind is not made up of *physical descendents*, but rather of *like characters*, and Esau was not the 'source' of these, but the *first* and *chief representative*. Since elsewhere he clearly states that the 'head' is the 'first and best part' of the body,[37] that is almost certainly what he means here.

(d) Least helpful of the types of evidence advanced, is the claim that amongst the ancients the head was often regarded as the source of a variety of substances and influences pertinent to life.[38] The claim itself need not be doubted, but how is it *relevant?* Just because, say, Artemidorus (late 2nd century A.D.) maintains that 'the head is the source of light and life for the body' does not mean that the writer considered "source" to be a *sense* of the *word* 'head'. Our employers are the source of our income, books are the source of our knowledge, and the good well-watered land the source of our food, but no one in their right mind would suggest that "source" is a *sense* of the *words* 'employer', 'book', or 'land'. Such would be a classic case of the confusion between the 'sense' of a word and (adjunct) properties of the thing-in-the-world the word denotes. At best a continual reference to the head as a source of life-supporting elements for the body *might* give rise to a metaphorical use of 'head' as source, but what needs to be shown is that what *might have been* did *indeed happen*. Just such a process can be demonstrated for the use of 'head' with the sense "ruler",[39] but we are not aware of any instance of 'head' unambiguously used with the sense "source" before the third century A.D. Such evidence *may* of course turn up; but until it does it remains linguistically less than responsible to say "source" was one of the (pre-Christian) *senses* of the word *kephalē*. At most we may *surmise* that the basis for such a usage was developing at some time in the period before Athanasius' day (mid-fourth century A.D.), if indeed the re-doubtable Father did not merely misconstrue this sense from Paul's wording.

In other words, as far as we can tell, "source" or "origin" was *not* a conventional sense of the word *kephalē* in Paul's time. This does not preclude the possibility that Paul himself began to use the word in such a way, but we would need very strong evidence to support such a view, and in our judgement nothing like such strength of evidence is forth-coming. And the point relevant to our distinction between lexical sense and word usages is that the distinction is important for deciding wheth-er or not a particular sense is liable to be what a reader would imme-diately perceive. In what follows we shall mainly (but not exclusively) be concerned with how lexical senses are understood.

5.2.2 Clarifying What We Mean By the 'Sense' of Word

It is hard to define what we mean by the words we use in a way that entirely satisfies others; and the word 'sense', in this context, is certainly no exception. Most would agree that when we talk of a (lexical) sense of a word we are referring to some sort of more-or-less discrete bundle of meaning, a segment of the language users' understanding of their world, conventionally bound to a particular lexical form. The 'sense' of a word is thus a cognitive construct. Beyond that, however, we discover considerable diversity—and, as we shall see, even the assertion that senses are 'discrete' bundles of meaning is challenged.

In this section we shall look at two of the different approaches to elucidating 'sense'. Though the approaches differ they both clarify im-portant aspects of what we mean by 'sense', and teach us something about how to analyze word meaning. We shall call the two approaches 'concept orientated' and 'field orientated' for reasons that will become obvious.

To avoid endless qualifications in what follows let us state here that we are only discussing 'descriptive sense' not connotation or affective meanings (as when we apply the word 'pig' to a greedy person, or 'rat' to someone who lets us down).[40] And when we use such pre-theoretical language as 'the sense of the word "cup" ' we do not deny homonymy or polysemy; we simply wish to avoid such inelegant qualifications as 'the sense of the word "cup" when that word is used in its most frequently recognized sense, as opposed to in one of its less common senses, "chalice", "trophy", etc.'

5.2.2.1 Concept Orientated Approaches to Word Sense   This may be regarded as a more traditional approach. Roughly speaking, the descriptive sense of a word is taken to be the bundle of meaning we might otherwise call the concept denoted by that word. Accordingly, if we want to know the sense of the word 'cup', we sit down and puzzle out a definition of 'cup' that encompasses its characteristic and distinctive features. This is then regarded as the sense of the word cup.

In ordinary one-language dictionaries, such definitions may for reasons of space be minimal, e.g. 'a small open container, usually having one handle, used for drinking from'[41]—a definition which incidentally would include mugs, and not absolutely exclude tin cans, glasses, etc., since a handle appears to be optional.

Alternatively, in careful attempts at lexicography, they may be relatively complete, as in Wierzbicka's two-page definition.[42] Her definition of cup starts with a statement of the purpose of a cup, because she thinks this is determinative for understanding its features. The fact that they are for the drinking of *hot* liquids, for example, dictates that they cannot be much wider than they are high. And that it is intended that they will be put down on a surface (e.g. a table), between sips, governs other features (e.g. that they may be provided with a saucer, on which to catch any drips; that if they have handles [to protect from the heat of the fluids] they need only be small ones [as opposed to mugs, which are made to be carried about, not replaced on a surface, and so need sturdier handles and construction]).

She goes on to provide a list both of the features regarded as *essential* to the concept of a cup (and Wierzbicka argues this includes neither handle nor saucer for example in the case of Chinese tea cups), and of the features which make up the *stereotype* of 'cup': i.e. those which one would normally include in the description of a typical or *prototype* cup[43] (and this would include saucer, handle[s], shape and design, conventional use, and so forth). The essential qualities and the stereotype together define the concept of "cup", and so may be regarded as the 'descriptive meaning' or 'sense' of the word cup. This possibly gives the most satisfactory account of what is traditionally meant by 'sense', and comes very close to identifying 'sense' and 'concept' (as the title of Wierzbicka's book—*Lexicography and Conceptual Analysis*—suggests). Shorter definitions of 'cup', or whatever, should perhaps simply be regarded as convenient abridgements.

A number of important objections can be raised against this sort of understanding of word sense. (1) It is not clear that all the features specified as part of the concept of 'cup' are actually in semantic focus every time we use the word 'cup'; so in what way may they be regarded as part of the *sense* of the word? Related to this, (2) many people who appear quite competently to use the word 'cup' in a wide range of contexts are nevertheless apparently unaware of what Wierzbicka regards as important elements defining the concept of a cup (e.g. the relation of height to diameter); so in what way are these elements necessary parts of the 'sense' of the word 'cup' *for them?* (3) 'Concepts', because they are mental objects, are not accessible to objective analysis, and so theories of meaning should not be based on them. We may consider these in turn.

(1) In fact, Wierzbicka does not suggest that all the features she specifies are actually in semantic focus every time we use the word 'cup' (though it must be admitted she takes pains to include no merely encyclopaedic information). But this is, in any case, a general feature of utterances—that is, the situational and semantic context modulates the sense of included lexical units, highlighting some components of the meaning of a lexical unit and backgrounding others.

Thus 'There are those who have made themselves eunuchs for the sake of the kingdom of God' (Mt 19.12) highlights the *worth* of the kingdom of God; 'If I, by the finger of God, cast out demons, then the kingdom of God has come upon you' (Lk 11.20) highlights it as liberating *power*; 'You shut the kingdom of heaven in men's faces' focuses God's kingdom (assuming 'heaven' is a circumlocution for God) as a realm or state of affairs to be entered, and 'I will not drink again of the fruit of the vine until the kingdom of God comes' (Lk 22.18) focuses it as a still-future hope. Unless one is prepared to say we have several *different* lexical units here, each sentence appears to give prominence to a distinct aspect of some more general concept of "the kingdom of God" in Jesus' teaching, while ignoring other features of the concept.

A context may promote what would normally be regarded as a merely stereotypical feature of a concept (or no more than an 'expected' trait of a sense) and make it an essential feature (or 'criterial' trait),[44] or *vice versa*. For example, in, 'The minister preached a pretty good sermon', an expected (though not essential) trait of the sense "minister" would be "male person", but in the alternative sentence, 'The pretty minister preached a good sermon', an *unexpected* trait of the concept "minister", namely "female person", has become *essential* to the sense. The fact that not all proposed components of the concept "cup" are actually brought to focus in any one sentence need not be a serious objection to Wierzbicka's definition. Rather this is to be understood as a normal feature of utterances.

(2) Theoretically more serious is the second objection. What if some of the elements of the proposed definition do not even appear to be highlighted in any of a *wide range* of normal utterances about cups? Does such a phenomenon not show that Wierzbicka has confused her simultaneously much fuller and yet more precise *concept* of a cup with what we normally mean by the *sense* of the word 'cup'? Against this charge Wierzbicka would argue that all the characteristics she includes are properly part of the sense, and that even the most unreflective would immediately ask questions if the context made clear that something corresponding to one of her essential elements was *missing*. To take another example, we may not immediately think the following description is *necessary* to the sense of the word 'bicycle':

at one end of the frame there is a thin movable part which sticks out on both sides of the frame
to support one's hands
so that by turning this part to one side with one's hands one can cause the whole thing to turn to that side.[45]

But once we try to imagine a 'bicycle' without handlebars (other than one from which they have merely been temporarily removed), we may be inclined to agree with Wierzbicka that they are actually a fundamental part of our concept of a bicycle, and that *anyone* (not just fussing lexicologists) would probably hesitate to apply the word 'bicycle' to a machine that was not expected to have them.[46] So something like 'handlebars' are part of the conventional sense of 'bicycle', even if not often a contextually focused part. What Wierzbicka is essentially claiming is that even those who could not themselves actually articulate a full def-

inition of 'cup' or 'bicycle', are nevertheless aware of the necessary in-
gredients for defining the sense (through their extensive knowledge of
prototypes of these things?).

(3) The third objection is potentially the most important. It cannot be
shown that we invariably visualize any kind of images or 'natural signs'
to correspond with our use of words, and so a theory that defines word
meaning strictly in terms of the concepts elicited in our use of the words
must inevitably appear problematic.[47] However, the sort of 'concept'
Wierzbicka is talking about is not a hypothetical mental image, but a
verbal description of a set of related elements of meaning that together
form a coherent and discrete abstraction. Both her 'concept', and its
relation to word-meaning, are directly accessible to scrutiny—and diagnostic sentences can readily be composed to test whether the elements
of her 'concept' of bicycle are indeed actually part of the sense of the
word 'bicycle'. An English speaker would thus normally accept as *semantically* anomalous such sentences as:

'It's a bicycle, but it has pedals, two wheels and a chain.'

'It's a bicycle, but you steer it with handlebars.'

'It's a bicycle, but you ride it.'

While a sentence like

'It's a bicycle, but it's painted tartan'

would be regarded as linguistically entirely acceptable, even if affirming
an unusual situation. In rejecting the first three sentences as internal
contradictions, he or she confirms that the elements apparently excluded from "bicycle" by the adversative clauses are in fact usually regarded as criterial traits of the *sense* "bicycle". And it is hard to see how
language users come to such a conclusion unless by testing the new
sentences put to them against some abstraction of a bicycle (or of its
elements and properties) which is effectively a 'concept' of a bicycle.[48]
And as Wierzbicka's 'concept' of a bicycle (as it comes to expression in
her definition) amounts to a listing of the criterial and expected traits
of the word 'bicycle' (as these are highlighted in a wide range of sentence contexts) it is hard to deny that her 'concept' of "bicycle" is closely
related to (if not indistinguishable from) the lexical sense of the word
'bicycle'. Essentially, then, we are inclined to agree with Jerrold Katz that
a 'sense' may be viewed as "a concept linguistically connected with a
word or expression and thereby providing its referential conditions or

the contribution it makes to the truth conditions . . . of the sentences in which it can occur"—as long as we distinguish (as he does) this narrower use of the word 'concept' from a more general use such as when people speak of 'Science's concept of the atom', 'a European's concept of an American', or 'Plato's concept of the noumenal world'.[49]

The traditional approach to lexical sense, which roughly defines it in terms of the 'concept' linguistically associated with a lexical form, can be expected to be most fruitful when applied to concrete nouns like 'carrot', 'pencil', 'table', 'jug', and the like. This is partly because people have seen and handled many prototypes of these things, and partly because they do not encounter many problematic cases of the sort that make them ask 'Is this, or is this not (say) a carrot?' They have, therefore, a relatively clear concept of them, which they bring to any context. Some of this apparent clarity is perhaps illusory, for, as W. Labov and others have shown, it is all too easy to create a cup which is virtually indistinguishable from a bowl or from a vase, thus putting a question mark over whether our concept of a cup is *really* a discrete bundle of meaning, separable from our concepts of 'bowl' and 'vase'.[50] But arguably, at least in this instance, much of the alleged fuzziness can be removed by observing that part of the sense of 'cup' is its intended and stereotypical use—a feature of the concept which distinguishes it from the senses of 'bowl' or 'vase'. Other words may have a much more general sense (e.g. 'middle-aged', 'bald', 'justice', etc), but it should still be possible to define what would be regarded as essential and stereotypical elements of the predicate. It may be felt, however, that field-orientated approaches to sense (discussed below) provide a more useful avenue for discussion of the senses of such lexical units.

In relation to exegesis of texts written in ancient languages, concept-orientated approaches to sense require special care. We do not have living speakers of the language to whom we can pose diagnostic questions in order to elucidate whether elements of our reconstruction were essential, or merely stereotypical features of their concepts. Often we have a very restricted number of occurrences of the lexical unit in contexts which do not allow us to draw assured conclusions. For example, for all Paul's (regular) insistence that he is an 'apostle (of Christ)',[51] we are still far from sure what he means by it; not least because in the early church, while there may have been no doubt that Peter and James were such, it *was not clear* (at least not to the Corinthians!) that Paul was one, and some appear to have thought Paul's opponents (in 2 Cor. 10-13) *were* apostles—while Paul thinks they have simply misunderstood the nature of apostleship. In short, the concepts of "apostle (of Christ)" in the earliest church were somewhat fuzzy, if not diverse—and it would consequently be problematic to relate them to a lexical sense. What elements of people's differing concepts could actually be counted part of an 'established sense' of the word in Christian circles? Or do we need here to speak of a minimal and slightly ambiguous 'established sense' supporting a flourishing growth of differing personal concepts?

This leads us to a second important potential problem; that of confusing a concept which might have a good claim to be called the lexical *sense* of a word with some broader concept present in a context. Conceptorientated approaches to defining senses are clearly able to build on the fact that lexical senses are a special *type* of concept. Given that a concept is a cognitive construct, a discrete bundle of meanings composing an independent unit of meaning with a central, or prominent element, further defined by other delimiting elements, we might then define the concept "bicycle" in terms of a central component [vehicle], qualified by the delimiting elements [with two wheels], [for one person], [pedal-propelled], [handle-bar steered] etc. The relation of this to the 'lexical sense' of 'bicycle' should then be relatively clear.

> Though if the components of a concept (the elements included in bold brackets) are regarded as *transcending* their expression in any one language, as Baldinger argues, then "with two wheels" is not simply identical with [with two wheels], but the former is the expression in English of the latter meta-linguistic entity.[52]

Arguably all word senses are concepts of some such type, or are very closely related to them. But the reverse is certainly not true. "My Uncle George's old red bike" expresses a concept (and we only need to supply the extra delimiting elements [old], [red], and [belonging to the speaker's Uncle George] to the ones given above in order to define it), but it is not a word-sense; at least, there is no single lexeme in *English*, for which "old", "red" and "belonging to the speaker's uncle" are recognized elements of *the sense*.

The danger we mentioned earlier should now be recognizable. If, word senses are concepts, and if concepts are readily expanded by further contextual elements, *the broader concept produced by a context may be confused with a word sense*. A speaker may keep referring to his Uncle's bike, but (having formally introduced it earlier, as it were) now just speaks of it as 'the bike'. Because the expression 'the bike' now still *refers* to Uncle George's old red one, this is all included in the concept denoted by the expression 'the bike' *in the speaker's discourse*, even though it is not properly part of the sense of the expression 'the bike' as such. We need to distinguish here between what we might call *lexical concepts* (i.e. the sense of the respective lexical units) and *discourse concepts*[53]—the latter being used to denote not only the lexical sense of the expressions involved, but also germane elements of meaning contributed by the context. Oldness, redness and to-Uncle-George-belongingness would not be part of the lexical concept "bike", but would belong to the *discourse concept* "the bike" in this particular situation.

If the reader is inclined to suspect that all this about red bicycles is nothing but a herring of the same hue, let it be said that the phenomenon we are discussing lies precisely at the heart of the Kittel/Barr dispute earlier.[54] In terms of the distinctions we have just introduced, Barr is accusing Kittel of equating discourse concepts with lexical concepts or lexical senses. The two are certainly easy to confuse.

For example, in Gal. 4.4-6, there is a discourse concept of "Son of God" that has a central element [being], and delimiting elements which include the components [pre-existent], [related to God as the Son], [incarnate], and [sent to redeem]; but to what extent can they be said to be the *sense* of Paul's expression 'the Son of God'? When Paul uses the expression elsewhere he may well have these and other elements of meaning in mind—for they are part of his broader *conception* of Jesus' divine sonship—but how many of these components can be said to be *linguistically* included in the *sense* of the expression "(the) Son of God" as such? As far as genuinely *lexical* sense is concerned, perhaps only [being] and [related to God as Son] could be included; and even the second of these would be meant in the widest sense: anything from a charismatic figure who seemed divinely empowered, to a mortal granted immortality by the gods, or (in Judaism) from a pious Israelite to an angel, and (possibly) Israel's awaited messiah, could be called a 'son of God'.

If it could be established that Jews at the time widely expected an eschatological messianic figure of David's ilk, reflecting God's glory, and that they usually (or at least often) referred to such a figure as the 'Son of God', then [related to God as the (messianic) son] could be justified as part of a specialized sense of the expression, at least for apocalyptic Judaism. But we do not have the required evidence; we only have such evidence as would justify the claim that 'Son of God' was perhaps *beginning* to be used as a messianic title in certain sectors of Judaism.[55] If that is so, it was not an established, and so 'lexical' sense. And however much Paul and his congregations used the term, in discourses that associated it with new components of meaning, these additional components cannot be regarded as part of the lexical sense of the expression until well beyond Paul's generation (if at all).

In his lifetime, the extra components could at most become part of an idiolect sense (one belonging to Paul himself) or of a specialized sense specific to a small group. But the real question is whether these extra components (such as [pre-existent], [sent to redeem], etc.) can legitimately be regarded as part of the *sense* of the term 'Son of God' for Paul at all. Are they not simply attributes of the one who *is* the 'Son of God'? How do we decide which of the attributes of Jesus have become, for Paul, linguistically included in the *sense* of the term 'Son of God', and which are merely associated (whether integrally or tangentially) with Paul's *broader conception* of the Son of God? The test would be whether Paul regarded as *semantically* anomalous (on the grounds that the adversative clause denies a major element of the sense of the initial clause of each) such sentences as

'He's the Son of God, but he was before the world.'

'He's the Son of God, but he was sent to redeem us.'

Unfortunately we cannot ask Paul. But it would require some courage to maintain he would so regard them. It is more easily believable that for him the sense "Son of God" did not include such components as [pre-existent] and [sent to redeem], but that these were important for his *broader* concept of Jesus' divine sonship. The Kittel dictionary regularly short-circuited this problem of the distinction between what belonged *linguistically* to the sense of a word or expression and what belonged either contextually or by association to some broader concept.

Concept-orientated approaches to *sense* have their problems, then; chief amongst which is that of deciding which components of the variety of discourse concepts are properly part of the lexical concept or sense of an expression. They remain within our provisional definition of sense as a relation of meaning between one word and other words in the language, only because the 'concepts' with which we are concerned are verbal definitions of the essential and expected traits of a lexical unit.

5.2.2.2 Field-Orientated Approaches to Word Sense[56]   Granted that it is extraordinarily hard to give definitions of many of the words we use, how is it that for the most part we still use them competently? One of the fundamental insights of modern linguistics has been that we understand words in relation to other possible words. And this provides the second main approach to what we mean by 'sense'.

Let us use an analogy taken from colour terminology. Our use of the term 'red' is afforded narrowly specific content by the fact that we can contrast it with 'brown', 'pink', 'yellow', 'orange', 'indigo', and 'violet'. 'Red' thus belongs to a 'field' of colour terminology, and gets its meaning from its contrasting relationship with other members of the field. Now if we were Bassa speakers from Liberia we would only have two colour terms (in addition to black and white); *hui* denoting everything from violet to green in the spectrum, and *ziza* to cover the spectrum from yellow to red. *Ziza* would thus be correspondingly less specific in sense than our 'red' because of the absence of the possibility of contrast with pink, yellow and orange.[57]

Similarly, the availability of comparable and contrasting terms provides a vital part of our notion of word meaning. The child learns the meaning of 'dress', not merely by having dresses pointed out to her, but by gradually learning to distinguish them from her mother's blouses, smocks, skirts, suits, coats, and trousers too. The 'sense' of the word 'skirt' (when this word is used to denote an article of clothing) is determined in part by its relationship to generic terms like 'garment' and 'clothes', and to subclasses like 'underwear', 'hosiery', and 'overclothes', and in part by how it contrasts with 'dress' (which is used for garments that simultaneously cover the upper and lower parts of the body) and 'trousers' (which cover the lower parts, but entirely encircle and separate the legs).

'Skirt' belongs to a field of words related to each other by the fact that they describe clothing, and its meaning derives from its comparable and contrasting relationships with other words in the same field. If we removed the word 'trousers' from the vocabulary of ladies garments (and refused to substitute some other lexeme), 'skirt' (as the available lexeme for lower-body garments) would probably have to absorb the sense now attached to 'trousers', with corresponding reduction in the specificity of its sense. What we are saying is that the sense of a word depends on the availability of other words in the same field of meaning, and on the word's relationship to those other words (and their respective meanings).

With this understanding, J. Lyons can introduce a chapter which he entitles 'Webs of Words: The Formalization of Lexical Structure'

People often think of the meanings of words as if each of them had an independent and separate existence. But . . . no word can be fully understood independently of other words that are related to it and delimit its sense. Looked at from a semantic point of view, the lexical structure of a language—the structure of its vocabulary—is best regarded as a large and intricate network of sense-relations: it is like a huge, multidimensional, spider's web, in which each strand is one such relation and each knot in the web is a different lexeme.[58]

In the context of this understanding, Lyons can tersely define sense:

The *sense* of an expression is, quite simply, the set of sense-relations that hold between it and other expressions.[59]

It should be noted Lyons is not speaking of the sense relationship a word has to other words *in the context of an utterance* here; he is talking rather of the meaning that any one lexical unit takes by virtue of its relationship to other words with related senses in the language in general. We shall need to give a brief account of the type of sense relationships he envisages before we come back to evaluate this idea of word sense, and of its contribution to the possible elucidation of the New Testament vocabulary.

5.2.3 Types of Sense Relationships Existing Between Words.

There are two basic types, substitutional (usually called paradigmatic) and collocational (usually called syntagmatic).[60] They are not as mysterious as they sound.

5.2.3.1 *Collocational Sense Relations*   Certain combination of words are both appropriate and meaningful in utterances, others are not. We are

happy with 'she ate spaghetti', but not with 'she ate Chianti'. You cannot 'eat' wine. 'Eat' refers to the consumption of solids, wine does not belong to this category—so the horizontal combination (along the 'line' of the sentence), what we call the collocation, is 'wrong'.

The use of a word restricts the possibilities of what may follow; sometimes to a lesser extent ('good' could be followed by a wide variety of nouns and participles), usually to a greater (only certain nouns could fill the blank in 'he smashed his head in with a _____'). A word may even be utterly specific in its collocates: what is 'rancid' other than butter, what can be 'addled' other than eggs (or, figuratively, brains); what licks but a tongue? The point is that there is a sense relation between (e.g.) 'kick' and 'feet' which makes it *inappropriate* to continue an utterance beginning (say) 'he kicked him . . .' by the words 'with his fingers (or 'with his ears')'. There is something to the claim that you can tell the sense of a word from the company it keeps.[61]

W. Porzig[62] has developed a whole field theory of word meaning based on how words tend to govern (and in turn to be modified by) what follows linearly in the sentence. But while collocations are extremely important for determining the sense of expressions (note, for example, how most of the possible senses of the Greek words *pneuma* ['spirit'] and *akathartos'* ['unclean'] are immediately eliminated by the collocation of the two words in *'pneuma akatharton'* ['an unclean spirit'; Mk 3.30, etc.]), and in the initial construction of semantic fields, nevertheless, the study of collocational sense relations has been less productive than that of substitutional relations in the determination of sense relations of words.

5.2.3.2 *Substitutional Sense Relations*[63]

In the sentence, 'Blood began to ooze from the wound', we can imagine the verb as occupying a slot in the sentence, which could have been filled in many different ways. Other verbs lie to hand, like so many rounds of ammunition in the magazine of a gun, waiting to be loaded into the breech. Each of the new verbs we substitute stands in some kind of sense relation to the verb it replaces.

We might substitute 'to seep'. In this instance the substitutional (or paradigmatic) sense relation would be of an overlapping kind which we call *synonymy*—here in fact true contextual synonymy, for there would be no distinguishable difference of meaning in this context.

Alternatively, we might substitute 'to dribble' or 'to trickle'. In this case the relation is still an overlapping sense relation, but now only *'near synonymy'*; for the amount of fluid, and the rate of flow envisaged, is greater, and focus perhaps shifts to movement *away* from the wound, rather than through the wound tissue. Similarly, we might substitute 'to leak'. This too would be a case of near synonymy, for while 'Blood began to leak from the wound' could be used to describe the same event as 'Blood began to seep from the wound', the focused element of meaning is that of *escape* of a fluid, and 'to leak' *could* suggest a faster flow than would be normal of the verb 'to seep' (cf. 'The blood leaked rapidly from the wound').

Or, yet again, we could substitute 'to gush'; this would be an *antonym* for 'to ooze'. 'To ooze' and 'to gush' are not what we call *'binary antonyms'* (i.e. not the kind of opposites we have in 'married' and 'unmarried' or 'true' and 'false'—which apply exclusive of other possibilities and of each other); nor *'converses'* (like 'buy' and 'sell'; 'borrow' and 'lend'; 'parent' and 'child'—in which cases e.g. x sells [to] y, requires y buys [from] x); rather these are *'gradable antonyms'* (like 'love' and 'hate'; 'easy' and 'difficult'); that is, they are at opposite ends of a continuous spectrum of meaning related to movements of liquids.

Or, as a final example, we could substitute 'to run' or 'to pour'. The former would be in near synonymy with 'to trickle', and the latter in near synonymy with 'to gush' (and 'to run' is a near synonym for 'to pour'; the latter suggesting, however, a greater or more rapid volume of flow). But in relation to 'to ooze' or 'to seep' these verbs could only be described as having a *contiguous* sense; that is a relationship of meaning which is quite closely associated ('to ooze' and 'to pour' both describe types of liquid flow), but within this relationship they do not overlap in sense.

All these possibilities stand in substitutional or paradigmatic sense relationships to 'to ooze', and of course we could go on to consider the noun slots; for 'blood' we might substitute 'pus', 'discharge', or 'fluid'. Blood would be in *contiguous* relation to the first, and in *'included'* or *'hyponymous'* relation to the third (that is to say blood belongs to the class 'fluids'; so it stands in the same relation to 'fluid' as 'house' does to 'building'; 'bike' to 'vehicle' and 'machine', 'rose' to 'flower' and both to 'plant', etc.). For 'wound' we could substitute 'sore', 'blister' (standing in contiguous relationship, all being pathological conditions of the body), or a part of the body (*just* contiguous), or even 'ceiling'—a possibility we mention not to be gruesome but as a viable example of a word that would be in *'incompatible'* sense relation with 'wound' (the house of one of the writers had dying rats in the roof).

We may summarize these relationships diagramatically as in figure 4:

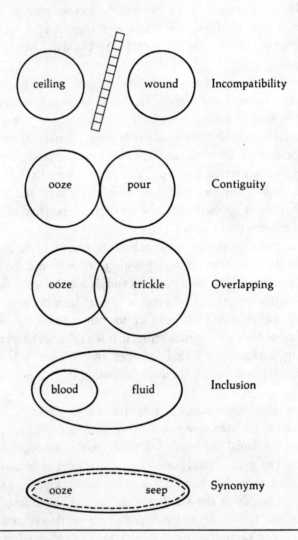

Figure 4.

Of these sense relations, contiguity and synonymy are perhaps the most important. Contiguity we shall deal with later, but a further note on synonymy is advisable as the term is prone to such diverse use.

A Clarifying Note on Synonymy[64]

Absolute synonymy hardly ever occurs (for there is little point in a language retaining two words with exactly the same range of sense, connotations, habitual collocations, and social register). But between absolute synonymy and the phenomenon exemplified above of *near synonymy* (mere overlap of meaning between otherwise distinguishable senses) we may usefully speak of *partial synonymy*. By *partial synonymy* we mean a true identity of meaning between two lexemes in at least *some*, rather than all contexts; or for some of the senses of the lexeme, if not for all.[65] Thus while *absolute* synonymy is very rare, it is common to find two or more lexemes which would communicate virtually the same sense in a given context, or specified range of contexts.

> For example, it is possible to substitute any one of a range of adjectives in a sentence such as 'My father was a fine man', (remarkable, outstanding, admirable, good) and yet still yield approximately the same meaning. It is, perhaps, a danger of exegesis that we tend to demand a precision in the use of words which our everyday experience should tell us is not to be expected, and to find differences in meaning where none is demonstrably intended. A case in point is John 21 and the alternation between two Greek words for "love" in Jesus' questioning of Peter. It is probable that we are right in seeing significance in the three-fold question in vv.15-17, less probable, however, that the change in *word* is significant.

Synonymy is a relationship of identity of *sense* between two linguistic expressions (whether lexical units, lexemes or more complex units). Because lexemes usually have a variety of senses (polysemy), it is to be expected that lexemes may be truly synonymous for one or even several of their senses (partial synonymy), but much less probable that they will be synonyms in all of their senses and habitual collocations. Thus we can say 'profound' is a synonym for 'deep' in: 'You have my deepest sympathy', and in 'We had a deep discussion of Ontology', but would recognize that the words were not synonymous in such contexts as: 'The river was deep'.

Similarly we can use 'ripe' and 'mature' synonymously of, say, tomatoes, but not of people; and 'wide' and 'broad' synonymously of roads, but not of Aberdonian accents. Collocated with 'sympathy', both 'deep' and 'profound' carry their sense "intense", and so are interchangeable. Both words also have the sense "intellectually demanding", and so are again interchangeable as adjectives qualifying 'discussion'. 'Deep' also has the purely spatial sense "extending linearly far down from a surface" (from which, arguably, the others are derived by metaphoric transfer and shift), and this is clearly what is meant when the word is collocated with 'river'; but the word 'profound' does not bear such a sense in English, and so could not be used as a synonym for 'deep' in this context.

Similarly, while in the sentence 'My father was a fine man', 'fine' is synonymous with 'outstanding' or 'remarkable'. Nevertheless in such a sentence as 'There was a fine difference between their positions', substitution of the words 'outstanding' or 'remarkable' would now convey the opposite sense to 'fine', for here 'fine' seems to mean something like "very small", and that is definitely not a sense of either 'remarkable' or 'outstanding'.

It may be alleged, however, by those who maximize homonymy, that this second example does not illustrate another sense of the same word 'fine$_1$', but that of an entirely different lexeme, 'fine$_2$'; in which case all we have shown is that 'fine$_1$' is a synonym for 'admirable', while the quite different word 'fine$_2$' is not (and why should it be?). But we are inclined to the view we have a genuine case of polysemy here: 'fine' has the senses (i) "of superior quality", (ii) "delicate", "exquisitely fashioned", "not coarse" (and hence) "attenuated", and (iii) "admirable". It is sense (ii) that is meant in 'There was a fine difference between their positions', and, as this sense is related (by shift) to (iii), it may reasonably be claimed we have to do with the same lexeme in our two example sentences.

In sum, a word has a range of senses (polysemy). The context of the sentence usually indicates which sense of a particular word is intended. If amongst its range of senses a different lexeme shares the same meaning, it may act as a synonym for the former word in the given context, and in like contexts; that is, it can be substituted for it without significant conceptual change.

Often, even in quite scholarly writings, the terms 'synonym' or 'synonymous' are used when co-referentiality is in fact meant. For example, a recent doctoral dissertation extensively speaks of *pistis* (faith), *logos* (word) and *alētheia* (truth) as 'synonyms' in Paul's writing for *to euangelion* ('the good news'). What the writer meant is that Paul uses the expression *'the* word' (not just 'word'!)—usually additionally qualified by (such constructions as) 'of God', 'of truth', etc.—*interchangeably* with 'the gospel' in certain contexts. But that does not mean the terms are 'synonyms' or even near synonyms: for they do not carry the same *sense* at all, they merely apply simultaneously to the same *referent*. And it is inadvisable to confuse synonymy and co-referentiality. For example, a reporter might refer to Mrs. Thatcher's participation at a public meeting by saying either, 'The Leader of the Conservative Party attended the convention', or, 'The Prime Minister attended the convention'—the terms 'the Leader of the Conservative Party' and 'the Prime Minister' being interchangeable if, say, referring to Mrs Thatcher in 1988, because she was the thing-in-the-world to which both expressions truly referred. The interchangeability here would not, however, imply that 'The Leader of the Conservative Party' should be taken to carry the same *sense* as the expression 'the Prime Minister'. They are co-referential, but not synonymous expressions in these utterances. Similarly with the use of a pronoun to take the place of a noun phrase in a discourse to avoid repetition; that we replace the expression 'the Prime Minister' with 'she' does not mean 'she' is a synonym for 'the Prime Minister'!

5.2.4 'Sense': Concept or Sense Relations?
What we have done to this point, for simplicity, is to consider sense relations between possible substitutions *in single utterances:* it needs to be said that those working with a field-orientated idea of 'sense' are talking about similar sets of relationships between words *in the whole language*, or in some specialized corpus of literature; say, the Pauline epistles. But the principles are sufficiently similar to allow us to return to the question of what we mean by 'sense'.

We have earlier pointed to some of the problems facing concept-orientated definitions of 'sense'. It is often not easy objectively to define our concepts, nor is it easy to decide how much of the concept in question is actually part of the established sense of the word. But difficulties also face a field-orientated definition of sense, which speaks of the sense of a word as its sense relations to other expressions in the language.

Such a definition may have the advantage of affording an objectivity difficult to attain in concept-orientated approaches, for it is relatively easy to decide such questions as, for example, whether or not word *a* is a hyponym, or contiguous with, word *b*. And a field-orientated approach to lexical analysis obviously sharpens our perception of the sense of a word by posing the question of how it is to be distinguished from other closely related words.

Thus 'to stew' is defined in one of the standard concise dictionaries as "to cook . . . by long slow simmering". Corresponding to this, a semantic field analysis would show 'stew' as a hyponym of 'simmer', 'simmer' of 'boil₁' (contrasted with 'steam', 'fry', 'roast', etc.), and this, in turn, of 'cook': see figure 5. But the field analysis will also turn up 'poach' and 'braise' as contiguous hyponyms of simmer, as well as 'boil₂' and 'steam'. This both extends our understanding of the sense 'stew' (by showing that it is related to these other terms) and requires us to sharpen it by distinguishing it from them: e.g. 'poach' means to simmer very gently in water to preserve the food's shape; 'braise' to simmer with a small amount of water in a closed vessel, after first browning, etc.[66]

Furthermore, a field-orientated approach can also help us to analyze what are normally regarded as related senses of the *same word*. The word 'mouth' as used in 'Peter's mouth', 'the squid's mouth', 'the mouth of the cave', 'the mouth of the bottle', and 'the mouth of the river', is usually, and perhaps properly, regarded as one polysemous lexeme—for all the senses are transparently related. But in the last occurrence, the sense could be defined in terms of the following meaning relationships which are not shared with any of the other examples: 'mouth' stands in relation to 'source' as opposites; in part-whole relation with 'river'; as coordinate parts (of river) with 'bed', and as a hypernym of 'estuary'. Indeed this set of sense relations is so distinct that it could be used as an argument for homonymy, rather than polysemy; though it is probably preferable (with Cruse) to speak of the sense relations establishing a *local sense* in the *sense spectrum* of 'mouth'.[67]

But field-orientated approaches to sense are also open to objections. The most important is that theoretically we cannot know the sense of a word until we know all the other words in the associated lexical field, *and* have a rough idea of *their* senses too. This objection was raised with considerable force by Wierzbicka against W. Labov, who, complaining he

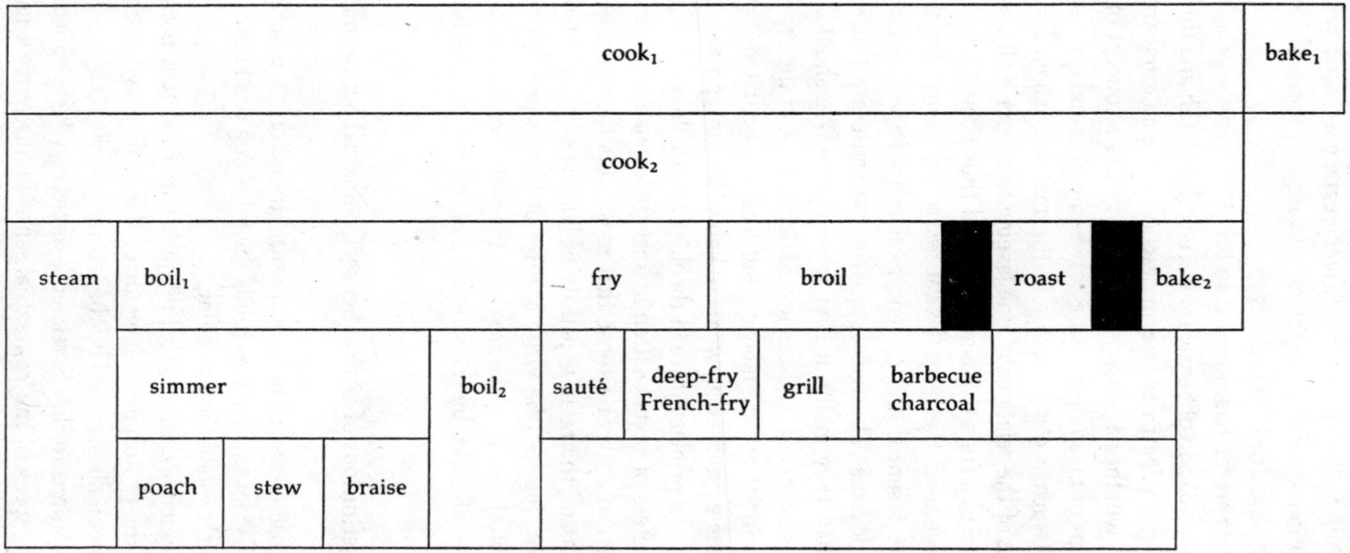

Figure 5. Synonymns appear in the same square. Incompatible terms are separated by vertical lines. Shaded areas indicate overlap. *Grill* is largely subordinate to *broil* (in American English), but there is some overlap with *fry*. The diagram is taken from A. Lehrer, *Semantic Fields & Lexical Structure*, p. 31.

had been struggling to define 'cup' for fifteen years, concluded 'we cannot write a definition of *cup* without taking into account the entire lexical field of containers and drinking utensils'.[68]

The biblical interpreter has no need to arbitrate between these approaches to the elucidation of sense; they are both helpful, and they are clearly complementary. Nor need he, in practice, make an *oversharp* distinction between whether a sense is best analyzed as a concept or as a set of relationships of meaning existing between words and expressions (however crucial such a distinction is in the metalanguage). For any formal statement of the relations of one lexeme to others is also bound to be an abstraction, a cognitive construct, and thus some *kind* of concept. And we have used the term 'lexical *concept*' for verbal definitions incorporating the essential and stereotypical traits *linguistically* bound with use of the lexeme. The two approaches to sense are thus more closely related than they might at first appear to be. We should, nevertheless, perhaps note that field-orientated definitions, of the type that interest the semanticist, are arguably not sufficiently orientated towards the interests of the exegete (who wants to know the conceptual content of word uses) to take primary place in theological lexicology.

As the interpreters of texts written in ancient languages we have to forge an approach to analyzing sense that most suits the materials we are working with and the relative paucity of linguistic data available to us. In the light of this we (the writers) offer at least a pre-theoretical definition that will clarify how we are using the word 'sense', and which we consider to be informed by the strengths of the two approaches we have discussed.

5.2.5 Towards Definitions of Lexical Sense, Contextual Sense and Specialized Sense

We suggest the use of the term 'lexical sense' to indicate a descriptive meaning of a 'full'[69] lexeme such as fulfils the following conditions:

(a) It is a publicly established meaning.

(b) It can be embodied in a verbal definition that includes both the essential and the prototypical elements of the quality, event, object, or concept potentially signified by the lexeme.

(c) Its sense relations to closely related lexemes may be specified.

We may then also speak of the 'contextual sense' or 'discourse sense' of a lexeme or expression. By this we shall signify the descriptive meaning of a lexeme or expression which fulfils the following conditions:

(a) It is the contextually determined descriptive meaning (and both presupposition pools and cotext may be part of the context).

(b) It can be embodied in a verbal definition that includes both the essential and the semantically focused elements of the specific 'token' (or 'type') quality, event, object, or concept actually signified contextually by the lexeme.

(c) Its sense relations both to the lexical sense (whether semantic narrowing or extension or both) and to closely related senses may be specified.

The distinction between lexical and contextual sense is important (and too often overlooked by e.g. the Kittel dictionary), and our definition of the latter allows us to include within its scope special usages, and lexemes that carry a great deal of theological conceptual freight, such as 'baptism', often simply called *technical terms*. It allows us, for example, to avoid both the Scylla of defining the sense of 'baptism' in Col. 2.12 in such minimalist terms as 'Christian initiatory water-rite', and the Charybdis of reading into this occurrence Paul's whole concept of the theological significance of baptism (the sort of error the Kittel dictionary frequently perpetrates). Such a definition as we have proposed invites us to specify, as a contextually focused part of the sense of 'baptism' here, that the rite is assumed to involve a uniting of the believer with Christ such that effects a participation in the Christ event. It is only on such an assumption that Paul's claim that we have been buried with him and raised with him, in baptism, makes sense; so we may regard this element as a semantically focused part of the word usage here. That is, it is baptism *qua an expression of the uniting of the believer with the crucified and risen Lord* that Paul intends here.

Our modified view of the concept-orientated approach to sense also allows for sense relations with other semantically associated lexemes to be recognized as part of the sense of a word or expression. This is not merely the addition to a concept-orientated approach of an alien view of 'sense'; the two approaches are mutually refining. Our understanding of the distinction between cups, glasses, mugs, chalices, and other potential drinking vessels, sharpens our understanding of essential qualities (both characteristic and distinctive) of, say, our concept of 'cup', and so partly determines its descriptive meaning for us. Similarly, our view of the sense of the word *hagios*, 'holy', in the New Testament will depend not merely on some concept(s) of 'holiness' that we might arrive at on the basis of examining all the occurrences of the word (and, hopefully, much else besides) in the New Testament, but also on an analysis of how it differs in sense and usage from the closely related words *hieros, hagnos, hosios, katharos*,[70] etc. (all of which could be translated 'holy' or 'pure'). We shall illustrate this further when we discuss Componential Analysis below.

But mediating between lexical sense and contextual sense there is room for a third term, which we may call specialized sense, which could either be an idiolect sense,[71] or a sense specific to a particular group, arising out of its distinctive interests. Paul's teaching on baptism, righteousness, charismata, etc., will gradually build up in his churches generally accepted senses of the respective words which are neither lexical senses (for they are not yet sufficiently widely established to be labelled such), nor are they purely Paul's personal usages, or special discourse senses, because they have become part of the general linguistic usage of the Pauline congregations. Specialized senses are not widely established, but common to an individual (in which case they are idiolect senses) or to a particular minority group (e.g. the Church, or particular congregations). Some lexemes no doubt developed specialized senses common to virtually the whole of the apostolic Church (e.g. 'the saints' as a term for Christians). Many more were developed in senses that became specific to particular circles of Christians, and may not have been common in other apostolic churches (e.g. John's use of 'eternal life' to designate our *present* experience in Christ of the type of life which belongs to the age to come [5.24; 17.3, etc.]).

It is because of the twin phenomena of innovative discourse senses and specialized senses that biblical scholars are rightly cautious of explaining the sense of a word in Paul by the sense of the 'same' word in John or Luke. Only usual lexical senses are liable to be held in common. Similarly with more complex expressions; thus when Paul uses the expression 'to receive the Spirit' the sense of his expression may be extrapolated from a careful analysis of his teaching about the function of the Spirit. To 'receive the Spirit' is to begin to experience the Spirit as the presence of new covenant life (cf.2 Cor. 3), as the eschatological Spirit giving us a first instalment of resurrection life (2 Cor. 1; 1 Cor. 15; Rom. 8), and as the Spirit *of Christ* (Rom. 8.9ff)—i.e. both as the Spirit mediating the presence of Christ and as the Spirit recreating in us Christ's nature and filial relationship to God (Rom. 8.15, Gal. 4.4- 6). When Luke speaks of 'receiving the Spirit' he means the inauguration in a man of a Christianized version of the gift of the Spirit promised by Joel (cf. Acts 2.14-39), i.e. the organ of (usually charismatically expressed) communication and revelation between the disciples and the Father or the risen Lord. As a result the senses of 'receive the Spirit' in the respective communities are complementary, and indeed overlap significantly, at a deep level, but they are *not simply the same.*[72]

5.2.6 Relating Senses to Semantic Domains: Introducing the UBS *Greek New Testament Wordbook*

We have already pointed out some of the difficulties that lie in wait for those who try to lump all the senses of a word under some general idea, ignoring both homonymy and polysemy (see 5.1.3). The fact is that words like 'dribble', 'trickle', 'pour', 'gush', 'spurt' are *closer in sense* to the word 'run', in a sentence like 'You left the tap running', than any of the other senses of the (phonological) word 'run' itself are. This phenomenon would be explained by some semanticists primarily in terms of the verb 'run' in this sentence belonging to the semantic domain of words describing movements of liquid masses.[73] Whereas the homonym 'run' in 'he ran the business efficiently' belongs to the semantic domain of words describing organization of function (with 'supervise', 'control', 'manage', 'operate', etc.), and further senses of 'to run' belonging to yet different semantic domains.

A new dictionary of the Greek New Testament due to be published by the United Bible Society will present the different senses of each word classified in its appropriate semantic domain. On looking up *pneuma*, instead of being given a list of possible English translation equivalents like *movement of air, wind, breath, spirit, disposition, influence, frame of mind, emotion, desire, spirit, ghost, Holy Spirit, God's Spirit*, the user will be directed to the relevant semantic domains: e.g.[74]

a) supernatural being—Holy Spirit—879

b) supernatural being—ghost—899

c) psychological event—inner self—9102

d) physical event—wind—2164

e) physiological event—breath—3386 etc.

(figures refer to subdivisions of the lexicon)

The reader will then find occasions where *pneuma* is used in the New Testament with a sense belonging to domain (d) discussed (at section 2164) alongside other terms for different kinds of movement of air, e.g. the near synonyms *anemos* and *pnoē*, and *pneō* 'to blow', etc. Their common and contrasting features will be compared.

Similarly (or so we are led to assume from advance descriptions of the work) where *pneuma* is used of 'spiritual beings' of one type or another the reader will find these uses discussed under domain (b), along with other terms like *angelos* ('angel'), *exousiai* ('powers'), *stoicheia* ('elemental spirits'[?]), *phantasma* ('apparition'), *daimonion* ('demon'), etc., once again with an indication of common and contrasting components of meaning, and an analysis of their sense relations.

And in subdivisions of domain (c) we should expect an account of the relation of *pneuma* to other so-called anthropological terms such as *kardia* ('heart'—when this is used as seat of will, intuition or thought; not when used as a physical organ: that sense of 'heart' would be treated along with the domain of words for organic parts of the body), *nous* ('mind'), *psychē* ('soul'—as in 'Love the Lord . . . with your whole . . . soul'), etc., as well as a discussion of the varieties of use of *pneuma* denoting 'inner influences' e.g. in such constructions as 'a proud spirit', a 'spirit of gentleness', 'a quiet spirit' (1 Pet. 3.4 = a quiet disposition), and the like. *The different senses of a single phonological word (which may include several distinct lexemes each with a plurality of lexical units) are a function of the different semantic domains in relation to which the word is used.*

It will be obvious to the reader to what extent such a dictionary is governed by a field-orientated concept of sense; lexemes being treated according to the domains of meaning to which they belong, and in comparison and contrast with other lexemes in the same domain.[75] This new approach to New Testament lexicography can only help us to sharpen our understanding of the senses of New Testament words. Of course the user will still have to be wary. The different domains to which the word *pneuma* may potentially belong can be determined relatively objectively using syntagmatic field analysis (to find out what words *pneuma* regularly collocates with) and paradigmatic field analysis (to find out what words might be substituted for it). Thus if we find that *pneuma* regularly collocates with Greek verbs for 'to gust' or 'to blow', and that other Greek words such as those for 'wind', 'breeze', etc. tend to substitute for *pneuma* with the same verbs (or in similar collocations), then we can be sure that *pneuma* (in *one* of its senses) belongs to the domain of what Louw and his colleagues call 'physical events'.

But we can be a little *less* certain that the editor of the Wordbook and his colleagues have necessarily successfully identified the domain to which any *specific New Testament occurrence* of the word *pneuma* belongs: for that will involve a considerable element of *interpretation*, not merely objective analysis.

It may be hoped, nevertheless, that the advent of the Wordbook, and its use by students, will increase the awareness of the sharp differences that often exist between different senses of what, at first sight, appears to be a single word. The frequently expressed desire for 'literal' translations—i.e. ones which attempt to translate a single Greek word consistently with the same English word, so always translating e.g. *sarx* as 'flesh'—appears especially misguided in the light of semantic domain analysis. No doubt the desire for such a translation is fuelled by the belief that somehow all the senses of *sarx must* belong mysteriously together. This is in a sense yet another form of the misunderstanding of homonymy and polysemy. The recognition that different senses of a (phonological) word often belong to entirely different semantic domains heightens our awareness of the *radical difference* of the senses that might be associated with a single lexical form.

For example, *sarx* (or the English 'flesh', the senses of which owe much to translations of the Greek New Testament) has the sense 'bodily tissue covering the bones'. By synecdoche (the use of a lexeme denoting a part to denote the whole instead) it came to mean 'body', and we are still in the same semantic domain (body and bodily parts). When, however, it is used in such expressions as 'The Lord . . . of all flesh' the word means 'human and animal creatures', 'natural beings', and is now a generic term belonging with words designating the semantic domain of natural animate entities. In the use in Luke 3.6 and parallels—'all flesh shall see the salvation of the Lord'—*sarx* is used to mean 'people' (cf. also John 17.2; Acts 2.17, etc.), and stands alongside such lexemes as 'mankind', 'humanity', 'man'. Here 'flesh' stands in much closer relation of meaning to these *different* words than it does to 'flesh' meaning "body tissue".

Different again is Rom. 11.14, where those who press for a 'literal' translation would have to render Paul 'in order to make *my flesh* jealous, and thus save some of them'. Here *sarx* is an example of terms belonging to the semantic domain of kinship; it goes together with words like 'generation', 'relatives', 'tribe', 'family', 'race', 'nation' (so RSV appropriately translates 'in order to make *my fellow Jews* jealous'), and belongs with them much more closely in sense than it does with the word 'flesh' meaning "bodily tissue or parts".

Quite differently again, John 1.13 speaks of birth 'of the will of the *sarx*'. The word 'flesh' now belongs to the domain of abstracts of quality, contributing the sense 'natural sexual' (in an ethically neutral sense). In sharp contrast, when Paul warns against *ta erga tēs sarkos* in Gal. 5.19, much of the list of so-called 'works of the flesh' which follow have nothing to do with sex at all, nor even anything necessarily to do with the body: the idolatry, witchcraft, hatred, discord, jealousy, selfish ambition, dissensions, factions and envy, which are instanced, could all presumably be cheerfully indulged in by disembodied spirits! *Sarx* here means 'sinful nature', and it belongs with 'spirit', 'inner influence', 'disposition' to the general domain of what Nida and Louw mean by 'psychological events' (though it should be borne in mind that the word 'event' here is being used in a semitechnical way). *There is no parallel sense in English usage of the word 'flesh' to correspond to Paul's usage of sarx here.* In English, 'flesh' does not denote the source of such activities as 'witchcraft' and 'envy'; of 'debauchery' and 'adultery' perhaps, but not of 'idolatry'. So RSV (and others) are *simply misleading* to translate *ta erga tēs sarkos* by 'works of the flesh'. And NIV (and others) are arguably *right* here to translate *sarx* by 'sinful nature'; and NEB *perhaps* right to translate 'lower nature', as long as this is not taken to mean purely "sensuous", "sexual" or "bodily" nature, but to mean "lower nature" in the sense of "man in rebellion against God".[76]

5.2.7 Distinguishing Related Senses of a Single Lexeme or of Related Lexemes: Componential Analysis

Componential analysis grew out of the conviction that 'senses' are rather like molecules; they are built out of smaller universal 'atomic' concepts. On such a view the sense "boy" is composed of the 'atomic' concepts HUMAN, MALE, and NON-ADULT all combined together;

similarly "chair" is allegedly a combination of such atomic concepts as FOR SITTING ON, WITH LEGS, WITH BACK, FOR ONE PERSON. An obvious advantage of the analysis is that it allows a ready explanation of the sense relations between related words—these can be elucidated in terms of their shared and distinctive atomic concepts. The domain of terminology for human beings includes, for example, 'man', 'woman', 'boy', and 'girl'. The sense relations of the words in this field could be regarded as specified in their shared and distinctive atomic concepts, represented in figure 6.

	human	male	adult
man	+	+	+
woman	+	-	+
boy	+	+	-
girl	+	-	-

Figure 6.

And componential analysis can easily be expanded to give an account of the meaning of whole sentences. As a philosophical explanation of meaning (whether simply meaning of words, or meaning of more complex units), however, the whole approach is controversial; it is not clear that the so-called atomic concepts are indeed universals, and the system suggests a rigidity which is not empirically confirmed (after the Greeks, for example, we call Cupid a 'boy', but is HUMAN then an essential component of the word for it to make sense?).[77]

But while componential analysis is perhaps inadequate as an exhaustive *theory* of meaning, a modified form of it—especially as developed by Eugene Nida[78]—has proved most useful *in practice*. It is useful both for analyzing the focal or prototypical meaning of a word like 'boy' (rather than its peripheral senses, as e.g. in application to Cupid!), and even more important it is useful for analyzing related senses of words to see what they have in common and what differentiates them.

For example, for furniture used for seating we might compose a grid as in figure 7.

	1	2	3	4	5	6
chair	+	+	+	-	+	-
sofa	-	+	+/-	+	+	+
armchair	+	+	(-)	+	+	+
stool	+	-	+	-	+	-
bench	-	(-)	+	(-)	+	-
pew	-	+	+	(-)	+	-
pouffe	+	-	-	-	-	+

Where 1 = For seating one person, versus more than one person

      2 = With back

      3 = With legs

      4 = With arms

      5 = With hard frame

      6 = With full, versus minimal or no cushioning

Figure 7.

Three points require comment. Firstly, it must be emphasized that componential analysis is usually related to components of *prototypical* objects of analysis. We can envisage both stools with backs, and pews with arms, but these are not features of a prototype stool or pew; they do not fall within the focal extension of the words, only within the peripheral and atypical features. This distinction is important, and we should always be prepared to say whether what we label a component of a sense of some word is actually essential to the meaning of the word, or whether it is rather prototypical of it, or merely peripheral to it.

Secondly, it should be obvious that the whole form of analysis owes much to field theories of sense (though not all field theorists approve of it). It is a useful tool within such an approach for sharpening our awareness of the components within a 'sense', and of how other words share some of these components, but differ precisely by not sharing the full combination of components (except in full synonymy), having, rather, some *contrasting* components.

Thirdly, it will be clear that no claim is being made that the components of meaning used to compare and contrast the different forms of seating are in any sense the 'atomic concepts' of a more philosophical theory of meaning: few indeed would be prepared to support the admission of such elements as (1) and (6) into a inventory of universal primes! The component (6) has been included in the grid for a purely pragmatic reason, namely its power as a distinguishing factor. Here, then, we have a componential analysis that is tailored to the task of elucidating the contrasts of sense between related terms, rather than attempting to provide the grounds for a more wide-ranging theory of meaning.

The approach has been reapplied in substantially different fashion by V. S. Poythress[79] to the holiness word group. Poythress offers a set of contrasting components of four key words belonging to the holiness domain in the NT period (figure 8).

Whereas all the pluses in the line for 'chair' indicated components that would be expected to be present in a chair, whether essentially or prototypically, this does not follow for Poythress's analysis of *hagios*. When *hagios* is used to denote cultic purity (corresponding to the plus in column 1), areas of meaning 2, 3, and 5 are usually excluded from the sense (despite the pluses in their respective columns). In other words, the vertical columns do not correspond to sense components which can be added together horizontally. *Hagios* does not denote a type of holiness that is cultic + moral + related to God + consecration, though on any one context it may comprise one or more of these elements, and this distinguishes the use of *hagios* from that of *hosios*, which has no cultic sense, and *hieros*, which has no moral sense.

Both types of componential analysis can be expected to yield useful results, though that which strictly analyses the essential and prototypical components of a single sense, and compares it with related senses of other words, is potentially more useful than Poythress's approach,[80]

	1	2	3	4	5	6
hagios	+	+	+	-	-	+
hagnos	?	+	+/-	?	+	+
hieros	+	-	+	-	-	-
hosios	-	+	+	+	-	-

1 = Can denote *cultic* 'holiness'

2 = Can denote positive moral-ethical quality

3 = When used of men can designate the quality of a man's relationship to God

4 = Can denote positive quality of man's relation to other men

5 = Can denote positive quality in relation to self, viz. individual integrity, purity

6 = Connotes consecration or setting apart from ordinary sphere

---

Figure 8.

which examines rather the plurality of potentially relevant aspects of a sense, and explains different collocational distributions. The former works especially well where we are dealing with *contiguous* (related, but not overlapping) senses, and the problem Poythress has is that he is attempting to analyze words which are not contiguously related but *partial synonyms*. Poythress's point, of course, is that *hagios* has usurped the ancient use of *hieros* and become a catch-all word that has to be used to cover all instances where one wants to designate an item as 'sacred', 'consecrated' or 'set apart for God's service'. Its 'sense' is correspondingly lacking in specificity. This does not mean, for Poythress, that we cannot determine, say, Paul's *concept* of holiness—he himself provides just such an account, and one that is both ground-breaking and painstakingly careful in methodology—but it does mean that Paul's concept cannot be read off an examination of the *words* 'holy', 'holiness' or 'sanctify'.

THE GRAMMAR OF WORDS: LEXICAL SEMANTICS

5.2.8 Concluding Comments

We have probably said enough in this long section to warn the student against cowboy approaches to word study. An adequate description of how one *should* go about the enterprise would itself require a full volume, and so is beyond our ability to provide in the allotted space. We hope the reader will remember that we have dealt so far only with descriptive meanings, and have made no attempt to deal with emotive or 'affective' language (on which see below, 9.2). The sense of 'rat', when applied as an emotive term to someone who has let us down, is less susceptible of the types of analysis we have introduced. We have attempted only to indicate some of the major features of modern linguistics-orientated approaches to word meaning—largely ignoring the more complicated question of special collocations (like 'the Holy Spirit'). Our hope is that the reader will have learned enough to begin to understand how words relate to 'meanings' in language, and to be able to go on to study with profit the works of Biblical lexicology that are beginning to emerge.[81]

5.3 CONTEXT AND THE CHOICE OF SENSES

Whereas most words are polysemous, it cannot be emphasized too strongly that this should not be taken to mean that a word is normally capable of a full range of meanings in its use in any one utterance. The context of the utterance usually singles out (and perhaps modulates[82]) the *one* sense, which is intended, from amongst the various senses of which the word is potentially capable. Of course occasionally we come across accidental, or even deliberate, ambiguity;[83] and occasionally we get deliberate *double entendre*, or word-play as in the familiar pun (for example the use of *pneuma* in John 3.8 to denote both 'wind' and 'the Spirit'). But these are the exception, not the rule. They are more common to some genres of literature than to others (to poetry more than to prose narrative) and there are usually contextual markers for what is happening (cf. the 'in the same way' of John 3.8b). When an interpreter tells us his author could be using such-and-such a word with sense *a*, or he could be using it with sense *b*, and then sits on the fence claiming perhaps the author means *both*, we should not too easily be discouraged from the suspicion that the interpreter is simply fudging the exegesis. He may of course be right, but while *we* may *often* not be sure which of several possible meanings an author intends, it is less regularly the case that *the author himself* was uncertain. Often more patient exegesis resolves what at first appears to be an ambiguity.

Thus in one commentary (chosen at random) on 1 Thess. 4.17—'We who are alive . . . shall be caught up *(harpazein)* together with them in the clouds to meet the Lord'—the interpreter informs his readers that the verb *harpazein* here means "to catch away speedily"; "to seize by force"; "to claim for oneself"; "to move to a new place"; and "to rescue from danger". All the senses are regarded as applicable. Now perhaps *harpazein* can mean all these things in appropriate contexts. And perhaps Paul believed all those things might be fulfilled at the Parousia. But *here*, i.e. in this sentence, it is difficult to see how Paul could mean all these things simultaneously. He appears to mean the first ("to catch away"), and the first only. The rest do not easily make sense, as an attempt to substitute them in Paul's sentence will make clear.

The Greek word *kosmos* is used with the following senses (amongst others):

1) the whole created universe: earth, heavens, heavenly bodies, etc.,

2) "earth" as opposed to heaven, or the heavens,

3) "mankind"; i.e. the 'world' of people,

4) the condition of mortal life; 'life in the world',

5) the beings (human and supernatural) in rebellion against God, together with the systems under their control, viewed as opposed to God,

6) the system of earthly and social structures (including its joys, possessions, and cares),

7) "adornment" or "adorning".

It is difficult to see that more than one of these senses is viable in any of the following relatively typical utterances:

(a) 'God so loved the *kosmos* that he gave his only Son that whoever believes in him shall not perish.' (John 3.16)

(b) 'Do not love the *kosmos* or the things in the *kosmos*. If anyone loves the *kosmos*, love of the Father is not in him.' (1 John 2.15f)

(c) 'Your beauty should not come from outward *kosmos*, such as braided hair.' (1 Pet. 3.3)

(d) 'Now, Father, glorify me in your presence with the glory I had with you before the *kosmos* was.' (John 17.5)

(e) 'and those who use the *kosmos* as though they were not engrossed in it.' (1 Cor. 7.31)

(f) 'We brought nothing into the *kosmos*, and we can take nothing out of it.' (1 Tim. 6.7)

For some of these there is little if any room for doubt. In the case of the utterance in 1 Pet 3.3, *kosmos* can only mean "adorning" (i.e. [7]), and none of the other senses is credible. It is likewise difficult to see how *kosmos* in 1 Cor 7.31 could denote other than the system of earthly and social structures (i.e. [6], as the broader context confirms). Only slightly more difficult is John 17.5: taken out of the Johannine context it could be jostled to fit most of the senses (1) to (7). But as part of John's Gospel, the utterance is bound to be read in the light of e.g. 1.1-14, where the Word is the cosmic creator. It must therefore be sense (1) that is intended; and once that is accepted the other senses become redundant. Similarly, 1 Tim. 6.7 denotes the condition of mortal existence (i.e. [4]) marked by its entry at birth and exit at death; the utterance would be transparently untrue if sense (6) were meant (we *do* contribute to the social world, and take things out of it), and the rest make only awkward sense if any (though a Gnostic could perhaps accept senses [1] or [2]).

We are left with the first two (Johannine) sentences. Arguably, these are only saved from blatant contradiction by the assumption that two *different* senses of the word *kosmos* are intended. For 1 John 2.15 we might be tempted to think *kosmos* means (6), in which case we shall think the warning is an injunction to asceticism. But in the broader context of John's usage this is seen to be improbable; and what is not to be 'loved' (and the examples are given in v. 16) is the cravings, lust and pride which mark the people and institutions belonging to the 'prince of this world' (cf. John 12.31; 16.11), and so constitute 'the world' (cf. 1 John 4.5; 5.19) which opposes what the believer stands for. So the sense of *kosmos* intended here is (5); and the readers are enjoined not to 'love' this world in the sense that they are not to desire to be part of it, moulded by its hostility to God's will.[84]

John 3.16 is possibly the most ambiguous of the uses of *kosmos*; and the interpreter is liable to be torn between (3) and (5)—other senses being excluded by the fact that the 'world' here is clearly one of *people* (for only people can 'believe'). There are clear contextual markers that the 'world' in view is one that needs saving, and that might predispose us to opt for sense (5). But later John distinguishes between those, on the one hand, 'who *shall* believe' and those, on the other, who are '*of* the world', and who may even simply be called 'the world'; Jesus prays for the former, but *not* for the latter, in 17.20 and 17.9 respectively. This suggests that it is not John's intention to affirm that God loves the world when this is viewed specifically in the sense of an order in rebellion against him, and so a more neutral sense of 'world' is perhaps required in Jn 3.16—favouring (3).

Six examples do not even begin to establish a case; but they could be multiplied many times over, and here they are simply given as typical examples of what would appear to be a more general rule. That is that, in any utterance, each occasion of a word will *normally* only carry one of its possible senses, and that sense is the one determined by the linguistic and extra-linguistic context.

5.4 SUMMARY OF IMPLICATIONS OF LEXICAL SEMANTICS FOR THEOLOGICAL WORD STUDIES

As this has been a long chapter it may be worth our while to draw the strands together in the form of some guidelines for exegetical practice.

5.4.1

Word formation and etymology *may* guide the reader to the meaning of the word, but cannot be counted on so to do. Words are not always transparently related in meaning to the blocks from which they have been built: lexical forms are liable to acquire a range of new senses through innovative usage, and senses that were once the usual meaning may become obsolete. Only word studies based on a *synchronic* analysis of the language should be allowed to inform interpretation; that is, only a study of the senses of a word known to be current at the time of the writing of a discourse is of primary relevance to its interpretation.

5.4.2

Usually a lexical form (that is, the abstract phonological or graphic form [e.g.] *run* [together with its purely inflectional variants, *runs*, etc.]) has *several* senses—either because we have a plurality of lexemes with the same form ('run$_1$', 'run$_2$', etc.—i.e. homonymy) or because we have lexemes with multiple senses (polysemy), or both. The different senses associated with any single lexical form enter the the history of the language at different stages, and are liable to evolve separately when they do. The attempt to give the words sharing a common lexical form a 'basic' sense which is then made to account for all the other senses of words with the same lexical form is to be resisted. In cases of homonyms there may be no shared component of meaning. In instances of polysemy there is usually *some* component of meaning shared between a number of the senses, but it is not always the case that every sense of the word shares a single common component of meaning, far less that it is a *central* component of meaning.

Different words sharing a common lexical form may actually be more closely related in meaning to words with an entirely different lexical form than they are to words having the same lexical form. Thus among the words sharing the lexical form *run*, one (let us say 'run₁') is more closely related in sense to words with the entirely different forms *trickle* and *dribble* than it is to another word with the same form *run*—for example, the word 'run₂', meaning "to manage (e.g. a business)". We must allow for the full diversity of senses that might be associated with any one form (not try to lump them together) and for the fact that the different senses will probably belong to entirely different semantic fields or domains.

5.4.3

Given the last two points it should be clear that if we wish to establish (for example) that it would be natural for Paul to use the word *stoicheia*, to denote certain planetary powers, we have to show not merely that the lexical *form stoicheion* was current, but that there was already current a lexeme which combined the lexical form *stoicheion* with the required *sense* "elemental spirit". In other words we have to show that "elemental spirit" (or the like) was a lexical sense of the form *stoicheion in Paul's day*.

5.4.4

As a rule of thumb we should recognize that, in any one context, a word will only carry *one* of its possible senses; the question of which single meaning is the most appropriate to the context is what needs to be settled. Deliberate *double-entendre* is relatively rare, and preferably only to be invoked when there are clear markers of it.

5.4.5

The sense of a word is a discrete bundle of meaning, the content of which may be clarified using two approaches.

(1) An attempt may be made to compare and contrast the sense of the word in question with other words with related senses. Thus our view of what *hagios* ('holy') means will depend in part on what relations of meaning it contracts with other words like *katharos* ('clean'), *agathos* ('good'), *euprosdektos* ('acceptable'), as well as with its near synonyms *hosios*, *hieros*, and the like. *Ideally* we would plot the lexical and semantic fields of each word, but it cannot be pretended that the task is an easy one, and it must be left to those who have both the competence and the necessary time.

(2) An attempt may be made to define the concept lexicalized. *Ideally* one would attempt to stipulate what features were *essential* to the sense, and further, what components would be regarded as belonging to a *typical* member of the class of thing denoted. At all times, however, care would need to be taken to avoid the danger of including within the lexical concept features which are not *linguistically* tied to it, but are merely *part* of the *discourse concept* in question (or even merely associated with its *referent):* how much of what Paul has to say about Jesus as the 'Son of God' is properly part of the sense of 'the Son of God' either (a) for Paul himself or (b) for his readers?

5.4.6

In the light of the distinction just made between lexical senses and discourse concepts, it is not unlikely that many interpreters will conclude that it is actually the broader *discourse concepts,* rather than the lexical, contextual or specialized *word senses,* with which they are primarily concerned! In that case they will still need to attempt to define the essential and prototypical elements of the concept which they seek to elucidate, but now they will have to cast the net more widely. For the concept of, say, 'Christian love' cannot be determined merely by looking up 'love' in a concordance and examining the relevant passages. The concept may well be elucidated in passages that do not use the *word* 'love' at all; but use other expressions to refer to the same reality, or do not actually explicitly refer to the reality at all, merely (in the context of another discussion) offer what may be considered examples of it. Concept analysis is undoubtedly more significant for theology than word study, even if it is also as difficult to execute, if not more so. But it is beyond the scope both of this chapter on word *sense*, and of this book introducing aspects of the linguistic semantics of exegesis.

Notes

[1] Good introductions are available in J. P. Louw, *The Semantics of New Testament Greek*, Philadelphia, Fortress, 1982, pp.23-66; J. R. Hurford and B. Heasley, *Semantics: A Coursebook*, chaps. 3 and 5; M. Silva, *Biblical Words and their Meaning*, pp.101-36; C. R. Taber, *IDB* (Supplementary volume) pp.800-4; A. C. Thiselton, 'Semantics and New Testament Interpretation' in I. H. Marshall (ed.), *New Testament Interpretation*, pp.78-93, and L. Zgusta, *Manual of Lexicography*, pp.1-118. For a fuller account see especially E. A. Nida, *Componential Analysis of Meaning*, The Hague, Mouton, 1975 passim, and, above all, D. A. Cruse, *Lexical Semantics*, Cambridge, CUP, 1986.

[2] Cf. especially de Saussure, *Course in General Linguistics*, pp.67ff.

[3] For a very simple introduction to English word formation see e.g. J. R. Hurford and B. Heasley, *Semantics: A Coursebook*, p.19; in more detail, however, see V. Adams, *An Introduction to Modern English Word-Formation*, London, Longmans, 1973 (p.33 for the example just given) or L. Bauer, *English Word-Formation*, Cambridge, CUP, 1983.

[4] For a brief account of semantic constituents and indicators in compound words see D. Cruse, *Lexical Semantics*, Cambridge, CUP, 1986, pp.22-40.

[5] J. Lyons, *Language and Linguistics*, Cambridge, CUP, 1981, p.145, and D. A. Cruse, *Lexical Semantics*, Cambridge, CUP, 1986, 2.7 and 2.9.

[6] See B. Metzger, *Lexical Aids for Students of New Testament Greek*, Princeton, 1971, M. Stehle, *Greek Word-Building*, Missoula, Scholars Press, 1976, and J. H. Moulton, *A Grammar of New Testament Greek*, Edinburgh, T. and T. Clark, 1920, vol. 2, pp. 267-410.

[7] See R. A. Waldron, *Sense and Sense Development*, London, Deutsch, 1979[2], p.186, for the definition of metonymy offered; and for a fuller discussion of the nature and reasons for lexical change see S. Ullmann, *Semantics: An Introduction to the Science of Meaning*, Oxford, Blackwell, chap. 9, and R. A. Waldron, *Sense and Sense Development*, part II. For the reasons for such changes in the Biblical languages see e.g. G. B. Caird, *The Language and Imagery of the Bible*, pp.62-84; M. Silva, *Biblical Words and their Meaning*, pp.53-97.

[8] No one has made the above points more clearly than de Saussure, *Course in General Linguistics*, part 1, chaps.3, 6-8, and the whole of parts 2 and 3.

[9] See further, M. M. B. Turner, 'Spirit Endowment in Luke-Acts: Some Linguistic Considerations', *Vox Evangelica* 12 (1981), pp.50-3.

10The most recent repetition of this, of which we are aware, is to be found in D. Prior, *The Message of 1 Corinthians*, Leicester, IVP, 1985, p.62.

11See J. Louw, *Semantics of New Testament Greek*, p.26f.

12In addition to Barr (as above) see e.g. J. Louw, *Semantics of New Testament Greek*, chap. 4, and D. A. Carson, *Exegetical Fallacies*, Grand Rapids, Baker, 1984, pp.26-32.

13So it has been argued by K. Hemphill, *The Pauline Concept of Charisma*, unpublished Ph.D. dissertation, Cambridge 1976, chap. 3.

14D. Prior, *The Message of 1 Corinthians*, pp.221-3.

15For these examples thanks are due to D. A. Carson, *Exegetical Fallacies*, p.32f.

16See e.g. the careful summaries of the evidence in the commentaries by E. Lohmeyer or P. T. O'Brien.

17For elementary accounts of polysemy and homonymy see R. Kempson, *Semantic Theory*, Cambridge, CUP, 1977, pp.79-83; G. N. Leech, *Semantics*, Harmondsworth, Penguin, 1981[2], pp.227-9; J. Lyons, *Language and Linguistics*, pp.146-8, and *Language, Meaning and Context*, London, Fontana, 1981, pp.19-22 and 42-5. For fuller treatment see J. Lyons, *Semantics*, Cambridge, CUP, 1977, pp. 550-69.

18For this definition see D. A. Cruse, *Lexical Semantics*, pp. 76-80; for the distinction between Cruse's use and that of Kempson and Lyons (differently) see ibid., p. 81.

19On the problems of 'basic' or 'core' meanings to account for the variety of senses see Zgusta, *Manual of Lexicography*, pp.64ff., and e.g. J. P. Louw, *Semantics of New Testament Greek*, pp.33-7.

20For an analysis of 'run' into different semantic domains see E. Nida, *Componential Analysis of Meaning*, The Hague, Mouton, 1975, pp.138-50, and compare the discussion of homonymy and polysemy of 'run' in R. M. Kempson, *Semantic Theory*, Cambridge, CUP, 1977, pp.80-3. For an explanation of semantic domains see further at 5.2.6.

21See Louw, ibid., p.51 and G. B. Caird, *The Language and Imagery of the Bible*, pp. 64-8.

22P. G. W. Glare, 'Liddell and Scott: Its Background and Present State' in R. Burchfield (ed.), *Studies in Lexicography*, Oxford: Clarendon, 1987, p.13.

23Similarly Louw, *Semantics of New Testament Greek*, p.53f., complains against Bauer's lexicon that while the sense "to lie before, be present, be set before" is appropriate to *prokeimai*, the sense "be exposed to public view, be exhibited", at Aeschylus *Septem* 965 and *Jude* 7, is merely a contextual entailment in those discourses, not part of the sense of *prokeimai* itself.

24For example, as J. J. Meuzelaar, *Der Leib des Messias: eine exegetische Studie über den Gedanken vom Leib Christi in den Paulusbriefen*, Assen, Van Gorcum, 1961, p.122, observed, here, as in Eph. 4.16, the words '*from whom*' are masculine (agreeing with an assumed 'Christ'), not feminine, in agreement with *kephalē*, requiring the translation *'from which'*. The 'body' is thus not precisely said to grow from the 'head'—suggesting 'head' means "origin" or "source"—but from the one who is the Head (and we are free to take this as 'the Lord').

[25]For documentation see W. Grudem, 'Does *Kephalē* ("Head") Mean "Source" or "Authority Over" in Greek Literature? A Survey of 2,336 Examples', *Trinity Journal* 6 (1985), pp.38-59, p.39f.

[26]D. Prior, *The Message of 1 Corinthians*, p.181.

[27]See e.g. Philo, *Life of Moses* 2.30; *On Rewards and Punishments* 1.25; Plutarch *Cicero*, 14.4; *Galba* 4.3; and *Table Talk* 7.7 for the clearest examples; these and others (less clear) are dealt with in Grudem, ibid., p.55f.

[28]Undeniably at Judges 10.18; 11.8, 9, 11; 2 Kings (= 2 Sam.) 22.44; 3 Kings 8.1; Ps. 17 (18).43; Isa. 7.8,9; Lam. 1.5 and cf. *Test Reuben* 2.2.

[29]S. Bedale, 'The Meaning of *Kephalē* in the Pauline Epistles' *JTS* 5 (1954) pp.211-5.

[30]But even here it may simply mean the river divided into four 'heads' (= tops of river; *rosh* often has the sense 'top'), rather than 'sources' in the sense of that from which something comes. *BDB* does not list 'source' as a sense of *rosh* at all.

[31]C. K. Barrett, *The First Epistle to the Corinthians*, London, Black, 1971, p.248.

[32]G. D. Fee, *The First Epistle to the Corinthians*, Grand Rapids, Eerdmans, 1987, pp.503f.

[33]See the discussion by Grudem, 'Does *kephalē* Mean "Source" or "Authority Over"?', pp.45f., though note the criticism of P. B. Payne in A. Mickelsen (ed.), *Women, Authority and the Bible*, Downers Grove, InterVarsity Press, 118-32.

[34]P. B. Payne in A. Mickelsen (ed.), *Women, Authority and the Bible*, pp. 118-32.

[35]G. D. Fee, *The First Epistle to the Corinthians*, pp.502f.

[36]*Congr. qu. er. gratia* 61.

[37]*De praemiis*, 125.

[38]For the evidence for this see C. Kroeger, 'The Classical Concept of "Head" as "Source" ' in G. G. Hull (ed.), *Serving Together: A Biblical Study of Human Relationships*, New York, 1987, pp.97-110. We have had available to us only a prepublication draft of this paper.

[39]See Grudem, 'Does *kephalē* Mean "Source" or "Authority Over"?', pp.54ff. In Philo see *de Somniis* 2.207; *de Vita Mosis* 2.30 (cf. 2.82); in Plutarch see especially *Table Talk* 7.7, but such usage goes back to Herodotus (7.148.17) and Plato, *Timaeus* 44D.

[40]For a succinct account of connotative and affective meaning see G. Leech, *Semantics*, chaps. 2 and 4.

[41]So the *New Collins Concise English Dictionary*. One-language dictionaries are not

attempting to give exhaustive definitions—especially in the case of words which it can be assumed any user of the dictionary is bound already to know if he is sufficiently linguistically competent to be using the dictionary at all!

[42]Anna Wierzbicka, *Lexicography and Conceptual Analysis*, p.33f., and pp.19-76 justifying the definition.

[43]The words 'prototype' and 'stereotype' are possibly clear enough for the average reader to understand the point; but they are also used as technical terms (albeit slightly differently) in e.g. Hurford and Heasley, *Semantics: A Coursebook*, chaps. 8 and 9, and J. Lyons, *Language, Meaning and Context*, pp. 71f. With Hurford and Heasley we use 'prototype' to mean 'a *typical* member of the extension' and 'stereotype' to mean a list of the typical characteristics to which the predicate applies.

[44]For the language of 'criterial', 'expected', 'unexpected', and 'excluded' traits of a sense, and their relation to the use of 'prototypes' and 'stereotypes', see D. A. Cruse, *Lexical Semantics*, pp. 16-22. On promotion, demotion, highlighting, and backgrounding of traits in sentence contexts see Cruse, pp. 50-4.

[45]Wierzbicka, *Lexicography and Conceptual Analysis*, p.112.

[46]If the bicycle had a steering wheel instead, that might still roughly fall within the terms of the definition supplied. All that would need changing perhaps would be the word 'thin'. The invention of a sit-back, two-wheeled, manually propelled vehicle, with battery-operated steering, would challenge our notion of the sense "bicycle", but *if* we decided to call it a bicycle it would be recognized at first that this was merely an extended usage, and eventually it might contribute to a change of sense, but Wierzbicka does not contend senses are immutable. And she is perfectly willing to distinguish between invariants and merely prototypical elements in the definition of sense.

[47]See e.g. the discussion and objections to conceptualism in J. Lyons, *Semantics*, pp.109-14.

[48]See e.g. the defence of 'concepts' in relation to word-meaning in G. A. Miller and P. N. Johnson-Laird, *Language and Perception*, Cambridge, CUP, 1976, chap. 4.

[49]J. J. Katz, *Semantic Theory*, London, Harper and Row, 1972, p.450.

[50]See e.g. W. Labov, 'The Boundaries of Words and their Meanings' in C.-J. N. Bailey and R. W. Shuy (eds.), *New Ways of Analysing Variations in English*, vol. 1, Washington, Georgetown University Press, 1973.

[51]The Greek word *apostolos* could, of course, simply be used to mean 'envoy', 'messenger', or 'representative' as at 2 Cor. 8.23; Phil. 2.25.

[52]K. Baldinger's, *Semantic Theory*, Oxford, Blackwell, 1980, is the most sophisticated defence of conceptualism in English of which we are aware: part 2 (taking over and developing earlier work by E. Coseriu, B. Pottier and, especially, K.

Heger) specifically argues that concepts are distinct from, but determinative of 'senses'. The latter are a property of words in specific languages, he agrees, but the former are supra-linguistic. For the analysis of concepts into components, and the relation to a more general theory of meaning, see 5.2.7 below, on Componential Analysis.

[53]The distinction is made in Beekman, Callow, and Kopesec, *The Semantic Structure of a Written Communication*, pp.41ff.

[54]See chapter 4.2 above.

[55]See e.g. M. Hengel, *The Son of God*, London, SCM, 1976, pp.42-5.

[56]The best English introduction to the whole subject is possibly still A. Lehrer, *Semantic Fields and Lexical Structure*, London, North-Holland, 1974.

[57]On colour perception and semantics see e.g. G. N. Leech, *Semantics*, pp. 233-6, A. Lehrer, *Semantic Fields and Lexical Structure*, pp. 152ff., and G. A. Miller and P. N. Johnson-Laird, *Language and Perception*, pp. 333-360, with the literature they cite.

[58]J. Lyons, *Language, Meaning and Context*, London, Fontana (Collins), 1981, p.75.

[59]Lyons, *Language, Meaning and Context*, p.58; and compare Lyons, *Semantics*, pp.204-6.

[60]We follow the more transparent language of J. Lyons, *Language, Meaning and Context*, p. 91, rather than the more usual terminology which goes back to de Saussure. Compare Leech's use of 'selectional' and 'combinatory' for the same contrast, in *Semantics*, p.11.

[61]This was a major plank in J. R. Firth's theory of meaning: see the essay 'Modes of Meaning' in his *Papers in Linguistics, 1934-51*, London, OUP, 1957: for summary, developments and reactions see A. Lehrer, *Semantic Fields and Lexical Structure*, pp. 173ff; F. R. Palmer, *Semantics*, chap.5, and R. A. Waldron, *Sense and Sense Development*, pp. 40-5.

[62]W. Porzig, *Das Wunder der Sprache*, Bern, Francke, 1950. For an English summary of Porzig's work see e.g. J. Lyons, *Semantics*, pp.261-6.

[63]See further e.g. Lyons, *Semantics*, chap. 8.4, and chap. 9; D. A. Cruse, *Lexical Semantics*, pp.84-294, especially pp.84-111. For elementary introductions to sense relationships see e.g. Hurford and Heasley, *Semantics: A Coursebook*, §§ 10-11, 16-17; Waldron, *Sense and Sense Development*, pp.95-110; F. R. Palmer, *Semantics*, chap. 4.

[64]For a brief but helpful discussion see Lyons, *Language, Meaning and Context*, pp.50-5; S. Ullmann, *Semantics*, chap. 6, and Zgusta, *Manual of Lexicography*, pp.89-113; for fuller treatment compare e.g. K. Baldinger, *Semantic Theory*, pp.212-59; D. A. Cruse, *Lexical Semantics*, chap. 12.

[65]This distinction is most sharply defined in J. Lyons, *Language, Meaning and Context*, pp.50-5.

66See A. Lehrer, *Semantic Fields and Lexical Structure*, pp.30-5, for further detail.

67Lehrer, *Semantic Fields and Lexical Structure*, argues the use of participation in different semantic fields (here e.g. 'parts of the body' versus 'parts of a river') as a criterion for homonymy (pp.8-10, 201); in contrast see Cruse, *Lexical Semantics*, pp. 71-4, from which the example above is taken.

68See Wierzbicka, *Lexicography and Conceptual Analysis*, p.73f.

69As opposed to what J. Lyons, *Language, Meaning and Context*, pp. 47ff., calls 'empty' lexemes, such as 'to', 'and', etc.

70For a careful discussion of the appropriate method and of the limits of word study in relation to *hagios* in the Pauline literature see above all V. S. Poythress, *Structural Approaches to Understanding the Theology of the Apostle Paul*, unpublished D.Th. dissertation, Stellenbosch 1981, chap. 3.

71See above, 1.4.

72For justification of this see e.g. M. M. B. Turner, 'The Significance of Spirit Endowment for Paul', *Vox Evangelica* 9 (1975), pp.56-69; 'The Significance of Receiving the Spirit in Luke-Acts', *Trinity Journal* 2 (1981), pp.131-58, and 'The Spirit of Christ and Christology' in H. H. Rowdon (ed.), *Christ the Lord*, Leicester, IVP, 1982, pp.168-90.

73See the discussion in A. Lehrer, *Semantic Fields and Lexical Structure*, chap. 11.

74The description is taken from Professor Louw's own introduction to the enterprise as given in 'The Greek New Testament Wordbook', *BT* 30 (1979) pp.108-17. Since this chapter was completed the UBS dictionary has been published. It differs in minor details from the description we have given here.

75On the setting up and structuring of the semantic domains themselves see Louw, 'The Greek New Testament Wordbook', *BT* 30(1979); Louw, *Semantics of New Testament Greek*, pp.58-68; Nida, Louw and Smith in R. W. Cole (ed.), *Current Issues in Linguistic Theory*, London, Indiana University Press, 1977, esp. pp.158-64, and Nida, *Componential Analysis of Meaning*, chap. 6.

76See E. A. Nida and C. R. Taber, *The Theory and Practice of Translation*, for a full discussion.

77For brief introductions see e.g. A. Lehrer, *Semantic Fields and Lexical Structure*, chap. 3, and R. Kempson, *Semantic Theory*, pp. 18-22, 86-102. In more detail, J. J. Katz and J. A. Fodor, 'The Structure of a Semantic Theory', *Language*, 39 (1963), pp.170-210, and J. J. Katz, *Semantic Theory*, passim. For a detailed attempt to justify a modified version of universal sense components, and the relation to lexemes, see A. Wierzbicka, *Semantic Primitives*, Frankfurt, Athenäum, 1972. For a critique of philosophical componential analysis see Lyons, *Language, Meaning and Context*, pp.75-84 or (in more detail) Lyons, *Semantics*, pp.317-35, but for a spirited defence of an attenuated form of it see G. N. Leech, *Semantics*, chap. 6, especially pp.117ff.

[78]See E. A. Nida and C. H. Taber, *The Theory and Practice of Translation*, chap. 4, but especially E. A. Nida, *Componential Analysis of Meaning*, The Hague, Mouton, 1975.

[79]See Poythress, *Structural Approaches to Understanding the Theology of the Apostle Paul*, 11.347.

[80]Compare the apparently similar approach of A. Vivian on the lexical field of 'separation' as summarized by Silva, *Biblical Words and their Meaning*, p.163.

[81]In addition to the basic introductions mentioned see also especially the following works which use the techniques described of J. Barr: 'The Image of God in the Book of Genesis—a Study of Terminology', *BJRL* 51 (1968), pp.11-26; K. L. Burres, *Structural Semantics in the Study of the Pauline Understanding of Revelation;* R. J. Erickson, *Biblical Semantics;* M. Klemm, *EIPHNH im neutestamentlichen Sprachsystem*, Bonn, BLB, 1977; E. Nida, *Componential Analysis of Meaning;* V. S. Poythress, *Structural Approaches to Understanding the Theology of the Apostle Paul;* and J. Sawyer, *Semantics in Biblical Research.* The simplest introduction to the whole area is M. Silva, *Biblical Words and their Meaning;* the best is E. Nida, *Componential Analysis of Meaning.* J. Lyons, *Structural Semantics*, Oxford, Blackwell, 1966, while not on biblical lexicology, but investigating especially an area of Plato's language relating to craft, wisdom, and knowledge, was a pioneering work well worth the detailed attention of the courageous.

[82]See above, section 5.2.2.1.

[83]See Silva, *Biblical Words and Their Meaning*, pp.48-56 for examples and discussion of the problems here.

[84]See e.g. I. H. Marshall, *The Epistles of John*, Grand Rapids, Eerdmans, 1978, pp.142-4.

6. Sentences & Sentence Clusters

6.1 SENTENCES

6.1.1 Introduction

When used as part of the communication process, words are sequenced, produced linearly and coherently. These ordered sequences are readily perceived as having limiting boundaries, and it is through this perception that we intuitively identify the existence of the sentence.

Although we have stated that sentences are produced linearly, and this is obviously the case, there are linguistic features which are *prosodic*, extended over the word sequences, features such as the intonation pattern. Unfortunately for us we have no indication of such prosodic features in the biblical text: we have to assume on other, and more subjective grounds, that when Paul wrote to the church at Corinth:'Already you are filled! Already you have become rich! Without us you have become kings!' (1 Corinthians 4.8) he was probably being ironical.

The coherence to which reference has been made is a coherence both of syntactic structure and of meaning. The words that are used are expected to exhibit appropriate *syntagmatic* and *paradigmatic* relationships. *Syntagmatically* it is expected that any one word will relate semantically to the other words in the sentence. We refer here to collocation: words either do or do not co-relate to other words. Colours are bright, clear, shining, pure, but not spongy, salty or even *colourless*.[1] Syntagmatically we refer also to such matters as concord of number and gender, as appropriate. In Greek we take particular note of the case system which goes some way towards clarifying the relationships between the elements of the sentence. The significance of the individual words of the sentence may then further be clarified through a consideration of *paradigmatic* relationships: words which might have been used in place of those actually occurring in the sentence to give similar meaning or, possibly, opposite meaning.

These two features of sentence coherence, syntagmatic relationships and paradigmatic relationships, might be seen as respectively the horizontal and the vertical components of meaning. In his first letter to the church at Corinth Paul commented:

I wrote to you in my letter not to associate with immoral men. (1 Corinthians 5.9)

The horizontal collocations enable us to understand what Paul had written (a letter) and the nature of the non-association for which he had argued (with immoral men). Further to understand the sentence we might note the paradigmatic relationship of 'associate' with 'meet', 'befriend', 'welcome' or 'accompany', and the word 'immoral' could similarly be explored paradigmatically. It is by a consideration of the similarities and contrasts in meaning introduced by replacing the words actually used in a sentence by other words that the meaning of a particular string may be established.

In fact the sentence considered above represents one translation of Paul's original words, *egrapsa hymin en tē(i) epistolē(i) mē synanamignysthai pornois*, and the syntagmatic and paradigmatic investigations which might lead to an understanding of Paul's communication would necessarily relate to these words and not to any derived sequence. The nominal form *pornois* is, perhaps, not best rendered as 'immoral men'. We note that C. K. Barrett renders *pornois* 'people guilty of fornication',[2] suggesting that the word 'immoral' at this point has too general a meaning for Paul's actual concern. Such a conclusion could readily be reached by a paradigmatic and syntagmatic consideration of *pornos*, noting, for example, 5.11, where *pornos* is distinguished from greed and idolatry and drunkenness and robbery.

Here we merely confirm what has already been said, that a word is no more than a token, a sign, available for use in the communication process, and given meaning by the context and cotext within which it appears.

6.1.2 Defining the term 'Sentence'

The concept of 'sentence' is commonly defined in terms of completeness. Classically Leonard Bloomfield defined it in terms of independence:

> In any utterance, a linguistic form appears either as a constituent of some larger form . . . or else as an independent form, not included in any larger (complex) linguistic form. When a linguistic form occurs as part of a larger form it is said to be in *included position;* otherwise it is said to be in *absolute position* and to constitute a sentence.[3]

Robins comments, 'Traditionally the longest structure within which a full grammatical analysis is possible has been taken as the sentence'.[4] David Crystal defines it as 'The largest structural unit in terms of which the grammar of a language is organised.'[5] But Crystal goes on ruefully to comment 'Innumerable definitions of sentence exist, ranging from the vague characterisations of traditional grammar (such as 'the expression of a complete thought') to the detailed structural descriptions of contemporary linguistic analysis.'

We do not propose to adopt any formal definition of the term here, but the notion of grammatical completeness is at least helpful. However it must be noted that utterances must always be understood in context and from cotext: the existence of *oun* in Romans 12.1 is a reminder that if the sentence can be fully explicated grammatically from within itself, it cannot be explicated *semantically* without reference to chapter 11. We note also the occurrence of pro-forms within a sentence where the antecedent lies outside the sentence boundary (John 3.2, *auton*, referring back to John 2.24).

6.1.3 The Classification of Sentences

Sentences may be classified so as to distinguish between syntactically marked sentences, say, interrogative sentences and command sentences;

or in terms of *form*, simple sentences and expanded sentences; or in terms of context,[6] sentences which may initiate a discourse (for example interrogative sentences), sentences which may conclude a discourse (the interrogative sentence could not [normally]), and sentences which serve to continue a discourse, following from something previous, and requiring something further.

A useful classification of sentences is into just two groups: productive sentences, or *major-pattern sentences (favourite-pattern sentences)*, and *minor-pattern sentences* which are non-productive. Major-pattern sentences include the vast majority of sentences, and they are productive in the sense that by substitution of alternative nouns and verbs and adjectives an infinite range of sentences may be produced. Thus 'Jesus came to Nazareth' is a major-pattern sentence and parallels 'Peter came to Nazareth' or 'Jesus went to Nazareth' or 'Jesus came from Nazareth' or 'Jesus came to Jerusalem'. The minor-pattern sentence is non-productive. Thus 'Not on your life' has a particular meaning which is not determined by any consideration of the lexical constituents or the semantic structure of the string. And although we may substitute other lexical items we may produce a grammatical sentence: 'Not on your bed', the *meaning* of that sentence bears no relation whatever to the meaning of the 'original' minor-pattern sentence. When Jesus arrived at the wedding in Cana, his mother told him 'They have no wine.' Jesus responded *ti emoi kai soi, gynai*, a minor-pattern sentence which is exceedingly difficult to render into English as witness the remarkable range of translations offered:

'Woman, what have I to do with thee?'   AV
'O woman, what have you to do with me?' RSV
'Dear woman, why do you involve me?'   NIV
'You must not tell me what to do, woman.' GNB
'Your concern, mother, is not mine.'   NEB[7]

A second sentence classification is also, initially, into two groups, simple sentences and expanded sentences. Expansion is seen to result from two distinct syntactic features, co-ordination processes and subordination processes. Co-ordination processes lead to *compound* structures, and subordination processes lead to *complex* structures in which some included part of the sentence attains the status of a clause, with its own verbal form. Thus in co-ordination processes we have elements of equivalent grammatical structure joined together: two nouns, two noun phrases, two sentences. But in subordination processes the structures related by the process are not equivalent.

We note, for example, the words of Jesus:

hymeis phōneite me ho didaskalos KAI ho kyrios (John 13.13)

'You call me teacher AND lord'

KAI kalōs legete   'AND you say well'.

There is no particular difficulty in this expanded sentence: in fact it could readily be processed as two short sentences for the co-ordinating particles introduce no complexity of relationship.

Contrast this with John 3.3:

ean mē tis gennēthē(i) anōthen,

ou dynatai idein tēn basileian tou theou.

'Unless one is born again

one cannot see the kingdom of God.'

Here two statements are made, but the first is the condition of the second, and the two statements cannot be processed independently without losing the essential meaning of the whole.

6.1.4 The Concept of Expansion: Kernel Sentences

It is possible to view long sentences as expansions of more basic structures. In fact, as any sentence is produced various possibilities for expansion are continuously available. The occurrence of a noun makes possible an expansion by the addition of a series of adjectives, the existence of a verb makes possible the addition of qualifying adverbs.

This suggests the reduction of compound and complex sentences to basic structures. Thus the enormously complex sentence which constitutes Ephesians 1.15ff. may be reduced to the basic sentence

ou pauomai eucharistōn hyper hymōn

'I do not cease giving thanks for you'

and this is itself an expanded and modified form of an even more basic structure

'I give thanks'

from which the obtrusive negative has been removed as well as the explanatory *hyper hymōn*. As we shall see in 6.2.2 below this concept of kernel sentences may be employed in the analysis of long and complex sentences to facilitate the important process firstly of identifying the meanings of the individual kernels, and secondly of identifying the relationships between the kernels.

The term 'kernel' was used in a highly formalized way in transformational grammar, and in a less formal way in the translation process characterized by E. A. Nida and C. R. Taber and developed by them in *The Theory and Practice of Translation*.[8] It is this latter approach that we shall develop below, 6.2.2. At this point it is enough to note that compound and complex sentences may be reduced back to a small number of basic sentence forms or kernels by removing modifiers, eliminating the results of subordinating and co-ordinating processes, turning negatives into positives and passives into actives.

6.1.5 The Question of Form and Meaning

We have noted above that it is possible to categorize sentences as interrogative sentences, command sentences, and so on. In many languages there will be found objective grammatical, lexical and syntactic markers which identify particular sentence forms.

At the semantic level, however, the categorization might well be less satisfactory. To take the interrogative form as an example, when the writer to the Hebrews asks 'how shall we escape?' (2.3) he is not inviting suggestions. On the contrary he is making a strong assertion that there can be no escape in the circumstances posited. When Job is asked 'Where were you when I laid the earth's foundations?' (Job 38.4) he is not expected to provide an answer. A similar measure of caution is required when interpreting the imperative mood. Dwight Bolinger distinguishes between the imperative-command and the imperative-hortatory[9] and this is a useful distinction when interpreting 'the first and great commandment' (Matthew 22.38) where Greek *agapēseis* is *not* an imperative, and Philippians 4.4, *chairete!* which is an imperative, but must be understood as hortatory. For this very important subject see in great detail John Lyons, *Semantics*, 16.2.[10]

6.2 SENTENCE CLUSTERS
6.2.1 Introduction

The smallest potentially independent unit of meaning in a text or discourse is, arguably, the concept. At the other end of the scale, the largest unit of meaning is the *whole* discourse, whether a novel, a play, or a scientific monograph trying to prove some particular thesis. Each of these may be called a unit of meaning because it (hopefully) has coherence.[11] By contrast a magazine would not normally be considered a *unit* of meaning, because it lacks the required element of coherence; it is rather a compilation of units of meaning, the separate articles, advertisements, notices and so forth. There is no cohesion between the separate units to make them a single coherent entity.[12]

Between the concept and the complete discourse lies a whole hierarchy of units of meaning. Concepts can be built together into a proposition, and the propositional content can be expressed in a variety of forms of sentence.[13] Such sentences can be clumped together into sentence clusters; these, in turn, combined to make paragraphs, and paragraphs to compose the sections which together make up a chapter. At each level of the hierarchy the unit concerned will display both internal coherence and what Ruskin called the 'law of principality'. If we are inclined to think Joos' famous illustrative sentence "I have never heard a green horse smoke a dozen oranges" is *not* a *unit* of meaning, it is because it appears to us to lack internal coherence: horses are not usually green; nor do they smoke. Were they so to do, it would be unlikely to be oranges they smoked (and even less a plurality of them), and smoking is not an activity one would naturally think of as being 'heard'. To put it another way 'smoke' does not collocate with 'oranges' nor 'green' with 'horse' nor 'hear' with 'smoke'. What we have is a pastiche of meanings but the pastiche lacks the necessary internal coherence of meaning which would make this 'sentence' a *unit* of meaning, unless we posit the most extraordinary circumstances.

By 'law of principality' we mean simply that amongst the various components of any meaning one component is usually the more marked, or prominent; the rest being subsidiary or delimiting—and it is usually the marked element, and its relation to the rest, which gives the required coherence to the unit of meaning. In the concept lexicalized by the word 'boy', the component of meaning "animate being" is central, those of "human", "male", and "non-adult", delimit or qualify the central and most prominent element.[14] In a simple sentence the most prominent element is usually the verb; while in a complex sentence it is usually the verb in the *main* clause, though some other element may be given prominence by being specially marked: as for example in such an utterance as 'It was the *bread* you were meant to eat, not the meringue!'

Similarly, in a paragraph, one sentence usually dominates and so gives coherence to the rest. While in a longer unit, such as a whole sermon, if there are not just a few *prominent* points, to which the rest are sub-ordinated, the hearer will come away wondering whether there was any real point at all. If everything is *equally* stressed, little if anything is *communicated*.

The sentence cluster, or short paragraph, is perhaps the basic unit of communication in a discourse. Single sentences (unless they are very long) are not usually capable of carrying all the information and information structure that the speaker or writer wishes to convey at one time. The sentence cluster or paragraph is the unit most suited to this purpose.

A paragraph will normally be a recognizable unit with internal coher-ence and prominence.[15] Consider Peter's attempt to translate a section of the New Testament prescribed text, Hebrews. He is a second-year student, who has done his homework and learned the basic vocabulary. He is picked on in class to translate 2.1-4, and it comes out something like this:

> [Verse 1] On account of this . . . um . . . it is necessary for . . . us more closely to pay attention to the things heard, lest we drift away. [Verse 2] Er . . . For if the word spoken by angels became . . . or was . . . confirmed, er . . . and every transgression and disobedience received a just recompense, . . . [Verse 3] how shall we escape . . . ignoring such a great salvation, which . . . er . . . um . . . having re-ceived its origin to be spoken by the Lord . . . was confirmed to us by those hearing . . . er . . . [Verse 4] God himself witnessing with them with signs and wonders and various miracles and distributions of the Holy Spirit according to his will.

If you have felt the need to reach for your own Bible to try to make sense of the passage we have made our point. Though the wording has been translated without any great inaccuracy, the whole passage still fails to communicate, because, presented this way, it offers neither co-herence nor prominence. The *structure* of thought of the passage remains inchoate.

This, of course, may not be the student's fault. He cannot do too many jobs at once, and here he has not only to find English word substitutions but also restructure a complex network of sentences. And if he is like most students he will have been taught quite a lot about the former, and very little if anything about the latter. If he has had a classical English education he may be able to analyze the structure of a single *sentence*, but very few students will ever have been offered help in analyzing longer sections of *discourse*. On the analysis and understanding of *sentences* there is a wide range of readily available literature to which we simply direct the reader;[16] and the commentators indicate the relevant grammatical and syntactic considerations for elucidating the structure of individual sentences in Biblical writings. But the analysis of larger sections is less frequently given formal treatment: we shall examine below three approaches that are at present in use, if not widely known: kernel analysis, diagramming methods, and full semantic structure analysis. But before we do we should comment provisionally on the aims of such analyses. What can they hope to accomplish?

Kernel analysis breaks down the complex discourse section by section, into very simple sentences, and thus virtually provides us with a list of the basic propositions stated by the discourse. That in itself may be a useful contribution, but it does not tell us *how* the propositions are related. It only *clarifies* the task by identifying the propositions that need to be related. The other two approaches seek in different ways to provide a framework within which to express the *results* of our analysis of the relationships between the propositions. And one of them—semantic-structure analysis—offers a grid of most of the *possible* types of relationship between two propositions, which clarifies what sort of decisions we have to make.

But no system performs the middle and all-important stage, that of actually determining the relations between the propositions. Here the interpreter will have to make complex decisions based on syntax, logic, and careful analysis of cotext. The main aim, then, of the approaches we are about to describe, is to clarify the questions, not to provide solutions. And building up a picture of the semantic structure of a passage is rather like making a model of a molecule while we are still engaged in researching its structure. The model is not the structure, but our emerging hypothesis about it. The model does not provide us with *new information* but may be expected to give us an *overall perspective* of the structure when we have examined the relations of the individual pieces.

6.2.2 Kernel Analysis

This is not a standard linguistics approach to analysis but is perhaps best understood as an off-shoot of Chomsky's earlier work on transformational grammar, but adapted to take an important part in a coherent system for translation work by, above all, E. A. Nida and C. R. Taber.[17] Kernel analysis would begin from the assumption that complex sentences and sentence clusters are produced from hypothetically simple kernel sentences such as introduced above, 6.1.4. Resolving the complex form *back* to the kernel sentences allows us to see what actually was being affirmed. It will be remembered that kernels are the simplest possible forms posited to lie below the surface-structure sentences in the text; with all passives given as active forms, and all tense indications removed. The kernels for verse 2 of the Hebrews passage would thus be:

A. They announce it.

B. He confirms it (or, perhaps, 'It is valid').

C. He breaks it.

D. He disobeys it.

E. He recompenses him.

Kernels D and E may surprise the reader, for there does not appear to be any verb in the English 'translation' offered by our student to correspond to them—and there is none in the Greek either. But it should be remembered that practitioners of kernel analysis argue that *nouns* which represent *actions* are transformations of kernel sentences; so the word 'transgression' stands for a hypothetical kernel sentence 'he transgresses' or 'he breaks the rule'. The purpose of these resolutions down to verbal forms is usually to facilitate translation. Most languages have corresponding kernel sentences, but not always a parallel noun structure for the *nomen actionis* (the noun denoting an action or event).[18] Arguably, having to resolve down to kernel sentences also clarifies to the English reader the meaning that attaches to some of his abstract nouns.

For ordinary exegetical purposes the resolution down to absolute kernels is unnecessarily cumbersome, and may obscure important information. With Nida and Taber it is better to resolve down to what we may call 'nuclear sentences' instead; that is, simplified forms of the surface-structure sentences such as still retain tense markers and indications of subject and object, but remove the expansions.[19] We would therefore obtain:

A'. Angels announced a word/message.

B'. God confirmed it (or, perhaps, 'The word was valid').

C'. God recompensed them [transgression and disobedience of the word/message].

We could now rearrange the nuclear sentences, and feed back the other features of the surface structure which have temporarily been ignored, to arrive at a translation such as:

God confirmed the message the angels spoke [= the Law]; he gave appropriate recompense for every transgression and act of disobedience to it.

or

The message spoken by the angels was valid; God gave appropriate recompense for every transgression and act of disobedience of it.

It does not matter that we have not precisely followed the Greek ordering; English may need to restructure the Greek ordering of kernel sentences in order properly to express the meaning.[20] If we now take the whole section and resolve down to nuclear sentences we would obtain:

1. It is necessary for us.

2. We hold firmly to them [the truths of the gospel].

3. We heard them [the truths of the gospel].

4. We drift away.

5. The angels announced a message.

6. God confirmed it.

7. God punished them [every transgression and disobedience].

8. We shall [not] escape.

9. We ignore it [the message about how God saves us].

10. The Lord first announced the message.

11. Some heard it.

12. They confirmed it to us.

13. God also witnessed to it.

Here we have represented all verbs by corresponding nuclear sentences, and we have spelt out the significance of the noun 'salvation' (in parenthesis to nuclear sentence 9) as it occurs in this context, but we have not resolved such words as 'sign', 'wonder', 'miracle', 'distributions [of the Holy Spirit = gifts of the Holy Spirit]', or 'will' into respective kernel or nuclear sentences. If we were to be systematic we should require to resolve 'wonder' into two nuclear sentences such as 'God performs an act' and 'It [this act] causes men to wonder', and provide corresponding analyses for the other nouns. But for the English reader these senses are not problematic, and so to give a full analysis would simply clutter the presentation.

Dividing the text into nuclear sentences should clarify the basic propositions that are being affirmed, and so facilitate understanding and translation. Once the basic nuclear sentences are established, it is easier to perceive the relations that exist between them, though the kernel analysis has not focused on this as such. The next two approaches attend more explicitly to the phenomenon of the relationships between the nuclear (or kernel) sentences.

6.2.3 Diagramming Methods of Analysis

A number of introductions to exegesis (such as those by W. Kaiser[21] and G. D. Fee[22]) offer a form of diagramming as a method of analyzing the semantic structure of a passage. In simple terms, the procedure recommended is that students put the subject and main verb on the left hand side of the page and inset qualifications of either, underscoring words that indicate sentence relationships. Fee's[23] analysis of 1 Cor. 14.1-3 can be seen in figure 9.

To undertake to provide such a diagram for any section of the NT would no doubt help the student to clarify for himself the thought structure of the passage concerned. Here verses 2 and 3 clearly emerge as providing the grounds for part of the exhortation in verse 1; and the fact that the ground offered consists primarily in a contrast between the nature and function of tongues and prophecy is also highlighted.

A disadvantage of the system emerges on consideration of the first verse. Because the main verbs are the imperatives, and because 'that *you might prophesy*' subordinates the verb *prophēteuein*, the analysis appears to assume that the former two verbs, and the kernel sentences they represent, are the most *prominent* sentences of the section. As a result we might then expect that what follows would go back to qualify the first half of the verse. But in fact the whole discourse as Paul planned it is about the use of *prophecy and tongues*, and, though *grammatically* subordinate, the sentence 'that you might prophesy' is *semantically the most prom-*

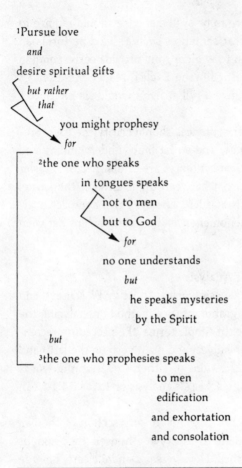

¹Pursue love
    and
desire spiritual gifts
    but rather
        that
            you might prophesy
                for
        ²the one who speaks
                in tongues speaks
                    not to men
                    but to God
                        for
                    no one understands
                        but
                            he speaks mysteries
                            by the Spirit
            but
        ³the one who prophesies speaks
                            to men
                            edification
                            and exhortation
                            and consolation

Figure 9.

inent part of the section. The first imperative, 'Pursue love', merely defines the *manner* or *circumstance* in which spiritual gifts are to be sought, and the second, '*seek* spiritual gifts', stands in a generic relation to the specific '[Desire especially] that you might prophesy'. The latter is made prominent by being marked by the expression 'but rather' or 'especially', and by the way the discourse continues to focus on this element. The verse would better have been represented as in figure 10. This is an example of the common phenomenon in language of a skewing between grammatical and semantic structure. Whereas we would expect prominence to attach to one of the main verbs, it in fact focuses on a sub-

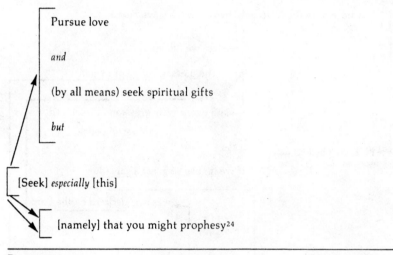

Figure 10.

ordinate clause and the elided verb to which it relates.

A more theoretically considered and systematic approach to diagramming sentence relationships is provided by Louw.[25] He is careful to ensure that any ellipsis (the missing out of a verb to avoid its repetition) is duly allowed for, and to bring out the semantic ranking of the elements of the section in question. His system of analysis focuses on what he calls the colon, which essentially is a sentence unit consisting of a nominal and verbal element together with all their syntactically dependent expansions. Compound sentences would be treated as several cola each corresponding to the individual sentences from which they were composed.

Using a simplified form of his analysis on the Hebrews passage we might obtain three cola; one corresponds to Heb.2.1, a second to 2.2-3 (for the conditional clauses in both qualify 'How shall we escape?'), and a third provided by the genitive absolute[26] beginning in 2.4. But the third is possibly better analyzed as a further qualification on the way the message of salvation was delivered, and so as subordinate to 2.3b—as figure 11 suggests.

The analysis offered sets a foot on the path towards clarifying the semantic structure of the passage. The whole of 2.2-4 is seen to provide the grounds for the exhortation in 2.1. The grounds given are offered in the form of a contrast between the giving of the Law and the giving

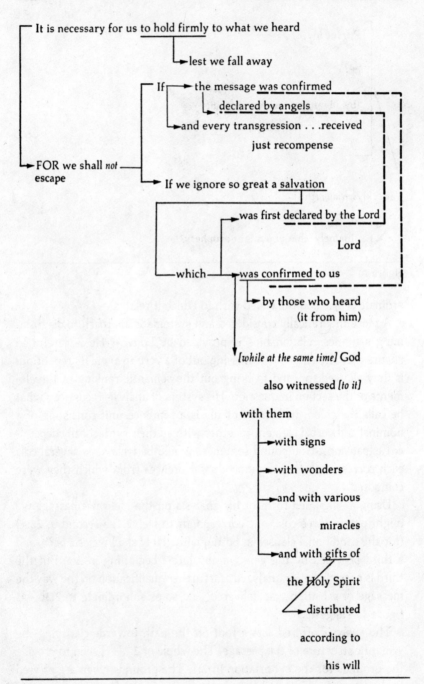

Figure 11.

of the gospel. Certain aspects of the contrast appear to be highlighted: If the Law was confirmed by God, and departure from it punished, how much more sure would be the fate of those who turned back from the gospel. For the Law was but a message *declared by angels;* whereas the gospel was *announced by the Lord himself* (the parallelism here is too obviously marked to be other than deliberate). The Law was, for the generation of the writer of Hebrews, something merely given to their ancestors, while the gospel was confirmed to the readers by those who had themselves heard the Lord who gave it. What is more, *God himself* had confirmed the proclamation of the gospel to the readers with signs performed by the first witnesses(?) and by distributions of the Spirit amongst the readers themselves (the amount of space devoted to this consideration signals its importance). If a man ignored all this, and let go of his hold on the gospel, how could he hope to escape future judgement?

The attempt to represent the thought structure in a diagrammatic form is usually liable to be fruitful, at least in helping the reader to explore the ranking of the subordination. But it is not yet a systematic and explicit statement of the relationship between the parts. A line on a piece of paper may suggest that a relationship between parts exists, but a line does not specify the nature of that relationship as such.[27]

6.2.4 Towards a Full Semantic Structure Analysis

If, as is generally assumed, all complex sentences are the result of embedding simple sentences in each other, then it should be possible both to isolate the 'deep-structure' sentences (kernel analysis) and to state the relationships that exist between them in the resultant 'surface structure'.[28] The same should potentially be possible for sentence clusters that are not just a single compound (or complex) sentence, but extend over *several* sentences. There does not seem to be any good reason why one should be able to analyze the structural relationships of the two nuclear sentences in 'Give him a pay rise because he has worked hard for it!' and yet expect an utterance of the form 'Give him a rise! He has worked hard for it!' to resist such clarification.

In the first instance the two simple sentences are admittedly linked *syntactically*, while in the latter they are not, but the same *semantic* relation holds for both. In each case the sentence 'He has worked hard for it' offers the grounds for the exhortation 'Give him a rise!' In the first instance the semantic relationship has been indexed *lexically*, with the word 'because', while in the second the relationship had to be *inferred*, but otherwise there is no significant difference. And it would have been possible to lexicalize the relationships in the second example without subordinating the second part to the first *syntactically;* thus, 'Give him a rise! For he really deserves it!'

Again, we may observe that in the Greek of Ephesians, the whole section 1.3-14 (and, for that matter, also 1.15-23) is just one long cumbrous sentence. But the meaning relationships between the kernel sentences of which it is composed do not magically change when the passage is split up into shorter sentences as in Nestle-Aland, or in the various English translations. The semantic structure of a sentence cluster composed of separate sentences is not necessarily different from that of the same material presented as a large compound sentence.

Already in their guide to translation, Nida and Taber had insisted that elucidation of the relations *between* the kernels should follow the breaking down of a text into its deep-structure kernel sentences. Only following such an elucidation can we restructure the kernel sentences into an apposite translation that still retains the same meaning relationships between the kernels. Thus, for example, for Eph. 2.8, "For by grace are ye saved through faith; and that not of yourselves: it is the gift of God: not of works, lest any man should boast" they suggest the following kernels:[29]

1. God showed grace.
2. God saved you.
3. You believed.
4. You did not save yourselves.
5. God gave it.
6. You did not work for it.
7. No man should boast.

And they specify the relations as:

1. Kernel 1 is the means of kernel 2.
2. Kernel 3 expresses an attendant circumstance or instrumentality of the event in kernel 2.
3. Kernel 4 stands in contrast with kernel 2.
4. Kernel 5 is in contrast with kernel 4, and is a confirmation and re-

emphasis of kernel 2.

5. Kernel 6 is a further amplification of kernel 4.

6. Kernel 7 states the result of this entire process.

And on the basis of this they offer the following translation to reflect both the kernel analysis and the elucidation of the semantic structure the sentences together compose:

> God showed his grace to you, and in this way he saved you through your trusting in him. You yourselves did not save yourselves. Rather, God gave you this salvation. You did not earn it by what you did. Therefore no one can boast about what he has done.

Our interest focuses on the central step of the process outlined here; in six terse statements the authors set out the meaning relationships that subsist between the kernels in Eph. 2.8. The brevity and apparent simplicity of these statements must not beguile us; behind the authors' elucidation there stands both a relatively sophisticated classification of possible relations between sentences, and a fairly systematic procedure for stating the actual relations of each kernel to the others.

Nida, Louw, and others, give a fuller account of their classification of relationships in their 1983 conference proceedings, "Style and Discourse", but we may perhaps better see what is going on in works produced by the Summer Institute of Linguistics to introduce translators to this type of analysis, and which refine and elucidate the system still further.[30] The student is first introduced to the different types of relationship that exist between any two nuclear sentences (or, more precisely, to the relationships between the propositions represented by such sentences), then, later, he learns how to handle relationships in clusters of more than two propositions or nuclear sentences. We shall examine the issues in the same order. Our material is heavily dependent, in this section, on the Summer Institute manuals.

6.3 MEANING RELATIONS BETWEEN PAIRS OF SENTENCES OR PROPOSITIONS

We may begin by distinguishing the two major classes of relationship. A nuclear sentence either relates to the *whole* proposition encoded in the other nuclear sentence; or, alternatively, it may qualify *only one* of the words or concepts in the other sentence. We take the latter case first.

6.3.1. Nuclear Sentences Delimiting Parts of other Nuclear Sentences

In Luke 2.4, 'And Joseph also went up . . . to the city of David, which is called Bethlehem', we have two nuclear sentences:

Joseph went up to it [= the city of David].

It is called Bethlehem.

The second sentence in no way qualifies the idea of 'Joseph going up'; it qualifies only the concept 'the city of David'. This restriction of focus is actually signalled lexically in the surface structure of the Lucan sentence by the relative pronoun *hētis* ('which'), but the same relationship would have had to be inferred even if Luke had omitted the relative.

We have met other examples of this type in our passage from Hebrews. For example, Heb. 2.2a, literally 'if therefore the by-angels-spoken word was confirmed', may be resolved down to two nuclear sentences

The 'word' was confirmed.

It was spoken by angels.

the second relates to the first only as providing an amplification of the concept 'the "word" ', not as qualifying the whole of the first sentence. Similarly, in 2.3, the words 'If we ignore so great a salvation . . . which . . . was confirmed to us' could be resolved down to two nuclear sentences

We ignore it [= so great a salvation].

It was announced by the Lord.

Here, once again, the second sentence qualifies not the whole of the first; only the concept 'so great a salvation'. In this case the relationship is again indexed lexically by a relative pronoun (*hētis* 'which') agreeing in gender with the antecedent 'salvation'.

In the type of relationship we have been discussing, in which one proposition or nuclear sentence qualifies only *one* of the concepts embedded in another proposition, the function of the delimiting sentence may be either to *identify* the concept delimited, or to amplify it with further descriptive information that will be relevant within the discourse. In the two examples just instanced from Hebrews it is a case of amplifying *description*, not of *identification;* the added information serving chiefly to underscore that ignoring one message is potentially more serious than ignoring the other. Whereas the second nuclear sentence of Luke 2.4 ('It is called Bethlehem') serves simply to *identify* which city is being spoken of.

6.3.2 Nuclear Sentences Relating Holistically

Whereas it is not uncommon to find nuclear sentences relating merely to a single concept *within* another nuclear sentence, more usually one nuclear sentence relates to the totality of another. Typical examples would include:

1. And he *healed* many . . . , and *cast out* many demons. (Mark 1.34)
2. If you have been raised with Christ *seek* the things above. (Col. 3.1)
3. I . . . beseech you, that *you lead a life* worthy of your calling. (Eph. 4.1)
4. So then, brethren, *stand firm,* and hold to the traditions you were taught by us. (2 Thess. 2.15)

Each of these contains a pair of kernels, and in each case the two kernels relate to each other in a total way. They are however examples drawn from two distinct classes of relation. In sentence 1 the two kernels are of equal prominence, because (in this instance) the two actions are simultaneous and neither is stressed more than the other. This general class of relations is called *Addition Relations.* In each of the other three examples one nuclear sentence (that which is underlined) achieves some semantic prominence either logically or contextually. This type of relationship is called a *Support-HEAD* relationship, and the last three of the four examples given above correspond to the major subdivisions of this class of relationship.

Sentence 2 illustrates a broad sub-class of what we term *Argumentation Relationships;* in this case a particular type of Argumentation Relation in which the first nuclear sentence is offered as the *grounds* or *motivation* for the *exhortation* offered in the second nuclear sentence. Sentence 3, by contrast, offers an example of *Orientation Relationships*. In this instance the second nuclear sentence states the *content* of the first: it tells us *what* Paul besought them to do (the *content* of his act of beseeching), and so the pair is an example of *orienter-CONTENT* relations. Sentence 4 is different again. It provides a case of the sub-class of *Clarification Relationships*. The example in question is one of the *HEAD-amplification* type, in that the second nuclear sentence restates and amplifies the semantic content of the first. Holding onto the tradition is what *Paul means* by the exhortation 'Stand firm!' We shall now introduce the classes, sub-classes and lesser subdivisions more fully.

6.3.2.1 *Addition Relationships* The term *Addition Relationships* is used to describe relations between nuclear sentences of *equal prominence*. Of these there are four types, two of which specify some kind of *chronological* relation between the kernels, the other two of which do not. In sentence 1 above (Mk. 1.34) we have already met an example of the former. The two nuclear sentences 'he healed many' and 'he cast out . . . demons' summarize two sets of activities performed by Jesus on the same evening in Capernaum. By contrast in the sentence

They stripped him of the purple cloak and put his own clothes on him (Mark 15.20)

the two actions are again regarded as equally prominent, but now clearly as in sequence. Mark 1.34 offers a case of *Simultaneous Relations;* Mark 15.20 one of *Sequential Relations.*

Over against these two types we may set a pair of *non-chronological* types of kernel relation: *conjoined* and *alternating* relationships respectively. Of the latter we may offer Mt. 27.17 and 1 Cor. 4.21 as examples:

Shall I release Barabbas to you? Or shall I release Jesus . . . ?

Shall I come to you with a rod, or (shall I come) with love in a spirit of gentleness'?

When we refer to these as *non-chronological*, of course, we do not mean that there is no possible chronological relationship; merely that any chronology in the relationship is not the focus of the discourse.

In *alternating* relationships both kernels are equally prominent, but either one, *or* the other applies, not both. In contrast, in *conjoined relationships* both kernels are equally prominent and *both* apply. For example,

Love bears all things, believes all things, hopes all things, endures all things.(1 Cor. 13.7):

here, in fact, we have *four conjoined* nuclear sentences all in one sentence. We may summarize these relationships diagrammatically as in figure 12.

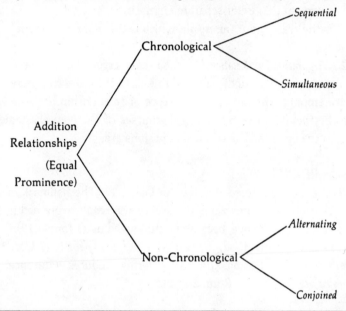

Figure 12.

6.3.2.2 Support-HEAD Relationships   While Addition Relationships denotes types of relation between two kernels of *equal* prominence; in *Support-HEAD* relationships one kernel is more prominent than the other, and the less prominent kernel plays some supporting role. In what follows, the more prominent kernel will usually be called the 'HEAD', and, where this is not so, the role that is naturally the more prominent will be capitalized. For example, in Gal. 2.12, Paul reports that when certain men came from James to Antioch, Peter drew back from eating with the Gentiles; according to Paul,

'He separated himself, fearing the circumcision party.'

In this case, the nuclear sentence 'he feared them' gives the reason for Peter's act, while 'he separated himself' indicates the result of his fear. This would be called a *reason-result* relationship, and because the *result* is normally the more prominent kernel it would be designated a *reason-RESULT* relation. It needs to be noted, however, that not all *reason-result* relationships focus on the result. The discourse can reverse the normal polarity; as, for example, were Paul to have written

It was because he feared the circumcision party [as opposed to some other reason] that Peter separated himself.

Here it is the reason, not the result, which is the more prominent.

6.3.2.2.1 Argumentation Relationships (also called Logical Relationships)

We have already met two subdivisions of this class; there are five more, and they are amongst the most common type of relationship between kernels to be found in the expository discourses of the New Testament; that is, in the epistles. The seven subdivisions are:

(A) Reason-RESULT

We have just encountered this type in Gal. 2.12. The hallmark of the type is that one kernel explains the *why* of the result expressed in the other kernel: e.g. 'We love, because he first loved us' (1 John 4.19); 'I fed you . . . not with solid food, for you were not ready for it' (1 Cor. 3.2); 'We rejoice in our suffering, knowing suffering produces endurance . . .' (i.e. *because* we know . . . : Rom. 5.3), etc.

(B) Means-RESULT

The essence of this relationship is that one kernel explains *how* the result expressed in the other was obtained: e.g. 'And having been set free from sin, you have become slaves of righteousness' (Rom. 6.18); 'By one man's obedience [kernel = 'He obeys'] many will be made righteous' (Rom. 5.19); 'In doing this, you will heap burning coals on his head' (Rom. 12.20b); 'By setting forth the truth plainly we commend ourselves to every man's conscience' (2 Cor. 4.2b).

It is quite easy to confuse *reason-RESULT* with *means-RESULT* relations; and in many cases the matter simply is not clear, at least not on purely linguistic grounds—for example the form 'Your faith has saved you' (Mark 5.34; cf. Luke 7.49) could be resolved down to the nuclear sentences 'You believed' and either 'It saved you' or 'God saved you'. If the former, then a *means-RESULT* relationship would be suggested; if the latter, either might be meant; that is, we could translate either 'God saved you *by means of* your believing', or, 'God saved you *because* you believed'. Logical or theological considerations would have to be brought to bear to settle the case.

(C) MEANS-Purpose

These relationships are also easily confused with *means-RESULT* ones. What marks them off from the latter is the focus on *intention*. When Paul says 'Our old self was crucified with him so that the sinful body might be destroyed, and we might no longer be enslaved to sin' (Rom. 6.6), the co-crucifixion is the *means* intended by God to fulfil two stated *purposes*. A minor rewriting would change the whole relationship into one of *means-RESULT* by eliminating the notion of intention: thus, 'Our old self was crucified with him so that [i.e. with the result that] our sinful body was destroyed, and we were no longer enslaved to sin'. The notorious exegetical crux in Mark 4.11-12 hangs very much on the question whether for those outside 'Everything is in parables *with the result that* they see but not perceive' or whether the teaching is given in parables *'in order that'* they might not perceive.

More easily recognizable instances of *MEANS-purpose* relations are provided by such examples as Luke 5.32, 'I have not come to call the righteous'; 1 Cor. 1.27f, 'God chose what is foolish in the world to shame the wise'; 1 Cor. 9.23, 'I do all for the sake of the gospel, that I might share in its blessings' (cf. 9.24 'So run that you may obtain it [the prize]'; but this is really *grounds-EXHORTATION* on which see below); or Heb. 12.10, 'God disciplines us for our good, that we may share his holiness'

(D) Grounds-CONCLUSION

In the case of *grounds-CONCLUSION* relations, one kernel offers the evidence on the basis of which the second is to be accepted. If we were told 'Mark must have passed his exam because he was grinning all over his face!', we would be unlikely to conclude that Mark's examiners had been lenient because they appreciated the candidate's cheerful disposition. We recognize this is not liable to be a *reason-RESULT* relationship, despite the 'because'. Rather, 'He was grinning' would probably be understood as the evidence on the basis of which we should infer that Mark must have passed. It is the *grounds* offered for the particular conclusion.

Similarly, in Acts 2.15 Peter argues

'These men are not drunk, for it is only the third hour of the day.'

This may look like a *reason-RESULT* argument, but further consideration suggests it is not. Peter is hardly offering a logically necessary reason for their state of non-drunkenness (for indeed men *could* be drunk at such a time); but reasonable *grounds* for the *conclusion* that they are not drunk; namely that it is an unlikely explanation of unusual behaviour at this time of day.

Another well-discussed case is Luke 7.47. When Jesus here announces '(I tell you) her many sins have been forgiven, for she loved much', he is not offering a *reason-RESULT* relationship, to be paraphrased 'God forgave her because she loved so much', but *grounds* for the *conclusion* that she has been forgiven; viz., her outpouring of love demonstrates she has experienced his forgiveness. Jesus words mean: 'Because of this conduct (I say), I can infer that her many sins have been forgiven, namely because she loved much.'[31]

(E) Concession-CONTRAEXPECTATION

In pairs of kernels related this way, the prominent kernel expresses an event or state of affairs that would be *unexpected* given the information offered in the other kernel. We have already met an example earlier in Col. 1.21f: '[Although] You were formerly alienated from God . . . God has [nevertheless] now reconciled you.' Compare also e.g. ' . . . though he was rich, yet for our sakes he became poor . . .' (2 Cor. 8.9); 'For though we live in the world, we are not carrying on a worldly war' (2 Cor.10.3); 'His letters are weighty . . . but his bodily presence is weak, and his speech is of no account' (2 Cor. 10.10).

(F) Grounds-EXHORTATION

Examples of this type are provided in cases where one kernel gives the grounds or motivation for an exhortation in the other kernel. We have met an example in 1 Cor. 9.24b; others are plentiful throughout the NT from Matt. 1.20 ('Do not fear [to take Mary as your wife] . . . for that which is conceived in her is of the Holy Spirit') through to Rev. 22.10 'Do not seal up the words of the prophecy, because the time is near.'

(G) Condition-CONSEQUENCE

This subdivision encompasses all cases where one kernel provides the condition which, if fulfilled, leads to the consequence related in the other kernel: for example, 'If any man would follow me, let him deny himself . . .' (Mark 8.34); or 'For whoever is ashamed of me [= if a man is ashamed] . . . the Son of Man shall be ashamed of him . . .' (Mark 8. 38). The careful reader will note that these two examples differ in type of semantic relationship; though both are *condition-CONSEQUENCE*, the former is also in *MEANS-purpose* relationship (it is *by* denying oneself that a man will enter on discipleship), while the second expresses a *reason-RESULT* relationship. *Condition-CONSEQUENCE* related kernels can occur in any of the other six argumentation relations as well as in the *Condition-CONSEQUENCE* mode itself.

Thus, 2 Cor. 11.20 ('For you bear it if a man makes slaves of you') is both *condition-CONSEQUENCE* and simultaneously *concession-CON-TRAEXPECTATION*; while Col. 3.1 ('If you have been raised with Christ, seek the things above') clearly expresses condition and consequence yet is simultaneously *grounds-EXHORTATION*. Again, Luke 16.31 is evidently conditional, yet 'If they did not hear Moses and the prophets, neither would they be persuaded by someone rising from the dead' also expresses a *grounds-CONCLUSION* relationship.

6.3.2.2.2 Orientation Relationships This class is composed of support-HEAD relationships in which the supporting kernel gives information about the setting or background of the head sentence, or introduces it. The label *introduction-HEAD* is used to describe those occasions where one kernel acts as a discourse marker introducing a whole section to follow, as in

'Now concerning the matters about which you wrote. It is well for a man not to 'touch' a woman. . . .' (1 Cor. 7.1; cf. 8.1),

'To what shall I liken this generation? They are like children. . . .' (Matt. 11.16; cf. 13.24; 22.2; 25.1 etc.),

'Now about the dead rising—have you not read in the book of Moses . . .', (Mark 12.26),

and we might similarly introduce a new section in a lecture with something like, 'We now come to our third point. Jesus could not have meant . . . etc.'

Another important subdivision is *orienter-CONTENT* relations. Verbs of saying, thinking, perceiving, desiring and evaluating often form constructions of the type 'I tell you, something greater than the temple is here' (Matt. 12.6), where the one kernel describes the content of what is said to be uttered, meant, perceived, considered best, or whatever, in the other kernel. Examples abound:

'It is good for a man not to marry.' (1 Cor. 7.1b)

'To the rest I say this . . . If any brother has a wife . . .' (1 Cor. 7.12)

'What I mean, brothers, is that the time is short.' (1 Cor. 7.29)

'I would like you to be free from concern.' (1 Cor. 7.32)

'I think I too have the Spirit of God.' (1 Cor. 7.40)

The third subdivision of this class is that of *setting-HEAD* relations: in these, one kernel provides the time at which *(time-HEAD)*, the place at which *(location-HEAD)* or the circumstance in which *(circumstance-HEAD)*, the event of the more prominent kernel takes place: e.g.

When Christ . . . appears, then you also will appear with him in glory (Col. 3.4): *circumstance-HEAD*

That evening, when the sun was set, the people brought to Jesus . . . (Mark 1.32): *time-HEAD*

When they arrived at Salamis, they proclaimed the word of God . . . (Acts 13.5): *location-HEAD*

6.3.2.2.3 Clarification Relationships This provides the last class that we need to look at; but it is an important one. Of the two subdivisions of this class, the more significant is that which deals with relations in which one kernel restates, in some way or another, the content of another. A familiar type will be the *HEAD-equivalence* relationship of Semitic parallelism, where essentially the same proposition is restated in other words for emphasis, e.g.

What is man that thou art mindful of him, and the son of man that thou dost care for him? (Ps. 8.4; and cf. Ps. 18.4-8)

But we also meet it in less conspicuous forms, such as 'Let the children come to me, and do not hinder them' (Luke 18.16); 'I speak the truth in Christ—I am not lying' (Rom. 9.1); or 'Let us rejoice, and be glad' (Rev. 19.7).

More commonly the restatement either gives *extra* information, re-stating the more prominent kernel, but also going beyond it in scope—in which case we describe the relations as one of *HEAD-amplification*—or the restatement gives specific examples of something that is said more generically in the head kernel: so, for example,

'I tell you this, and testify to it in the Lord . . .' (Eph. 4.17); *GENERIC-specific* (here 'to testify' is a hyponym of 'to tell'; a specific form of telling).

'He was devout, fearing God . . . , giving alms generously, and pray-ing to God regularly' (Acts 10.2); *HEAD-amplification* (threefold ampli-fication).

'So then, brethren, stand firm, and hold to the traditions you were taught by us' (2 Thess.2.15); *HEAD-amplification* (or is it *GENERIC-specific?*).

The other subdivision of this class does not involve restatement. It in-cludes three types: *HEAD-manner* (e.g. 'To this end I labour, struggling with all his energy [which so powerfully works in me]'; Col. 1.29); *HEAD-comparison* (e.g. 'Just as Moses lifted up the snake in the desert, so the Son of Man must be lifted up'; John 3.14), and *HEAD-contrast* (e.g. 'I did not receive it from any man . . . ; but I received it by a revelation of Jesus Christ'; Gal. 1.12).

6.3.3 Summary

We may conveniently summarize the various types of kernel relation-ship diagrammatically as in figures 13 and 14.

We have dealt with most of the types of kernel relationship envisaged in expository discourses (that is, in discourses that expound concepts and ideas) and hortatory discourses; other specialized terminology is used to cover kernel relations in narrative genres and in conversations,

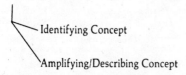

Identifying Concept

Amplifying/Describing Concept

Figure 13. Nuclear Sentences Qualifying Concept Embedded in Other Nuclear Sentences (6.3.1 above)

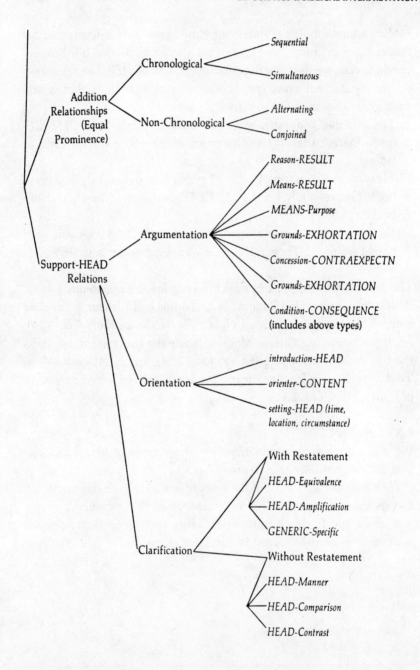

Figure 14. Holistically Relating Nuclear Sentences (6.3.2 above)

but these need not concern us at present. We have omitted mention only of those types of kernel relation which are only partial relationships; the *comment* (a qualifying remark loosely connected by association) and the *parenthesis* (which appears almost entirely peripheral to the meaning of the discourse).[32]

6.4 THE NUCLEAR SENTENCE RELATIONS IN HEBREWS 2.1-4

We obtained the the following nuclear sentences in our earlier provisional analysis of the passage:

1. It is necessary for us.
2. We hold firmly to them [the truths of the gospel].
3. We heard them [the truths of the gospel].
4. We drift away.
5. The angels announced a message.
6. God confirmed it.
7. God punished them [every transgression and disobedience].
8. We shall [not] escape.
9. We ignore it [the message about how God saves us].
10. The Lord first announced the message.
11. Some heard it.
12. They confirmed it to us.
13. God also witnessed to it.

(a) Nuclear sentence 1 relates to nuclear sentence 2 in *Orienter-CONTENT* manner.

(b) Nuclear sentence 3 describes or identifies the object of nuclear sentence 2.

(c) Nuclear sentence 2 stands in *MEANS-Purpose* relation to nuclear sentence 4; *by* holding to what we heard we purpose to avoid drifting away.

(d) Nuclear sentence 2 is formally a CONCLUSION to the *Grounds* offered in sentence 8 and its dependent nuclear sentences. But it serves semantically as an EXHORTATION[33] for which the other sentences are *Grounds*. The rhetorical question 'How can we escape', resolved in nuclear sentence 8, is simply an expressive form of the statement '(otherwise) We shall not escape (wrath)'; and this is the motivation offered for holding firm.

(e) Nuclear sentence 6 either gives a *Reason* for the *RESULT* expressed in nuclear sentence 7,[34] or the two are *Conjoined*.

(f) Nuclear sentence 8 is the *CONSEQUENCE* of fulfilment of the *Condition* in nuclear sentence 9. Nuclear sentence 6 and nuclear sentence 7 *together* provide the *Grounds* for the *CONCLUSION* in nuclear sentence 8 and nuclear sentence 9 *together*.

(g) Nuclear sentences 10 to 13 describe and amplify the 'message of salvation' which is the object of nuclear sentence 9.

(h) The relation between nuclear sentence 12 and nuclear sentence 13 is unclear. The genitive absolute construction of sentence 13 could suggest a merely circumstantial or temporal link, hence that between 12 and 13 we have an orientation relation specifying *Circumstance*, or perhaps a *simultaneous* addition relation. But nuclear sentence 13 could equally be *Conjoined* with sentence 12, as the parallel with nuclear sentence 6 and nuclear sentence 7 suggests. And this last possibility does more justice to the evident importance of the nuclear sentence 13, with its considerable expansions, in the semantic structure of the whole.

The description has now almost become too complex to take in, as it involves a delicate structure of ranking. It is to this subject we now turn.

6.5 RANKING NUCLEAR SENTENCES IN COMPLEX PROPOSITION CLUSTERS

We have so far confined ourselves mainly to discussing relations between just two kernels or nuclear sentences. In discourses, however, we do not meet the material neatly divided this way. One nuclear sentence may relate to several others, and at different levels in the hierarchy of the paragraph. Let us take the second nuclear sentence in the Hebrews passage ('We hold firmly to them'). It is related to nuclear sentence 3 ('We heard them'), which defines the things that are to be held firmly; they are 'the things we have heard', the object of the verb in sentence 2 (see figure 15).

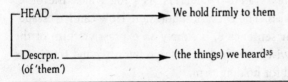

┌─HEAD ─────────────────────→ We hold firmly to them

└─Descrpn. ─────────────────→ (the things) we heard[35]
  (of 'them')

Figure 15.

But the nuclear sentence 'We hold on firmly to them' also relates more broadly: in the first place it relates as *CONTENT* to the *Orienter* 'It is necessary' in nuclear sentence 1. As sentence 3 is *grammatically embedded* in sentence 2 it will be included as part of the *CONTENT* to which sentence 1 provides the orienter. We may reflect this inclusion by placing the more general and inclusive relation further to the left in the mapping out (see figure 16).

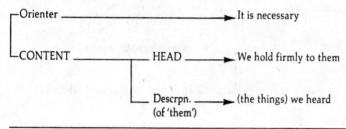

Figure 16.

Together, these form an exhortation. But there is still another nuclear sentence to be accommodated somewhere in the structure; sentence 4 'lest we drift away'. It is clearly a purpose clause; the 'lest' being equivalent to 'in order that not'. But what is the corresponding *MEANS?* It must be sentence 2; but is it sentence 2 alone, or in combination with sentence 1? The latter is more probable, for 'It is necessary' seems to function here merely as an auxiliary verb; something like 'We *must* hold on'. And as the whole serves as an exhortation we may represent the combined semantic structure as in figure 17.

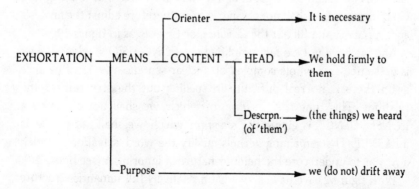

Figure 17.

We have said Hebrews 2.1 consists of an exhortation, verses 2-4 provide its grounds. But the structure of this is not uncomplicated. The 'if', which begins verse 2 with a conditional clause, and the main verb in the rhetorical question 'how shall we escape'—equivalent to 'we shall *not* escape'—form the backbone of the motivation: it is a *condition-CONSEQUENCE* relationship (see figure 18).

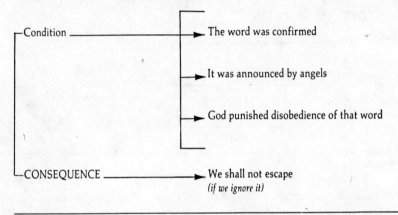

The word was confirmed

It was announced by angels

God punished disobedience of that word

We shall not escape
(if we ignore it)

Figure 18.

The relations within the *Condition* need to be spelt out. The logic appears clear; if God punished those who ignored the angels' message, the Law, we shall not escape (if we ignore the message we received). If this is the logic then the *Condition-CONSEQUENCE* is structured in the form of a *Grounds-CONCLUSION* relationship. That is, God's ancient dealings with Israel are offered as the grounds for the conclusion that if we ignore God's message we shall not escape. We can therefore adjust the analysis appropriately, and fill out the *Condition*, or *Grounds*, as in figure 19.

And we have not, so far, simplified the *CONCLUSION*, which in fact is presented as a whole complex of nuclear sentences (9-13). But once again there is no real difficulty in spelling out the structure of the relations. This time the *Condition*, of which 'we shall not escape' is a *CONSEQUENCE*, is giving the *reason* for which 'we shall not escape' is a *RESULT*. The remaining kernels qualify the word 'salvation', in such a way as to underscore the heinous nature of ignoring it (see figure 20).

With figure 21 we have arrived at a relatively full semantic structure analysis of the passage concerned; and it should be clear where the

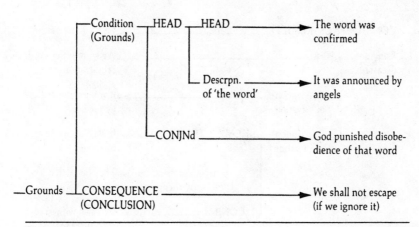

Figure 19.

passage is going, and how the parts relate. The meaning of the passage is partly a function of the individual nuclear sentences but also substantially of the structure of the relationships between them.

6.6 SEMANTIC STRUCTURE ANALYSIS OF EXTENSIVE DISCOURSES

To this point we have discussed only the semantic relations that exist between nuclear sentences. But because the relations discussed are *meaning* relationships they are applicable to the ways larger units combine too. For example the paragraph we have just analyzed in Hebrews stands in a particular relationship to what precedes and to what follows. The most prominent element in Hebrews 2.1-4 is the *Exhortation*. Everything else in the paragraph turns around this. But the 'therefore' with which 2.1 commences shows that chapter 1 is already furnishing other grounds for the exhortation in this paragraph. A similar analysis of that first chapter would show its most prominent nucleus to be the statement that God has finally spoken in a Son (v.2) who is supreme over the angels (v.4). This, then, provides the *grounds* for the *exhortation* to hold all the more firmly to what was announced by the Son, rather than to what was merely announced through angels in 2.1-4.

We could go on to specify how Heb. 2.1 relates also to the subsequent paragraphs, but that is beyond the scope of this chapter.[36] Often the paragraphs are related through their most prominent nuclear sentences (the HEAD of the paragraph), but this is not always the case. Just as

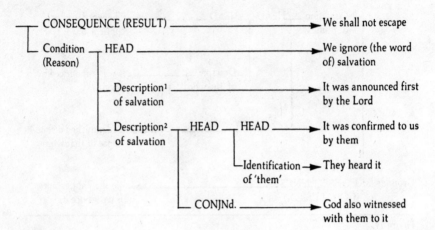

Figure 20.

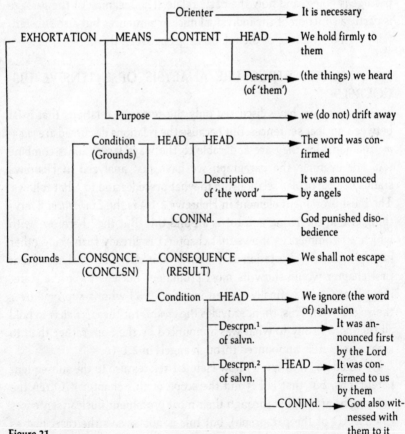

Figure 21.

some nuclear sentences qualify a concept embedded in another nuclear sentence, rather than the whole sentence as a unit, so a paragraph may relate to one nuclear sentence that was not central to another paragraph; it may take up and expound an idea only briefly mentioned there before the main theme is returned to in a subsequent paragraph. Analyses that pursue the semantic structure through large sections of discourse are called literary-semantic analyses, and they are an important, but an all too often neglected aspect of exegesis. Such an analysis of a relatively short section of Titus is given in figure 22, taken from Barnwell's *Introduction to Semantics and Translation*.[37] The methods involved have been introduced in this chapter, but are dealt with in more detail by Barnwell and others.[38] We can only be sure that we have explained the argument of a section if we can show that the proposed argument is consonant with a lexical semantic analysis of the passage.

6.7 SEMANTIC STRUCTURE ANALYSIS AND NEW TESTAMENT EXEGESIS

So far we are aware only of one book written in English that has made any detailed attempt to use semantic structure analysis as part of the task of New Testament exegesis—C. C. Caragounis' *The Ephesian "Mystērion"*[39]—and even that was written before the technique was brought out of its infancy. Nevertheless Caragounis was able to relate lexical and conceptual analysis of *mystērion* to the semantic structure of the passages which included the term (1.3-10; 3.1-13), and thereby to define more precisely what the writer intended by his use of the language, and how it related to the background of associated concepts in the apocalyptic tradition based on Daniel.

It may be hoped that commentators in the future will adopt the method, at least as a way to check their own understanding of how the argument of a passage is progressing. Already the great commentators struggle earnestly with the problem of the relationship of immediately adjacent nuclear sentences—Cranfield's *Romans* is a model of how a careful attempt can be made to see how each nuclear sentence is modified by the expansions which follow and which precede in the discourse. The same writers usually also attempt to examine the development of the argument or of theme from one major section to the next. However, the intermediate structure—the way meaning is organized in the individual

SECTION CONSTITUENT 2:1-10 (Paragraph; role: head of 2:1-15)

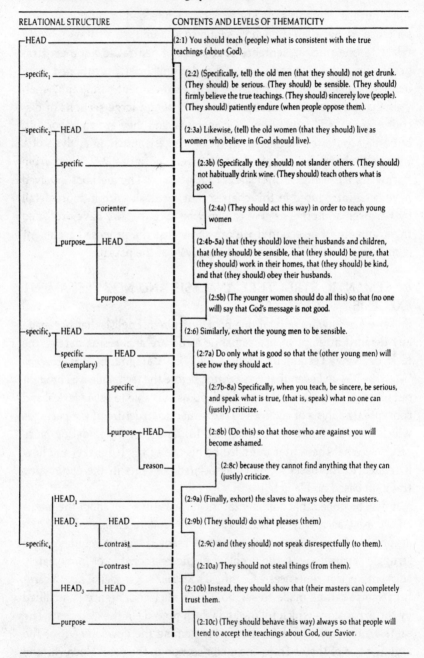

RELATIONAL STRUCTURE	CONTENTS AND LEVELS OF THEMATICITY
HEAD	(2:1) You should teach (people) what is consistent with the true teachings (about God).
specific₁	(2:2) (Specifically, tell) the old men (that they should) not get drunk. (They should) be serious. (They should) be sensible. (They should) firmly believe the true teachings. (They should) sincerely love (people). (They should) patiently endure (when people oppose them).
specific₂ — HEAD	(2:3a) Likewise, (tell) the old women (that they should) live as women who believe in (God should live).
specific	(2:3b) (Specifically they should) not slander others. (They should) not habitually drink wine. (They should) teach others what is good.
orienter	(2:4a) (They should act this way) in order to teach young women
purpose — HEAD	(2:4b-5a) that (they should) love their husbands and children, that (they should) be sensible, that (they should) be pure, that (they should) work in their homes, that (they should) be kind, and that (they should) obey their husbands.
purpose	(2:5b) (The younger women should do all this) so that (no one will) say that God's message is not good.
specific₃ — HEAD	(2:6) Similarly, exhort the young men to be sensible.
specific (exemplary) — HEAD	(2:7a) Do only what is good so that the (other young men) will see how they should act.
specific	(2:7b-8a) Specifically, when you teach, be sincere, be serious, and speak what is true, (that is, speak) what no one can (justly) criticize.
purpose — HEAD	(2:8b) (Do this) so that those who are against you will become ashamed.
reason	(2:8c) because they cannot find anything that they can (justly) criticize.
HEAD₁	(2:9a) (Finally, exhort) the slaves to always obey their masters.
HEAD₂ — HEAD	(2:9b) (They should) do what pleases (them)
contrast	(2:9c) and (they should) not speak disrespectfully (to them).
contrast	(2:10a) They should not steal things (from them).
HEAD₃ — HEAD	(2:10b) Instead, they should show that (their masters can) completely trust them.
purpose	(2:10c) (They should behave this way) always so that people will tend to accept the teachings about God, our Savior.

Figure 22.

paragraphs—is often not treated. And while the discussion of how the clauses and prepositional phrases modify the main verb and its expansions is conducted with utmost syntactic rigour, the explanations of the development from one paragraph to another often appear relatively subjective and merely thematic. This is not for want of care or thought, but for want of *criteria* and of systematic analysis of structure. Semantic structure analysis at least provides a framework within which relations of meaning within a paragraph may be discussed systematically. And it also allows the possibility of testing theories of development of argument; does a literary-semantic analysis highlight, as the most prominent elements, those that the exegete has otherwise considered to be the high points of the discourse, and are these high points plausibly related in the way the exegete has supposed?

We need to remember here our earlier caution about the objectives of semantic structure analysis and our consideration of what it might *possibly* accomplish. We cannot claim for semantic structure analysis that it is liable to offer startling new insights, nor even that it can provide 'objective' 'scientific' precision. It is not a neutral 'tool' any more than redaction criticism and form criticism are. Like them, it involves the interpreter in making refined judgements on the basis of his literary and interpretative experience as well as on clearly indexed linguistic features of the text.

For example, to attempt a semantic structure analysis of Eph. 1.3-14 immediately throws up the question of the relationship of the two nuclear sentences in verse 3, 'God is blessworthy',[40] and 'he has blessed us with all spiritual blessing'. Formally and syntactically the latter is merely a relative clause further describing or identifying the subject of the first sentence. But the exegete is not likely to be content with that. His knowledge of parallel forms (the *berakhoth* of Jewish literature) suggests to him that the second sentence is providing the grounds for the conclusion that God should be blessed). With the most basic awareness of illocutionary acts he will soon enough conclude that even if the first statement is formally an indicative its illocutionary force is that of an *exhortation* to bless God, and that in turn will suggest that the second sentence provides the *motivation* or grounds. But this is not strictly *provable;* at best it might attain widespread assent, but only that sort of assent that is won by any strongly probable reading. Semantic structure analysis cannot prove the reading right; all it can do is state the range of *possible* relationships, and in particular suggest one particular framework of *hypothesized* relationships. Its contribution is not to solve the question, but to *pose* it in the sharpest possible way.

Similarly we might feel the most probable semantic relation between verse 3 and what follows in verse 4ff. of Ephesians chapter one is that of *Generic* to a series of *Specifics:* that is, that 'He chose us', 'he foreordained us to sonship' (v.5) and 'he revealed the mystery of his will to us' (v.9), are offered as specific examples of the *generic* statement that 'he blessed us with every spiritual blessing'. And not a few commentators have suggested something like this *might* be the case, even without the 'benefits' of having studied semantic structure. But once again *proof* eludes us. Perhaps all we can say is that the most plausible semantic structure that can be offered requires such a relation, and that *kathōs*, the conjunction between v. 3 and v. 4, can be translated 'since', 'for', or 'because', even if it is more usually comparative or modal; while for the more usual meanings of *kathōs*, no satisfactory semantic structure is readily offered.

The construction of a semantic structure for a paragraph, or for a longer discourse, has to be carried out in an environment informed by syntax and by linguistics. And the result is a model with which the meaning of a section may be compared. Because it is a *clear* and systematic presentation of the proposed structure of meaning, it should, like any good theory, fulfil two functions. It should help us to understand the phenomenon of the text. And it should bring to expression our interpretation with such lack of ambiguity that it is readily falsifiable. In other words, semantic structure analysis should be understood not as an iron sceptre with which to rule interpretation, but as a lamp to illuminate the possibilities.

Notes

[1]Cf. Noam Chomsky's renowned sentence, 'Colorless green ideas sleep furiously', *Syntactic Structures*, The Hague, Mouton, 1957, p.15, which is identified as grammatical using a limited definition of grammar which excludes meaning. See J. Oller, 'On the Relationship Between Syntax, Semantics and Pragmatics', *Linguistics* 83 (1972), pp.43-55.
[2]C. K. Barrett, *The First Epistle to the Corinthians* (Black's New Testament Commen-

taries), London, A. & C. Black, 1971², p.130.

³*Language*, London, Allen & Unwin, 1935, p.170.

⁴*General Linguistics*, p.190.

⁵*A Dictionary of Linguistics and Phonetics*, Oxford, Blackwell, 1985².

⁶M. B. Lewis, *Sentence Analysis in Modern Malay*, Cambridge, CUP, 1969, defines a grammatical sentence as 'that unit which has potentiality of indefinite silence both before and after it. It is grammatically complete' (p.66). See also C. C. Fries, *The Structure of English*, New York, 1952, who employs a similar concept for sentence classification.

⁷See above, 2.1.5 and cf. A. H. Maynard, 'Ti emoi kai soi', *NTS*, 31, 4(1985), pp. 582-6.

⁸Leiden, Brill, 1969, pp.39ff.

⁹*Meaning and Form*, p.184.

¹⁰And Bolinger's *Meaning and Form*. Lyons, *Language and Linguistics*, 5.5, 'Sentence Meaning and Utterance Meaning' provides a useful summary of the issues.

¹¹For much of the material in this section we are grateful to Beekman, Callow, and Kopesec, *The Semantic Structure of Written Communication*, chap. 2.

¹²On *cohesion* see M. A. K. Halliday and R. Hasan, *Cohesion in English*, London, Longmans, 1976, or more briefly in G. Brown and G. Yule, *Discourse Analysis*, 6.1.1. On coherence, see Brown and Yule, 7.1.

¹³On the complex relations between 'propositions' and 'sentences' see the contrasting approaches of J. J. Katz, *Semantic Theory*, 4.3f., and J. Lyons, *Language, Meaning and Context*, pp. 106ff.; Lyons also distinguishes between the different propositions a single sentence might affirm, in different *utterances*, and a more general concept of *propositional content*.

¹⁴See Beekman, Callow, and Kopesec, *The Semantic Structure of Written Communication*, chap. 5.

¹⁵This is not to say that determining the borders of paragraphs is always easy (contrast the different paragraphing of the various versions of the English Bible). On the criteria, see e.g. Beekman, Callow, and Kopesec, *The Semantic Structure of Written Communication*, chap. 9.

¹⁶See for example G. D. Fee, *New Testament Exegesis: A Handbook for Students and Pastors*, Philadelphia, Westminster Press, 1983, pp. 60-77, and the literature cited. For modern approaches to sentence analysis see *inter multos alios*, Jean Aitchison, *Linguistics*, chap. 7; J. Lyons, *Introduction to Theoretical Linguistics*, 5.2 and chap. 6, and W. R. Elkins, *A New English Primer*, London, MacMillan, 1974, passim. On the theoretical question of *how* sentences convey meaning see the different approaches of R. Kempson, *Semantic Theory*, chap. 7 (componential analysis); G. N. Leech, *Semantics*, chap. 8 (componential and predication analysis), and J. Lyons, *Language, Meaning and Context*, parts 3 and 4.

17For introductions to N. Chomsky's works see e.g. J. Aitchison, *Linguistics*, chaps. 14-16 (very elementary) or J. Lyons, *Chomsky*, London, Fontana, 1970 (fuller, but not so up to date). E. A. Nida and C. R. Taber's seminal *Theory and Practice of Translation* was first published in the *Helps for Translators* series sponsored by the United Bible Societies.

18See above all E. A. Nida and C. R. Taber, *The Theory and Practice of Translation*, passim but especially pp.39-55.

19E. A. Nida and C. R. Taber, *The Theory and Practice of Translation*, pp.51ff.; though Nida and Taber in fact retained the term 'kernels' for these semantically fuller sentences. The term 'nuclear structures' is, however, used by E. A. Nida (et al.) in *Style and Discourse*, chaps. 6-8.

20Cf. the general discussion in Nida and Taber, *The Theory and Practice of Translation*, chap. 7.

21W. J. Kaiser, *Towards an Exegetical Theology*, Grand Rapids, Baker, 1981.

22G. D. Fee, *New Testament Exegesis*, pp. 60-77.

23Fee, *New Testament Exegesis*, pp.74-6.

24R. P. Martin, *The Spirit and the Congregation: Studies in 1 Corinthians 12-15*, Grand Rapids, Eerdmans, 1984, p.57, wishes to take the first verb as imperatival, the second as indicative, and the *hina* clause as imperatival; yielding: 'Make *[this kind of]* love your goal; yet "*you are striving for spiritual gifts,*" but [I say] rather *that you should all prophesy.*' But it is unlikely that the Corinthians would read *zēloute* as an indicative when it follows immediately on an imperative. And imperatival *hina* is rare in the NT, and improbable after two finite verbs in the imperative. So the ellipsis is not of 'I say', but of a potentially repetitive 'seek': compare v.5 where the same wording and structure is clearly *not* a case of imperatival *hina*.

25Louw, *Semantics of New Testament Greek*, pp. 67-158.

26An absolute clause is one *grammatically separate* from the main clause; e.g. 'They *being on their way,* a certain man said . . .' (Lk 9.57). In the Greek the participle and its 'subject' (the pronoun 'they') are both inflected as genitives, which thus separates them syntactically from the rest of the sentence. Similarly, in Heb 2.4, the participle '[God] *bearing witness*' is genitival and so separated from the main verb in an 'absolute' construction.

27Though Louw goes on to state the relationships within the structure in some measure; and compare the fuller elucidation in E. A. Nida, J. P. Louw, A. H. Snyman and J. v.W. Cronje, *Style and Discourse*, chaps. 7 and 8.

28It should be clear we are not using 'deep structure', 'surface structure', 'transformation', etc. in the same technical sense as Chomsky, but in a looser, nevertheless comparable way. The 'deep structure' sentences are the kernels which are 'transformed' into the 'surface structure' sentences (i.e. those before us in the text) by addition of time indicators, spelling out of the phrase structure, and addition of expansions (including embedded sentences).

[29]Nida and Taber, *The Theory and Practice of Translation*, pp.53-4.

[30]E. A. Nida (et al.), *Style and Discourse*, chap. 7. For SIL approaches, see Beekman, Callow, and Kopesec, *The Semantic Structure of Written Communication*, chaps. 2, 7, and 8; also K. Barnwell, *Introduction to Semantics and Translation*, High Wycombe, SIL, 1980[2], and the pioneering work by J. Beekman and J. Callow, *Translating the Word Of God*.

[31]See e.g. I. H. Marshall, *The Gospel of Luke*, p.313; J. A. Fitzmyer, *The Gospel According to Luke I-IX*, pp.690ff.

[32]For discussion of these see Beekman, Callow, and Kopesec, *The Semantic Structure of Written Communication*, p.107f. As an example of *comment* they offer the statement that the Lord will punish Alexander in 2 Tim. 4.14b, while of *parenthesis* they offer the remarks about Erastus and Trophimus, and the request Timothy come to Paul before the stormy season, in 1 Tim. 4.20-1.

[33]That is, the illocutionary force of the statement is cohortative. The purpose of the writer is not merely to *inform* of the need to 'hold firmly', but vigorously to encourage his readers towards that goal.

[34]This is how the Jerusalem Bible has taken the relationship in translating it 'If a promise that was made through angels proved to be so true *that* every infringement . . . brought its own proper punishment.'

[35]It will be noted that we have not provided the nuclear sentence here, but, for convenience, the corresponding nuclear segment. By nuclear segment we mean a rearrangement of or transformation of a nuclear sentence such as more closely reflects the surface structure of the text, and yet may still be a simplified form of it.

[36]For extended treatments of the structure of Hebrews see, for example, L. L. Neeley, 'A Discourse Analysis of Hebrews', *OPTAT* 3-4(1987), pp.1-147; also A. Vanhoye, *La Structure Littéraire de L'Épitre aux Hébreux*, Paris, de Brouwer, 1975[2], and L. Dussaut, *Synopse Structurelle de L'Épitre aux Hébreux*, Paris, du Cerf, 1981.

[37]P.226.

[38]K. Barnwell, *Introduction to Semantics and Translation*, ch. 21; J. Beekman, J. Callow, and M. Kopesec, *The Semantic Structure of Written Communication*, chaps. 9 and 10; W. Pickering, *A Framework for Discourse Analysis* (passim).

[39]*The Ephesian "Mystērion": Meaning and Content*, Lund, Gleerup, 1977. Caragounis has used the technique to a lesser extent in his monograph on *The Son of Man*, Tübingen, Mohr, 1986, pp.96ff.

[40]See Caragounis, *The Ephesian "Mystērion"*, p.79f. for the argument that *eulogētos* does not mean 'blessed', but 'blessworthy'. The ellipsed verb is not therefore *eiē* but *estin*.

7. Discourse Analysis

7.1 INTRODUCTION

The term 'discourse' is used generally for any coherent sequence of strings, any coherent stretch of language. As we have already seen, some linguists would restrict the term to spoken language, but there is no compelling reason for us to do that. A conversation is discourse, but so is a novel or a poem or a dissertation. At the level of discourse we are past the discussion of sentences to a consideration of the fact that language is used primarily in coherent, structured sequences, not in unrelated phrases.

It is becoming increasingly clear that all discourse is carefully structured so as to ensure some measure of development through the discourse. To put it at the most elementary level, discourse has a beginning, a middle and an end, and the beginning could not be confused with the end: the parts could not randomly be interchanged and still leave recognizable discourse. Discourse, in fact, is characterized by *coherence*,[1] a coherence of supra-sentential structure and a coherence of topic. That is to say there is a relationship between the sentences which constitute any discourse, a relationship which involves both grammatical structure and meaning.

There are various features available to control discourse structures, in some measure related to literary genre, and it is these features which enable the reader or listener to make his way through discourse. As we shall see in Chapter 8, this is most clearly demonstrable in the case of conversation, where participants know what they are expected to do or say and when it is appropriate to take a turn in speaking. But regularity is there in all discourse.

In this book we have been concerned with the problems necessarily involved in the interpretation of biblical text. That text was generated in context. Jonah had its context, Revelation had a very different context, and the context which gave rise to 1 Corinthians was different again. Each of the texts (Jonah, Revelation, 1 Corinthians) represents a communication from an author to a reader or readers. Brown and Yule offer a simple definition of a text (later carefully modified): a text is 'the verbal record of a communicative event'.[2]

This important observation takes us back to Chapter 1 and the consideration of pragmatics. Semantics represents the study of the meaning of some particular string of words. But in the world of communication, the world where words are used in context, meaning is to be found not merely in semantics, but in the wider considerations of context and cotext, in the considerations of who said what to whom and where and when and why and how and with what accompanying gestures and with what consequences. The understanding of text, in fact, necessarily involves the interpreter in pragmatics. To quote Brown and Yule again:

> Any analytic approach in linguistics which involves contextual considerations necessarily belongs to that area of language study called *pragmatics*. 'Doing discourse analysis' certainly involves 'doing syntax and semantics', but it primarily consists of 'doing pragmatics'.[3]

Text, then, relates to the communication of an event, and the more skilled the communicator so the more carefully structured will be the text. Unfortunately for us, the term 'carefully structured' has its own linguistic horizon: it is relative to the perceptions of the author and his perceptions of his readers. We have already considered Hebrews 2.1-4[4] in some detail, but the writer's reference to 'the message declared by angels', a reference which is not further explicated, is simply incomprehensible to the average reader today, who would not be aware of the Jewish tradition that the Law was mediated to Moses through angels. The phrasing of the text and the sequencing of the phrases *is* carefully structured, but the structure is related to a particular historical and sociological context within which the communication was effected. And this is of the essence of text. Text relates harmoniously to a context, and is more than a mere sequence of plausibly related sentences.

We may readily construct a sequence of sentences which demonstrate a measure of coherence, but which do not constitute a text:

> Today is Friday. Man Friday was a character in a book. There are seven thousand books in our municipal library. Garbage collection is the responsibility of the municipal authorities. The Christian is expected to submit to authorities. Last night the wrestler Big Daddy got three submissions in less than two minutes.

The sentences in this concatenation are well formed, and each is objectively related to its neighbours. In this sense we have a coherent text. But there is no imaginable context for the sequence, which is not a *discourse* text. Texts are created in a context, and texts demonstrate structure.[5]

Let us consider the question of the structure of a discourse whose boundaries are given: say Paul's First Letter to the Corinthians. The total discourse will include the following components:[6]

1. The set of descriptions of the objects referred to in 1 Corinthians. This would include the local church (1.2), the city of Corinth (1.2), 'my letter' (5.9), 'your bodies' (6.15), and 'idols' (8.1).

2. The set of propositions included in 1 Corinthians, including, for example, 'The unmarried man is anxious about the affairs of the Lord' (7.32).

3. The set of actual sentences used.

4. The set of thematic nets identifiable in the letter. Any object of the discourse may have a number of propositions in the text relating to that object. The semantic significance of these propositions lies not only in their individual occurrence, but also in the net which might be cast over the total set of those propositions. This net is a thematic net. Thus the object 'body' in chapter 12 has a number of propositions made about it ('the body is one', v. 12; 'there are many parts, yet one body', v. 20; 'you

are the body', v. 27) and a thematic net relates them all.

5. The net of time reference. This net must be conceived of as embracing more than patently time-orientated words such as 'today'. The tense system also is included in the net, which would then take in 'called by the will of God' (1.1), 'there is quarrelling among you' (1.11), 'when I came to you' (2.1), 'I wrote to you'(5.9), 'when I arrive' (16.3).

6. The reference-relation diagram, a diagram which establishes the relationship between the discourse objects. The various discourse objects do not exist in the discourse independently of one another: their relationship to one another is an essential part of the coherence of the discourse.

The presence of the above six components in any given text serves to identify the text as a discourse rather than as a mere agglomeration of sentences. We have chosen an epistle as an example of a coherent text, but the presence or absence of a coherent net of time reference, of thematic nets meaningfully relating the propositions made about the discourse objects, or of the reference relationship diagram, makes possible the actual identification of discourse boundaries of all types of discourse.

Thus the time net relating to 1 Corinthians is quite distinct from that relating to, say, John's Gospel. The two are, in discourse terms, independent nets, but through the real world to which each net refers they may be related to each other. Obviously this process of net-relationship is of greater significance in the case of the Pauline *corpus* than in the case of a Pauline letter and a Gospel.

Before we advance any further into a consideration of discourse analysis as it relates to biblical exegesis, we must at least comment on the tentative nature of this particular aspect of linguistics. The fact is that at the present there are no firm conclusions, no generally accepted formulae, no fixed methodology, not even an agreed terminology. In these next two chapters we aim at bringing into biblical studies relevant and important concepts from a comparatively young and vigorously growing discipline. Michael Stubbs makes the point for us: 'I can only point out that no one is in a position to write a comprehensive account of discourse analysis. The subject is at once too vast and too lacking in focus and consensus.'[7] Since 1983, when Stubbs made his comment, certainly great advances in our understanding of discourse have been made, but discourse analysis, as a branch of linguistics, is still in the process of explosive growth.

7.2 DISCOURSE INDICATORS OF TIME

One of the most transparent of all discourse indicators is the time indicator. Of course in a thesis there might be little or no indication of time shift, and by contrast in anecdote the time shift might be the principal discourse feature. John 1.19—2.1 may be taken as an example of careful time indication.[8] A week of events is indicated:

Day one: The Jews send priests to John. (1.19)

Day two: John sees Jesus. ('The next day', 1.29)

Day three: John again sees Jesus. ('The next day', 1.35 and 'They stayed with him that day.' 1.39)

Day four: Jesus decides to go to Galilee. ('The next day', 1.43)

Day seven: The wedding at Cana (2.1)

Note also other possible indicators of passing time:

'At the Passover Feast'   (2.23)

'After this'   (3.22)

'When the Lord knew'   (4.1)

'Meanwhile'   (4.31)

'When evening came'   (6.16)

It is, of course, important to note that a phrase such as 'after this' is only potentially a time indicator in the sense of introducing a *subsequent* event. It may be nothing more than a semantically neutral way of indicating the close of one section of discourse and the beginning of a new section, without any necessary reference to a time relationship between the two sections.[9] The discourse regularities for time vary from one culture to another. In some languages it is not permissible to have 'flashbacks'; time must flow linearly, steadily forward, or even backward.

In general any text is made more difficult if the time sequence is not linear. Note in the following example from P. G. Wodehouse[10] just how difficult it is to get a clear idea of the flow of events, but note also that (fortunately) in this entirely trivial story appreciation of the story does not require the reader correctly to interpret the opening paragraphs.

The thing really began when I got back to Easeby, my uncle's place in Shropshire. I was spending a week or so there, as I generally did in the summer; and I had had to break my visit to come back to

London to get a new valet. I had found Meadowes, the fellow I had taken to Easeby with me, sneaking my silk socks, a thing no bloke of spirit could stick at any price. It transpiring, moreover, that he had looted a lot of other things here and there about the place, I was reluctantly compelled to hand the misguided blighter the mitten and go to London to ask the registry office to dig up another specimen for my approval. They sent me Jeeves.

I shall always remember the morning he came. It so happened that the night before I had been present at a rather cheery little supper, and I was feeling pretty rocky. On top of this I was trying to read a book Florence Craye had given me. She had been one of the house-party at Easeby, and two or three days before I left we had got engaged.

The reader might care to attempt to re-order the statements in their true chronological order.

The Greek language does not require that events in a discourse should develop linearly. The classical New Testament passage which illustrates the point is Mark 6.14ff.

In this passage we have great complexity of time reference, but it is possible to rearrange the kernel sentences into a time sequence. In the following there is no attempt to identify all the kernels. On the left-hand side we have indicated approximately the sequence in which the kernels are presented by Mark.

  8 Herodias married Philip.

  7 Herod married Herodias.

  9 John the Baptist kept telling Herod.

  10 Herodias held a grudge against John.

  11 Herodias wanted to kill John.

  6 Herod arrested John.

  13 Herod knew that John was a good man.

  12 Herod was afraid of John.

  14 Herod protected John.

  15 Herod listened to John.

  16 Herod became disturbed.

  17 It was Herod's birthday.

  18 Herodias' daughter danced.

  19 Herod promised to give her anything.

20 Herodias' daughter asked for John's head.

21 Herod had John executed.

2 Jesus' reputation spread.

3 The people said Jesus was John the Baptist.

1,4 Herod heard this.

5 Herod said 'He is John'.

The time indicators are just one example of what is more generally termed deixis (see 7.3.2, below), and we now turn to look at this feature of discourse.

7.3 DEIXIS

Deixis[11] is a term applied to utterances to indicate personal, temporal or locational aspects of an event. We may identify five categories of deixis: personal deixis, social deixis, temporal deixis, locational deixis, and discourse deixis.

7.3.1 Personal Deixis

The personal pronouns in a text may have clear antecedents so that when we read Mat. 17.2, 'And he was transfigured before them . . .' we have only to look back into the preceding verse for the antecedent of 'he'.

Much more interesting is the situation where a pronominal form cannot be directly explicated from the text and recourse has to be made to some wider context. Thus Acts 16.9-10 displays the intriguing introduction to the 'we' passages of Acts:

And a vision appeared to Paul in the night: a man of Macedonia was standing beseeching him and saying, 'Come over to Macedonia and help us.' And when *he* had seen the vision, immediately *we* sought to go on into Macedonia.

7.3.2. Social Deixis

This category is a special case of personal deixis. Wherever language is realized as utterance it is necessarily employed in a particular culture, where certain conventions are used with regard to human relationships. A man may be addressed as "Sir", "Doctor", "George", "Mate" and these labels are all deictic, indicating something of the man and something of the relationship between the man and the speaker. Some languages employ honorifics, special forms of pronoun or special forms of the verb, which at once indicate the relationship between any two people. We may note also the so-called T-V languages,[12] such as French, where 'tu' is used for a close friend, but 'vous' for anyone else or for more than one person.

Again there is the indirect address to royalty, still used in some parts of the world, where the pronoun 'you' is avoided altogether, and some alternative phrase is used: 'As your Majesty knows . . .' Note, for example, Nehemiah 2.3, 'May the king live for ever!' and 2.7, 'If it pleases the king . . .'[13] Note also the indirect mode of address used by Joseph to Pharaoh in Genesis 41.25ff.: 'The dream of Pharaoh is one; God has revealed to Pharaoh what he is about to do . . . It is as I told Pharaoh, God has shown to Pharaoh what he is about to do . . . And the doubling of Pharaoh's dream means . . . Let Pharaoh proceed . . .'

Social deixis is also evident in the formal greetings, common in all cultures, stylized adjacency pairs, which again provide a means of indicating a relationship between those who are exchanging greetings. The greetings may convey very little, 'Hello!', or may convey very precise information: in Mixe, a language of Mexico, a younger person greets an older person in one of two ways, depending on whether he lives uphill or downhill from where the younger person lives.

Of course social deixis is often paralinguistic: when another person enters the room it may be necessary to know exactly how far one should rise from one's seat. In Ethiopia this varies all the way from completely ignoring the person who has come through to standing up and not resuming the seat until invited to do so. It is important to understand the social conventions lying behind deixis, since the use of inappropriate forms of deixis, whether linguistic or paralinguistic, may be interpreted as insult. But of course in written discourse the social deixis may often be of great importance in identifying the roles of the participants. Note in the New Testament the use of *Kyrie!* (Luke 6.46) in the vocative, of *Rabbi!*, and *Gynai!* (Matthew 15.28).

The book of Esther not only illustrates some of the features of social deixis at the Persepolis palace, but also provides us with one of the most carefully sculpted dramas in the entire Old Testament. We note particularly chapter 5:

On the third day [pointing back to 4.16 and the requirement that the

Jews of Susa fast for three days on her behalf] Esther put on her royal
robes [she would be in the *herem*, the part of the palace reserved for
the king's women, and to which they would normally be confined;
she wears her royal robes both to indicate her peculiar privilege as
queen, and in recognition of the occasion: a formal audience] and
stood in the inner court of the king's palace, opposite the king's hall.
The king was sitting on his royal throne [not as though, naively, the
writer imagined that he sat there in solitary splendour all day, but
because this was the set day for the king to grant audiences, and
Esther knew so] inside the palace opposite the entrance to the palace;
and when the king saw Queen Esther standing in the court, she
found favour in his sight and he held out to Esther the golden sceptre
[confirmation that this was, indeed, a formal occasion] that was in his
hand. Then Esther approached and touched the top of the scepter.
We note that thus far not a word has been spoken, although much has
been communicated, and for those who understood the etiquette involved the new and highly dramatic events now to be narrated have
been persuasively introduced.

And the king said to her, 'What is it, Queen Esther? What is your
request? [It is apparent that like any other person attending the formal reception she has some specific request to make.] It shall be given
you, even to the half of my kingdom.' [On the one hand to be recognized as hyperbole, on the other hand to be seen in the context of
this narrative as an ironical glance forward to the time when Esther
will demand if not half of the kingdom at least the removal of the
second ruler and his replacement by Mordecai.] And she said, 'If it
please the king, let the king and Haman come this day to a dinner
that I have prepared for the king.' [No specific next step is mentioned,
but this dinner has already been prepared. As Clines points out the
crafting of the story involves the Jews in repeated fasting and the
Persians in equally repeated feasting (1.3, the banquet by Ahasuerus;
1.9, the banquet given by Vashti; 2.18, a second banquet by Ahasuerus, this time in Esther's honour; 3.15, a drinking session with the
king and Haman; 5.5 is Esther's banquet for the king and Haman; and
7.1 is the second banquet. In 8.17, after the dispatch of Haman, the
Jews' fasting symbolically turns to feasting.)][14]
However, the promise of the king to give Esther whatever she asks

'even to the half of my kingdom' has yet to be redeemed. And once again we are to be aware of the subtlety of court etiquette. Esther saves the king from any possible embarrassment resulting from his promise by making his coming to the second, as yet unprepared, banquet the condition for his redeeming his promise. If he thinks better of his promise then he need not attend the banquet. If he still intends to keep to his promise then she will be spared any embarrassment at making her request and he will be spared any doubts about meeting it. The social strategies appropriate to court life are delicately presented by a master of literary style.

7.3.3 Temporal Deixis
Temporal deixis has already been referred to, and at least four categories of deictic indicators may be identified. First of all there is the deictic element inherent in verbal tense systems. Then there is usually a range of nominals indicating time: 'today', 'Wednesday'. Thirdly, there are deictic conjunctions, 'before', 'while'. And then there are the aspectual verbs indicating intent: 'I wanted', 'I intended', 'I planned', 'I expected'. We note here particularly Romans 1.13, 'I want you to know, brethren, that I have often intended to come to you (but thus far have been prevented), in order that I might reap some harvest among you . . . so I am eager to preach the gospel to you also . . .' a Topic which is lost in a lengthy text from 1.16—15.21. when it is resumed with 'This is the reason why I have been hindered from coming to you. But now . . . I hope to see you in passing as I go to Spain.'

7.3.4 Locational Deixis
Locational deixis enables us to place any action spatially. Words used by any speaker have deictic reference to his own position or to some location indicated by him. Thus 'here' means where the speaker is, but 'there' means where he is not. Similarly 'this' preceding a nominal places the referent near to the speaker, where 'that' places it at a distance.

7.3.5 Discourse Deixis
Discourse deixis relates to indicators of structure within any discourse. Such words as 'therefore', 'following', 'subsequent', and phrases such as 'so then' point to some new stage reached in the discourse. It would

be misleading, however, to assume without further evidence that the use, for example, of *oun*, 'therefore', necessarily established a causal relationship between the new text and the preceding cotext: 'It does not always furnish a strictly causal connection, but may be used more loosely as a temporal connective in the continuation or resumption of a narrative.'[15] Luke, in Acts, repeatedly uses *oun* in this continuative sense (as in 2.30 and 33; in 8.4, 10.32, and 12.5, where *ho men oun Petros etēreito en tē(i) phylakē(i),*'Peter is kept in prison' not because of Herod's intention to bring him to trial after Passover, but simply as the inevitable next event in time.

7.4 DIRECT AND INDIRECT SPEECH IN TEXTS

In written text there are two ways of recording utterances: through direct speech or through indirect speech.[16] But the selection process is not necessarily arbitrary: in some languages, where a more important person is addressing a less important person direct speech is always used to record what was said, but indirect speech is used to record the words of an inferior addressing a superior. Again the choice of direct or indirect speech may be determined by the level of embedding in the sentence: 'I said to him "He told me that he would come today" ' and not 'I said to him "he told me 'I will come tomorrow' " ' although, obviously, it is usually possible to use direct speech forms if the context requires it: 'What did he actually say?'

The use of indirect speech may be indicated by some deictic word: 'He said *that* he would come' and in Greek, forms such as *hoti* and *pōs* may indicate indirect speech. However attention needs to be paid to cotext here, since Greek *hoti* recitative actually introduces direct speech and in some sense corresponds to our quotation marks ("). Note, for example, Luke 19.7-9:

All the people saw this and began to mutter
(hoti) 'He has gone to be the guest of a "sinner",'
But Zacchaeus stood up and said to the Lord,
'Look, Lord! Here and now I give half of my possessions to the poor,
and if I have cheated anybody out of anything,
I will pay back four times the amount.'
Jesus said to him,
(hoti) 'Today salvation has come to this house,

because this man, too, is a son of Abraham.'
This statement of Jesus does give rise to a grammatical problem because although it is made *pros auton*, 'to him', the man is referred to in the third person.[17] The problem may be resolved by making *pros auton* mean 'about him', so that Jesus, in fact, addresses the people, or by supposing that the direct quotation ends at 'house', or by assuming that after 'house' there is some indication of astonishment on the part of the listeners to the conversation, and the latter part of Jesus' words is addressed to them, not to Zacchaeus.

7.5 THE STRUCTURE OF DISCOURSE
7.5.1 Discourse Boundary
A discourse may consist of a limited sequence of utterances quite clearly separated off from all other verbal exchanges. Two students pass in the street:

'I'll see you later.'
'Right!'

The discourse boundary is unambiguous: silence.

At the other extreme we have extended discourse, long conversations, for example, where the discourse moves from greetings to a sequence of different topics and then to some closing formula. In such a discourse the main boundaries are clear, but within the main boundaries there will be further boundaries, marking, for example the transition from greetings to first topic and from first topic to second topic. It is already apparent from this brief introduction to discourse boundaries that we should expect to find discourse marked by some measure of structuring, demonstrating initiatory sequences, concluding sequences, and continuative sequences. Discourse is characterized by staging, the orderly progression in a necessarily linear sequence.[18]

The orderly sequence of which we speak, however, is not order merely for the sake of order, or order over against chaos. It is order which leads to some kind of *peak*. This is most readily demonstrable with respect to narrative, but is more generally true, for example, of ordinary correspondence. Longacre puts the point clearly:

Something like plot characterizes forms of discourse other than narrative. If we grant that any discourse is going somewhere, it follows that it does not simply start and stop but that it may have some sort

of culminative expression between.[19]
What is important is that discourse is never random, that it has marked initiation and conclusion, and that somewhere in between a peak is reached.

7.5.2 Initiatory Markers
These often include some indication of genre. 'Once upon a time' is both initiatory and genre-indicating. 'Good morning' has the same dual function. But the initiatory marker may be common to a number of genres. Thus a discourse might simply begin with a statement of subject: 'I want to talk about kangaroos.' In this initiation there is no indication of genre beyond the negative indication that this is not a fairy story. The sentence could introduce a formal lecture or could be the prelude to some kind of farce. It could prove to be the first line of a poem. In fact this sentence could only be identified as initiatory by reference to the cotext: it could be merely continuative, possibly marking a transition from a topic already being discussed to the topic of kangaroos which is what the speaker wishes to discuss.

7.5.3 Concluding Sequences
Concluding sequences are marked as such by some kind of transition formula or *colophon:* 'Amen' to end a prayer, 'Goodbye' to end a conversation, or a clearly identified cycle may be completed, for example the completion of the alphabet in the acrostic poem which constitutes Psalm 119, where each verse of any one section begins with the same letter of the Hebrew alphabet. The Old Testament displays many distinct concluding formulae.

Thus the six days of creation in Genesis 1, each conclude with the phrase 'And there was evening and there was morning . . .' Genesis later moves into a long succession of interrelated genealogies, *toledōth,* Genesis 25.19. Although these colophons are often taken as initiatory there can be little doubt that in fact each forms the conclusion to a family history, not the introduction to a genealogy. Thus at Genesis 5.1 we have the formula: 'This is the *toledōth* of Adam', but in fact chapters 2—4 have been concerned with Adam and all that remains to be said about Adam is a brief summary of some five verses.[20] The book of Judges presents another pattern in which successive cycles are organized in a set pattern: a statement that the people of Israel 'did what was evil in the sight of the Lord', the tracing of the consequences of the apostasy until a deliverer is granted and the conclusion of the cycle with some such phrase as 'the land had rest forty years' (3.7, 3.11). The complicated succession of rulers in the two kingdoms is handled by reference to the king's name, the name of his kingdom, the length of his reign, his mother's name and a concise religious assessment of the reign:

> Now in the eighteenth year of King Jeroboam the son of Nebat
> Abijam began to reign over Judah.
> He reigned for three years in Jerusalem.
> His mother's name was Ma'cah the daughter of Abishalom.
> And he walked in all the sins which his father did before him.
> (1 Kings 15.1-3)

The conclusion to a history is similarly signalled:

> And Rehoboam slept with his fathers and was buried with his fathers in the city of David. His mother's name was Na'amah the Ammonitess. And Abijam his son reigned in his stead. (1 Kings 14.31)

7.5.4 The Internal Structure of Discourse

The discourse structure of Ephesians is elegantly summarized by Markus Barth in his commentary:

> Paul's exhortation to married people (5.21-33)
> forms the first of three parts of the social ethics
> that constitutes the Haustafel. (5.21—6.9)
> The Haustafel is embedded among the general ethical admonitions to the whole Christian community and each of its members. (4.17—5.20)
> All ethical statements are in turn part of the teaching on the public testimony of the church which begins with 3.1 . . .
> and is grounded on the proclamation of the foundation and formation of the church. (1.3—2.22)

The actual boundaries and transitions in discourse are not usually overtly noted by the casual reader. It seems as though transitions are identified subjectively. In fact, objective markers of discourse transitions are invariably present and it is on the basis of these markers that the apparently subjective perception is possible. Thus subordinate discourse boundaries may often be discerned through the appearance of some new dominant lexical reference, for example, the reference to Laban within the long Jacob narrative[21] of Genesis. Laban is first mentioned in 28.2 as a new character in the narrative, and disappears from the narrative at 31.55 in a carefully crafted passage which artistically dismisses him:

> Early in the morning Laban arose, and kissed his grandchildren and his daughters and blessed them; then he departed and returned home.

The Laban pericope has its own structure, its own transitions, its own peak, all within the larger structure of the Jacob narrative. To deal with these complex structures a new kind of commentary is needed which can place lexical studies in their appropriate place but can give to the larger structures more careful consideration. Claus Westermann's *Genesis 12-36*, for example,[22] sets out the commentary in a series of identifiable pericopae, each of which is then discussed under six headings, literature, text, form, setting, commentary, purpose, and thrust. This format ensures that not only are the minutiae of the text examined, but the macroscopic relationships of the pericopae to one another are also carefully identified and discussed. Note for example the identification of the interrelated discourses of Genesis 27—33: 'The theme is a conflict or rivalry between the brothers Jacob and Esau. The conflict between Jacob and Laban (29—31) is set within it and into this that between Leah and Rachel'(p.407). We note also the innovative work of Walter Brueggemann whose commentary on Genesis (significantly subtitled 'A Bible Commentary for Teaching and Preaching')[23] includes a series of structure diagrams, aimed at allowing the student to see at one glance the involved structures of several chapters. Of course the most significant part of discourse structure is the marking of the peak, and it is to a consideration of peaking that we now turn our attention.

7.5.5 Peaking

In narrative stories it is normal to find a peak towards which the narrative advances, and from which there is a rather rapid descent. The peak is the point of the story: a question is posed . . . and then answered, a paradox is presented . . . and then resolved, a competition is described . . . and then a winner produced. The identification of the peak is vital to the appreciation of the narrative; it is not surprising, therefore, to find that the peak of a narrative is often explicitly marked. As some modern writers have discovered, if there is too great subtlety in presenting the peak the reader (or listener, in the case of oral literature) will simply fail to perceive it, and the story then fades out miserably.

Of course any extended narrative will have multiple peaks. Again the Jacob narrative provides an excellent example. The Laban pericope presents the conflict between Jacob and Laban which is resolved in stages:

Stage 1: Jacob's two wives: Laban wins by deceiving Jacob.

Stage 2: Jacob's wages: Jacob wins by the trick with peeled sticks.

Stage 3: Laban's threat to harm Jacob because of his trickery: Jacob wins by an unannounced escape.

Stage 4: Rachel threatens Jacob's "innocence" by stealing Laban's household gods. Jacob is (unknowingly) saved by Rachel's trick.

Stage 5: The pursuit. A final confrontation: will Jacob be caught and killed?

The ultimate peak. No one wins: the dispute is settled by a typical covenant-treaty, and this peak now becomes the start-point for the long-delayed confrontation between Jacob and Esau, and the resolution of the conflict between Jacob and Yahweh.

Delayed peaking. In most cultures peaking in narrative is deliberately delayed. This is so in the Jacob narrative. The conflict between Jacob and Esau is set aside in favour of the years of conflict between Jacob and Laban. But the expectation is always that eventually the story-teller will come back to the Esau theme. And note the way in which the actual confrontation between Jacob and Esau is deferred, although already announced in 32.6, '. . . he is coming with four hundred men . . .' The confrontation with the 'angel' at Jabbok postpones the meeting, which is again adumbrated in 33.1, 'Behold, Esau was coming, and four hundred men with him.' Yet again there is a delay, brief this time, while Jacob prudently organizes his family, and then in 33.4 in place of the expected fight, or massacre, the whole conflict is resolved when Esau 'ran to meet him, and embraced him'.

In a different literary genre entirely, Revelation displays the same kind of delay in peaking. The successive cycles of seven provide a framework, but repeatedly the seventh sign is deferred. Note 6.12, the sixth seal, but then there is a long interruption through chapter 7, and the seventh seal is opened in 8.1. Similarly with the seven trumpets: the

sixth is sounded at 9.13, and then there is a long interlude and the
seventh trumpet does not sound until 11.15. The new heaven and new
earth appear in 21.1 and the entire revelation is concluded within the
space of 32 verses. A similar pattern of deferment of peak is to be seen
in Job:

Introduction, The Divine Council	1—2
Job's complaint	3
Job and his three counsellors	4—31
AN EXPECTATION THAT YAHWEH WILL NOW RESOLVE THE INCONCLUSIVE DEBATE	
Delay: Elihu introduced	32—37
Yahweh speaks	38—41
Conclusion	42

Peaking in narrative text[24] is always marked, so as to ensure that the
reader is aware that the peak has been reached. Negatively this may be
effected simply by withdrawing specific and otherwise characteristic features of the syntax. Certain particles may disappear and reappear only
after the peak has been passed.

Positively we note especially three features:

1. *Concentration of participants.* This may take either of two opposite
forms: on the one hand the assembling of all of the characters involved
in the narrative, as in an Agatha Christie novel. On the other hand all
other participants may be removed so as to leave the stage to the principals only, as in the Jacob story, where Jacob sends away his attendants
and then his family so as to face Yahweh alone.

2. *Change of pace.* Here again two opposite means are available. Most
commonly there is a sudden abandoning of the delaying technique and
the reader is plunged into a rapid resolution of the text. In the Jacob
narrative this is particularly clear: we have waited a long time for Jacob's
confrontation with God, and yet it is all over within a sequence of ten
verses. Alternatively we may have a sudden flourishing of rhetoric: note
the remarkable peak in *A Tale of Two Cities* where Dickens makes use of
John 11.25, 'I am the resurrection and the life' to heighten the dramatic
impact of his story.

3. *Change of locus.* Peaking is often carefully located at some significant
place or at some particular time. Jabbok for Jacob, The day of Pentecost
and the Upper Room for the coming of the Spirit, Sinai for the giving

of the Law and the appearance of Yahweh, a mountain for the trans-figuration, the third day for the resurrection. The occurrence of the peak may also be recognized from the surrounding cotext: a delay text before a peak and a rapid *closure* after the peak. In non-narrative texts peaking will also be marked. Note the change in sentence structure between the end of 2 Timothy 3 and the beginning of chapter 4: the five appearances of Greek *pros* in 3.16-17 and the four appearances of *kai* in 4.1.

7.6 DISCOURSE STRUCTURE: A SUMMARY

Any address, any conversation, any book, any discourse, has structure. It would be absurd to attempt to impose any rigorous model of that structure on discourse, since it would be a matter of little difficulty to produce an example of discourse minus the structure. But discourse is not a random sequence of utterances, or an unrelated collection of sentences. In discourse we have sequences, words which are grammatically related and semantically connected, and this grammatical and semantic relatedness extends across sentence and paragraph boundaries to embrace the entire discourse. We note also that there is not merely coherence; there is also progression: a discernible development leading to some kind of peak. There is, in simplistic terms, a beginning, a middle, and an end.

However, these three terms demand further explication. We may tentatively identify and label six rather typical elements which appear in narrative discourse, recognizing that the prominence and significance of any one element will depend on the particular discourse:

1. *Title.* A formula which introduces or identifies genre. Notice Job 1.1, 'There was a man in the land of Uz whose name was Job.' It is this which informs us of the narrative to follow, in contrast to, say, Philippians 1.1, 'Paul and Timothy, servants of Christ Jesus, to all the saints in Christ Jesus who are at Philippi', which in turn contrasts with Revelation 1.1, 'The revelation of Jesus Christ which God gave him to show to his servants what must soon take place'.

2. *Stage.* There is a need to identify the problem, the conflict, the question. This is effected by staging it: presenting it in some suitable form. It may be stated propositionally as in Romans 3.1, 'Then what advantage has the Jew?' or in dramatic form as in the prologue to Job,

chapters 1 and 2. In the case of Revelation the stage is set by the seven letters, which are by no means to be dismissed as a mere preamble.

3. *Pre-peak episodes.* Only rarely does discourse move directly from the staging of the issue to its resolution. An intermediate text is used further to explicate the issue, perhaps to highlight the significance of the issue. As we have seen these pre-peak episodes may be used to delay the peak and so to increase the tension.

4. *Peak*, possibly followed by an explanatory or confirmatory post-peak.

5. *Post-peak episodes.* Usually brief, and non-controversial, merely to move the participants on to where they are next needed or to tie up loose ends.

6. *Closure.* Paul concludes his second letter to Timothy, 'The Lord be with your spirit. Grace be with you.' Revelation concludes appropriately, 'The grace of the Lord Jesus be with all the saints. Amen.' In Job the post-peak episode includes the rebuke to Eliphaz, but the closure begins at 42.10 with the account of Job's ultimate prosperity.

These elements of discourse may now be illustrated from 2 Samuel 13, the account of the rape of Tamar.

7.7 THE RAPE OF TAMAR

The two boundaries of the Rape of Tamar (RT) pericope[25] are readily identifiable. On the one hand the preceding section is tidily concluded at 2 Samuel 12.31 with the return of the principal actors in the story of the destruction of Rabbah back to Jerusalem. On the other hand at 13.23 we have the interposition of an interval of two years which has the effect of closing off what is the main event in the history and of reminding us that RT is only part of a very much larger discourse, involving far more than the principal actors directly engaged in it.

2 Samuel 12.31 serves to clear the stage of the previous actors; 13.1 serves to introduce in a highly significant way the actors in the new discourse. Three factors signal the new Topic. We have been at Rabbah: we are now in Jerusalem. We have been involved with David and Joab and 'all the people', now we have a limited cast: Amnon, Tamar, and Jonadab. Thirdly, we have been concerned with great events where individual relationships mattered not at all; now we are concerned with a microcosm in which personal relationships are everything. The preced-

ing event was an epic. Now we come to human tragedy. The new episode is introduced by the familiar transition formula, 'And it happened
after this . . .'. We are, in discourse terms, dealing with stage, scene
setting for the discourse.

The two principal actors appear at once: Tamar and Amnon. Tamar
is deliberately introduced: 'Absalom, David's son, had a beautiful sister,
whose name was Tamar.' By bringing the name of Absalom to the front
we are forced into an awareness that this is not in fact a story about
Tamar so much as part of the ongoing story of Absalom, and this pericope in its fullest sense does not end at 13.22 or 13.39 but at 18.33, with
the death of Absalom. But the significant phrase occurs a second time:
'he-loved-her, Amnon, son-of-David.' The verb here, unlike those that
follow, does not indicate an action, but it forms part of the static background to the events which are subsequently described: in modern language we might render the clause: 'he was in love with her was Amnon,
this son of David.' For the phrase *ben-dawid* is used not merely to identify
objective relationships pertinent to the discourse, and delicately to hint
at the scandalous nature of Amnon's passion,[26] but also to point back
to David's own lax sexual morals to explain, although not to excuse,
Amnon's conduct.

In fact, in the opening words of the chapter we are concisely informed
of the beginning of the new pericope, introduced to Absalom as the
principal character in the new major division of the text, and reminded
that although we do have a new section we are nonetheless still in the
general context of the succession narrative. RT is not to be isolated from
the context within which it is deliberately set.

Of course we must also note here that what we have recorded in RT
is not a novel,[27] freshly created, but a history of events already well known
to the reader/listener. As the royal chronicle is read aloud it is read to an
audience whose presupposition pool already includes a knowledge of this
story. It is precisely because of this shared knowledge that the writer dares
to be so economical, so allusive, in his style. As Conroy comments:

> The narrator plays on the fact that the (first) readers share with him
> a certain amount of background knowledge. Hence he can merely
> allude to certain points, aware that his brevity will stimulate the
> readers to draw on their own knowledge, to respond as it were with
> a knowing nod.[28]

The initiating stage of the discourse is now complete and the story can begin its development. Verse 2 sets the problem and verse 14 its final resolution, and in between a carefully planned series of obstacles is identified and in turn overcome. Tamar is Absalom's sister and so Amnon's sister, too, although by a different mother. Tamar is a virgin, and so she is carefully chaperoned. More probably the reference to her virginity is a cynical commentary on the morals of the royal court: had she been married she would have been available. Fornication was forbidden but adultery was not. That this is the more probable explanation of the significance of the term virgin, *bethulah*, in v.2 is confirmed by the fact that Tamar is permitted to visit her brother in his private apartment (v.8), and moreover there is no mention of her being accompanied by her women. And there is a further problem: Tamar's own resistance to Amnon's advances. These obstacles are to be overcome as the story develops.

The opening episode carries within it the coherence term which will carry the narrative forward into the second episode: Amnon is sick with love: 'he made himself ill because of his sister Tamar'. The sickness is apparent and enables Jonadab to be brought into the story. But the sickness, too, is significant. Although Amnon hides his lust behind the temporizing euphemism 'it seemed impossible to Amnon *to do anything to her*', his sickness finds an echo both in The Song of Solomon (5.8, 'I adjure you, O daughters of Jerusalem, if you find my beloved, that you tell him I am sick with love') and in Egyptian love poetry.[29] It is part of the irony of the text that as in that particular literary genre so here, in sober narrative, one's beloved is designated one's 'sister' (Song of Solomon 4.10-12, 'How sweet is your love, my sister, my bride . . . a garden locked is my sister, my bride . . .'). Amnon has a lust appropriate to pagan society, a lust which is neither more nor less than a debased noble passion. But a passion it is, as the text itself exemplifies through 'a series of gasping sighs . . . A somewhat exaggerated effect is achieved by repeated alliteration of *'alep* followed by -o and -a sounds with a few gutturals thrown in for good measure.'[30]

The second episode (vv.3-5) may be passed over briefly. Jonadab is introduced as the means of resolving the problem of bringing Tamar onto the scene, but he is quickly dismissed, having served that purpose. Yet there is one significant point that is made with the sureness and yet delicacy of touch which is typical of RT. Jonadab is 'the son of Shimeah,

David's brother.' As Conroy points out 'there are two camps, as it were, Tamar being in Absalom's and Jonadab in Amnon's; the future conflict between these two is insinuated already.'[31] The episode is quite deliberately crafted in a stolid, unimaginative way, to convey an impression of an unimpressive, easily dominated Amnon: 'Lie down . . . pretend to be ill . . . say to him . . . So Amnon lay down, and pretended to be ill . . . Amnon said . . .'.

Episode 3 (v.6): The flat repetition then carries the action forward into the third episode, which now introduces the last of the important actors in the drama, David himself, who comes to visit his son who is 'sick'. At this point it may well be crucial to recognize that we are dealing with an erotic theme, and that erotic literature has its own allusive character. This observation may bear on the fact that in this third episode Amnon departs from Jonadab's suggested request, and asks not for bread (v.5) but for 'a couple of cakes' (Hebrew *lebibōth*). McCarter connects this nominal with the verb *libbēb*, which in the Song of Solomon 4.9 refers to an erotic arousal: 'You have *ravished* my heart, my sister, my bride, you have *ravished* my heart with a glance of your eyes, with one jewel of your necklace.'[32]

In another literary genre this interpretation of Amnon's terminology would properly be seen as highly improbable. Even here we are confronted with a double problem: if the language is suggestive why did David approve of Amnon's suggestion, and why did Tamar obey? There are ready answers to both question: David's own morals, which enabled him to perceive the *double entendre* and cynically go along with his son's desires, and Tamar's innocence: she is consistently presented in the pericope as of high moral standard, perhaps as too high-minded even to imagine what Amnon was planning. Conroy notes (with approval?) a comment from Brockington that the cakes 'were intended to bewitch Amnon to full health; secretly Amnon would expect them to intensify passion and enable him to take her by surprise'.[33] Amnon knew quite well what he was about, Tamar most certainly did not. The king's perception is less clear. Is it, perhaps, significant that David avoids Amnon's reference to a couple of *lebibōth*, and uses the word originally used by Jonadab? The interpretation of this general point of Amnon's word does turn on the question of the moral climate of the court.

The speech by Jonadab does lend support to the impression of a general collapse of morale and of morals at the king's court: dismissively he refers to the king as simply 'your father', indicating an absence of respect (which is not shared by the chronicler, who refers twice to 'the king' [v.6]).

Verse 7 now quietly furthers the action, simply fulfilling the expectations of the reader of the story, and constituting episode four. But the verse does mark a clear division in the developing drama. To this point very little has really *happened*. The first four episodes do little more than set the scene for the event, the rape of Tamar. But we must conceive of the event as being already known to the reader or listener, who has simply been picking up the various nuances of the unfolding story. But with episode five there is a clear change signalled by the appearance of action verbs: 'A rapid succession of narrative verbs . . . creates an impression of bustling activity.'[4] The structure here has a clear function: it enables the reader to visualize the scene, and the detail gives clear indication that now we are past the introductory stage and into the real story. At the same time the detail has the effect of heightening tension: of delaying the peak.

This episode is characterized by the activity of Tamar and the passivity of Amnon who, from his couch, is closely watching her. But we are left to infer the presence of others, assisting Tamar who, after all, is no mere palace servant. Verse 9 then neatly concludes the episode through the completion of Tamar's task, the totally unexpected refusal of Amnon to eat what she has prepared, and the brusque command from Amnon which dismisses all the actors from the stage except the two principal actors.

Episode six now shifts the role of main participant from Tamar to Amnon. It is Amnon who orders the servants away, it is Amnon who calls Tamar into his room, it is Amnon who waits until, for the first time, she is within physical reach of him (v.11), and then takes hold of her. The sibling word 'my-sister' is used here directly addressed to Tamar by Amnon for the first time in the story. She has, of course, been spoken of in that term at several points in the story, but at this point its use comes as a shock: as no doubt is intended. Amnon has used a base trick to entice her within his grasp knowing that she would not come willingly, and now addresses her in this term of sibling affection.

The episode is characterized by a series of commands from Amnon and the corresponding submissive actions by the servants and Tamar. And now the expectation is that Jonadab's plan will reach a successful conclusion. But the chronicler introduces another delay: Tamar is by no means ready to submit to Amnon.

Episode seven introduces a long delaying speech which surveys the consequences of what Amnon plans for her and for him, and which proposes an alternative which would both allow Amnon his desire and preserve some measure of decency: let Amnon speak to the king for her. The episode concludes with the peak event, the anticipated outcome, the rape of Tamar. The form of the episode is typical of pre-peak text: a long, rather dull, monologue, and then the sudden, dramatic conclusion expressed with great economy of words.

Of course, although in one sense RT is now complete we have been aware from the very beginning of the pericope that while Amnon and Tamar are the principals involved here, in the longer view it is not these two, but Absalom and David who are the prime concern. So RT is carried forward beyond the rape and on into its consequences for Amnon, for Absalom, and ultimately for David, into what is a post-peak episode of considerable importance and the typical closure of 13.22, 'But Absalom spoke to Amnon neither good nor bad; for Absalom hated Amnon, because he had forced his sister Tamar.'

Here in this minimal story we have an example of great writing. We are constantly made to look back, to the sexual excesses of David and particularly the Bathsheba episode, forward, to the convoluted court politics involving David and Joab and Absalom, within the text to the delicately selected vocabulary, the carefully distributed verbal forms and the snatches of dialogue, and out to the context, to what we can glean of sexual morals at David's court. Although the central event is itself uncomplicated, it is only careful attention to text, cotext and context, careful attention that is focused by some knowledge of linguistics, that enables the reader fully to appreciate the communication being effected.

Notes

[1]There is a most useful collection of relevant essays in English (although most of the contributors are not native speakers of English) in W. Dressler (ed.), *Current Trends in Textlinguistics*, Berlin, de Gruyter, 1978. Note particularly the explanation of coherence given by T. A. van Dijk and Walter Kintsch in a

discussion of the connection between pairs of propositions: 'Connection is a specific kind of *coherence*, defined over sequences of propositions, not only in terms of relations between facts, in some possible world and relative to a topic of discourse, but also in terms of intensional and extensional relations between "parts" of propositions . . .' (p.68). See also T. A. van Dijk, *Text and Context*, London, Longmans, chap. 4, 'Coherence', and M. A. K. Halliday and R. Hasan, *Cohesion in English*, London, Longmans, 1976.

[2]*Discourse Analysis*, p.6.

[3]Ibid., p.26.

[4]See above, 6.1.4.

[5]Brown and Yule, *Discourse Analysis*, pp.190-9.

[6]Cf. H. Rieser, 'On the Development of Text Grammar' in W. Dressler (1977), p.13. He in turn is summarizing Petofi's proposals.

[7]*Discourse Analysis*, Oxford, Blackwell, 1983, p.12. See also the important discussion by Stephen Levinson of Discourse Analysis and Conversation Analysis in chapter six of his *Pragmatics*.

[8]Although the indications of time here have also been construed as primarily theologically orientated. See particularly R. Schnackenburg, *The Gospel According to St John*, p.325, for a consideration of Boismard's suggestion. C. K. Barrett, *The Gospel According to St John*, p.158, discusses the significance of the seven days marked out in the first two chapters of John and the further week similarly marked at the end of the Gospel.

[9]Cf. Barrett, *The Gospel According to St John*, p.162, '*meta touto* and *meta tauta* are frequent, and synonymous, indications of the transition from one narrative to another. It is impossible to tell (unless further evidence is given) whether a long or short interval is intended.' In fact John is not particularly concerned to set his events in a strict chronological order (although the *theological* connections are most carefully made), and it is unwise to deduce anything about chronology from these two phrases.

[10]*Carry on Jeeves*, Harmondsworth, Penguin, 1925(!) and many reprints.

[11]On deixis see Brown and Yule (1983), pp. 50-8 and Longacre (1983), 3.7, where a rather different concept of deixis is presented. See also Levinson, *Pragmatics*, chap. 2.

[12]On the so-called T-V languages see D. Bolinger and D. A. Sears, *Aspects of Language*, New York, Harcourt Brace Jovanovich, 1981[3], pp.212-6.

[13]Although the NIV's indirect speech at 2.5, ' . . . if your servant has found favour in *his* sight, let *him* send me' does not represent the Hebrew original, which uses the second person in both places, as AV and RSV.

[14]David Clines, *The Esther Scroll* , *JSOT* (Supplement Series, 30), 1984. This entire study is beautifully executed and repays careful reading.

[15]Blass-Debrunner, *A Greek Grammar of the New Testament and Other Early Christian Literature*, ed. R. W. Funk, Chicago, University of Chicago Press, p.235.

[16]See especially A. T. Robertson, *A Grammar of New Testament Greek*, pp.1027ff. for a very full discussion of direct and indirect speech. See also Nigel Turner, *A Grammar of New Testament Greek*, vol. III, p.325.

[17]'*pros auton* would normally mean "to him", but since the saying is couched in the third person it may mean "about him" ', I. Howard Marshall, *The Gospel of Luke*, Exeter, Paternoster, 1978, p.698. Arndt in his commentary agrees with this viewpoint, but see Plummer's ICC commentary *per contra*. Some texts at this point resolve the difficulty by replacing *pros auton* with *pros autous*.

[18]Brown and Yule (1983), chap. 4.

[19]R. E. Longacre (1983), p.20. It is worth noting here that the placing of the peak is itself part of the significance of the peak, but that the placing of the peak may in some measure reflect on the character and purpose of the author. A letter may be written to transmit an important item of information. The placing of that information at the beginning, followed by trivia, in the middle, preceded by trivia (so as to minimize shock?), or at the end (to maximize shock?) is an important part of the message.

[20]See R. K. Harrison's comments in *Introduction to the Old Testament*, Grand Rapids, Eerdmans, 1969, pp.542ff., and P. J. Wiseman's *Clues to Creation in Genesis*, edited by D. J. Wiseman, London, Marshall, Morgan and Scott, 1977.

[21]See especially William McKane, *Studies in the Patriarchal Narratives*, Edinburgh, The Handsel Press, 1979; chap. 1 offers an invaluable history of this fascinating literary genre. On the Jacob narrative see Heather A. McKay, 'Jacob Makes It Across the Jabbok', *JSOT* 38 (June 1987).

[22]Minneapolis, Augsburg, 1981.

[23]Atlanta, John Knox Press, 1982.

[24]Longacre (1983), pp.25-38.

[25]We acknowledge with appreciation the work on this pericope by Ms Jennie Smith, M.A., formerly a student at London Bible College.

[26]Cf. Leviticus 18 and especially v.9 which explicitly covers the case of Tamar and Amnon, and Deuteronomy 27.22. Of course it is arguable that the laws recorded here were not formulated in David's day but were a later idealization. Even if that were so there must have been some parallel code of sex morals operating in Israelite society in general and in court circles in particular.

[27]But see Dan Jacobson, *The Rape of Tamar*, London, Andre Deutsch, 1985[2] (first published in 1970), for an imaginative re-creation of the event.

[28]Charles Conroy, *Absalom, Absalom!*, Rome, Biblical Institute Press (Analecta Biblica 81), 1978, p.113.

[29]For details, bibliography, etc., see P. K. McCarter, *II Samuel* (Anchor Bible), New

York, Doubleday, 1984, p.320.

[30]McCarter, *II Samuel*, p.321.

[31]Conroy, *Absalom, Absalom!*, p.27.

[32]*II Samuel*, p.322; 'Amnon, by asking that Tamar prepare the dumplings . . . is privately anticipating more than the restoration of his health, as the use of *libbeb* in Cant. 4.9 suggests.'

[33]Charles Conroy, *Absalom, Absalom!*, p.29, n43.

[34]Conroy, *Absalom, Absalom!*, p.30.

8. Discourse Analysis: The Special Case of Conversation

Language is used in human communication both impersonally, through its written form, and personally through such forms as sermons, after dinner speeches and lectures, and through the less obviously structured conversation.

In its simplest form conversation may involve only two people, but commonly several people will be involved and it is intuitively apparent that a process of this nature, involving several individuals, a potentially infinite range of topics, and a multiply infinite range of sentences must be structured if it is to lead to successful communication. The structure must make provision for some kind of turn-taking amongst the participating individuals, must be sufficiently flexible to allow for ambiguities to be cleared up as the conversation proceeds and must take account of the existence amongst the participants of shared knowledge.

8.1 THE PRESUPPOSITION POOL
We have already encountered this important concept in Chapter 3. The

term was introduced by T. Venneman[1] and helps to explain the way in which speakers include certain pieces of information in what they say, but exclude other pieces of information which may, in fact, be equally important to the perception of what is being said. Any speaker will necessarily make certain assumptions about his listeners and will fashion what he has to say accordingly. For example, he will not unnecessarily explain such technical terms as he may use unless he is fairly sure that explanation is required; the gratuitous supply of an unnecessary explanation may become part of the communication and may be perceived as patronizing. On the other hand failure to provide a necessary explanation may be perceived as deliberate one-upmanship, as exhibitionism, as (Chapter 3) sesquipedalian. Under these circumstances the listener may determine not to ask for clarification of the new word and so allow the communication to fail. In either case misunderstanding of the actual contents of the presupposition pool is likely to lead to an undesirable alteration in the character of the conversation.

How are the contents of the presupposition pool to be determined? It is apparent that the contents will be best known by an individual when that individual is familiar with all the members of the group. Within the family the contents of the pool are very well known. In the lecture situation the pool is to some extent created by the common participation in the formal study of a chosen discipline. But as the relationships between the members of any group become more and more diffuse, so the contents of the presupposition pool become less and less clearly defined and the possibilities for mis-communication increase. Clearly the contents of the shared presupposition pool become smaller as the group involved becomes larger, unless the group has some particular homogeneity: a group of physicists, for example, or a gathering of theologians.

In the normal social context that measure of homogeneity is not commonly found, and as a result the presupposition pool of a large group is rather small. This in turn may lead to large group conversations which tend to tedium. In order to make such conversations intelligible to the whole group, explanations must be given which are needed only by part of the group and which are superfluous for the rest. It is certainly interesting to observe the way in which large groups tend to reform into several smaller groups each consisting of up to half a dozen people, so allowing for the expansion of potential conversational topics on the basis of the expanded presupposition pool. The alternative may be to discuss the weather!

The presupposition pool may include such matters as knowledge of certain people about whom anecdotes might be shared, an expertise in certain subjects, such as music or theology, and certain prejudices, so that, for example, jokes about the Scottish character might not be acceptable. The concept of the presupposition pool is important for biblical exegesis, since we may move from a perception of what is being said in a conversation to a recognition of what the speaker has already assumed to be in the pool and so has not overtly expressed. Thus in Matthew 19.16-30, Jesus tells his disciples: 'I tell you the truth, it is hard for a rich man to enter the kingdom of heaven.' This statement is greeted with astonishment (v.25) by his listeners.[2] They were astonished, as probably any Jew would have been, because their presupposition pool included the belief that riches were actually a reward for righteousness. Since that belief was in their presupposition pool it was unnecessary for Jesus to add, as he might have done in a modern context, 'Of course it is usually assumed that a rich person must be a godly person but . . .' Today we would probably be more astonished to be told that it is hard for a *poor* man to enter the kingdom of heaven.

We should note that frequently the biblical writers are aware of the existence of two quite distinct presupposition pools relevant to their text. The first is that appropriate to those involved in the original events being recorded, and the second is the pool shared by the contemporary readers of the text. In John 4.9 we have a parenthetical comment for the sake of John's readers, 'For Jews do not associate with Samaritans.' This comment is part of the evidence relevant to the determination of the date of the text and of the nature of the audience for which the text was written. Clearly it was *not* prepared for a community which had that piece of information already in its presupposition pool. Again, from the Old Testament, we have the explanation in Ruth 4.7, explaining to the reader a custom which would have been entirely familiar to Boaz and his contemporaries but not to the expected readership of the story.

8.2 FIVE PRINCIPLES GOVERNING CONVERSATION

H. H. Clark and E. V. Clark in *Psychology and Language*[3] identify five principles which govern conversation:

1. Knowledge of the listener
2. Co-operation in the conversation
3. The reality principle: the principle of relevance
4. Context appropriateness
5. Appropriateness to the participants and especially to their linguistic skills.

8.2.1 Knowledge of the Listener

This knowledge would include some understanding of the common pre-supposition pool, but would also include knowledge *about* the listener. The total knowledge of the listener would enable the speaker to determine how much explanation to include in the message: whether to refer to 'Anne', to 'My next door neighbour, Anne', or, perhaps, to 'That woman Anne'.

In John 4.16 there is an important transition in the conversation between Jesus and the Samaritan woman. From verse 7 to verse 15 the conversation is about water. At verse 16 Jesus introduces a totally new Topic (a procedure which is itself both very unusual and highly significant), 'Go, call your husband, and come here.' Jesus is somehow aware of the tangled marital relationships of the woman and that awareness informs the conversation.

Again, in Acts 23.6 we find Paul before the Jewish Council. It occurs to him that the Council is necessarily divided: there are Sadducees present and there are Pharisees. He is himself a Pharisee. Rightly or wrongly he makes use of this perception to throw the Council into confusion: 'I am a Pharisee . . . with respect to the hope and resurrection of the dead I am on trial.'[4]

8.2.2 The Principle of Co-operation

It is generally unacceptable to attempt to pursue a conversation with a person who does not wish to co-operate. In fact the principle of co-operation is sometimes seen as the most important principle governing conversation.[5] However it must not be assumed that all conversations proceed in a spirit of co-operation, but from the principle itself it follows that where co-operation is withheld *that* constitutes part of the communication and helps to direct the development of the conversation.

Co-operation implies that any contribution will be as informative as is necessary (bearing in mind the implicit awareness of the contents of the common presupposition pool), that it will be as accurate as possible (that there will at least be no intention to mislead or deceive), that what is said will be relevant to the subject of the conversation (so that if what is said *appears* to be irrelevant the listener will be right in further processing the speech in search of an alternative and relevant meaning) and that what is said will be kept clear and appropriately brief. Of course these maxims will be observed with varying degrees of success, depending on the linguistic abilities of the participants and on the sociological components relating to the conversation. But without their presence in some degree conversation simply becomes impossible.

The foundational work of H. P. Grice in this aspect of discourse is summarized by Levinson[6] in terms of four maxims which exemplify the principle of co-operation in conversation.

The Co-operative Principle is: *make your contribution such as is required, at the stage at which it occurs, by the accepted purpose or direction of the talk exchange in which you are engaged.*

The Maxim of Quality is: *try to make your contribution one that is true, specifically:*
(i) do not say what you believe to be false;
(ii) do not say that for which you lack adequate evidence.

The Maxim of Quantity is:
(i) make your contribution as informative as is required for the current purposes of the exchange;
(ii) do not make your contribution more informative than is required.

The Maxim of Relevance is: *make your contribution relevant.*

The Maxim of Manner is: *be perspicuous, and specifically:*
(i) avoid obscurity;
(ii) avoid ambiguity;
(iii) be brief;
(iv) be orderly.

There are, obviously, occasions where a conversation is conducted under

the stress of conflicting or competing goals.[7] In the Bread of Life discourse, which reaches back into John 5 with its introduction of Moses
(v. 45),[8] and covers the whole of chapter six (the events on the two sides
of the lake are clearly intended to be related to each other), the topic of
conversation as perceived by the crowd conflicts with the topic determined by Jesus. Actually the two are so related as to enable the discourse
to proceed calmly enough until Jesus' topic becomes unambiguously apparent, at which point (v. 41) the conversation moves to conflict.

There are innumerable ways of analyzing chapter six. As Moloney
expressed it:

> The division and structure of the discourse on the Bread of Life is
> so strongly influenced by each scholar's stance on the content of the
> discourse that there are nearly as many theories as there are inter-
> preters.[9]

The chapter has obvious eucharistic overtones. There is also clear reference back to Moses and the miracle of the manna. In particular we
note the messianic expectation attested to by 2 Baruch 29.8, (to be dated
around A.D. 100), the expectation that the miracle of the manna would
be repeated by Messiah.[10] There is the allusive use of Psalm 78.24 or
Exodus 16.4-5[11] in v.31. And we must throughout any balanced consideration of the Bread of Life discourse be aware of the meaning of the
confrontation as it originally occurred and the intention of John in including the narrative at this point in his Gospel.[12]

It must be admitted that the majority of commentators do not consider
the discourse to represent anything approaching a reliable record of a
historical event.[13] Here we shall approach the text assuming that it is a
reliable, but obviously edited[14] account of a genuine event. In taking this
line we must note that to some important questions regarding the presupposition pool(s) assumed for the conversation we have no firm
answers, although the text may supply intelligible clues. And perhaps it
should be added that there are several such pools in evidence, not one
single pool. There is the pool common to Jesus and the crowd as a whole.
There is the pool common to Jesus and the more sophisticated 'Jews',
leaders of the crowd. There is a third pool, common to Jesus and his
immediate disciples, and another common to Jesus and the larger crowd
of uncommitted disciples. And at least one further presupposition pool
must be noted, that presupposed by John as relating to his readership.

The discourse begins with the arrival of the crowd, v.25, and their commonplace and perhaps self-conscious question: 'Rabbi, when did you come here?' Jesus responds crisply, 'Truly, truly, I say to you, you seek me, not because you saw signs, but because you ate your fill of the loaves.' Schnackenburg comments: 'The experience of the feeding did not lead these people to a deeper vision. Their eating of "the loaves" . . . gave them pleasure, but it was enough for them to have their stomachs filled. Their thoughts and searching have no higher object.'[15] Haenchen clearly dislikes the scenario: 'The crassest possible misunderstanding is thereby presupposed, viz, that man seeks Jesus only in the hope that he may be satiated by him in an earthly sense.'[16] And yet that *is* the immediate concern of the man who is neither a philosopher, nor a theologian. Crass it may be, but the sentiment is true to human nature.

But there *is* a conflict of topic. That the topic is 'bread' or possibly 'manna' or perhaps the more general 'food' is quite apparent. In the earlier part of the chapter (v.15) there was a move to make Jesus king, but that matter is never raised in the new conversation. Bread, loaves, manna are mentioned 16 times in vv.25-51. The conflict arises and is allowed to arise out of the topic Jesus himself sets: the elucidation of the term bread. He is the bread from heaven. What they want is the bread from heaven. But the one bread is spiritual, the other material. And Jesus warns them of the folly of what they have done in pursuing him across the lake: 'Do not labour *for the food which perishes* but *for the food which endures to eternal life*', at the same time verbalizing and summarizing the nature of the conflict of topic.

The conversation continues naturally. The crowd must not labour for the wrong thing. Very well then, 'What must we do . . . ?' And the answer is a demand for faith . . . in Jesus. And entirely reasonably again the crowd demands a sign that would justify the call to faith. But the nature of the sign demanded is significant: 'Our fathers ate the manna in the wilderness; as it is written, "He gave them bread from heaven to eat." ' The implication is clear: it is for you to do the same. Jesus' response is in the form of a correction: he is preparing the way for what he must shortly say, and the demand of the people for a manna-sign makes the way forward clear. He can use their misapprehension to further the conversation: 'It was not Moses who gave you the bread from heaven.' To allow Moses to stand as the giver of the manna would not helpfully further the argument. It was, in fact, God who gave the manna, and it is similarly God who gives the new 'bread from heaven'.

Still respectful, the crowd asks for that bread: 'The Jews have understood only that Jesus is talking about an unusual bread offered by God, but they misunderstand him to mean a miraculous earthly food. They ask for some (in respectful tones, as did the Samaritan woman, 4.11,15) and thereby confirm Jesus' remark that they are only concerned with food which passes away.'[17] It is at this point that Jesus makes his topic clear. There is no manna, there is no earthly bread to be obtained from him. He himself is the 'bread of life', he himself has been sent down by God. The conversation sharpens from this point on. In v.41 'The Jews then murmured at him', and his further explanations (all talk of actual bread has now disappeared from the conversation) simply deepen the hostility: 'Then the Jews began to argue sharply among themselves . . .' (v.52): an argument and disagreement which is now fuelled by an even more outrageous statement: ' . . . unless you eat the flesh of the Son of Man and drink his blood you have no life in you' (v.53), a hard saying which leads to a characteristically Johannine 'division', with even the disciples dismayed, and the Twelve perplexed but yet knowing that although they do not understand what has been said any more than the rest of the crowd, they have nowhere to go, no other refuge, no other hope.

In this particular example we have limited co-operation: despite the different goals set for the conversation by Jesus and by the crowd each co-operates to the extent of talking about bread. A conversation here would have been impossible if Jesus had set the topic 'bread', but the crowd had chosen the topic 'the Samaritans'.

8.2.3 The Reality Principle[18]

Because in the course of conversation we are frequently required to *guess* at the meaning of certain words or phrases there is an assumption that the guessing process will be used responsibly. Clark and Clark refer to the innovative compound 'alligator-shoes'[19] which would be reasonably construed as 'shoes made from the hide of the alligator' and not as 'shoes to be worn by an alligator' (cf. the parallel compound 'baby-shoes', probably 'shoes for a baby', but contrast 'tennis-shoes', not 'shoes for a tennis' but 'shoes to be worn when playing tennis': noun-noun compounds of this kind may be interpreted in many ways).

The reality principle is involved in the John passage we have considered above. Jesus tells the people that they must eat his flesh and drink his blood, and the reality principle requires that the people should see that he cannot mean that they should there and then devour him. Quite properly they respond with a question: 'How can this man give us his flesh to eat?' (6.52).

8.2.4 The Principle of Context-appropriateness

We all of us make use of a number of idiolects, personal dialects, each idiolect appropriate to a particular context. There is one for the family, one for business colleagues, another for preaching, one for one's peers and another for one's superiors. It is expected that in conversation all participants will correctly identify the level of language, the idiolect, that is appropriate to it.[20] Whether the level of language I adopt is too high or too low the result will be the same: annoyance on the part of the other participants, and possible personal embarrassment.

We may assume that the rabbis who encountered Jesus would have been in doubt as to the contextually appropriate mode of address and level of language to be employed in conversation with him. On the one hand it was well known that he was not in the formal sense of the word a rabbi. On the other hand he certainly taught the people as though he were a rabbi, and he gathered a group of disciples, *mathētai,* around him as a rabbi would. Nicodemus addressed him as 'Rabbi . . .' but it is, of course, quite possible that this was mere irony.

8.2.5 Conversations Are Obviously Also Limited by the Linguistic Competence of the Participants

This may mean that certain subjects will not be discussed at all, simply because some participants entirely lack linguistic competence in the topic, or it may merely mean that the subject will be discussed, but with the use of circumlocutions, paraphrases, analogies, where such devices are no more than a concession to the perceived incompetence. In particular instances the linguistic incompetence may have a spiritual origin.

So in 1 Cor. 3.1-2 Paul comments ironically, 'I could not address you as spiritual but as worldly—mere infants in Christ. I gave you milk, not solid food, for you were not yet ready for it. Indeed, you are still not ready.' There was no point in carrying on a spiritual dialogue with an unspiritual people simply because the terminology necessary to such a dialogue would have signified different things to the different contributors. The irony here is the more poignant in that Paul is writing in order to counter those in Corinth who offered a super-spiritual esoteric teaching which, in the very act of claiming spirituality closed the minds of the hearers to true spirituality.[21] His 'milk' was in fact 'meat', but their preoccupation with their illusory 'meat' meant that they could not properly perceive what he was offering. The outcome of their conversation was, inevitably, frustration. A change of perception was needed.

All conversations are to a greater or lesser degree determined by these five principles and an awareness of the principles may be helpful in interpreting biblical conversations.

8.3 TURN-TAKING

Conversation must also make provision for turn-taking. Conversation may be considered as consisting of a number of units, each consisting of a complete contribution by one participant.[22] In most societies there is provision for a highly stylized prefatory stage to conversation, involving formal greetings, inquiries about health, and so on. These may be prolonged, as is frequently the case in contemporary African societies, or very brief, as in much of Western society. In Semitic societies prolonged greetings are the rule, which helps to explain both Elisha's prohibition of any exchange of greetings by his servant Gehazi (2 Kings 4.29),[23] and the similar prohibition by Jesus when he sent out the seventy (Luke 10.4). I. Howard Marshall comments: 'Oriental greetings were important, long, and time consuming.'[24]

The actual initiation of the greetings is culturally determined: it was normal for the inferior to greet the superior, a practice reflected in Jesus' characterization of the scribes and Pharisees in Matthew 23.7, 'as loving greetings'. There is an interesting passage in Josephus referring to the confrontation between Jaddus, the high priest, and Alexander, just outside Jerusalem, and Josephus says of Alexander: ' . . . he approached alone and prostrated himself before the Name and first greeted (*prōtos espesato*) the high priest',[25] that is he initiated the series of greetings, accepting the subordinate place after Jaddus. The scribes and Pharisees did not merely 'love greetings'; what they loved was having others initiate greetings, so acknowledging the superior status of the Pharisees.

8.4 ADJACENCY PAIRS

Even where conversation involves several people it is conducted essentially between pairs, dyads. This is, clearly, one of the features which distinguish conversation from more formal oral language genres, where speech is directed at a group, and not, particularly, at any one member of the group. And even here one is aware of the fact that a group has no ears: as a *group* it cannot hear, and actual communication still takes place dyadically. In addition to the importance of participant-dyads in genuine conversation we note the fact that conversation proceeds by means of sequences of paired utterances, adjacency pairs. In John's account of the events in the Upper Room before the arrest of Jesus, Jesus addresses the whole group:

' . . . one of you will betray me',

Simon Peter uses paralinguistic gesture to the Beloved Disciple urging him to ask the obvious question ('Who?'), and the Beloved Disciple does so:

'Lord, who is it?'

The conversation is furthered again by an act, the giving of the 'morsel' (John 13.26) to Judas, after which Jesus speaks to Judas:

'What you are going to do, do quickly.'

This again is followed by an act, the real, but also symbolic, departure of Judas into the night, after which Jesus addresses the whole group once more:

'Now is the Son of man glorified. . . .'

to which Peter alone responds

'Lord, where are you going?'

The dyads here change rapidly, as is normal in conversations involving a group:

> Jesus to the group
> Peter to the Beloved Disciple
> The Beloved Disciple to Jesus
> Jesus to the Beloved Disciple
> Jesus to Judas
> Jesus to the group
> Peter to Jesus

Jesus to Peter

but although the conversation is immediately between one dyad the entire group present is involved in the dynamics of the conversation.

8.4.1 Initiation

We have seen that the initiation of a conversation, however brief, is through a series of formal greetings, Greetings-Pairs. Such pairs may display the formal grammatical markings of interrogation, but they are commonly semantically neutral; the utterance 'How are you?' is not primarily an enquiry after someone's health, but a formal exploration of that person's willingness to engage in conversation. Indeed, even where a semantically appropriate response is given to such an initiating question it might bear no relation to the facts at all. In a Semitic culture I greeted a neighbour. He was well. His wife? She was well, praise be to God! And the children? They, too, were well. The cattle and the sheep? All was well. But when after perhaps five minutes of such formal Greetings-Pair dialogue we moved on to actual facts I discovered that he was on his way to the hospital to visit his wife who was to undergo surgery that day, and that two of his children were ill with whooping cough. He himself was suffering a severe attack of gastritis. . . . Notice here the parallel with 2 Kings 4.25ff., part of the account of the Shunammite woman who went for help to Elisha. Elisha sees her coming and sends Gehazi running to her to find out what was wrong:

'Is it well with you?
Is it well with your husband?
Is it well with the child?'

And she answered:

'It is well.'

In fact, the child was dead.

8.4.2 Topicalization

Some conversations do not proceed beyond the initiation stage: having exchanged greetings-pairs the speakers are at liberty to go about their business without causing ill feelings. But commonly dialogue moves on to the discussion of some substantive subject, the topic.[26] It is by no means easy to produce a satisfying and comprehensive definition of this elusive term. Topic is sometimes presented as a single noun: 'Pacifism', sometimes as a noun phrase, 'The real meaning of peace', sometimes as a statement of intent: 'To show that religion by itself is not a sufficient guarantee of salvation' (as a topic description for the Nicodemus pericope).

The difficulty is simply that topic may be differently perceived and so differently expressed by different participants in a conversation or by different observers of the conversation. And obviously the perception of topic by participants will be affected by their own expectations, prejudices, intentions. Here two things must be said: firstly that topic may change very rapidly as different participants contribute to the conversation, but secondly that the broad area of the topic will usually change only gradually. In other words topic might be something to do with holidays in Spain, move to holidays in Greece, and then to Greek architecture, followed by trends in contemporary architecture, but within a single topic, however defined, contributions to the conversation will reflect the five principles of conversation we have already examined. And transitions may commonly be objectively identified. It has to be said that topic in the context of conversation is whatever it is intended to be *by the current speaker*, and this conforms with our earlier insistence that authorial meaning, the intention of an author, is the only real meaning that may be assigned to a text. In summary, then, we may say that it is extremely unlikely that any extended conversation will have a readily definable single topic, that topic may be perceived quite differently by participants, that the current speaker's intended topic is, temporarily at least, the legitimate topic of the conversation, and that topic transition is effected logically.

But the questions remain: how do we identify topic and how is it defined? A key concept in answering these questions is that of relevance.[27] Just as any text may be incomprehensible without its context, so any conversation is potentially incomprehensible if isolated from its context. If we take the utterance 'We can't use the table today', neither the meaning nor the significance of the utterance can be determined apart from some further explication of the context of the utterance. If now we set the conversation of which the sentence is part in a field we might at once discard 'dining room table' as the referent of the sentence, but might still have doubts as to the actual referent intended. The topic might be something to do with mathematical tables, or possibly a picnic table, or again might bear on the local water table. If those involved in the discussion are distinctly non-mathematicians, or if it is fairly certain that they would be very unlikely to have any knowledge of water tables (water tables are not in the presupposition pool), and if, further, there are twenty-two men in white flannels and white shirts wielding bats standing in the field, then topic is likely to be perceived as at least related to cricket, since the specially prepared area of the field on which important matches are played is termed the table.

The term 'table', then, brings into my consciousness a very large number of possible topics for the discussion, many of them at once excluded as being *irrelevant* in the actual context. It is worth noting at once that the actual range of possible topics is determined by my own presupposition pool, and by my knowledge of the presupposition pool shared by the participants in the conversation. If my presupposition pool does not include a particular piece of knowledge then a possible topic related to that piece of knowledge would not be known to me, and similarly if I am aware of the fact that others in the group lack knowledge (which I have) which would suggest a particular topic then that topic can be dismissed as a probable topic for the current discussion. We do not normally introduce a topic into conversation unless members of the conversing group can handle it (Clark and Clark's reality principle taken with their principle of linguistic competence).

The concept of relevance, then, in terms of conversation, implies relevance for the group of participants, and the assumption made by participants is that each contribution made by any speaker is relevant both to the context (the actual setting of the conversation), and to the cotext (what has already been said by others, and particularly what was said by the last speaker). However, it is important to notice that with the introduction of the concept of relevance we have again moved into the realm of the subjective in interpretation. The fact is that real language cannot be explicated with a rigorous objectivity. The complex semiotic system of gesture, dress, proxemics, and so on, and the complex structures of spoken language produce communications the significances of which are perceived more or less accurately by human observers[28] who make assumptions which may or may not be justified about the relative probabilities of this or that interpretation being correct. As Sperber and Wilson comment:

It is true that a language is a code which pairs phonetic and semantic representations of sentences. However, there is a gap between the semantic representations of sentences and the thoughts actually communicated by utterances. This gap is filled not by more coding but by inference.[29]

This acute observation in one sense takes us away from the search for an objective and thoroughly scientific study of semantics. It takes us beyond the search for a semiotic whose code could unambiguously be deciphered. At the same time Sperber and Wilson put us firmly back into the business of interpreting real language, admitting once more that semantics plus semiotics will do no more than point us in the right direction as we seek to interpret discourse.

And all of this helps to explain the generally unclear concept of topic. We identify topic in conversation as what the current speaker perceives himself to be talking about, although we recognize that other participants in the conversation may perceive topic differently. Topic is not necessarily identical with grammatical subject, nor necessarily with any particular statement made by a speaker, nor yet with any particular word in the conversation, however great its frequency of occurrence.

For the purposes of exegesis, however, what is more important is the way in which topic is determined. What the *ultimate* topic of any conversation is likely to be simply cannot be predicted. But in some measure even that unpredictable terminus is decided by the first topic set. In each culture there is a recognized hierarchy which determines who sets first topic. Although there can be no absolute law here, there is some measure of regularity. On occasions the regularity may be disturbed by a strong individual who introduces first topic although in the culture he should not, or a diffident individual who will not introduce first topic although in that culture he should, still cultures do exhibit some degree of regularity in providing for the initiation of first topic.

The initiation of first topic then leads into some kind of response, providing us with the second category of conversational adjacency pair, the proposition-response (P-R) adjacency pair.

8.4.3 Questions and Answers
Conversation is commonly developed through questions. As we have already seen, an interrogative does not necessarily signify a question,

and the absence of any interrogative form does not necessarily mean that no question is being asked. A provocative statement, 'You must be born anew' (John 3.7), may have the same effect as a direct question, demanding a reply of some kind, and so involving a different speaker in the conversation.

This observation directs attention onto the existence of principles governing the participation of individuals in any kind of group discourse. Clark and Clark identify a schema of three related rules:[30]

The next turn goes to the speaker addressed by the present speaker.

The next turn goes to the first to speak when the present speaker pauses.

The next turn goes to the present speaker if he resumes before anyone else speaks.

These three rules are arranged in order of priority. We would not wish to speak of 'rules' so much as 'regularities', and we would also want to note that if we identify the regularities appropriate to one culture there can be no certainty that those regularities may be transferred across to another culture.

We may illustrate these points by reference to the conversation in Luke 7.36-50. It takes place at a meal in the house of a Pharisee, and this latter fact is of double significance: the fact that Jesus was invited to the meal suggests that Simon the Pharisee had a high regard for Jesus' attitude to Torah, and the fact that Simon was a Pharisee explains his shock when the 'sinner' of v.37, moreover a woman, dares to minister to his guest. The events are not formally annotated for us, but the sequence involved is important:

i. Jesus is at the home of Simon the Pharisee.

ii. A lacuna; Luke's failure to describe the customary washing of the guest's hands and feet is not the mere omission of unimportant detail: in this case the omission marks an omission, and for dramatic effect the *fact* of the omission is not overtly noted so as not to spoil the effect of Jesus' comment on it later in the conversation.

iii. He is eating a meal.

iv. A 'woman of the city who was a sinner' is present: she has apparently come specifically to minister to Jesus (v.37 and v.45).

v. She is crying. Her tears fall on his feet . . . her hair becomes a towel. She anoints his feet with perfume which she has brought with her. We are not told why she is crying.

vi. Simon disapproves; his expression reveals his thoughts, which, however, remain unspoken, 'If this man were a prophet . . .' The dialogue thus far has been unspoken, and yet is as transparent as if it had all been verbally expressed. Indeed, it is arguably better expressed non-verbally.

vii. Jesus observes Simon's disapproval.

viii. Jesus 'replies' (RSV), *apokritheis*, 'responds', to the silent dialogue: the Greek at this point neatly illustrates the point that a question may be asked non-verbally and without even the paraphrase containing an interrogative. Simon is directly addressed so that his is next turn: 'Simon, I have something to tell you.'

ix. 'Tell me . . .'

x. 'Two men owed money . . . which of them will love him more?' A direct question to Simon, who again takes next turn.

xi. 'I suppose the one who had the bigger debt cancelled.'

xii. 'You have judged correctly.' At this point it would have been appropriate for Simon to have asked for an explanation of the unexpected and rather trivial anecdote, but Clark and Clark's third rule comes into play: Jesus takes next turn when Simon, surely perplexed by the odd story, doesn't quite know how to carry the conversation further.

xiii. 'Do you see this woman?' And now the point of the anecdote is mercilessly driven home. Jesus had not commented on the discourtesy displayed towards him in omitting the foot-washing, but he had noted both the omission and its significance. Simon was curious enough to invite Jesus to his home, sure enough of his ritual purity not to feel threatened by his presence in the home, but Simon had no intention at all of treating Jesus with that respect he would inevitably have accorded a 'man of God' (in his own terms).

xiv. 'Your sins are forgiven.' Although directly addressed to the woman, the sentence is clearly also directed at Simon and the others present at the meal, and is a continuation of the explanation of the anecdote: its meaning has been explained, and now its significance for the woman is made clear. This very brief saying is the peak[31] of the discourse, and the post-peak episode involving the other guests is typically brief and is not explicated at all.

xv. 'The other guests began to say . . .' The provocative nature of Jesus' words now draws the whole group into the discourse.

xvi. 'Your faith has saved you.' The conversation could not have ended at this point, but for Luke's purposes this saying by Jesus is a suitable point at which to terminate the record.

Question-Answer adjacency pairs (Q-A Pairs) are commonly used to further conversation, and we note that this may be so even where the formal markers of interrogation are absent.

8.4.4 Repair-Resolution Pairs

There are occasions in conversation where the speaker is prepared to move on to the next stage and assumes that others also are prepared to move on, but another speaker is not yet prepared for the advance. In a committee meeting, for example, the chairman might be prepared to move to a decision, the implications of which are still not entirely clear to others on the committee. In such a case a *repair* [32] is inserted into the conversation: 'So if we agree to this proposal it will *not* mean raising more money?' The insertion makes it clear that the speaker has recognized the assumed next step, but is insisting on a return to an earlier stage and a satisfactory completion of that stage before the next step is taken. In computer terminology *repair* represents a loop in the programme.

In the conversation between a 'lawyer' and Jesus in Luke 10 the conversation is initiated by the lawyer:

'Teacher, what must I do to inherit eternal life?'

'What is written in the Law? How do you read it?'

'Love the Lord your God . . .'

'You have answered correctly. Do this and you will live.'

The question has been answered, and the conversation is to be terminated. It is left only for the lawyer to leave. However, the questioner is not satisfied that the answer to his question is a clear one. There remains some ambiguity, and so a Repair insertion is made which takes the conversation back to the point *before* the commendation by Jesus,

'And who is my neighbour?'

'A man was going down from Jerusalem . . .

which of these three do you think was a neighbour

to the man who fell into the hands of robbers?'

'The one who had mercy on him.'

'Go and do likewise.'

And now the conversation *is* completed, the ambiguity is resolved, the repair is complete. The injunction 'do this', *touto poiei*, has been replaced by the referential 'do likewise', *poiei homoiōs*, and the lawyer may leave.

8.4.5 Conclusion

Conversation concludes when time runs out, or when the participants run out of things to say, or when the topic is satisfactorily concluded, the problem resolved to the satisfaction of the participants.

The conclusion may then be signalled by an appropriate series of formalized exchanges corresponding to the initiating Greetings pairs, by a form expressing simple agreement, 'O.K.!', or, less commonly, by the participants simply dispersing.

An interesting example of the need for some formal signal of the end of a dialogue is provided by extemporaneous prayer meetings in British Protestant circles. It is rarely clear just when such a meeting is to close, and in many such groups the signal is, in fact, given by whoever considers himself to be the last speaker, prefacing *his* prayer by the word 'So . . .', or 'So, then . . .' Even more interesting is the confusion that often follows in such a prayer meeting if someone is unaware of the significance of the 'So' signal, and inserts another prayer after what was intended to be the closing prayer. It is somehow perceived by the group that another 'So' signal is inappropriate; the problem is often resolved by introducing the words of the Benediction; no one can miss the finality of *that!*

8.5 ANECDOTAL PAIRS

We return to a consideration of the question of change of topic and of the effect this has on the total conversation. The first speaker may offer a single topic, or more probably will offer a comment which might open up any one of several topics. We shall simplify matters by considering the situation where just two topics are offered, A and B. If A is accepted by the other participants then it becomes the substantive topic, and topic B is lost. Alternatively, if B is taken up then topic A is lost. The lost, or rejected, topic is in practice very difficult to reintroduce. Indeed if it is reintroduced it is usually preceded by some explanatory comment which itself acknowledges that what is being done is in some sense irregular: 'Going back to what you were saying about cats . . .' The explanatory comment ('By the way', 'Incidentally', 'Apropos of nothing at all', 'Going back to what we were saying') is termed a *misplacement marker*[33] and signals a recognition that the normal conversational process is for some reason being abandoned.

One reason for the difficulty in reintroducing a rejected topic is that during the discussion of topic A a further potential topic, C, may be introduced, and the conversation may then continue either with topic A or with topic C as the new substantive topic. But the line of continuity with the original topic has been broken, and conversation depends heavily on topical continuity. The process of topic change may be illustrated quite simply as in figure 23.

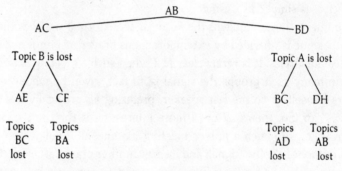

Figure 23.

The principle is, perhaps, best illustrated by reference to the kind of experience most of us have. We are sharing in a conversation. The topic is holidays and particularly sea experiences. We have an appropriate anecdote which we would very much like to contribute. But before the anecdote can be inserted a new topic is introduced: still related to holidays, but now concerned with mountains. Intuitively we recognize that 'sea experiences' are now lost from the topic area, and reluctantly we accept that the anecdote must be discarded. Conversation normally develops, advances, and any gambit that returns the conversation to an earlier stage tends to be rejected.

The conversation between Jesus and the Samaritan woman in John 4 illustrates changing topic very well. The setting of the conversation is made clear, since the location, Jacob's well, suggests topic, ('a drink of water'?) as soon as the two actors appear on the stage. The time is midday. As R. E. Brown points out[34] the chore of fetching water was normally done in the morning or in the evening, and we are told about the time of the encounter not merely to suggest heat and consequent tiredness in Jesus, but principally to signal the aberrant conduct of the woman who comes to fetch water from the well. The woman herself, then, *must* have expected Jesus to comment on her unexpected appearance, if, indeed, he deigned to make any comment at all to a woman, and a Samaritan woman at that. Schnackenburg accepts the general understanding of the story, that as a notorious sinner ('the man you now have is *not* your husband') she would want to avoid conversation with other people[35] and has come to the well at midday for that very reason.

The topic which hangs over the ensuing conversation is that of her conjugal relationships. Jesus intends to reach that topic eventually; she is determined to evade it. Coulthard refers to 'skip-connecting' where speakers repeatedly attempt to introduce different topics, and labels the general phenomenon topic conflict.[36] The initial and changing topics all in fact relate to the threatening potential topic. Jesus does *not* begin the conversation with a comment on her odd conduct, but begins with a request for water. In one sense this is a natural request, but since she is a woman and a Samaritan no request could be entirely natural. The successive contributions offer a variety of possible topics, which are noted in figure 24.

There are two major breaks in the developing conversation, points at which new topics are introduced for which there has been no preliminary text at all: the break which introduces the 'husband' motif, and the break which introduces 'worship'. But neither break is as radical as surface structure suggests. As has already been indicated, above, the question of the woman's background and the reason for her coming to the well at an unsocial hour was always a potential topic. And the way into the topic 'worship' was found in the designation of Jesus by the woman as a prophet, one with special knowledge, indicated by his detailed knowledge of the woman's private life. The topic conflict arises here not because of the woman's desire to discuss worship, but because of her desire not to discuss her conjugal relationships.

Utterance	Topics offered	Topic agreed
Give me a drink	Drink, thirst, water (Jews-Samaritans Men-women)	Drink
You are a Jew	Drink, thirst, water Jews-Samaritans	Drink
If you knew	Drink, water The gift of God	Water
The well is deep	Water, well, Jacob	Water
Whoever drinks . . .	Drink, water, thirst	Water
will never thirst	eternal life	
Give me this water	Water	Water
Go, call your husband	Husband	Husband
I have no husband	No-husband	No-husband
You have had five . . .	No-husband Truth	No-husband
You are a prophet	Prophets, worship Jerusalem	Worship

Figure 24.

8.6 NICODEMUS

8.6.1 Introduction

The Nicodemus pericope in John offers an obvious example of conversation which exhibits a number of intriguing features. We shall attempt to identify the context of the conversation and to determine the limits of the directly relevant cotext, and so to exegete the passage in some detail. The text will be treated seriously in its own terms as a description of a real conversation.[37] It must at once be stated that the majority of scholars do *not* take this view of the pericope.[38]

Of course the passage is an edited record. John's redaction involves the selection of this particular confrontation between Jesus and Nicodemus, as well as a selective description of the context. The inclusion of the event here, by John, is particularly significant in that the event is either unknown to the synoptists, who do not even mention the name of Nicodemus, or deliberately omitted by them. Accepting this necessary level of redactional activity by John we will proceed on the assumption that we have an accurate, if incomplete, record of a real event. The intention is to determine whether or not the pericope can fairly be presented as a real event, whether or not the description conforms to what we know of the principles governing real conversations. If it does conform to the principles of real conversation then it would certainly be possible to argue for the historicity of the pericope. Of course it would also be possible to argue that it simply illustrates John's ability to create fictitious conversation.

8.6.2 The Discourse Boundary

We have deliberately refrained thus far from indicating the text boundaries of the pericope. The fact is that the traditional chapter division tends to conceal the essential continuity of John's text between chapters two and three. Indeed, from 1.19 to 5.47 we have a continuing topic area, which might loosely be designated 'Various ways in which people related to Jesus'. It is entirely clear from 3.2 that the boundary introduced by the chapter division is an intrusion. John records of Nicodemus, 'This man came to *auton* by night', and the antecedent to the pronoun appears in 2.24.

Furthermore there is an interesting and semantically important continuity across the chapter boundary provided by Greek *anthrōpos*: there was no need for anyone to bear testimony concerning *anthrōpou*, because Jesus knew what was in *anthrōpo(i)*, although there was an *anthrōpos* named Nicodemus . . . Verse one of chapter three is linked with chapter two by *de*. The importance of a word is not to be measured by its length, and the occurrence of *de* here neatly illustrates the point. John is not prodigal in his use of *de*[39] and this does make it rather surprising that the adversative force of the particle is missed by all the major English-language translations. That we are intended to make the connection between the 'men' of chapter 2 and the 'man' of chapter 3, is made clear by the resort to the unusual phrase 'a man of the Pharisees' (*anthrōpos ek tōn Pharisaiōn)*, a phrase which is, as Leon Morris has noted, as unusual in Greek as it is in English.[40] So then we are presented with a crowd of people who in some sense believed on Jesus, but Jesus, knowing all about them, did not commit himself to them. *However* there was a certain Pharisee . . .

The discourse boundary closing the pericope is, for a different reason, also unclear. RSV places a section break after verse 21, but Nicodemus has disappeared from the text long before that. The Nicodemus pericope in fact appears to end at verse fifteen, and what follows is the writer's own commentary on the role of the Son of man who has descended from heaven. Verse twelve retains the first person subject for the verb, 'If *I* have told you . . . if *I* tell you heavenly things', and this is then joined to the following text by *kai* (v.13). The phrase 'Son of man' is used by Jesus of himself elsewhere, and we are thus carried forward into verse 15. But the record of the conversation appears to end there.

Precisely how the actual conversation ended we do not know. For John's literary purposes the record ends with the reference to the 'Son of man', just possibly reflecting the *anthrōpos* theme set at the beginning.

8.6.3 The Plurals of the Discourse

It is commonly assumed by commentators that the conversation between Jesus and Nicodemus took place between the two individuals, with no other participants.[41] Both sociological considerations and the text itself make this highly improbable. It is unlikely, for example, that Nicodemus, an eminent rabbi, should be walking about Jerusalem with none of his disciples in attendance. Birger Gerhardsson refers to the story of the two students who 'one evening hid themselves in their teacher's bedroom where he slept with his wife. When the teacher suddenly discovered them he was naturally angry, but they defended themselves by arguing in all innocence that this too involved Torah, and they wanted to learn'.[42]

But the text itself at the very least suggests, even if it does not require, that there were others present in addition to Jesus and Nicodemus. In 3.2 Nicodemus says '*oidamen*, we know, that you are a teacher . . .' Nicodemus speaks on behalf of an undefined group of other people. This has been taken to be one or other of four groups:

1. The *archontes*, the body of the Sanhedrin of which Nicodemus was

a member. This suggestion runs directly counter to 7.48, where the Pharisees themselves comment, 'Has any of the rulers or of the Pharisees believed in him? No!'

2. His own disciples who accompanied him, or, less likely, a representative group of rabbis who were with him. This suggestion has a high level of probability.

3. *All* the people, with Nicodemus speaking on behalf of the masses (so Archbishop Bernard).[43]

4. The *polloi* of 2.23. But if we are right in seeing *de* in verse 1 as adversative we can scarcely now set Nicodemus as representative of the *polloi*.

We would suggest, then, that Nicodemus was not unaccompanied. But we would also suggest that Jesus, too, had his disciples with him. In v.11 Jesus echoes the comment of Nicodemus: *oidamen*, 'we know', and the most obvious explanation of the plural is the presence of Jesus' disciples.

8.6.4 The Occasion
The conversation is commonly set in a house in Jerusalem at night. However there is no good reason for setting the conversation in a house. Although Jesus did eventually have a house available to him in Bethany, it can be no more than conjecture to suppose that the house of Mary, John Mark's mother (Acts 12.12), presumably in Jerusalem, would have been available to him at this point. It is surely more reasonable to set the conversation *not* in a house, but somewhere in the city, possibly in the Temple area, where Jesus was sitting with his disciples, and to which place Nicodemus came with *his* disciples.

We do have explicit reference to the time: *nyktos*, v.2. This has been interpreted in at least four ways:

1. As a simple chronological marker.

2. As reflecting a desire for anonymity on the part of Nicodemus. This is not explicitly stated. In 19.39 Nicodemus is described as the one who came to Jesus *nyktos to prōton*[44] but this need be nothing more than a means of drawing attention to his earlier appearance in the Gospel.

3. As reflecting the redactor's concern with the symbolism of night, over against day, of darkness, over against light. The symbolism is explicit in 1.8-9 and in 11.10,30, and it is certainly arguable that this sym-

bolism provides one element of coherence in the structure of the Gospel, in some measure relevant to each part of it.

4. As reflecting the known custom of the rabbis of using the 'night' for theological discussion.[45] John's failure to explain this reference to 'night' would then be explained by his confidence that the fact that rabbis preferred to have their theological discussions at night time was part of the presupposition pool.

In deciding between these alternatives we should note that John does not mark *nyktos* by bringing it to the head of the sentence. The mobility of this element of the sentence may be demonstrated by reference to Acts 9.24-5, ' . . . the disciples took him by night', where *nyktos* closes the clause, Matthew 28.13, referring to the 'stealing' of the body of Jesus, 'His disciples came by night . . .', where *nyktos* precedes the main verb, and Luke 21.37, 'at night he went out and lodged on the mount called Olivet', where *nyktos* immediately follows adversative *de*. John could have marked *nyktos* by fronting it. The fact that he chose not to do so suggests that its use here is no more than as a chronological marker, with the assurance that readers would recognize the suitability of the time for the kind of debate which occurred.

8.6.5 The Initiating Stage of the Conversation
The salutation 'Rabbi!' must have followed the customary greetings, but their omission allows John to bring into marked position the highly significant word 'Rabbi'.[46] Of course the term itself had its conventional meaning: a Jew trained in an appropriate school in rabbinic method. In the person of Nicodemus there was an example of a self-confident rabbi there in the centre of the situation. But it is by no means certain that Nicodemus really intended to accord to Jesus the dignity of a rabbi. The fact is that the opening statement by Nicodemus carries a certain ambiguity: ' . . . we know that you are a teacher . . .' Plummer comments: 'There is a touch of Pharisaic complacency in the words: "Some of us are inclined to think well of you." '[47] Westcott is even more definite: 'There is . . . a symptom of latent presumption in the word. Nicodemus claims for himself and for others like him the peculiar privilege of having read certainly the nature of the Lord's office in the signs which he had wrought.'[48] If Westcott is right in his perception there is an ironic twist in the phrase, glancing back to the statement that Jesus *did* know what

was in man (2.25). The high level set for the discussion by the use of the term 'rabbi' by Nicodemus awaits confirmation in the subsequent text.

Nicodemus continues his initiating statement, 'Rabbi, we know that you are a teacher come from God'. The word *didaskalos*, 'teacher', collocates well with 'Rabbi', and is qualified by *apo theou*, 'from God', the qualifying phrase being fronted, brought ahead of *didaskalos*, modifying what might otherwise be perceived as a very modest assessment of Jesus. Despite the fronted qualification, the use of *didaskalos* rather than, say, *prophētēs*, suggests a very conservative estimate of the status of Jesus by Nicodemus.

The ground for identifying Jesus as a teacher from God is found in his signs. If we consider this passage merely as a text, the appearance of *tauta* at this point presents a difficulty. There is no immediate example of these *sēmeia* in the cotext, although we note *sēmeia* in 2.23 (a possible further indication of the intrusive nature of the chapter division). However if within the context of the original discussion we ask 'Which signs?', Nicodemus would respond with an expressive wave of the hand, 'These signs, the signs which Jesus has recently been showing.' John has already recorded one sign; other selected signs will be recorded in the appropriate places. Others still will not be recorded at all. In the context of a real conversation Nicodemus feels no need to be specific in the matter of signs: they have been demonstrated.

In his initiating words Nicodemus is offering substantive topic. In fact he offers several. The conversation could now proceed by a discussion of the rabbinate, or of the office of *didaskalos*, or of the signs which Jesus has been doing, or of the significance of the phrase *apo theou*, 'from God'. But in taking the initiative in this way Nicodemus has assumed that his is the right to set topic. The assumption is entirely understandable: he is 'the' teacher of Israel (v.10), a recognized rabbi, a member of the Sanhedrin. Jesus is a wandering teacher accorded the title Rabbi tongue-in-cheek, or at best only by a great stretch of the imagination. Normally it was almost certainly the more important participant who set topic for a conversation: a Rabbi would certainly expect to set topic in any teaching situation. We note also that in the abnormal context of a capital trial it was the least important who spoke first, suggesting that normally the more important spoke first.[49] Thus it appears that in Jewish circles of the day it was the lesser person who initiated greetings, and the more important person who set topic, leaving him with the decision as to whether or not he wished to develop a conversation beyond the level of mere greetings.

8.6.6 Complex Repartee

Although Nicodemus has offered Jesus a number of possible topics, Jesus appears to ignore them all: 'Truly, truly, I say to you, unless one is born anew, he cannot see the kingdom of God.' It is a remarkable fact that commentators largely ignore the disparity between Nicodemus' opening gambit and Jesus' response.[50] It is very difficult to understand what Jesus says as a response to Nicodemus. It has every appearance of a normal *opening* statement. In fact we are here confronted by what Longacre refers to as *complex repartee*.[51] He comments on the consequence of a speaker refusing to follow offered topic: 'When this happens the first speaker is himself faced with a decision as to whether he will accept the dialogue on the new terms suggested by the second speaker.' Of course what happens in the present example is that Jesus rejects the topics offered by Nicodemus and offers new topics as a challenge to the assumption made by Nicodemus *that he has the right to set topic*. If Nicodemus now chooses to continue the conversation on the new terms he will also be accepting Jesus' assessment of the relative status of the two participants. And if we are right in thinking that disciples of both men are present then acceptance of the new terms, and the implications of that acceptance, will be known to them, too. In the event he decides to continue the conversation, accepting topic as set by Jesus: being born anew.

8.6.7 Being Born *Anōthen*

It is true that the Greek at this point is ambiguous: the reference could be to being born *again* or to being born *from above*. The problem need not detain us since we make the simplifying assumption that the discourse represents a genuine conversation which would, in fact, have been not in Greek but in Aramaic, where a parallel ambiguity would not occur.[52] In our written record there is no suggestion at all that Nicodemus found Jesus' words ambiguous: he goes at once to the meaning 'being born *again*'.

It is significant here that Jesus does not give him any explanation of his surprising statement. We must assume, therefore, that Jesus knew that an understanding of the concept of a second birth was in the presupposition pool. Nicodemus could have understood the concept from his awareness of the significance of proselyte baptism as effecting a new birth. R. E. Brown comments:

> Jewish proselyte baptism could have come to his mind, a custom wherein the baptised proselyte was compared to a newborn child (the custom of proselyte baptism seems to have taken hold in Judaism some time in the first century A.D.).[53]

In fact we can probably take Brown's dating into the period before the destruction of the Temple, since the three essential conditions to be fulfilled by the proselyte were circumcision, baptism and *sacrifice*, which must have ceased with the destruction of the Temple.[54]

Nicodemus, however, chooses to be obtuse. His response, 'How . . .' lacks any of the subtlety to be expected of a learned rabbi engaged in theological debate. If the pericope is to be taken as an imaginative creation by John, then the obtuseness reflects on John's knowledge of contemporary Pharisaism. If the pericope is taken to represent a genuine conversation, then the obtuseness reflects the psychologically understandable reaction of Nicodemus to the rebuke implied by Jesus' rejection of topic as offered by Nicodemus. Nicodemus offers only limited co-operation. Even so, Jesus agrees to further the conversation by explaining his remark: Jesus amplifies his statement, ' . . . unless one is born of water and the Spirit', and, as Haenchen comments, 'That can only refer to Christian baptism.'[55]

There could now, surely, be no excuse for Nicodemus failing to perceive that Jesus was referring to the conversion process, the process of 'entering the kingdom'. And even if the practice of proselyte conversion did not occur to him there was an even more startling example of baptism to hand:

> John's baptism was at that very moment producing so profound a sensation in Israel that the first thought of Nicodemus on hearing the phrase 'born of water' could not fail to turn to that ceremony.[56]

John had extended the practice of proselyte baptism to include the baptism of repentant Jews. Jesus is making a dual advance on this contemporary practice: first of all he is insisting that water baptism is *not* enough: to it must be added birth from the Spirit; and secondly he is extending the need for new birth from proselyte baptism to John's baptism of repentant Jews to the universal *'hymas*, you-all, must be born again' (v.7). The Greek construction here is open to at least three interpretations. *Hydatos kai pneumatos* might represent a simple co-ordination, in which water baptism is distinguished from spirit baptism. Alternatively we might have *kai pneumatos* taken as epexegetical, 'born of water, that is to say of the Spirit'. Thirdly we might have an example of hendiadys ('the co-ordination of two ideas, one of which is dependent on the other').[57] The grammar of the phrase does not assist us in deciding between the three interpretations. However, in view of John's careful distinction between water baptism and spirit baptism in 1.32-4 the first of these three possibilities would appear to be the most plausible.

If this is a correct understanding of the original saying of Jesus it is not surprising that Nicodemus is startled by such a radical idea. The emphatic plural form, here, suggests a sweep of the hand from Jesus: all of you, you, Nicodemus, your disciples, my disciples (although Jesus precisely does *not* say 'we-all'). Or again, Nicodemus might have understood Jesus' reference to water and Spirit through Ezekiel 36.25-27:[58] 'I will sprinkle clean water upon you, and you shall be clean from all your uncleannesses, and from all your idols I will cleanse you. A new heart I will give you, and a new spirit I will put within you; and I will take out of your flesh the heart of stone and give you a heart of flesh. And I will put my spirit within you.'

In this case we would understand Jesus as not referring to any contemporary baptismal practice, but to a theologically and eschatologically orientated prophecy of which Nicodemus should be fully aware. Nicodemus, however, responds with another 'How?', possibly a single word in the Aramaic of the original conversation. Indeed, it is apparent that Nicodemus has been steadily reducing his contributions. In the Greek text these reduce from 24 words (v.2) to 18 words (v.4), to 4 words (v.9) and to zero in response to Jesus' question in verse 10. Barrett interprets this gradual diminution to a loss of interest in him as a person by the redactor: 'As the discussion proceeds he is quickly forgotten . . . We are made to hear not a conversation between two persons but the dialogue of church and synagogue.'[59] An alternative perception might be that what we in fact have is Nicodemus steadily withdrawing from the conversation as his position as religious leader is progressively challenged. He does *not* have the right to take the lead in the debate, he is *not* willing to investigate the implications of the very theology he purports to embrace, and he is as much in need of new birth as are the proselytes or, indeed, his own disciples. In fact Nicodemus abandons the principle of co-operation (Clark and Clark again) which alone makes dialogue a possibility, and Jesus is necessarily driven to monologue.

The application of discourse analysis to the Nicodemus conversation leads to a very different interpretation of the encounter from those reached by more traditional methods. Of course it is true that if it is assumed that we have a record of a real conversation then such an analysis becomes possible, just as it is true conversely that if we assume that we do *not* have a record of a real conversation then a very different interpretation must be found. What has been demonstrated, however, is that if the text is treated as a (necessarily) edited account of a genuine conversation it is possible to reconstruct the original event with plausibility. To the extent that this attempt has succeeded, the necessity for any one of the many proposed reinterpretations is brought into question.

Notes

[1]T. Venneman, 'topic, sentence, accent and ellipsis', in E. L. Keenan (ed.), *Formal Semantics of Natural Language*, Cambridge, CUP, 1975.

[2]Although the modern reader would not be at all astonished by the statement. In our presupposition pool we have the belief that wealth is somehow spiritually dangerous, and this knowledge actually goes back, at least in part, to the Matthew 19 tradition. This is a good example of our earlier contention that meaning must be separated from significance, and that neither meaning nor significance lies solely in words.

[3]New York, Harcourt,Brace, Jovanovich, 1977, pp.225-6.

[4]See the discussion on this preliminary hearing in Ernst Haenchen, *The Acts of the Apostles*, Oxford, Blackwell, 1971. He sees the passage as 'the illustrative composition of the author' (p.643).

[5]See particularly H. P. Grice, 'Logic and conversation', in P. Cole and J. L. Morgan (eds.), *Syntax and Semantics*, New York, Academic Press, 1975, and R. Wardhaugh, *An Introduction to Sociolinguistics*, Oxford, Blackwell, 1986, chap. 12.

[6]*Pragmatics*, pp.101f.

[7]M. Coulthard, *An Introduction to Discourse Analysis*, p.78.

[8]Of course we must distinguish the discourse as perceived by the crowd in the second part of John 6 from the very much longer discourse as perceived by the reader of the Gospel. The point is an important one; the writer is at liberty to craft his text as he sees best in the interest of his readers, but cannot, with integrity, do the same for the original actors in his discourse.

[9]F. J. Moloney, *The Johannine Son of Man*, Rome, Las, 1976, p.89. But see especially the detailed structuralist analysis of John 6 by J. D. Crossan, and the essay by Gary A. Phillips in *Semeia*, 26 (1983).

[10]'And it shall come to pass at that self-same time that the treasury of manna shall again descend from on high.' But see the discussion in, for example, R. Schnackenburg, *The Gospel According to St John*, on 6.31.

[11]Peder Borgen argues that what we have here is a midrash on the Exodus 16 pericope dealing with bread from heaven, parallel to similar midrash from Philo *(Bread from Heaven*, Leiden, Brill, 1965). The proposition is worked out with great ingenuity and erudition.

[12]Whatever meaning is given to 'this point'. Schnackenburg, for one, transposes chapters five and six although he admits to being without manuscript evidence for making the change *(The Gospel According to St John*, vol.II, pp.5-9).

[13]But there is little unanimity amongst the commentators as to the relative importance to be given to various factors which are, or might be, relevant to the interpretation of the text. Thus the assertion by Weiss that there is nothing against the view that the evangelist was an eyewitness to these events is dismissed by Haenchen as rash *(John*, vol.1, Philadelphia, Fortress Press, 1984, p.271). Again, Haenchen approves of Bauer's view that the Elisha story probably served as the model for this narrative, but Bultmann insists that there is no proof of such a dependency, and Wellhausen does not so much as consider the possibility. Haenchen surveys the views of various scholars on the status of 51b-59 and admits 'There is a note of uncertainty in most of these exegetes' (Haenchen, op.cit., p.297).

[14]But *not* falsified, and *not* merely created by author, editor, or redactor.

[15]Schnackenburg, p.35.

[16]Haenchen, p.290.

[17]Schnackenburg, p.43.

[18]See also D. Sperber and D. Wilson, *Relevance*, London, Blackwell, 1986, especially chap. 3, for an incisive examination of this aspect of the interpretative process in conversation.

[19]*Psychology and Language*, p.226.

[20]See Peter Trudgill, *Sociolinguistics*, Harmondsworth, Pelican, 1983[2], chap. 5, and Ronald Wardhaugh, *An Introduction to Sociolinguistics*, Oxford, Blackwell, 1986, chap. 4, 'Choosing a Code'.

21See G. D. Fee, *The First Epistle to the Corinthians*, Grand Rapids, Eerdmans, 1987, pp.121-7.

22See especially R. E. Longacre, *The Grammar of Discourse*, chap. 2, 'Repartee', and R. Wardhaugh, *How Conversation Works* and *An Introduction to Sociolinguistics*, pp.287ff., 'Some Features of Conversation'. Both of Wardhaugh's books are published by Blackwell.

23L. Bronner, in *Pretoria Oriental Series*, 6(1968), 'The Stories of Elijah and Elisha as Polemics against Baal Worship', made the interesting suggestion that Gehazi was primarily sent ahead of Elisha to ensure that the child was not buried before the prophet could arrive (quoted in G. H. Jones, *I and II Kings* [The New Century Bible Commentary], London, Marshall, Morgan & Scott, 1984, p.408). However, Gehazi's comment when he returned to Elisha from his errand, 'The child has not awaked', militates against the suggestion.

24*The Gospel of Luke*, Exeter, Paternoster, 1978, p.418.

25Josephus, *Ant.*, 11,331.

26G. Brown and G. Yule, *Discourse Analysis*, especially chap. 3, 'Topic and the representation of discourse content'. We note their perceptive comment, ' . . . the basis for the identification of "topic" is rarely made explicit. In fact, "topic" could be described as the most frequently used, unexplained, term in the analysis of discourse' (p.70). See also Wardhaugh, *An Introduction to Sociolinguistics*, pp.291-2.

27See Dan Sperber and Deirdre Wilson, *Relevance*, Oxford, Blackwell, 1986. The sub-title of this important book, 'Communication and Cognition', makes it clear that Sperber and Wilson treat language as primarily a means of communication and focuses attention on the vital role of participants in interpreting discourse, rather than on the fixed and objective semiotic systems they employ. See also Brown and Yule (1983), 3.4, and the much earlier work by H. P. Grice, for example 'Logic and conversation', in P. Cole and J. Morgan (eds.), *Syntax and Semantics*, New York, Academic Press, 1975.

28The whole question of the relationship between language and the person using the language is explored in a highly compressed but very readable book by John B. Carroll, *Language and Thought*, in the Foundations of Modern Psychology series, Englewood Cliffs, New Jersey, 1964.

29*Relevance*, p.9.

30Clark and Clark, *Psychology and Language*, p.228. See also M. Coulthard, *An Introduction to Discourse Analysis*, pp.52-62.

31Longacre, *The Grammar of Discourse*, 4.3.

32Wardhaugh, *An Introduction to Sociolinguistics*, p.293.

33See Michael Stubbs, *Discourse Analysis*, p.183.

34*The Gospel According to John* (The Anchor Bible), London, Chapman, 1966, vol. I, p.169.

35R. Schnackenburg, *The Gospel According to St John*, London, Burns & Oates, 1968, vol.I, p.424. He also comments, 'The time given, about midday, explains his being tired and thirsty.' This is certainly true, but the time indicator has greater importance than that.

36M. Coulthard, *An Introduction to Discourse Analysis*, p.78.

37See F.P. Cotterell, 'The Nicodemus Conversation', *Expository Times* 96, 8 (1985); and 'Sociolinguistics and Biblical Interpretation', *Vox Evangelica* 16 (1986).

38It is very difficult to satisfy the critics. Thus Schnackenburg comments on the reference to Passover at verse 4, 'The meaning of the remarks about the nearness of the Passover . . . is also not chronological but theological', but at verse 10 comments on the 'much grass', 'which would only be found in spring, near Passover, on these mountain slopes of Galilee' (*The Gospel According to St John*, vol. II, p.14). If the presence of confirmatory circumstantial detail of this kind is to be dismissed out of hand it makes the scholarly refutation or confirmation of any proposed interpretation effectively impossible. To the linguist the *meaning* of the remark on Passover must be chronological until it can be shown to be something different. What the *significance* of the reference may be is a different issue, and we would assume that this is Schnackenburg's point.

39If we take Luke as a basis for comparison, the comparative frequencies are: Matthew 94%, Mark 49% (Luke 100%), and John 52%. In John *de* is more than a stylistic copulative.

40*The Gospel According to John* (New London Commentaries), London, Marshall Morgan & Scott, 1971, p.209, n2.

41Cf. Leon Morris, 'The first "Discourse" is a private talk to a single listener' (*The Gospel According to John*, p.208), and Bernard, 'Nothing is said in c.3 of any one being present at the interview between Jesus and Nicodemus' (passing over *oidamen*), but he adds ' . . . on the other hand, there is nothing to exclude the presence of a disciple', *The Gospel According to St John* (International Critical Commentary), vol. I, p.101.

42*The Origins of the Gospel Traditions*, London, SCM, 1979, p.18.

43*St John* (International Critical Commentary), Edinburgh, T. & T. Clark, 1928, vol. I, p.101.

44And Bezae imports this description into 7.50.

45It is interesting here to compare the Qur'an, 73.5, 'We shall cast upon thee a weighty word; surely the first part of the night is heavier in tread, more upright in speech, surely in the day thou hast long business' (Arberry's translation, Oxford, OUP, 1983). Muhammad's meditations were located in the first part of the night because the day was too busy.

46See Brown and Yule, *Discourse Analysis*, 4.2. It is a fact that very similar information may be conveyed in a range of syntactic structures: 'Jesus came yesterday', 'It was yesterday that Jesus came'.

[47]*The Gospel According to St John* (The Cambridge Greek Testament), Cambridge, CUP, 1882, ad. loc.

[48]*The Gospel According to St John*, London, Murray, 1892, ad. loc.

[49]*Sanhedrin* 4.1: 'In civil suits and in cases of cleanness and uncleanness, we begin with (the opinion of) the most eminent (of the judges); whereas in capital charges we commence with (the opinion of) those on the side (benches).' See also J. Neusner, *There we sat down*, New York, Ktav, 1978[2], p.95, for a description of the attitude of the disciple to his *rab*. In *A Life of Yohanan ben Zakkai*, Leiden, Brill, 1970, Neusner includes an account of the visit by a group of the Rabbi's disciples to comfort him on the death of his son. Each begins his address to the Rabbi: "Master, by your leave, may I say something to you?" (p.101). The Rabbi expected his students to listen: he spoke first.

[50]S. Mendner, in *Journal of Biblical Literature* 77 (1958), pp.293-323, considers the problem but, unable to reconcile what Jesus says to the opening remark by Nicodemus, responds by dismissing parts of the text from the dialogue. Haenchen handles the problem by restating the comment from Nicodemus. 'We know that you are a teacher . . .' becomes an 'assertion . . . that he, Jesus, will be incontestably legitimized by miracles for everyone who sees his works' (*John 1*, p.200). There seems to be an element of Humpty Dumpty here (see 1.2, above).

[51]R. E. Longacre, *The Grammar of Discourse*, pp. 51-3.

[52]But see Haenchen, *John 1*, p.200 for a discussion of *anōthen*.

[53]*The Gospel According to John*, p.222. See also R. J. Werblowsky, 'A Note on Purification and Proselyte Baptism', in J. Neusner (ed.), *Christianity, Judaism and other Graeco-Roman Cults*, Leiden, Brill, 1975.

[54]Of course we are aware that the provisions laid down for proselyte conversion could have been theoretical and ideal only, but there is no particular reason for taking such a view. Indeed, there is good reason for taking John chapter 3 as evidence to the contrary.

[55]*John 1*, p.200. Haenchen makes reference to Acts 19.5 to make the connection between baptism and the receiving of the Spirit, rightly contrasting John's baptism with Christian baptism, the former being no more than an external confession of repentance. In the Acts 19 passage, John's disciples are rebaptized *and* have Paul's hands laid on them, when they receive the Spirit. Even here there is no *mechanical* association between baptism and the receiving of the Spirit.

[56]F. L. Godet, *Commentary on St John's Gospel*, Edinburgh, 1889, vol. II, p.49.

[57]F. Blass, A. Debrunner, *A Greek Grammar of the New Testament*, R. W. Funk (ed.),

Chicago and London, University of Chicago Press, 1961, p. 228.

[58]See Linda Belleville, 'Born of Water and Spirit', *Trinity Journal*, 1,2 (1980), p.140.

[59]*The Gospel According to St John*, London, SPCK, 1978[2], p.202.

9. Non-Literal Language

9.1 SUBJECTIVE MEANING IN UTTERANCES

In Chapter 1 we briefly investigated the inherent complexity of real language, human language being used in the communication process. If I read in an old-fashioned school primer the *sentence*, 'The cat sat on the mat', I would probably recognize that the sentence has been produced solely for the book and has no particular reference to any real cat or real mat anywhere.

If, however, in real life I encounter the very similar sequence of monosyllables, 'The cat sat on the board', the meaning of the *utterance* is by no means clear. What cat? Which board? Why would any cat sit on a board? Why should anyone bother to comment to me on such an event? Is the 'cat' in fact Miss Tolwell-Entwistle, and is the 'board' in fact the Board of Governors of the local grammar school, and was she merely a member of the Board or did she sit on it in the sense of intimidating it, dominating it?

In the real-life situation, meaning is multiply ambiguous, and this is so not merely because of the very large number of possible referents for the words that I choose to employ, dozens of possible cats, for example (although *not* all existing cats, just the cats which happen to swim in my presupposition pool), but also because there exists a second stream of meaning of which specific notice must now be taken: figurative, non-literal, meaning. Miss Tolwell-Entwistle may literally sit on a literal board, or she may figuratively sit on a figurative board and the two meanings of the two identical sets of word forms are utterly different the one from the other. We have already seen (4.2.3) that there exists some ill-defined relationship between a concept, that of "boy", a form (or sign), the dictionary entry 'boy', and some actual boy in the real world.[1] The form 'sit' has many potential meanings and so does the form 'board' and the same is true of most forms, and it is this general phenomenon of polysemy which is in part responsible for the imprecision of human communication.

In this chapter we are concerned with another source of imprecision: the existence within the human communication system of two strands of meaning, uncomfortably labelled literal and non-literal. An example illustrates the distinction. If I observe 'It's raining cats and dogs', I am not speaking literally. If I point to the garden and comment 'There are five dogs and six cats in the garden', I am speaking literally. Caird helpfully and candidly comments:

> 'Literality is easier to illustrate than to define, but provisionally we may say that words are used literally when they are meant to be understood in their primary, matter-of-fact sense.'[2]

We would not wish to support the notion of a simple dichotomy between literal and figurative language. In utterances we would be quite wrong in supposing that the meaning of *any* sentence is simply the sum of the meanings of its constituents. Meaning is inextricably bound up in context and cotext. Even the most trivial word takes on additional, non-literal, subjective, meaning when it abandons the dictionary for the street.[3]

9.2 AFFECTIVE LANGUAGE

The fact is that language as communication is both an expression of an emotion and the creator of an emotion. Just as there can be no music other than mood music, so there can be no utterance which is not emotive, and to that extent non-literal. Isaiah 5.7 offers an example:

> For the vineyard of the Lord of hosts
> is the house of Israel,
> and the men of Judah
> are his pleasant planting;
> and he looked for justice,
> but behold bloodshed;
> for righteousness,
> but behold, a cry!

The concluding phrases are striking in English, but the euphony has inevitably been lost:

> *wayequ lemishpat wehinneh mispah*
> > *letsedaqah wehinneh tse'aqah.*

Just why we rhyme and balance clauses, and how the rhyme and balance affect the meaning of the resultant text is unclear: but that a particular emotion is created by such linguistic forms is not in dispute.

However, such forms are more than merely decorative: they are also informative.[4] One such linguistic form is *chiasmus*. As the term suggests the form involves a *crossing over* in which words, phrases, sentences and even longer texts are sequenced not linearly, but in a cross-pattern. A good example is furnished by the well-known saying in Matthew 7.6; RSV processes the text linearly:

> 'Do not give dogs what is holy;   a
> and do not throw your pearls before swine,   b
> lest they trample them under foot   b'
> and turn to attack you.'   a'

It is the swine which would trample the pearls under foot, and it is the dogs which would turn to attack.

This particular example carries no theological significance, but the possible chiasmus in Philemon 5 is more important:

> 'I hear of your love   a
> and of the faith   b
> which you have toward the Lord Jesus   b'
> and all the saints.'   a'

If this is a genuine instance of the phenomenon, then Paul is affirming that Philemon has *love for all the saints*, and he has *faith toward the Lord Jesus*, but not *faith toward all the saints*.[5]

With respect to more extended texts, Talbert, to give one example, has attempted to show that both Luke 10.21—18.30 and Acts 15.1—21.26 are to be understood in terms of chiasmus,[6] and somewhat more convincingly C. Blomberg has argued that Luke used a chiastic parable *source* for the *former* section, to which he has added.[7] J. Bligh has even argued that the *whole* of Galatians is one vast chiasmus containing an intricate network of smaller chiasmi.[8]

While these hypotheses may be viewed with various degrees of confidence, it is at least attractive to suggest that in Galatians Paul takes up the two criticisms made of him and after stating the criticisms responds to each at length, but in the reverse order:

his Gospel is *kata anthrōpon*	Gal.1.11	a
his Gospel is *para anthrōpou*	Gal.1.12	b
it is *not* in fact *kata anthrōpon*	Gal. 1.13—2.21	b'
it is *not* in fact *para anthrōpou*	Gal. 3.1—6.10	a'

Chiasmus is far more a Semitic phenomenon than a Greek phenomenon and is a particular feature of Hebrew poetry:

Deliver me, O my God!
For
thou dost smite all my enemies on the cheek,

thou dost break the teeth of the wicked
Deliverance belongs to the Lord. (Psalm 3.7-8)

This combination of non-literal language and carefully crafted clauses serves to communicate more than information: we have what is called *affective language*. The intention is to communicate to the reader an attitude, an opinion, a judgement, an emotion. When Paul referred to 'mutilators of the flesh' (*katatomē*, Phil. 3.2) he was concerned less with the denotative meaning of the word than with its affective power. When in 2 Cor.12.11 he used the term 'superlative apostles', he was probably using irony and his intention was affective.[9]

Utterances fall along a spectrum, with a very high level of figurative language at one end of the spectrum, and a very low level of figurative language at the other end of the spectrum. Even in the utterance, 'It's raining cats and dogs', I recognize the literality of the rainfall. In the real world of human communication we cannot banish either literality or affective language. John Locke, the rationalist philosopher, expressed deep suspicion of the non-literal use of language, because of its essential ambiguity. To speak of things *as they are*, he felt, requires that we abandon rhetoric: 'If we would speak of things as they are we must allow that all the arts of rhetoric . . . are perfect cheats.' And yet in expressing his objection Locke makes use of non-literal language: can an art *cheat*?

It can be argued that it is impossible for us to evade metaphorical language. To speak of a particular flower as a *tulip* is to describe it *not* in terms of itself but in terms of other flowers which in this or that respect it resembles (it is, obviously, identical with none of them).[10] To speak of this-which-I-hold-in-my-hand in terms of itself is not only dull, it is also necessarily uninformative. Cognition appears to require an escape from literal language into the non-literal. Non-literal language is employed so as to convey a level of meaning which may well prove to be beyond objective analysis. The expression, 'It's raining cats and dogs', conveys something different from the similar expression, 'It's raining very hard', or from the objective expression, 'One inch of rain fell in less than an hour yesterday afternoon in Preston'. The three expressions might each be used to describe the same event, but each would convey different information and each would be appropriate in a particular but distinct context.

Although the biblical text abounds with examples of non-literal communication, Hebrew poetry, as exemplified in, say, Isaiah, offers perhaps the most persuasive examples. In addition to the apparent figurative language *parallelism* is sometimes employed, as in the following example, both to explain and to extend the meanings of the figures employed:

> Comfort, comfort my people,
> says your God.
> *Speak tenderly* to *Jerusalem*,
> and *cry* to *her*
> that her *warfare* is *ended*,
> that her *iniquity* is *pardoned*,
> that she has received from the Lord's hand
>   double for all her sins.

A voice cries:
'*In the wilderness* prepare the *way of the Lord*,
Make straight *in the desert* a *highway for our God.*
Every *valley* shall be *lifted up*,
and every *mountain and hill* be *made low*;
the *uneven ground* shall become *level*
and the *rough places* a *plain.*' (Isaiah 40.2-4)

We notice here the striking way in which one word is explicated by its parallel: warfare is related to the iniquity of Israel, and the warfare is ended only by the granting of Yahweh's pardon. Note, too, the initial metonymic use of the word 'Jerusalem', where 'the people of Judah' is meant. There is antithetic parallelism, too: valleys are lifted up and mountains are made low. But of course the important point to be made is that the communication achieved by these rhetorical devices is quite different from what would be achieved by a more literal genre, perhaps in the following approximate equivalent:

Tell Judah that they have now been sufficiently punished and so their sins are forgiven. But they must end the wrongs they are committing, and they must begin to do what the law requires, so that Yahweh may again act on their behalf.

The interpretation of passages such as this requires the reader to distinguish between the literal meaning of the text and the figurative meaning of the 'same' text. The literal meaning of Isaiah 40 includes the sense of hills being levelled and of valleys being filled in, so as to produce a vast plain. The concept itself is not a difficult one, (although more difficult is the concept of someone standing outside the city of Jerusalem and speaking to *it*.) The non-literal meaning can only be correctly discerned by those whose presupposition pool is that shared by the prophet himself. That meaning includes the concept of sin as pride and disobedience, and a recognition that Yahweh is in some sense the absentee God of Israel, preparing himself to return to his people. But the meaning is conveyed through an *emotional appeal* as much as through the bare semantics of the constituent sentences.

The key to the interpretation of the passage is not given to the casual reader since the oracle is not intended for anyone who does not already hold that key. The key must be found elsewhere: in the case of the contemporary people of Judah from within their own prophetic tradition, and in our case by a scholarly recovery of the key from that same tradition. But those who hold the key and are able to perceive the prophet's connotative meaning will find that the meaning involves both a cognitive and an emotive element. And the repeated 'Comfort!', '*na-hamu!*' which stands at the head of the poem has a particular poignancy to supply to the sonorous phrases that follow.

A similarly careful process of interpretation is required in the case of the well-known saying of Jesus, 'If any one comes to me and does not *hate* his own father and mother and wife and children and brothers and sisters, yes, and even his own life, he cannot be my disciple'(Luke 14.26). Most other usage of *misein*, 'hate' in the New Testament is understandable to the Christian reader (although note Romans 9.13), but what are we to make of the requirement that we 'hate' our closest relatives? As Caird reminds us,[11] Matthew presents us with the same teaching but in a different form: 'He who loves father or mother more than me is not worthy of me; and he who loves son or daughter more than me is not worthy of me; and he who does not take his cross and follow me is not worthy of me' (Matthew 10.37-8).[12] In the Lucan saying we have non-literal language, hyperbole. The strength of the saying lies precisely in the emotive response of the reader and the immediate recognition that the literal meaning cannot be the intended meaning.

9.3 METAPHOR

Comparative language is used so that what is unknown may be understood in terms of what is known. It is usual to distinguish between *simile* and *metaphor* although the two figures of speech shade imperceptibly into each other: 'every metaphor presupposes a simile, and every simile is compressible or convertible into a metaphor.'[13] All comparisons hold only to a limited extent: to say that a narcissus is *like* a daffodil is to relate narcissi and daffodils to one another, with an underlying assumption that daffodils are known, but narcissi are a novelty. Again, to say that a field of poppies looked *like* a sea of blood is to explain what a field of poppies looks like. In each case there is an observer who has seen and knows, and there is someone who has not seen and does not know, but would like to know.

It is sometimes suggested that the former example is a simile, the narcissus is a plant with a stem and leaves and a flower, and so is a daffodil, but the latter example is a metaphor because a poppy is not a splash of blood. Similarly, 'My love is like a red, red, rose' is a metaphor because she isn't a rose but a person.

Another approach to differentiating between simile and metaphor is to concentrate on the presence or absence of a linguistic marker such as 'like': 'My love is *like* a red, red, rose' is then a simile and not a metaphor. However, it is not clear that there is any distinction in meaning between the 'simile' of the Good News Bible, 'Benjamin is *like* a ravening wolf', and the 'metaphor' of the Revised Standard Version, 'Benjamin *is* a ravenous wolf' (Genesis 49.27).

Without attempting any formal distinction between the two figures, it is, perhaps, worth noting that in English, at least, the writer who uses a metaphor such as 'Benjamin is a ravenous wolf' is formally lying. Benjamin is not a wolf. Similarly, the Christians at Corinth were *not* the body of Christ (1 Cor. 12.27).[14] It is this conflict between what is stated and what is known to be the case that supplies metaphorical language with its dynamic.

Metaphor, like all comparisons, consists of two parts, the imprecise element which is to be explained, and the alien, surprising, incongruous, or unexpected element which is used to supply the explanation. The unexpectedness lies in the transfer of a linguistic label from a context where it is well understood to an alien context. And the more alien and unexpected the context the more vivid the metaphor. In Hosea 5.12, we have two vivid metaphors which present God in terms of a moth and of dry rot in a house. The word 'moth' here is the *vehicle* of the metaphor, the known, but the word is transferred to a new sphere entirely, to God, the *tenor* of the metaphor. And it is precisely in the unexpectedness of the designation of God as *moth* and as *dry rot*, that the power of the metaphor lies. In Matthew 5.13-14 the people of God are designated as metaphorical lights, a metaphor which is readily intelligible, and as metaphorical salt, which is less intelligible, certainly to us today, and to that extent more striking.

The use of metaphor is a creative act,[15] and there can be no certainty that the interpretation of the metaphor will follow the intention of its creator. The receiver must search through his own experience, and must employ his own imagination, and if necessary engage in his own

research, and only so can the meaning of a metaphor be realized. But
that experience and that imagination are his, and not those of the creator of the metaphor, so that the use of metaphor inevitably opens up
the way to misunderstanding.

Our understanding of metaphor depends on our knowledge of the
presupposition pool of the creator of the metaphor, and is further enhanced by the availability of a cotext from which the purpose of the
metaphor might be deduced. Metaphorical language is like any other
manifestation of real language in that it is to be understood only in a
context. However, it is not difficult to see that metaphor depends for
its effectiveness on the existence of some feature common to both parts
of the metaphor, but a feature which is not normally identified as common.

If we take the metaphor of the body we might illustrate this concept
in triangular form as in figure 25:[16]

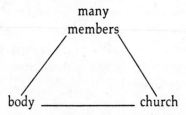

Figure 25.

The metaphor is used by Paul in 1 Corinthians 12 because he wishes
to draw on the idea of the essential unity of the body despite its many
members. However, although Paul uses the same terminology elsewhere (Ephesians 1.22; Colossians 1.18) the triangle of relationships is
not necessarily retained: a new point of comparison is in mind. Colossians 1.18 states that Christ is 'the head of the body, the church', although in 1 Corinthians 12 the 'head' of the body is apparently to be
understood as some self-important member of the church (v.21).

So then metaphorical language draws attention to some feature
shared by two terms, a feature not usually recognized as common to the
two, but a feature which, when once presented, commends itself to the
hearer of the metaphor as appropriate and illuminating. In other words
metaphor is not merely an adornment to language: it contributes positively to communication.

In fact the meaning of metaphor is properly elucidated by an encyclopaedic evaluation of the two terms being used, and the attempt to
identify some common feature which is congruous both with the cotext
and the context within which the metaphor appears. Thus in interpreting the metaphor which relates church to body, we require an encyclopaedic knowledge of what a church is, and of what a body is, and a
study of the text of 1 Corinthians 12 to discover which of the many
possible matches Paul actually had in mind when he employed the metaphor. What the metaphor might *mean* elsewhere is another issue entirely: it would need to be determined in its new context.[17] In the case of
the body metaphor of 1 Corinthians 12 we have little difficulty in seeing
the point of the metaphor. The metaphor is itself so productive that Paul
elaborates his imagery so that we are in little doubt of his intentions.
But this is by no means always true of metaphorical language.

One further observation needs to be made: effective metaphor depends on a common perception between the creator of the metaphor and
the hearer. In other words there must be an appropriate common presupposition pool from which the hearer could correctly perceive meaning. The modern reader of the Bible might not have that presupposition
pool, as the following example shows.

9.4 BURNING COALS (ROMANS 12.20)
The fragility of metaphor is well illustrated by Paul's approach to the
question of how Christians ought to deal with their opponents:

> Bless those who persecute you; bless and do not curse them. Rejoice
> with those who rejoice, weep with those who weep. Live in harmony
> with one another; do not be haughty, but associate with the lowly;
> never be conceited. Repay no one evil for evil, but take thought for
> what is noble in the sight of all. If possible, so far as it depends on
> you, live peaceably with all. Beloved, never avenge yourselves, but
> leave it to the wrath of God; for it is written, 'Vengeance is mine,
> I will repay, says the Lord.' No, 'if your enemy is hungry, feed him;
> if he is thirsty, give him drink; for by so doing you will heap burning
> coals upon his head.' Do not be overcome by evil, but overcome evil
> with good. (Romans 12.14-21)

The metaphor in verse 20, 'You will heap burning coals upon his head',
elicits no appropriate response in the thinking of the modern reader of

the Bible. If the modern reader goes to other parts of the Bible for his explanation of the burning coals he is almost certain to conclude that the idea of *judgement* is primary. Nadab and Abihu are destroyed by fire from the Lord in Leviticus 10.2. Sodom and Gomorrah are destroyed by fire out of heaven in Genesis 19.24. Psalm 11.6 warns 'On the wicked he will rain coals of fire and brimstone'. Ezekiel prophesies in the name of Yahweh, 'I will blow upon you with the fire of my wrath' (Ezekiel 21.31). Peter describes the day of judgement in terms of the heavens being 'kindled and dissolved', and Revelation describes the 'second death' as a lake of fire (20.14). The metaphor is then interpreted as indicating that the Christian who forgives his enemies, in the very act of renouncing retaliation himself, hands his enemy over to the fiery judgement of God. This interpretation has the merit of conforming to 2 Esdras 16.53: 'Let no sinner say that he has not sinned; for God will burn coals of fire on the head of him who says, "I have not sinned before God and his glory",' but conflicts with the central thrust of Romans 12.20 which is forgiveness, *not* judgement.[18]

An alternative approach which would render the problematic words by something like 'burning with shame' has little to commend it, since it appeals to a culturally bound figure of speech.[19] It is true that this idiom is current, although it is becoming more rare, in English-speaking society, but there is no corresponding idiom in Hebrew, and no firm evidence of it in Greek of the time[20] so that we would be guilty both of a synchronic error and of a cross-cultural error if the idiom were pressed into service to explain Paul's metaphor.

A third possibility is the appeal to some contemporary activity involving coals of fire. William Klassen, in his detailed study of the coals of fire metaphor,[21] quotes J. E. Yonge who confidently asserts that 'it is generally agreed that the metaphor is taken from metallurgy', and former missionary John Steele who suggests that the metaphor referred to the work of the blacksmith. However the understanding of the phrase used by Paul may be recovered by reference to the original usage of the metaphor in Proverbs 25.21-2. We give here the relevant verses together with the following verse, verse 23, the significance of which will become apparent shortly:

If your enemy is hungry, give him bread to eat;

and if he is thirsty, give him water to drink;
for you will heap coals of fire on his head,
and the Lord will reward you.

The north wind brings forth rain;
and a backbiting tongue, angry looks.

Verse 23 has perplexed commentators, some of whom have resorted to
conjectural emendation of the text to resolve the problem, since in Palestine it is simply not the case that the north wind brings rain.[22] The
Jewish commentator A. Cohen admits as much: '. . . the north wind
which is said to herald fair weather . . . whereas it is the wind from the
east and the west which brings rain.'[23] However, the statement *is* true
for Egypt, and it has been suggested that the origin of the metaphor in
verse 22 and of the statement about the wind in verse 23 is Egypt and
not Palestine.

Klassen points for an explanation to an Egyptian text first published
by F. L. Griffith, *Stories of the High Priests of Memphis*,[24] from which it
appears that a penitent would go to the individual he had wronged,
bearing on his head a clay dish containing burning coals. The meaning
of the metaphor as it is used in Proverbs then becomes clear: if a man
acts generously towards his enemy he may bring him to repentance.
And if this is the sense of the metaphor as Paul understood it, then he
is telling us that if a Christian has an enemy, and instead of threatening
him forgives him, then he is likely to bring his enemy to the point of
repentance; metaphorically the Christian is himself putting the clay
bowl of burning coals on the man's head and starting him on his way
to repentance. Is this a possible explanation for the metaphor? In response to the question five comments may be made:

1. It is not necessary that the actual *practice* attested in the metaphor
should have spread into Palestine: being geographically contiguous the
metaphor could spread even without the actual practice.

2. Proverbs itself comes from precisely that genre of literature which
might draw in contributions from a wide region: mottos, maxims, proverbs, apophthegms. The fact that verse 23 contains a statement appropriate to Egypt makes it at least possible that verse 22 has the same
provenance.

3. Negatively it must be admitted that the demotic text recording the Egyptian practice is later than Proverbs, but clearly the *practice* must have preceded the *recording* of the practice.

4. This interpretation agrees with the cotext both of the original Proverbs passage and of Paul's quotation of it.

5. Of course it must be emphasized that there is no necessary suggestion here that Paul was aware of the existence of an Egyptian repentance ritual involving a clay dish and burning coals. What Paul *did* know was the text of the Old Testament, and the contemporary understanding of the metaphor. We would suggest that that understanding of the metaphor conformed generally to that outlined above, for such a sense provides a more credible explanation of Paul's words in this context than the alternatives at present on offer.

Furthermore we should be wary of offering for the phrase 'coals of fire' and for the passage in which it stands any *retributive* sense. Paul is not unlikely to have known Jesus' teaching on loving one's enemies (Matt. 5.44; Luke 10.25-37), and on non-retaliation (Mt. 5. 38ff.). He might even have known the tradition that Jesus had rebuked his disciples when they wished to call down fire on unbelieving Samaritans (Luke 9.51-6). Unless he was quite unaware of all these strands of tradition (and others beside) he is unlikely to have intended a retributive teaching in Romans 12.20.

So then, in writing to the church at Rome, Paul faces the important question of how a Christian should respond to his enemies, reaches back into the Old Testament for the verses regarding feeding an enemy and giving him drink, and retains the metaphor which accompanied and completed the original text. The meaning of the whole must be a harmonious unity, but failure correctly to interpret the metaphor by some commentators has led to a measure of confusion in which the entirely natural, human, desire to see the enemies of God's people get their come-uppance is gratified at the expense of the consistent teaching[25] both of Jesus and of Paul. Ernst Käsemann summarizes: 'Whatever may be the meaning of the original text . . . the statement seems to point to an Egyptian penitential ritual involving a forced change of mind . . . This supports the opinion that the saying is not related to a divine penalty . . . but to the remorse and humiliation of the adversary.'[26]

Our discussion of metaphor so far has largely focused on examples that are not central in theological debates, but metaphor is so abundant in the New Testament that theologically controversial examples are available in plenty, too. Amongst the more celebrated of these are cases of the verb *baptizein*, "to baptize", "to immerse", "to deluge with", or "to overwhelm".

In one of its senses the verb had become a technical term for the initiation rite of Christian belief, i.e. "to baptize". Elsewhere, in the Gospels and Acts, especially when collocated with the word *pneuma* ("Spirit"), it usually has the sense "to deluge with"; and as the Spirit was not literally conceived as a liquid medium the usage is metaphor. The experience of Spirit, or of Spirit-and-fire, so denoted (see e.g. Mark 1.8; Luke 3.16; Acts 1.5, etc.) are thus pictured as *like* an overwhelming deluge of water, totally engulfing.[27]

However, in several Pauline texts, principally Gal. 3.27; Rom. 6.3; and 1 Cor. 12.13, we have instances which have perhaps incorrectly been assumed to be examples of the literal sense of 'to baptize'—i.e. taken to refer to water baptism—but which are arguably instances of a metaphorical use of the verb with the sense "to immerse into". RSV translates Rom. 6.3, 'All of us who have been baptized into Christ Jesus were baptized into his death'. The translators have taken the verb literally and have thus afforded a very high theology of the water rite of baptism. The modifying phrase 'into Christ Jesus' is construed merely to mean something like "with respect to Christ" or "for the sake of Christ".

In a recent Ph.D. thesis J. A. Brown has argued at length that taken with a prepositional phrase governed by *eis* ("into"), the verb *baptizein* would naturally mean "immerse into". The point in focus, then, is not that a water rite conducted 'with respect to Christ' has proved a water rite 'with respect to' Jesus' death. It is rather that the spiritual reality corresponding to conversion-initiation is pictured in terms of being "immersed (or plunged) into" the incorporative Christ. And it is affirmed that as a consequence of that real union with Christ which results—and because Jesus *died* —we too can be said to have been "immersed *into his death*".[28] Brown in no way attempts to sever the relation between this conversion-initiation unification with Christ and the water rite of baptism; indeed he believes that Paul may have chosen the metaphor 'to immerse (or plunge) into' *because* of the associative connection with baptism; but he insists, nevertheless, that it is not that water rite that is the topic of the sentence.

Similarly with respect to 1 Cor. 12.13, Brown argues for a sense corresponding roughly to the translation, "*By* the one Spirit we were all *immersed into* one body . . . and all were irrigated with the one Spirit."[29]

In each case, as in Gal. 3.27 also,[30] we have to do with a metaphor (after all, neither Christ nor a 'body' are liquid entities into which we might be *literally* plunged) for an engulfing and transforming union with Christ which (as 1 Cor. 12.13 emphasizes) is also union with other Christians in a *(metaphorical)* 'body'. Needless to say, the last sentence has raised the further and no less contentious matter of the status (literal or otherwise) of Paul's language of 'the body of Christ', and its correspondence to the spiritual realities he refers to. We cannot introduce here (far less enter into) that debate too; we merely observe that in 1 Cor. 12.13 we have no fewer than *three* difficult metaphors in immediate sequence: 'immersion' by the Spirit into Christ (cf. v.12), the 'body' of Christ, and 'irrigation by' the Spirit (or 'being caused to drink of' the Spirit, depending on how we translate *potizein*). The three metaphors in a single verse warn us of the potential prevalence of metaphors of considerable theological significance elsewhere in the New Testament.

9.5 PARABLE

In parable we have figurative language, but we move beyond a single word or phrase which is to be understood figuratively to what might be perceived as a *coherent* sequence of metaphors or the expansion of a single metaphor. The coherence or expansion frequently, but not invariably, arises from the existence of a core scenario: someone sowing seed, someone on a journey, a court appearance. The scenario is then expanded, and at various points the details of the scenario may be transferred so as to explicate the didactic point of the whole. The intention appears to be the persuasive communication of some central truth, although this does not rule out the identification of subsidiary truths which are being communicated along with the central truth. We should not unthinkingly surrender to Jülicher's insistence that parables have only one point to make.[31]

Linguistics includes within itself the discipline of *stylistics* which obviously concerns itself with the more subjective aspect of human language as communication. For convenience of discussion it is usual to divide figurative language into the two categories of *trope* and *scheme*. The *trope* is essentially a singular occurrence of a figure of speech, and the category includes metaphor, simile, irony, hyperbole and metonymy. The *scheme* involves a related series of figures of speech or a developed pattern of non-literal language, and these would include allegory, rhetorical questions, parallelism and what are termed congeries, carefully structured sequences of statements or phrases all cast into similar syntactical forms. The parable is clearly a *scheme*, not a *trope*.

It was Adolf Jülicher more than any other who directed New Testament scholarship towards a decisive attempt to understand the role of parable in the teaching of Jesus. The radical allegorizing of the parables was abandoned and the search begun for a key that would enable us to penetrate their true meaning. But as Jeremias made clear, 'His efforts to free the parables from the fantastic and arbitrary interpretations of every detail caused him to fall into a fatal error.'[32] The error was to insist not merely that a parable should be understood as conveying a single idea, but that the idea should be as general as possible. The result was a trivializing of profound teaching. Thus the parable of the Unjust Steward was supposed to teach nothing more profound than that a happy future depends on the proper use of the present. In fact it is well for every one who approaches the parables with the determination to understand them to take note of Schippers' warning:

> A man had to be on his guard when someone told him a parable, a *mashal*. For the narrator of a parable always meant more by it than the hearer would grasp on first hearing it.[33]

And this is at least an indication of the meaning of Jesus' words 'You shall indeed hear, but never understand, and you shall indeed see, but never perceive' (Matthew 13.14 equals Isaiah 6.9-10).[34] For in reading the New Testament although we have become accustomed to the *Greek* term 'parable', we forget that what we have is a *Semitic* linguistic form, the *mashal*, which was not merely a vehicle for transmitting the commonplace. Nor was the full significance of the parable likely to be immediately discerned. The linguistic form was usually intended to require of the hearer a willingness to dialogue, to question all presuppositions, to be prepared for the quixotic, the anomaly, the startling, the paradox, and a willingness to act on the perceived teaching of the parable. The hearer of a parable who was *not* prepared to have prevailing views, including his own, challenged would not, could not, perceive what would be plain to others.

There was a second level of error, also, into which Jülicher led his successors, the error of supposing that the presence of allegorical extensions in the interpretation of a parable must be due to the redactional activities of the early Church, since Jesus could not have used this more sophisticated, more developed, form of allegory.[35] This error led on to an impoverishment of the vehicle of parable, in the denial of the legitimacy of any attempt to extend the interpretation of the parable beyond the obvious making of a point. Thus in the parable of the Prodigal Son the question of the identity of the 'father' was taken to be an illegitimate question. It must be recognized that pressing the question could blur the focus of the parable: the younger son has sinned 'against heaven' as well as against his father, against his 'heavenly father' as well as against his 'earthly' father. We have too many fathers! But inevitably behind the story is the idea of the Father who did *not* wait at home for his sons and daughters to return, but sent his one and only Son to seek them out.[36]

Of course Jülicher was very properly reacting against the recurring tendency to find significance in all the details of a parable. Augustine makes reference to various attempts to find a significance in the thirty-fold, sixty-fold, hundred-fold fruitfulness of the Word of God: the hundred-fold represents the martyr, the sixty-fold is the virgin and the thirty-fold is the obedient wife. On another scheme the hundred-fold is the virgin, the sixty-fold the widow and the thirty-fold the obedient wife. And pursuing the matter further it was suggested that the virgin who represented a sixty-fold fruitfulness might reach the hundred-fold level through martyrdom![37] Such ingenuity is clearly misplaced. There is moreover a danger of supposing that because a certain distinction, say of literary genre, occurs in one language, that the distinction may be assumed to transfer across cultural boundaries.[38] There may well be a distinction in English literature between allegory and parable, but the distinction is less readily demonstrated in Semitic literatures. In the Septuagint the Hebrew *mashal* is represented by a number of Greek words, amongst them the word *parabolē*. The most common usage of *mashal* involves the concept of similarity: *this* is like *that*. But *mashal* may be used of a few words, 'Like mother, like daughter' (Ezekiel 16.44), or

of an extended discourse (Job 27.1: 'And Job again took up his *mashal*').
The *mashal* is the dominant form of Hebrew Wisdom writing so that
'Proverbs' begins, 'The *misheley* of Solomon, son of David . . .' This same
range of literary forms is discernible in the New Testament.[39] We have
the parabolic saying in Luke 16.13, 'No servant can serve two masters;
for either he will hate the one and love the other, or he will be devoted
to the one and despise the other. You cannot serve God and mammon.'
There are the parables of simple comparison: 'The kingdom of heaven
is like leaven which a woman took and hid in three measures of flour,
till it was all leavened' (Matthew 13.33), a parable which has an incipient
time-line, and there are narrative parables such as the parable of the
Prodigal Son, which has an extended time-line. Parabolic teaching is
characteristic of the teaching of Jesus. Indeed Mark informs us that
Jesus did not teach without using parable, and we would probably be
right here in assuming that Mark is referring to the whole range of
Hebrew *mashal* rather than to the single literary genre 'parable'.[40]

What we have said thus far should enable us on the one hand to
develop an understanding of what Jesus might have been intending
when he used parable, being aware of the danger of mere superficiality,
the teaching of a commonplace, and on the other hand of unwarranted
allegorizing. Augustine's handling of the Good Samaritan[41] is probably
the best known example of allegorizing, identifying elements of the
parable as in figure 26. Augustine has in fact changed Jesus' *parable* into
an *allegory* of salvation history, and the surest evidence that he is wrong
is the nonsense it makes of Jesus' summons to the lawyer to 'Go and
do likewise' (Luke 10.37).

A second error in understanding parable is failure to recognize the
existence of different categories of parable, parables of contrast and
parables of similarity, for example. Luke 18.1-8 presents the parable of
the Unjust Judge. The judge is plainly said to be unjust and to fear
neither God nor man, and he deals with the widow's case not out of a
concern for justice but merely to gain respite from her continual demand
for his help. It would be wrong, here, to press the detail of the woman
being a widow, but it would be even more wrong to suppose that just
as the judge was reluctant to act, and had to be bullied into doing justice,
so God must be coaxed and bullied and cajoled if he is to act on our
behalf. God is precisely *not* like the unjust judge.[42]

The traveller	is Adam.
Jerusalem	is the heavenly city of peace.
Jericho	means 'moon', and signifies our mortality because it waxes and wanes.
The thieves	are the devil and his angels who stripped Adam of his immortality.
Half dead	because Adam was left dead in sin but alive in the flesh.
Priest and Levite	are the priesthood and ministry of the Old Testament.
Samaritan	means 'guardian' and refers to Jesus.
Bound up his wounds	refers to the restraining of sin.
The oil	is the comfort of good hope.
The wine	is the exhortation to work with a fervent spirit.
The donkey	is the flesh of the incarnation.
Riding on it	means having faith in the incarnation.
The inn	is the church.
The two pence	are the present life and the life to come.
The innkeeper	is Paul.

Figure 26.

9.6 ALLEGORY

Allegories and parables have much in common, and we note in particular that each may appear as narrative, each may exhibit a 'time-line'. But allegory may be distinguished from parable to some extent by the intention of the parable to clarify but the intention of the allegory to mystify.[43]

The intention to mystify must be distinguished from a desire simply to confuse. The author of an allegory will expect his reader to be able to interpret his allegory correctly and therefore uses his symbols in accordance with accepted principles. This is particularly clear in the case of the employment of allegory in apocalyptic literature. We may note in passing that apocalyptic literature may well include prophetic elements in which the word of God is mediated with some clarity, as in the example of the letters to the seven churches in Revelation 2.1—3.22. The apocalyptic literature of the New Testament (including, for example, the 'Little Apocalypse' of Mark chapter 13, the Pauline apocalyptic material in, say, 2 Thessalonians 2.1-12, and John's Revelation) builds on that of the Old Testament, and also on the wider apocalyptic imagery of the ancient Near East. As Aune has commented:

> One common feature of Near Eastern Apocalyptic literature during the Hellenistic and Roman periods was the resurgence and revitalization of archaic patterns of cosmic conflict in which the transition from defeat to victory, chaos to order, sterility to fertility, is brought about by a messianic figure.[44]

Clearly the effectiveness of the use of allegory depends on the ability of the reader to interpret the symbolism appropriately, so that at least so far as the *symbols* employed are concerned, storms and eagles and earthquakes and crowns should have a correspondence to the real world which is an agreed correspondence, not an opaque, skewed correspondence. We have selected the allegory of Revelation 12 for attention because of the important, even decisive, role played by the section in the structure of Revelation. As G. R. Beasley-Murray comments:

> These chapters (12.1—14.2) constitute the most substantial parenthesis in the Revelation. Yet they are more than a parenthesis, for they form the central section of the book. Not only do they come at the mid-point of the work, they provide an understanding of the nature of the conflict in which the church is engaged, and into which John sees she is to be drawn to the limit.[45]

In studying the allegory we are at the same time studying the central theme of the book which is *not* 'the end of the world' but something like 'an explanation of the cosmic battle in which the church is necessarily engaged'.

Allegories make use of symbols. In Revelation 12 we have the term 'portent', *sēmeion*, used of the woman who is a principal character in the allegory which actually extends through two chapters of the apocalypse. An understanding of the inter-actions which constitute the time-line of the allegory depends on the correct interpretation of the signs employed. The principal signs here are three in number: the woman, her child, and the dragon. Michael and the angels also participate in the narrative, but they have not been allegorized: they are allowed to act as themselves precisely because the allegory presents a cosmic conflict involving two worlds: the transcendent world and the material world. The material world is allegorized so that its interaction with the transcendent world can become a possibility.

The identity of the dragon is in fact supplied in verse 9, which marks the end of the first part of the drama. He is 'that ancient serpent, who is called the Devil and Satan, the deceiver of the whole world'. This places the dragon firmly in the context of the Old Testament, universalizing the single act of deception in Genesis 3.13. More difficult is the identification of the woman and of her child. It is superficially tempting to identify the woman as Mary who gives birth to Jesus, and it is this interpretation which lies behind the Roman Catholic representation of Mary crowned with twelve stars (v.1). It is worth noting that such an interpretation would have no support at all from the rest of the New Testament (although this fact could not of itself preclude such an identification if John's language required it). At this point it is somewhat difficult to find a way forward in interpreting the allegory. The symbol of the dragon is interpreted for us, but the symbols of the woman and the child are not. For the symbol of the dragon we might, even without the apocalyptist's assistance, have found the right interpretation perhaps by combining Genesis 3.13 with Isaiah 27.1:

> In that day the Lord with his hard and great and strong sword will
> punish Leviathan the fleeing serpent, Leviathan the twisting serpent,
> and he will slay the dragon that is in the sea.

Good exegesis, here, requires us to look into the referent of 'that day', *ba-yyōm ha-hu'*, a phrase which is used as a discourse marker at 26.1, 27.1, 27.2, 27.12, 28.5, and at many other places in Isaiah, and, importantly, elsewhere in Jewish apocalyptic literature (cf. Jeremiah 4.9; 25.33; 30.7,8; 39.16,17; 48.41; 49.22; 49.26; 50.30). The occurrences of the phrase at 26.1 and 27.1 in fact neatly bracket a further part of Isaiah's prophecy which is strongly evocative of Revelation 12:

> O Lord, in distress they sought thee,
> they poured out a prayer
> when thy chastening was upon them.
> Like a woman with child,
> who writhes and cries out in her pangs,
> when she is near her time,
> so were we because of thee, O Lord;
> we were with child,
> we writhe,
> we have as it were brought forth wind.

> We have wrought no deliverance in the earth,
> and the inhabitants of the world have not fallen.
> Thy dead shall live, their bodies shall rise.
> O dwellers in the dust, awake and sing for joy!
> For thy dew is a dew of light,
> and on the land of the shades thou wilt let it fall.
> (Isaiah 26.16-19)

Translators of this passage make various attempts to represent the be-wildering changes of reference in the Hebrew text ('*Thy* dead shall live, *my* bodies shall rise', for example). The passage is best perceived as an antiphonal poem, involving the people, Yahweh, and other unspecified individual voices.[46] For our present purposes it is important to note that the poem brings into juxtaposition the principal features of the allegory of Revelation 12, the dragon, the pregnant woman, and the proximity of the day. Significantly, the poem is set in the context of a persecuted people, corresponding to the context of John's writing.

The poem, therefore, might point us towards an understanding of the woman as Israel, giving birth to a deliverer. This theme reappears in Isaiah 66.6-7, where by metonymy it is Zion that brings a nation to birth 'in one day . . . in one moment', v.8. The imagery, therefore, is not that of a single verse, but must have become part of the apocalyptic imagery of Israel, an imagery which John could safely assume to be part of the presupposition pool of his readers in a parallel setting but in a very different age. We note, however, that the Hebrew text of Isaiah 26.18 does not necessarily imply the birth of a single (messianic) deliverer: the immediate sense might be of the birth of a heroic generation of deliv-erers.[47]

What we have identified here is a means for recognizing the principal symbols of John's allegory, together with a basic framework for the events in the allegory. It is quite clear that parallel allegories existed in other Near Eastern cultures of the time; commentators make particular reference to the Ugaritic Baal cycle and to the Akkadian creation epic.[48] That the imagery had a continuing fascination is attested by the exis-tence of a Greek myth, in which Python, the great dragon, knows of the threat posed by the unborn son of Leto, but his plan to destroy the child is thwarted when Leto is carried off to an island which is then concealed beneath the waves. The infant, Apollo, is born and reaches his full strength at once, ultimately destroying the dragon. We note also an even closer parallel in the Qumran documents.[49] However, having identified the materials for the allegory already within Jewish tradition there is no reason to suppose that John had any knowledge of these other myths at all. What he has done is to develop the materials he found to hand in his own distinctive way.

The woman, then, is Israel, more precisely Mount Zion, symbolizing Israel, who gives birth to the Messiah. Satan is determined to destroy the child but is thwarted by the resurrection-ascension, which places the Messiah beyond his power. There is a superficial problem here, in that in conventional history the story would read as if the child were snatched away to heaven immediately upon birth. In allegory, however, although we can generally depend on time flowing conventionally from past through the present and to the future we cannot depend on the duration of any particular segment of the time continuum. This is, of course, one of the features of allegory which makes it so agreeable to the transmission of apocalyptic, where, as Peter insists, a day may be as a thousand years and a thousand years as a day (2 Peter 3.8).

For Christology it is significant that the next scene in the developing allegory involves war in heaven in which the dragon is defeated, not by the Messiah-child, but by Michael and his angels. The decisive action of Messiah is past, and complete, and it remains only for God's servants in heaven, led by Michael, and his servants on earth, the Church, to bring about in history what is already accomplished proleptically.

In developing this understanding of the allegory we note the controlling role of the one symbol that is identified for us: the dragon. A second controlling feature is the author himself. He is a Jew, using symbolism in a manner appropriate to a Jew. Thirdly we noted the literary genre: an allegory employed in the service of apocalyptic. And fourthly, in some measure a consequence of the preceding three, we were able to make use of *appropriate* parts of the Jewish Scripture, appropriate in the sense that it was apocalyptic literature and certain to form part of the presupposition pool both of the author and of his readers. On the other hand we have noted the existence of similar allegorical materials in other cultures and at varying points in history, but in the absence of any evidence to suggest that John could have known of them we have not found it necessary to draw on them in interpreting this text.

9.7 CONGREGATIONAL WORSHIP: 1 COR. 11.2-16

To provide a conclusion to this book we turn to one of the most perplexing of all New Testament passages, 1 Corinthians 11.2-16. Although
this is a relatively brief passage it illustrates a number of the aspects of
biblical exegesis which have been our concern. It bristles with problems
of interpretation, beginning with the very important metaphor of the
kephalē, on through the perplexing issue of head-coverings for men and
women, to a tightly constructed double chiastic sequence and finally an
apparently un-Pauline appeal to 'nature' and a last-ditch stand on church
tradition.

The boundaries of the pericope are reasonably clear, although it is
important to note that the text lies within a longer co-text concerned
generally with the problem of concepts of 'freedom' held within the
Corinthian church and specifically with the exercise of the gift of prophecy, a topic which carries forward to 14.40. Paul is not concerned merely
with women in the church, but with the proper and orderly conduct of
the church's worship.

The immediate boundaries of the section are indicated by the introductory commendation at verse 2, introducing the notion of 'tradition',
paradosis, and the somewhat peremptory conclusion at 11.16, which appeals to the traditional 'practice', *synētheia*, of the churches of God. This
of itself indicates the topic of the passage: the customary practice of the
churches of God in relation to the conduct of congregational worship.
The structure of the passage is important. It begins from a paradigmatic
presentation of the relationships which obtain between women, men,
Christ, and God. Then follows a section dealing specifically with women
who pray or prophesy in the context of public worship. Third is an
explanation of an admitted difference between men and women in respect of worship based on a consideration of the creation narratives of
Genesis 1 and 2. Fourth there is what appears to be a somewhat ingen-
uous appeal to 'nature' further to justify the distinction. And then comes
the conclusion which is in essence an appeal (if all else has failed to
convince) to the wider authority of the Christian churches. The text is
best examined by sections and by sentences as well as by words, since
there is scarcely a word or phrase here which does not offer a serious
contribution to an understanding of the whole. The English renderings
can only offer a very general guide to what is in the text, since all

translators agree as to the complexity of the ideas being expressed and, more importantly, perhaps, as to the problem posed by our almost total ignorance of the sociology of the situation under discussion.[50]

The word *kephalē*, 'head', occurs nine times in the passage, four times with a literal meaning, signalled by the collocation with 'hair', and five with a metaphorical meaning. The first, but by no means only, difficulty has been the understanding of the metaphor. In what sense are we to take *kephalē*? The metaphorical usages appropriate to this passage reduce to two: the word either means 'source' or it means 'chief'. The evidence is considered in some detail above (5.2.1) and we conclude (against Fee) that the metaphorical meaning here is 'chief', and that as in other New Testament passages we are presented with what might be termed an innocent subordination of women to men.[51]

The subordination is evident not only in the initial paradigm, but also in the later 'woman is the glory of man' (v.7), and his assertion that woman was created for man (v.9), an assertion which is, of course, entirely agreeable to Genesis 2.18-25.

This element of subordination then explains Paul's parenthetical and adversative 'Nevertheless, *plēn*, . . . woman is not independent of man nor man of woman; for as woman was made from man, so man is now born of woman' (v.11).[52] He is anxious to state an essential interdependence of man and woman that might in some measure counter what he could already anticipate as an indignant response from the feminists of the first-century church at Corinth.

The second fundamental question that must be settled before there can be any attempt at detailed exegesis is the question of the meaning of the words *gynē*, *gynaikos* and *anēr*, *andros*: are we dealing with the question of the relationship between husbands and wives, or the more general question of the relationship between men and women? The words themselves give us no assistance in resolving the question: they may be used indifferently of married or unmarried women and men. It is tempting to resort to 14.33ff. which perhaps informs us of the confusion being then produced in the church at Corinth by wives who involved themselves in public disputes in the context of worship. But it would not be safe to take this route if only because of the uncertainty surrounding both the authenticity and the interpretation of the relevant verses.[53]

However, the central part of the present pericope makes repeated reference to the Genesis creation narrative, and there to the creation of woman *for* man, the prototypical wife and husband. It would seem then that we would not necessarily be *wrong* in understanding the passage as dealing with husbands and wives, but it must be admitted that there are no strong grounds within the text for restricting the subject in this way.

9.7.1 The kernel sentences

The actual relationships between the propositions of the text are not difficult to determine, but an identification of the kernels does assist by making plain the structure of the argument. There are 47 kernels which together constitute the basic structure. The kernels are readily grouped into five clusters which may be considered in turn. We have indicated the places where the key words 'man', woman', 'head' appear.

1. I want you to understand.

2. The head of the man is Christ.
3. The head of the woman is man.   Section One: v.3
4. The head of Christ is God.

5. A man prays/prophesies.
6. His head is covered.
7. He dishonours his head.

8. A woman prays/prophesies.
9. Her head is not covered.
10. She dishonours her head.   Section Two: vv.4-6
11. It is the same thing.
12. She shaves her head.
13. A woman will not cover (her head).
14. She shaves (her head).
15. It is disgraceful.
16. A woman shaves (her head).
17. She covers (her head).

18. A man not-covers his head.

19. He is the image and glory of God.
20. Woman is the . . . glory of man.
21. Man (was) not (made) from woman.
22. Woman (was) (made) from man.
23. Man (was) not created for woman.
24. Woman (was) (created) for man.   Section Three: vv.7-12

25. A woman 'authoritys' her head.
26. The angels (require it) (the 'authority').
27. They are in the Lord.
28. Woman is not independent of man.
29. Man is not independent of woman.
30. Woman was (made) from man.
31. Man is (made) from woman.
32. Everything is (made) from God.

33. You judge (this matter).

34. It is appropriate?
35. A woman prays to God.
36. She does not cover (her head).
37. Nature teaches.
38. A man wears long hair.   Section Four: vv.13-15
39. It is disgraceful.
40. A woman wears long hair.
41. It is her glory.
42. It (long hair) is given to her.
43. It covers her.

44. He is contentious.
45. We do not recognize.   Section Five: v. 16
46. The churches (do not recognize).
47. You practice this.

9.7.2 Section One: A Basic Paradigm
The head of the man is Christ
But *(de)* The head of the woman is man (husband?)

And *(de)* The head of Christ is God.

The paradigm is reasonably clear: woman, man, Christ, God. The presentation of three dyads[54] is intended to make clear the proper relationship between the lowest pair, woman and man. As Christ relates to God, so man should relate to Christ, and so woman should relate to man. The relationship is clearly one of subordination. It is not unimportant that only four chapters further on in this epistle Paul is able to write:

> Then comes the end, when he delivers the kingdom to God the Father after destroying every rule and every authority and power. For he must reign until he has put all his enemies under his feet. . . . When all things are subjected to him, then the Son himself will also be subjected to him who put all things under him, that God may be everything to every one. (1 Corinthians 15.24-8)

Whatever we may consider to be the theological significance of this 'subordination' it is clearly present in some form in Paul's thinking at the time of writing this epistle.

Paul has begun by a reference to tradition; he will conclude with a further commendation of tradition. He has presented metaphorically what is presumably a tradition in the churches, the tradition of the subordination of women to men. That tradition is being questioned at Corinth, and women's hair is somehow the symbol of revolt. The second section deals with the visible symbol.

9.7.3 Section Two: The question of head and hair

	A man prays/prophesies
	His head is covered
	He dishonours his head
But *(de)*	A woman prays/prophesies
	Her head is not covered
	She dishonours her head
For *(gar)*	It is the same thing
As if *(kai)*	She shaves her head
For *(gar)*	A woman will not cover (her head)

Then *(kai)*	She shaves (her head)
But *(de)*	It is disgraceful
	A woman shaves (her head)
	She covers (her head)

The essential argument here appears to be that both men and women may take audible part in public worship, through prophesying and through praying. But men are not women. Women are not men. Women are subordinate to men and there should be visible evidence of that subordination. The visible evidence was the woman's head covering, but some at least of the women had abandoned it. It is not unlikely that the problem arose out of an exaggerated realization of the eschatological expectations of the church. With the *eschaton* would come the end of the distinction between male and female: then why should not that distinction be ended now?

It is entirely possible that Paul was partly responsible for the disorders in the church at Corinth. The phenomenon of glossolalia was out of hand . . . but Paul confesses that *he* spoke with tongues more than anybody (14.18)![55] Had his enthusiasm shown itself at Corinth and is he now regretting it? And does this in part explain Paul's evident lack of enthusiasm for the present argument? It was, after all, part of his own teaching that there was, now, in Christ, neither male nor female (Galatians 3.28). As Fee says of this passage, 'It lacks almost all of the evidence of rhetoric and emotion that pervades the rest of the letter.'[56] Is the lack of enthusiasm explained by Paul's awareness of the source of the problem: himself?

Alternatively we may ask if the situation was very much more serious than appears: had the blurring of the distinction between the sexes gone so far as to result in widespread homosexuality, that sin which seems to have been perceived by Jews as particularly a gentile vice, and to have been peculiarly loathed accordingly? Might this explain Paul's unaccustomed uneasiness in the argument? We note, however, that earlier in this same letter Paul had grappled with a distasteful moral issue (5.1-5) and there is no particular reason to suppose that he would not similarly have dealt firmly with the problem of homosexuality had it been the issue.

The distinction between the two sexes was to be seen in the head covering. Men were *not* to use a head covering, women *were* to use a head covering. Without further argument Paul simply states that the uncovered head of a man did *not* dishonour Christ, but the uncovered head of a woman *did* dishonour her husband. At this point it becomes clear that if the argument relates generally to the relationship between men and women, it is most convincingly presented as it affected the relationship between husbands and wives. It does not appear reasonable to suppose that if a woman prayed with her head not covered she dishonoured all the men in the church.

But we must ask, *how* is he dishonoured? The fact of being uncovered could not of itself dishonour him. The uncovering must, then, signify something dishonourable or, alternatively, (and what amounts to the same thing) be accompanied by something which is dishonourable. The problem is metonymic. And there are several more-or-less plausible solutions.

1. That the uncovering of the head was the failure to wear the shawl that was customary for women in Corinth, but which was dispensed with by prostitutes. The women in the church were then laying themselves open to being accosted in the streets, and in this way shamed their husbands. This is an attractive explanation, but the evidence either for women in general wearing a shawl over their heads in public, or for prostitutes not wearing the shawl in public is, to say the least, equivocal.[57] In the illustrations that we have from the period, some women are so covered, some are not, and we are not told whether any of those pictured are prostitutes.

As to the practice for men, the evidence concerning the adoption of the *tallith* head covering by Jews is too late for it to be of help in determining practice at this time.[58] The implication of this passage is that at least in the Christian congregation there was no such practice.

However we note that although there is no direct reference to a shawl or veil other than that in v.15, verse 5 reads *akatakalyptō(i) tē(i) kephalē*, crudely to be rendered as 'as to the head, uncovered'. The word *katakalyptomai* generally does refer to the wearing of some kind of head covering. It was not, in fact, required in either Roman or Greek society, either in secular or religious situations, that a woman wear a head-covering in public. However, according to Oepke it was the custom amongst Jews in the east, who characterized gentile women as those who would go unveiled in public. The argument, then, is that Paul is attempting to impose a specifically Jewish practice on the mainly gentile congregation at Corinth, a congregation which might well have responded entirely negatively to Paul's appeal to 'nature', in v. 14.[59]

2. A second explanation is generally similar to the first, but suggests that the passage does not deal with shawls or veils, but with literally letting the hair down.[60] It is said that women generally dressed their hair, and pinned it up, but that prostitutes allowed their hair to be *akatakalyptos*, 'uncovered', or 'loosed'. The word is certainly used in that sense in the Septuagint rendering of Leviticus 13.45, 'The leper who has the disease shall wear torn clothes and let the hair of his head hang loose.' Against this view it must be said that although *akatalyptos* may mean 'loosed', its more usual meaning is 'uncovered' and that 'uncovered' fits the context perfectly well. And we may at this point simply anticipate a comment to be made below, that in verse 15, when Paul comments that a woman's hair is given to her *anti* a shawl, we are not obliged to understand *anti* as 'instead of': it may simply mean "as" or "for", implying equivalence of function.

9.7.4 Section Three: An Appeal to the Events of Creation

For *(men gar)*	A man not cover his head	
(Because)	He is the image and glory of God	
But *(de)*	Woman is the glory of man	
For *(gar)*	Man (was) not (made) from woman	a
But *(alla)*	Woman (was)(made) from man	b
Neither *(kai gar)*	Man (was) not created for *(dia)* woman	a'
But *(alla)*	Woman (was) (created) for *(dia)* man	b'
That is why *(dia touto)*	A woman 'authoritys' her head	
Because of *(dia)*	The angels (require it)	
Nevertheless *(plēn)*	(They are) in the Lord	
Neither *(oute)*	Woman is not independent of man	b'
Nor *(oute)*	Man is not (independent) of woman	a'
For *(houtōs gar)*	Woman (was)(made) from man	b

| So *(houtōs kai)* | Man (is) (made) from woman | a |
| And *(de)* | Everything is (made) from God | |

The structure is clearly chiastic as the above outline shows, with the whole argument coming neatly back to the Genesis creation narrative from which it took its start. It is interrupted by the entirely unexpected and unexplained reference to *exousia* and the *angeloi* in verse 10.

It is at this point that the controlling significance of the initial metaphor of the head becomes apparent. If the initial metaphor means no more than that man is the *source* or *origin* of woman then the third section cannot be taken to imply any measure of subordination of woman to man, or of wife to husband. And this leaves the adversative 'nevertheless' of v.11 lacking in force, and the dependent clauses robbed of significance. Granted, however, that the initial metaphor is intended to establish a subordinate relationship for the woman, vv.11-12 take an entirely understandable ameliorating role: the fact is that 'in the Lord' these necessary distinctions ultimately lose their significance.

But the parousia is not yet, the distinction has not yet disappeared, there are still husbands and wives, there are still men and women, and it is entirely proper for their relationship to be decorously maintained and signalled. It seems to us difficult to deny the subordinating relationship implied by verses 8-9. According to these verses, woman not only came *from* man: she was actually created *for* man. The subordination cannot reasonably be removed from these statements, and they entirely conform to the expectations raised by the metaphors which stand at the beginning of the argument.

It is also important to the understanding of Paul's argument that woman is the 'glory' of man. It is of course true that Genesis 1.27 establishes the fact that man and woman were both created in the image of God, and thus are *his* glory. But Paul makes a careful distinction as he describes the condition of man and woman: the former was created in the image and glory of God, but woman is precisely *not* created in the image and glory of man. She is created in the *image* of God, but is the *glory* of man. Thus, as Morna Hooker clearly expresses it:

> The obligation which lies upon the woman is based on the fact that she is the glory of the man. In her case, therefore, her uncovered head will reflect his glory, both because she is his 'glory', and because

he is her 'head.'[61]

The uncomfortable insertion into the chiastic structure of the reference to *exousia* on the woman's head, and to the *angeloi* (v.10) requires some consideration although the verse does not appear significantly to advance the argument. The word *exousia* occurs ten times in this letter, each time indicating a kind of executive authority, the ability to do something: the ability to control the will (7.37), the ability to eat foods shunned by others (8.9), the ability to have food supplied by others (9.4) or to be accompanied by a wife (9.5), or absolutely, as in the reference to 'authorities' in 15.24. This makes RSV's 'veil' at 11.10 at first surprising,[62] although it is quite apparent that the translators see the veil or head-covering as a sign of authority, and *exousia* as being used metonymically.[63] What is less clear is whether the head-covering is intended to represent the fact that she accepts her husband's authority even though she is praying or prophesying in the congregation, or whether it is a signal to the attendant angels, that under the New Dispensation she has an *exousia* which she did not have under the Old.

The *angeloi* are mentioned in 4.9; 6.3; here; and in 13.1. It is possible to call in 6.3 to assist in interpreting the later reference: Paul confirms an implied hierarchy in 4.9, 'world, angels, men', and states that humanity is so far superior to angels as ultimately to act as their judges. It would then suggest that women are to cover their heads not, as sometimes suggested, so that the angels would not be seduced by the beauty of women, but to affirm a creation order, which might then be expanded to the sequence: world, angels, women, men, Christ, God.

The uncovered head would then be taken as a disavowing of the authority of the husband and by implication of the authority of God who is responsible for the ordering of creation. In deciding between this interpretation and that which sees the head-covering as signalling to the angels an innovative New Covenant authority[64] granted to the woman we once again look to the introductory metaphors and their controlling influence on the rest of the argument.

9.7.5 Section Four: An Ingenuous Appeal to Nature

> You judge (this matter)
> It is appropriate?

                                   A woman prays to God
                                   She does not cover (her head)

Does not *(oude)*   Nature teaches
                                   A man wears long hair
                                   It is disgraceful

But *(de)*   A woman wears long hair
                                   It is her glory
Because *(hoti)*   It (her hair) is given to her
                                   It (her long hair) covers her
                                   (anti, for a covering *[peribolaiou])*

The appeal to contemporary practice, not even the particular practice of
the church, is not typical of Paul. He is, of course, saying no more than
that at that time it was normal for men to have shorter hair and for
women to have longer hair, and that in contemporary society those who
went against this convention, whether men having long hair or women
having short hair, ran the risk of the strong disapproval of the community. It is not necessary to press the recognition that *anti* may mean
'instead of': it may also mean equivalence.[65] Woman has long hair in the
normal course of events, which suggests that she should cover her head.
There is, then, nothing odd in suggesting that in the congregation she
should wear some kind of head covering. Man does not have long hair
in the normal course of events, so it is not surprising that in the congregation he should not wear a head covering.

   Of course it is true that both man and woman have their origin in God,
and it is true that man is now born from woman. But it remains unal-
terably true that there is a creation distinction between the two, and it
is still true that woman is the glory of man, and that man must not be
glorified in the congregational worship. So the woman is to be covered.

9.7.6 Section Five: Conclusion: An Appeal to the Tradition of the Churches

If *(ei de)*   He is contentious
                                   We do not recognize

Nor *(oude)*	The Churches (do not recognize)
	You practice this

Ultimately Paul appeals to the common practice of the churches. Perhaps he is aware that his arguments are not entirely clear, nor totally convincing. He has not felt free to disclose what information he had about the practice of the women of Corinth, nor where he obtained that information (contrast his references to the letter written to him [7.1]; to the visit of Stephanas, Fortunatus, and Achaicus [16.17]; and the mention of Chloe's people [1.11]). He is unwilling to reveal his sources and that, arguably, weakens his hand. The final section of the argument allows us a glimpse of recent events at Corinth: the irregular practice of certain women had been commented upon, and some of the congregation had responded contentiously. Well, writes Paul, you may not accept my arguments on this subject, but you can't easily reject the practice of the other churches.

9.7.7 Summary

To summarize the argument, women may pray and prophesy in the congregation. But women are not men, the creation distinction between the sexes is not yet abolished, and the creation hierarchy must still be observed. Woman is still the glory of man as she was from the beginning, and in worship *man's* glory must not be on display. For the sake of good order women are to wear a head-covering, indicating that although in the New Covenant there is, before God, no differentiation between the sexes, all recognize that even in Christian society the differentiation between the sexes is to be acknowledged.

This comparatively brief text provides a useful example of the complexity of the method inherent in responsible New Testament exegesis. The use of metaphor and its relationship to the semantic content of the related structure, the objectively determined boundaries of the pericope, the chiastic structures at the heart of the argument, the clearly defined stages in the developing discourse, and the necessity of attempting exegesis without recourse to an artificial squeezing of the text into conformity with parallel passages, all illustrate the need for methodical analysis and interpretation.

And yet at the end of it all we are still left with uncertainty as to the meaning of what Paul wrote. The meanest member of the congregation at Corinth was in a better position than we are to understand the text. Real language can only satisfactorily be understood from cotext *and* context. The former we have. The latter is irrevocably lost.

Notes

[1] See John Lyons, *Language, Meaning and Context,* London, Collins (Fontana), 1981, p.19.

[2] *The Language and Imagery of the Bible*, p.133.

[3] We are, of course, aware of the fact that a word cannot 'abandon the dictionary for the street', as if it had a will of its own. But the metaphor is deliberately employed to signal the subjective process which enhances meaning and which is the subject of this chapter.

[4] See, for example, Umberto Eco on metaphor, *Semiotics and the Philosophy of Language,* p.89.

[5] See Beekman and Callow, *Translating the Word of God,* p.331, especially on the question of the significance to be given to the two prepositions used here, *pros* and *eis.* See also F. Blass and A. Debrunner, *A Greek Grammar of the New Testament,* 477(1), on the same verse. Alternatively it may be that the noun *'pistis'* is to be translated 'faithfulness' (so F. F. Bruce, *Paul: Apostle of Liberty,* p.393) or construed in two slightly different senses, depending on whether it is taken with Jews or the saints as its 'object'. For fuller discussion see P. T. O'Brien, *Colossians* (Word Biblical Commentary), Waco, Word, 1982, pp.278f., and the literature cited there.

[6] C. H. Talbert, *Literary Patterns, Theological Themes and the Genre of Luke-Acts,* Missoula, Scholars Press, 1974, pp.56-8.

[7] C. L. Blomberg, 'Midrash, Chiasmus and the Outline of Luke's Central Section' in R. T. France and D. Wenham (eds.), *Gospel Perspectives,* vol. III, Sheffield, JSOT, 1983, pp.217-62.

[8] J. Bligh, *Galatians,* London, St Paul Publications, 1969. His reviewers have not been convinced.

[9] At least if the 'superlative apostles' are to be identified with the earlier, self-vaunting, triumphalist 'false-apostles'; on this, see e.g. P. W. Barnett, 'Opposition in Corinth?', *JSNT* 22(1984), pp.3-17. Barrett *(inter alios),* however, argues that the term refers to the 'pillar' apostles, Peter, James, and John.

[10] See also S. McFague, *Metaphorical Theology,* New York, Fortress Press, 1982, p.16.

[11] *The Language and Imagery of the Bible,* p.111.

[12] In this particular case it is not necessary to assume that we have Matthaean redactional activity, recasting an original Semitic figure of speech into a more literal form. Jesus himself may well have used the same idea in two distinct

literary expressions on two distinct occasions for two different audiences.

13H. W. Fowler, *Modern English Usage*, quoted in Caird, *The Language and Imagery of the Bible*, p.144.

14Eco, *Semiotics and the Philosophy of Language*, p.89.

15But see Swanson, 'Towards a psychology of metaphor', in *Critical Inquiry*, 5.1 (1979), pp.163-8.

16Eco, ibid., p.92.

17For this whole discussion see Eco, *Semiotics and the Philosophy of Language*, chap. 3. Eco's *componential analysis* of the separate terms of a metaphor, and the resultant interpenetrating network of meanings when allied to cotext and context provide a powerful method for the explication of metaphor.

18See the convenient summary of various interpretations in C. E. Cranfield, *The Epistle to the Romans* (ICC), Edinburgh, T. & T. Clark, 1979, pp.648-50.

19Vincent Taylor, *The Epistle to the Romans*, London, Epworth, 1956, p.84.

20But note that Origen, Pelagius, and Augustine each interpreted the saying along those lines; see Cranfield, *Romans*, p.649.

21William Klassen, 'Coals of Fire: Sign of Repentance or Revenge?', *New Testament Studies* 9(1962-3), pp.337-50.

22Cf. Job 37.22, 'Out of the north comes golden splendour', a reference to clear skies, bright sun, and cold nights.

23A. Cohen, *Proverbs*, London, Soncino Press, 1945, p.171.

24Oxford, OUP, 1900.

25Cf. William McKane, *Proverbs* (Old Testament Library), London, SCM, 1970, who briefly considers the relevance of the Egyptian penitential ritual to the interpretation of the metaphor, and concludes, 'Certainly there is little doubt that it is the penitence of the enemy which is indicated by the use of this imagery' (p.592).

26*Commentary on Romans*, London, SCM, 1980, p.349.

27See M. M. B. Turner, *Vox Evangelica* 12(1981), pp.50-3.

28J. A. Brown, *Metaphorical Language in Relation to Baptism in the Pauline Literature*, unpublished Ph.D. dissertation, Edinburgh 1982, chap.4.

29Brown, ibid., chap.9.

30On which see Brown, ibid., chap.5.

31See Caird's criticism of Jülicher's views in *The Language and Imagery of the Bible*, chap.9.

32*Rediscovering the Parables*, London, SCM, 1966, p.12. But see also A. C. Thiselton, 'Reader-Response Hermeneutics, Action Models, and the Parables of Jesus', in R. Lundin, A. C. Thiselton, C. Walhout, *The Responsibility of Hermeneutics*, p.96, 'In all fairness to Jülicher, we ought not perhaps to accept without qualification the verdict of A. M. Hunter and others that his interpretations of the parables reduce them to nothing more than prudential platitudes.'

[33]R. Schippers, 'The *mashal* character of the Parable of the Pearl', in F. L. Cross (ed.), *Studia Evangelica* II, Berlin, Akademie-Verlag, 1964, p.238f.

[34]Note here A. C. Thiselton's important discussion of this crux in the study of the parable as a literary form, in his chapter 'Reader-Response Hermeneutics', in R. Lundin, A. C. Thiselton, C. Walhout, *The Responsibility of Hermeneutics*, pp.111ff. He concludes that the saying indicates that 'Jesus used parables *in order to prevent premature understanding unaccompanied by inner change'*.

[35]See R. E. Brown's helpful critique in chap. 13, 'Parable and Allegory Reconsidered' of his *New Testament Essays*, London, Chapman, 1967.

[36]See K. E. Bailey, *Poet and Peasant*, pp.188ff., for what he sees to be the Christological implications of the son's return.

[37]See P. Schaff (ed.), *The Nicene and Post-Nicene Fathers: First series, vol. III, St. Augustine*, Grand Rapids, Eerdmans, 1978, *De Virginitate*, p.434.

[38]See G. B. Caird, *The Language and Imagery of the Bible*, p.160: 'The problems presented by parable and allegory are quite different, arising largely from overzealous definition.'

[39]See article 'Parable' in *The Interpreter's Dictionary of the Bible*.

[40]But see the fuller discussion by C. E. Carlston, *The Parables of the Triple Tradition*, Philadelphia, Fortress, 1975, p.98f., and A. C. Thiselton, *The Responsibility of Hermeneutics*, p.86.

[41]C. H. Dodd, *The Parables of the Kingdom*, p.13. Jeremias deals with the same parable in *The Parables of Jesus* (New Testament Library), London, SCM, 1963. R. H. Stein's *An Introduction to the Parables of Jesus*, Philadelphia, Westminster Press, 1981, provides a fairly elementary introduction to the genre, although his key chapter 'Interpreting the Parables Today', offers four principles of interpretation of which the *first* is 'Seek the one main point'!

[42]But for a very different view see J. Derrett, *Studies in the New Testament* vol. I, Leiden, Brill, 1977, pp.32-47.

[43]Caird observes that parables and allegories form a continuous spectrum, but suggests that they are distinguished generally in that parables are similitudes having a high degree of development of detail (like allegories), but a relatively low degree of intended correspondence: *The Language and Imagery of the Bible*, chap.9.

[44]D. E. Aune, *Prophecy in Early Christianity*, Grand Rapids, Eerdmans, 1983, p.112. A. Bentzen commented, 'In late Judaism and in the Early Church we observe a "renaissance of mythology" ', *King and Messiah*, London, Lutterworth, 1955, p.79.

[45]*The Book of Revelation* (New Century Bible), London, Oliphants, 1974, p.191. We are pleased to acknowledge the work done on the allegory of Revelation 12.1-

9 by Ms. Susan Thomas, formerly a student at London Bible College.

[46]See especially the careful reconstruction by J. D. W. Watts, *Isaiah 1-33* (Word Biblical Commentary), Waco, Word, 1985, p.337.

[47]It is interesting that LXX at this point appears to interpret the text as messianic: ' . . . we have brought forth thy beloved *(tō[i] agapētō[i] sou)'.*

[48]See, for example, G. R. Beasley-Murray, *The Book of Revelation*, pp.192-3.

[49]Beasley-Murray, op.cit., p.194. He quotes Dupont-Sommer's translation of the Qumran thanksgiving hymn E, from *The Essene Writings from Qumran*, Oxford, Blackwell, 1961, p.207. Dupont-Sommers comments, 'Hymn E is one of the most important and the most difficult to interpret of the whole collection'.

[50]See Fee's mournful but realistic footnote on p.492 of his commentary *The First Epistle to the Corinthians*, Grand Rapids, Eerdmans, 1987.

[51]But see J. Murphy-O'Connor, *1 Corinthians*, p.107: 'There is not the slightest hint that he wants to inculcate the subordination of one sex to the other.'

[52]See Fee, p.522, n39.

[53]The grammatical structure makes it clear that we are dealing with three parallel dyads, and not with a single chain, as Murphy-O'Connor *(1 Corinthians*, p.108) seems to assume.

[54]See Fee, pp. 699ff., and Grudem, *The Gift of Prophecy in 1 Corinthians*, Washington, University Press of America, 1982, pp.239-55.

[55]Cf. Christopher Rowland, *Christian Origins*, p.277, and especially J. Drane, *Paul, Libertine or Legalist?* London, SPCK, 1975.

[56]Ibid., p.491. Indeed, one is disposed to say that Paul's arguments in this passage are not particularly convincing, and his final appeal to tradition peculiarly weak.

[57]But see the somewhat tendentious discussion in Florence Bulle, *"God Wants You Rich" and Other Enticing Doctrines*, Minneapolis, Bethany House, 1983, p.92f. Fee gives a judicious and scholarly summary of the facts in *The First Epistle to the Corinthians*, n80, p.511. The assumption relating the unveiled head to prostitutes is characterized by Fee succinctly: 'It seems to be a case of one scholar's guess becoming a second scholar's footnote and a third scholar's assumption.'

[58]Fee, ibid., p.507.

[59]See particularly the entry *katakalyptō* by A. Oepke in *TDNT*, vol. III. Oepke comments, 'In general one may say that etiquette as regards the veil becomes stricter the more one moves east' (p.562).

[60]J. B. Hurley, *Man and Woman in Biblical Perspective*, Leicester, IVP, 1981, and J. Murphy-O'Connor, *1 Corinthians*, pp.103-9.

[61]'Authority on her head: an examination of 1 Cor.xi.10', *NTS* X (1963-4), p.415.

[62]Cf. article *exousia* in *TDNT*, where W. Foerster refers to Kittel's suggestion that an Aramaic word had the two meanings, 'to conceal' and 'to rule'.

[63]Granted the metonymy there is no difficulty in seeing the head-covering as

indicating the husband's authority, no reason why it *must* indicate that of the wife. Of course it is convenient that the head-covering also served to conceal the *doxa* of the women from the gaze of the men. As several commentators note this was far more likely to produce disorder in the church's worship than was the lustful gaze of the angels! One wonders if Paul had this, also, pragmatically in mind, and that this, too, helps to explain his discomfort in the arguments he is employing.

[64]See the argument of Murphy-O'Connor at this point. Although he recognizes that verses 7-9 tend to 'make one think that Paul's purpose is to prove the subordination of women' he relates the *angeloi* to the Law-giving at Sinai (Gal. 3.19), and suggests that the covered head signals to the angels that the Law they had mediated had now been changed *(1 Corinthians*, pp.108-9).

[65]See Fee's helpful discussion, *The First Epistle to the Corinthians*, pp.528-9, and F. Blass and A. Debrunner, *A Greek Grammar of the New Testament*, p.208.

Bibliography

Adams, V., *An Introduction to Modern English Word-Formation*, London, Longmans, 1973.

Aitchison, J., *Linguistics*, Sevenoaks, Hodder, 1987.

Aune, D. E., Review of Hans Betz, *Galatians: a Commentary on Paul's Letter to the Churches of Galatia*, in *Religious Studies Review* 7,4(1981), pp.323-8.

_____. *Prophecy in Early Christianity*, Grand Rapids, Eerdmans, 1983.

_____. *The New Testament in its Literary Environment*, Philadelphia, Westminster, 1987.

Bailey, Kenneth, *Through Peasant Eyes*, Grand Rapids, Eerdmans, 1980.

Baldinger, K., *Semantic Theory*, Oxford, Blackwell, 1980.

Barnwell, K., *Introduction to Semantics and Translation*, High Wycombe, SIL, 1980[2].

Barr, J., *The Semantics of Biblical Language*, Oxford, OUP, 1961.

_____. *Biblical Words For Time*, London, SCM, 1962, 1969[2].

_____. *Old and New in Interpretation*, London, SCM, 1966.

_____. 'Common Sense and Biblical Language', Bib 49 (1968).

_____. 'The Image of God in the Book of Genesis—a Study of Terminology' *BJRL* 51 (1968).

Bauer, L., *English Word-Formation*, Cambridge, CUP, 1983.

Barrett, C. K., *The Gospel According to St John*, London, SPCK, 1978[2].

_____. *The First Epistle to the Corinthians*, London, Black, 1971.

Barth, Marcus, *Ephesians 4-6* (Anchor Bible), New York, Doubleday, 1960.

Beasley-Murray, G. R., *The Book of Revelation* (New Century Bible), London, Oliphants, 1974.

_____. *Jesus and the Kingdom of God*, Exeter, Paternoster, 1986.

Bedale, S., 'The Meaning of *Kephalē* in the Pauline Epistles', *JTS* 5 (1954).

Beekman, J., and Callow, J., *Translating the Word of God*, Grand Rapids, Zondervan, 1974.

Beekman, J.; Callow, J.; and Kopesec, M.; *The Semantic Structure of Written Communication*, Dallas, SIL, 1981[5].

Beker, J. C., *Paul the Apostle*, Edinburgh, T. & T. Clark, 1980.

Belleville, Linda, 'Born of Water and Spirit', *Trinity Journal*, 1,2(1980).

Berlin, Adele, *Poetics and Interpretation of Biblical Narrative*, Sheffield, The Almond Press, 1983.

Bernard, J. H., *The Gospel According to St John* (International Critical Commentary), Edinburgh, T. & T. Clark, 1928.

Betz, H. D., 'The Literary Composition and Function of Paul's Letter to the Galatians', *NTS* 21(1975).

Blass, F., and Debrunner, A., *A Greek Grammar of the New Testament and Other Early Christian Literature*, ed., Funk, R. W., Chicago, University of Chicago Press, 1961.

Bloomfield, Leonard, *Language*, London, Allen & Unwin, 1935.

Bolinger, D., *Meaning and Form*, London, Longmans, 1983[3].

———— and Sears, D. A., *Aspects of Language*, New York, Harcourt, Brace, Jovanovich, 1975[2].

Boman, T., *Sprache und Denken: Ein Auseinandersetzung*, Göttingen, VR, 1968.

Borgen, Peder, *Bread from Heaven*, Leiden, Brill, 1965.

Bourne and Ekstrand, *Psychology*, New Jersey, Holt, Rinehart and Winston, 1979[3].

Brown, G. and Yule, G., *Discourse Analysis*, Cambridge, CUP, 1983.

Brown, Raymond E., *The Gospel According to John* (Anchor Bible), London, Chapman, 1966.

————. *New Testament Essays*, London, Chapman, 1967.

Brueggemann, W., *Genesis*, Atlanta, John Knox Press, 1982.

Bulle, Florence, *'God Wants You Rich' and Other Enticing Doctrines*, Minneapolis, Bethany House, 1983.

Burchfield, R., ed., *Studies in Lexicography*, Oxford, Clarendon, 1987.

Burres, K. L., *Structural Semantics in the Study of the Pauline Understanding of Revelation*, unpublished Ph.D. dissertation, Evanston, Northwestern University, 1970.

Caird, G. B., *Paul's Letters From Prison*, Oxford, OUP, 1976.

————. *The Language and Imagery of the Bible*, London, Duckworth, 1980.

Callow, Kathleen, *Discourse Considerations in Translating the Word of God*, Grand Rapids, Zondervan, 1974.

Caragounis, C., *The Ephesian "Mysterion": Meaning and Content*, Lund, Gleerup, 1977.

————. *The Son of Man*, Tübingen, Mohr, 1986.

Carlston, C. E., *The Parables of the Triple Tradition*, Philadelphia, Fortress, 1975.

Carroll, John B., *Language and Thought* (Foundations of Modern Psychology), Englewood Cliffs, New Jersey, 1964.

Carson, D. A., *Exegetical Fallacies*, Grand Rapids, Baker, 1984.

Chomsky, Noam, *Syntactic Structures*, The Hague, Mouton, 1957.

———. *Current Issues in Linguistic Theory*, New York, Humanity Press, 1964.

———. *Language and Responsibility*, Hassocks, Sussex, Harvester Press, 1979.

Clark, H. H., and Clark, E. V., *Psychology and Language*, New York, Harcourt, Brace, Jovanovich, 1977.

Clines, David, *The Esther Scroll*, Sheffield, JSOT (Supplement Series, 30), 1984.

Cohen, A., *Proverbs*, London, Soncino Press, 1945.

Cole, P., and Morgan, J. L., eds., *Syntax and Semantics*, New York, Academic Press, 1975.

Cole, R. W., ed., *Current Issues in Linguistic Theory*, London, Indiana University Press, 1977.

Conroy, Charles, *Absalom, Absalom!*, Rome, Biblical Institute Press (Analecta Biblica 81), 1978.

Corner, J., and Hawthorn, J., *Communication Studies*, London, Arnold, 1980.

Cotterell, F. P., 'The Nicodemus Conversation', *Expository Times* 96,8 (1985).

———. 'Sociolinguistics and Biblical Interpretation', *Vox Evangelica* 16 (1986).

Coulthard, M., *An Introduction to Discourse Analysis*, Harlow, Longmans, 1977.

Cranfield, C. E., *The Epistle to the Romans* (ICC), Edinburgh, T. & T. Clark, 1979.

Cruse, D. A., *Lexical Semantics*, Cambridge, CUP, 1986.

Crystal, David, *A Dictionary of Linguistics and Phonetics*, Oxford, Blackwell, 1985.

Deissmann, A., *Light From the Ancient East*, London, Hodder, 1910, 1911[2].

Derrett, J., *Studies in the New Testament* I, Leiden, Brill, 1977.

van Dijk, T. A., *Text and Context*, London and New York, Longmans, 1977.

Dodd, C. H., *The Parables of the Kingdom*, London, Fontana (Collins), 1961[2].

Donaldson, T. L., 'Parallels: Use, Misuse and Limitations', *EvQ* 55(1983), pp.193-210.

Dressler, W., ed., *Current Trends in Textlinguistics*, Berlin, de Gruyter, 1978.

Dunn, J. D. G., *Christology in the Making*, London, SCM, 1980.

Eco, Umberto, *Semiotics and the Philosophy of Language*, London, Macmillan, 1984.

Elkins, W. R., *A New English Primer*, London, MacMillan, 1974.

Erickson, R. J., *Biblical Semantics, Semantic Structure, and Biblical Lexicology: A Study of Methods, with Special Reference to the Pauline Lexical Field of 'Cognition'*, unpublished Ph.D. dissertation, Fuller Theological Seminary, 1980.

Faur, José, *Golden Doves with Silver Dots*, Indiana University Press, 1986.

Fee, G. D., *New Testament Exegesis: A Handbook for Students and Pastors*, Philadelphia, Westminster Press, 1983.

———. *The First Epistle to the Corinthians*, Grand Rapids, Eerdmans, 1987.

Fish, S., *Is There a Text in This Class: The Authority of Interpretive Communities*, Cambridge, Harvard University Press, 1980.

Firth, J. R., *Papers in Linguistics, 1934-1951*, London, OUP, 1957.

Fitzmyer, J. A., *The Gospel According to Luke* (Anchor Bible), New York, Doubleday, 1981, 1985.

Friedrich, G., 'Die Problematik eines Theologischen Wörterbuchs zum Neuen Testament' in Aland, K., ed. *Studia Evangelica*, Berlin, Akademie Vlg., 1959, pp.481-6.

——————. 'Semasiologie und Lexikologie', *TLZ* 94 (1969), pp.801-16.

——————. 'Zum Problem der Semantik', *KuD* 16 (1970), pp.41-57.

Fries, C. C., *The Structure of English*, New York, 1952.

Gasque, W. W., and Martin, R. P., eds., Apostolic History and the Gospel, Exeter, Paternoster, 1970.

Gätner, B., *The Temple and the Community in Qumran and the New Testament*, Cambridge, CUP, 1965.

Gerhardsson, B., *The Origins of the Gospel Traditions*, London, SCM, 1979.

Glare, P. G. W., 'Liddell and Scott: Its Background and Present State' in R. Burchfield (ed.), *Studies in Lexicography*, Oxford, OUP, 1987.

Godet, F. L., *Commentary on St John's Gospel*, Edinburgh, 1889.

Grice, H. P., 'Logic and conversation' in Cole, P., and Morgan, J. L., eds., *Syntax and Semantics*, New York, Academic Press, 1975.

Grimes, J. E., *The Thread of Discourse*, The Hague, Mouton, 1975.

Grudem, W., 'Does *Kephalē* ("Head") Mean "Source" or "Authority Over" in Greek Literature? A Survey of 2,336 Examples', *Trinity Journal* 6 (1985), pp.38-59.

Gulkowitsch, L., *Die Bildung von Abstraktbegriffen in der hebräischen Sprachgeschichte*, Leipzig, 1931.

Güttgemanns, E., *Studia Linguistica Neotestamentica*, Munich, Kaiser Vlg, 1971.

Haenchen, E., *John*, Philadelphia, Fortress Press, 1984.

Halliday, M. A. K., *Language as Social Semiotic*, London, Edward Arnold (for the Open University), 1978.

——————. and Hasan, R., *Cohesion in English*, London, Longmans, 1976.

Harrison, R. K., *Introduction to the Old Testament*, Grand Rapids, Eerdmans, 1969.

Hayes, John H., and Holladay, Carl R., *Biblical Exegesis: A Beginner's Handbook*, Atlanta, John Knox Press, 1982 and London, SCM, 1983.

Hemer, Colin, *The Letters to the Seven Churches of Asia in their Local Setting*, Sheffield, JSOT, 1986.

Hemphill, K., *The Pauline Concept of Charisma*, unpublished Ph.D. dissertation, Cambridge, 1976.

Hengel, M., *The Son of God*, London, SCM, 1976.

——————. *The Atonement*, London, SCM, 1981.

Hesselgrave, David, *Communicating Christ Cross-culturally*, Grand Rapids, Zondervan, 1978.

Hill, D., *Greek Words and Hebrew Meanings: Studies in the Semantics of Soteriological Terms*,

Cambridge, CUP, 1966.

Hirsch, E. D., *The Aims of Interpretation*, Chicago, University of Chicago Press, 1976.

Hooker, Morner, 'Authority on her head: An examination of 1 Cor.xi.10', *NTS* 10 (1963-4).

Hudson, R., *Invitation to Linguistics*, Oxford, Robertson, 1984.

Hurford, J., and Heasley, B., *Semantics: A Coursebook*, Cambridge, CUP, 1983.

Hurley, J. B., *Man and Woman in Biblical Perspective*, Leicester, IVP, 1981.

Jacobson, Dan, *The Rape of Tamar*, London, Andre Deutsch, 1985[2].

Jeremias, J., *The Parables of Jesus*, London, SCM, 1963.

————. *Rediscovering the Parables*, London, SCM, 1966.

Jones, G. H., *I and II Kings* (The New Century Bible Commentary), London, Marshall, Morgan & Scott, 1984.

Kaiser, W. J., *Towards an Exegetical Theology*, Grand Rapids, Baker, 1981.

Käsemann, E., *Essays on New Testament Themes*, London, SCM, 1964.

————. *Commentary on Romans*, London, SCM, 1980.

Katz, J. J., *Semantic Theory*, London, Harper and Row, 1972.

————. and Fodor, J. A., 'The structure of a semantic theory', *Language*, 39(1963).

Keenan, E. L., ed., *Formal Semantics of Natural Language*, CUP, 1975.

Kempson, R. M., *Semantic Theory*, Cambridge, CUP, 1977.

Kittel, G., *Lexicographia Sacra, Theology*, Occasional Papers 7, London 1938.

————. and Friedrich, G., eds., *Theological Dictionary of the New Testament*,10 volumes, London, SCM Press, 1946-77.

Klassen, William, 'Coals of Fire: Sign of Repentance or Revenge?', *New Testament Studies* 9 (1962-3).

Klemm, M., *EIPHNH im neutestamentlichen Sprachsystem*, Bonn, BLB, 1977.

Knight, G. A. F., *A Biblical Approach to the Doctrine of the Trinity*, London, Oliver & Boyd, 1953.

Kroeger, C., 'The Classical Concept of "Head" as "Source" ' in Hull, G. G., *Equal to Serve: Women and Men in the Church and Home*, Old Tappan, Revell, 1987.

Langacker, R. W., *Language and Its Structure*, New York, Harcourt, Brace, Jovanovich, 1973[2].

Leech, G., *Semantics*, Harmondsworth, Penguin, 1981[2].

————. *Principles of Pragmatics*, London, Longman, 1983.

Lehrer, Adrienne, *Semantic Fields and Lexical Structure*, London, North-Holland, 1974.

Levine, D. N., *Wax and Gold*, Chicago, University of Chicago Press, 1965.

Levinson, S. C., *Pragmatics*, Cambridge, CUP, 1983.

Lewis, C. S., *Christian Reflections*, London, Bles, 1967.

Lewis, M. B., *Sentence Analysis in Modern Malay*, Cambridge, CUP, 1969.

Longacre, R. E., *The Grammar of Discourse*, London and New York, Plenum, 1983.

Louw, J. P. 'The Greek New Testament Wordbook', *BT* 30(1979), pp.108-17.

————. *Semantics of New Testament Greek*, Philadelphia, Fortress Press, 1982.

Lyons, J., *Structural Semantics*, Oxford, Blackwell, 1963.

————. *Introduction to Theoretical Linguistics*, Cambridge, CUP, 1968.

————. *Chomsky*, London, Fontana, 1977[2].

————. *Semantics*, Cambridge, CUP, 1977.

————. *Language and Linguistics*, Cambridge, CUP, 1981.

————. *Language, Meaning and Context*, London, Fontana (Collins), 1981.

Malina, B., *The New Testament World: Insights from Cultural Anthropology*, London, SCM, 1983.

Marshall, I. Howard, *The Gospel of Luke*, Exeter, Paternoster, 1978.

————. *The Epistles of John*, Grand Rapids, Eerdmans, 1978.

————. *Last Supper and Lord's Supper*, Exeter, Paternoster, 1980.

————. ed., *New Testament Interpretation*, Exeter, Paternoster, 1977.

Martin, R. P., *The Spirit and the Congregation: Studies in 1 Corinthians 12-15*, Grand Rapids, Eerdmans, 1984.

Mattill, A. J., 'The Jesus-Paul Parallels and the Purpose of Luke-Acts', *NovT* 17 (1975).

Maynard, A. H., 'Ti emoi kai soi', *NTStud* 31,4(1985).

McFague, S., *Metaphorical Theology*, New York, Fortress Press, 1982.

McKane, William, *Proverbs* (Old Testament Library), London, SCM, 1970.

————. *Studies in the Patriarchal Narratives*, Edinburgh, The Handsel Press, 1979.

McCarter, P. K., *II Samuel* (Anchor Bible), New York, Doubleday, 1984.

McKelvey, R. J., *The New Temple*, Oxford, OUP, 1969.

Meeks, W., *The First Urban Christians*, New Haven, YUP, 1983.

Mendner, S., 'Nikodemus', *Journal of Biblical Literature* 77 (1958), pp. 293-323.

Metzger, B., 'Methodology in the Study of the Mystery Religions and Early Christianity' in *Historical and Literary Studies*, Leiden, Brill, 1968, pp. 1-23.

————. *Lexical Aids for Students of New Testament Greek*, Oxford, Blackwell, 1980.

Meuzelaar, J. J., *Der Leib des Messias: eine exegetische Studie über den Gedanken vom Leib Christi in den Paulusbriefen*, Assen, Van Gorcum, 1961.

Mickelsen, A., ed., *Women, Authority and the Bible*, Downers Grove, InterVarsity Press, 1986.

Miller, G. A., and Johnson-Laird, P. N., *Language and Perception*, Cambridge, CUP, 1976.

Moloney, F. J., *The Johannine Son of Man*, Rome, Las, 1976.

Moo, D. J., 'Israel and Paul in Rom. 7.7-12', *NTS* 32 (1986).

Morris, Leon, *The Revelation of Saint John*, London, IVP, 1969.

————. *The Gospel According to John* (New London Commentaries), London, Marshall Morgan & Scott, 1971.

Moulton, J. H., *A Grammar of New Testament Greek*, vol II, Edinburgh, T. & T. Clark, 1920.

————— and Turner, Nigel, *A Grammar of New Testament Greek*, vol. III, Edinburgh, T. & T. Clark, 1963.

Mounce, R. H., *The Book of Revelation*, Grand Rapids, Eerdmans, 1977.

Mudge, Lewis, ed., *Essays on Biblical Interpretation*, London, SPCK, 1981.

Murphy-O'Connor, J., *1 Corinthians*, Wilmington, Glaziers, 1979.

Neill, Stephen, *The Interpretation of the New Testament, 1861-1961*, Oxford, OUP, 1964.

Nida, E., *Componential Analysis of Meaning*, The Hague, Mouton, 1975.

—————. *Exploring Semantic Structures*, Munich, Fink, 1975.

—————. and Taber, C. R., *The Theory and Practice of Translation*, Leiden, Brill, 1969.

—————. (et al.), *Style and Discourse*, Cape Town, BSSA, 1983.

Palmer, F. R., *Semantics*, Cambridge, CUP, 1976.

Pickering, W., *A Framework for Discourse Analysis*, Dallas, SIL, 1981.

Plummer, A., *The Gospel According to St John* (The Cambridge Greek Testament), Cambridge, CUP, 1882.

Poythress, V. S., *Structural Approaches to Understanding the Theology of the Apostle Paul*, unpublished D.Th. dissertation, Stellenbosch, 1981.

Prior, D., *The Message of 1 Corinthians*, Leicester, IVP, 1985.

Riches, J., *Jesus and the Transformation of Judaism*, London, SPCK, 1980.

Ricoeur, P., *The Conflict of Interpretations*, Evanston, Northwestern University Press, 1974.

Rieser, H., 'On the Development of Text Grammar' in Dressler, W., ed., *Current Trends in Textlinguistics*, Berlin, de Gruyter, 1978.

Robertson, A. T., *A Grammar of the Greek New Testament*, Nashville, Broadman, 1934[4].

Robins, R. H., *General Linguistics, an Introductory Survey*, London, Longmans[3], 1980.

Robinson, J. A. T., *The Body: A Study in Pauline Theology*, London, SCM, 1952.

Rowdon, H. H., ed., *Christ the Lord*, Leicester, IVP, 1982.

Rowland, Christopher, *Christian Origins*, London, SPCK, 1985.

Rudwick, M. J. S. and Green, E. M. B., 'The Laodicean Lukewarmness', *Expository Times*, 69 (1957-8).

Sanders, E. P., *Jesus and Judaism*, London, SCM, 1985.

Sandmel, S., 'Parallelomania', *JBL* (1962) 81.

Sapir, E., *Selected Writings in Language, Culture and Personality*, Berkeley, University of California Press, 1947.

de Saussure, F., *Cours de Linguistique Générale*, Paris, 1916. English translation: *Course in General Linguistics*, New York, Philosophical Library, 1959; London, Owen, 1960.

Sawyer, J., *Semantics in Biblical Research: New Methods of Defining Hebrew Words for Salvation*, London, SCM, 1972.

Schenk, W., *Die Philipperbriefs des Paulus*, Stuttgart, Kohlhammer, 1984.

Schippers, R., 'The *mashal* character of the Parable of the Pearl', in Cross, F. L., ed., *Studia Evangelica*, vol. II, Berlin, Akademie-Verlag, 1964.

Schnackenburg, R., *The Gospel According to St John*, London, Burns & Oates, 1982.

Silva, Moises, *Biblical Words and their Meaning*, Grand Rapids, Zondervan, 1983.

Sperber, Dan and Wilson, Deirdre, *Relevance*, Oxford, Blackwell, 1986.

Spurgeon, C. H., *Lectures to my Students*, London, Marshall, Morgan & Scott, 1954.

Stambaugh, J. E., and Balch, D. L., *The New Testament and Its Social Environment*, Philadelphia, Westminster, 1987.

Stehle, M., *Greek Word-Building*, Missoula, Scholars Press, 1976.

Stein, R. H., *An Introduction to the Parables of Jesus*, Philadelphia, Westminster Press, 1981.

Steinberg, D. D., and Jakobovits, L. A., eds., *Semantics: An Interdisciplinary Reader in Philosophy, Linguistics and Psychology*, Cambridge, CUP, 1971.

Stubbs, Michael, *Discourse Analysis*, Oxford, Blackwell, 1983.

Talbert, C. H., *Literary Patterns, Theological Themes and the Genre of Luke-Acts*, Missoula, Scholars Press, 1974.

Tångberg, K. A., 'Linguistics and Theology', *BT* 24 (1973), pp.308-10.

Taylor, Vincent, *The Epistle to the Romans*, London, Epworth, 1956.

Theissen, G., *The Social Setting of Pauline Christianity*, Edinburgh, T. & T. Clark, 1982.

————— . *The Shadow of the Galilean*, London, SCM, 1987.

Thiselton, A. C., 'Semantics and New Testament Interpretation' in Marshall, I. Howard, ed., *New Testament Interpretation*, Exeter, Paternoster, 1977, pp.75-104.

————— . *The Two Horizons*, Exeter, Paternoster, 1980.

————— . 'Reader-Response Hermeneutics, Action Models, and the Parables of Jesus', in Lundin, R.; Thiselton, A. C.; Walhout, C. *The Responsibility of Hermeneutics*, Exeter, Paternoster, 1985.

Tidball, D., *An Introduction to the Sociology of the New Testament*, Exeter, Paternoster, 1983.

Trier, J., *Der Deutsche Wortschatz im Sinnbezirk des Verstandes*, Heidelberg, Winter, 1931.

Tuckett, C., *Reading the New Testament*, London, SPCK, 1987.

Turner, M. M. B., 'The Significance of Spirit Endowment for Paul' *Vox Evangelica* 9 (1975).

————— . 'Spirit Endowment in Luke-Acts: Some Linguistic Considerations', *Vox Evangelica* 12 (1981).

————— . 'The Spirit of Christ and Christology' in Rowdon, H. H., ed., *Christ the Lord*, Leicester, IVP, 1982.

_____ . 'The Significance of Receiving the Spirit in Luke-Acts', *Trinity Journal*
2 (1981).

_____ . 'Spiritual Gifts Then and Now', *Vox Evangelica* 15 (1985), pp. 7-64.

Ullmann, S., *The Principles of Semantics*, Oxford, Blackwell, 1957.

_____ . *Semantics: An Introduction to the Science of Meaning*, Oxford, Blackwell, 1962.

Venneman, T., 'Topic, sentence, accent and ellipsis', in Keenan, E. L. ed., *Formal
Semantics of Natural Language*, CUP, 1975.

Vermes, G., *Jesus the Jew*, London, Collins, 1973.

Wagner, G., *Pauline Baptism and the Pagan Mysteries*, London, Oliver & Boyd, 1967.

Waldron, R. A., *Sense and Sense Development*, London, Deutch, 1979².

Wardhaugh, Ronald, *An Introduction to Sociolinguistics*, Oxford, Blackwell, 1986.

Watts, J. D. W., *Isaiah 1-33* (Word Biblical Commentary), Waco, Word, 1985.

Westcott, B. F., *The Gospel According to St John*, London, Murray, 1892.

Westermann, Claus, *Genesis 12-36*, ET by J Scullion, Minneapolis, Augsburg, and
London, SPCK, 1985.

Whorf, B. L., *Language, Thought and Reality*, Cambridge, MIT, 1956.

Wierzbicka, Anna, *Semantic Primitives*, Frankfurt, Athenäum, 1972.

_____ . *Lexicography and Conceptual Analysis*, Ann Arbor, Karoma, 1985.

Wiseman, P. J., *Clues to Creation in Genesis*, Wiseman, D. J., ed., London, Marshall,
Morgan & Scott, 1977.

Zgusta, L., *Manual of Lexicography*, The Hague, Mouton, 1971.

Author Index

Subject Index